CW00340961

THE HOUSE OF
GODWIN

THE HOUSE OF
GODWIN

THE RISE AND FALL OF AN
ANGLO-SAXON DYNASTY

MICHAEL JOHN KEY

AMBERLEY

For Tamasine Roberta Michele

First published 2022

Amberley Publishing
The Hill, Stroud
Gloucestershire, GL5 4EP

www.amberley-books.com

British Library Cataloguing in Publication Data.
A catalogue record for this book is available from the British Library.

ISBN 978 1 4456 9406 1 (hardback)
ISBN 978 1 4456 9407 8 (ebook)

1 2 3 4 5 6 7 8 9 10

Typeset in 10pt on 13.5pt Sabon.
Typesetting by SJmagic DESIGN SERVICES, India.
Printed in the UK.

Contents

Acknowledgements

In writing this book I am particularly indebted to those academics and scholars that have previously devoted their time and energy towards translating and editing the various important primary source documents that address this period of history, from Latin, Old English, or Norman French into modern English. I have relied heavily on many of these texts during my research and could not have completed it without their earlier endeavours.

I would also like to acknowledge the large library of secondary sources and the works and texts of many historians that gave me inspiration for the themes and direction of this book. They are too numerous to mention all of them here but are listed appropriately within the bibliography. However, I would wish to single out my gratitude to Frank Barlow, Stephen Baxter, Simon Keynes, Pauline Stafford, and Ann Williams, for their valuable research and enthusiasm in particular for all matters related to eleventh-century English history. A specific acknowledgement should also be directed towards the compilers and keepers of the *Prosopography of Anglo-Saxon England* database. With specific regard to a history on the Godwin dynasty and Godwin in particular, I am also grateful to the earlier research of Hubert Grills and Emma Mason.

Further thanks go to English Heritage at Battle Abbey, to the authorities at Waltham Abbey and Holy Trinity Church at Bosham, and to those unnamed individuals that have helped me with information and advice during my visits to some of the places named within the text. Thanks go to Shaun Barrington, Connor Stait and Nikki Embery at Amberley Publishing and in particular to Alex Bennett at Amberley for supporting the completion of this book through uncertain times in 2020 and 2021. Lastly, I would like to give a special mention to my partner, Alice, for her continued patience and support.

List of Maps and Tables

Introduction

This work tells the story of the House of Godwin, the life and times of Earl Godwin of Wessex and his family in eleventh-century England. The rise and fall of the Godwin dynasty is encapsulated within the major historic events that touched Anglo-Saxon English history in this period, and their story runs parallel with all the dramatic developments described in these chapters. I have attempted, as much as the primary sources have allowed, to relate the full drama of the Godwinson family dynasty within the pages that follow and hopefully given Godwin and his wife Gytha the necessary consideration they are due.

This was a period which saw England conquered twice by foreign invaders a half century apart, first the Danes and then the Normans. The Godwinson family were central to all the major developments that took place in England from shortly after the succession of Cnut until the appearance of William the Conqueror. The careers of Godwin and his eldest children are therefore inexorably linked to the volatile politics that characterised this period, and the major changes that took place both inside England and on a wider scale across western Europe and Scandinavia. As powerful as the Godwinsons were to become, they would prove unmindful as to the fateful role their dynasty was to play towards the last days of Anglo-Saxon hegemony.

After Godwin's death in 1053 much of the later chapters fittingly deals with ongoing events surrounding his offspring, particularly his son Harold and the developments relating to the Norman Conquest of 1066. That event looms large in what would be the closing years of Anglo-Saxon rule across England and remains one of the most defining moments in English history.

Godwin of Wessex was to fully emerge in the second decade of the eleventh century during the Anglo-Saxon and Danish wars between Edmund Ironside and Cnut. Within a short span he became by the early 1020s the most influential member of the nobility and chief adviser to Cnut, the new king of England, a position he was to hold under four monarchs for over thirty years, the last being Edward (later to be known as 'the Confessor'). Godwin's eldest daughter, Edith (aka Eadgyth), was to become queen after marrying Edward in 1045, and his son Harold was to reach the apex of power when he succeeded Edward as king of England several months before the Norman invasion in 1066. The Godwinsons were the most successful Anglo-Saxon dynasty of their time, surpassing their contemporaries in their perseverance, wealth, and longevity. After holding these positions of influence and significance for almost half a century their dramatic and irreversible fall from power would take only a matter of weeks, heralding the last days of Anglo-Saxon dominance across England.

For those readers acquainted with mid-eleventh-century English history, the dynastic name will be familiar through King Harold II Godwinson (i.e. son of Godwin). I have employed the inclusive 'Godwinsons' rather than using the more etymologically accurate 'Godwins' when referring to Godwin himself and generically to all other members of the Godwin dynasty, and I would kindly ask readers to bear with this principle. This rule also includes Godwin's daughters, although their correct patronym should be 'Godwinsdottir'. Using a patronym, adding 'son' to the father's name, or 'dottir' in the case of a daughter, was a practice particularly common in Scandinavia. Through Anglo-Saxon links to Scandinavia and the Germanic origin of the Anglo-Saxon tribes, the use of patronyms had become common practice in England by the eleventh century.

Having established himself as Cnut's right-hand man by the mid-1020s, Godwin was to safely steer his path through the storm of the Danish succession question between 1035 and 1042, and after Edward's succession he had arguably become as politically influential as the king. It is a sign of Godwin's character that he could manoeuvre through several diplomatically difficult situations, not only between 1035 and 1042 but more impressively in his reestablishment following his and his family's exile in 1051. His daughter Edith's marriage to Edward ('the Confessor') in 1045 was a masterstroke in the game of political influence, and between the 1040s and the Norman Conquest Godwin and his offspring were to dominate royal policy. The exploits and achievements of the sons Swegn, Harold and Tostig contrast each other dramatically, and the rift that developed between Harold and Tostig resulted ultimately in the direst of consequences for England.

In writing about Godwin and the Godwinson dynasty I was aware there was a contrast in the quality and quantity of primary source data and secondary texts relating to the life and career of Godwin in comparison to the greater data available about Harold and the events leading up to and including 1066. Choosing to write a book on the Godwinson dynasty, therefore, brought with it challenges in ensuring that the important events during Godwin's own life were given sufficient justice ahead of the later sections dealing with the dramatic events that overwhelmed his offspring. Much of the content has been devoted to the Godwinsons' contemporaries, the leading personalities that touched the lives of Godwin, his wife Gytha, or one or more of his children throughout this period. Several individuals were prominent in directing or changing the fortunes of the Godwinson dynasty, such as Cnut, Emma of Normandy, Edward, and William of Normandy. They are as central to the Godwinson story as the household members themselves, and a history of the Godwinsons cannot be complete without detailing the significance of these other important figures.

The text has been planned to flow as best as is possible along chronological timelines, beginning with an assessment of Godwin's father Wulfnoth Cild and ending with a summing-up and deliberation of the Godwinsons' dynastic legacy and their relevance in England's story. The first chapter considers Godwin's family background and his emergence during the Danish Conquest, and the next two follow his marriage to Gytha and the establishment of Godwin's dynasty under Cnut between the years 1017 and 1034. These are followed by chapters concerning Godwin's involvement in the Anglo-Danish succession disputes between 1035 and 1042. Chapter six considers his role under Edward ('the Confessor') during the 1040s, the advance of his sons Swegn and Harold, and his daughter Edith's royal wedding; the next chapter looks at the impact of the eldest child, Swegn, the 'black sheep' of the family. Chapters eight and nine discuss the dramatic exiling of Godwin and his family in 1051 and their even more dramatic return in 1052. Chapters ten and eleven follow the continued ascent of Harold after Godwin's death, the search for a royal successor, and the emergence of Tostig and his younger brothers in the years up to 1063.

Chapter twelve looks at Harold's infamous trip to Normandy in 1064, which encouraged William of Normandy to extend a claim for the English throne, and the next considers the rebellion of 1065 that removed Tostig from his earldom and led to the rift with Harold. Chapter fourteen addresses the death of Edward and Harold's ascension to the throne and his brief reign as monarch. The next five chapters (fifteen to nineteen) describe the build-up to and subsequent invasions of England by Harald Hardrada (Sigurdsson) of Norway and William of Normandy, the battle of Stamford Bridge, and the battle of Hastings and its immediate aftermath. The penultimate chapter looks at the fate of the Godwinsons who survived beyond 1066, and the concluding chapter considers their reputation and standing with relevance to the history of England.

There are a few topics that it would be useful to address in this introduction, and brief notes have been included here on generic descriptions, personal names, the medieval calendar, place names and locations. Readers will see that I have used the terms 'Anglo-Saxon' and 'English' interchangeably across the text. From 1016 until 1042, Danes and not Anglo-Saxons ruled England. While these were 'Danish kings', it is more fitting to describe them as 'Anglo-Danish kings' in the context of English affairs. Similarly, William (later to be known as 'the Conqueror') is defined using his correct title of Duke of Normandy prior to the Conquest, but for any references post-1066 'Anglo-Norman' is a more appropriate term for his reign. From the 1040s, the Norwegians again became an important factor in English history. Both Norwegians and Danes can be generically labelled as Scandinavian, more emotively as 'Vikings', but in almost all cases I have distinguished them appropriately as 'Norse' or 'Danish'.

It has been tempting to include more detail on the Godwinsons in terms of their physical appearance or personal characteristics. However, except for a few snippets added by the early twelfth-century chroniclers and some detail taken from Godwin's daughter Edith's comments in her text *Vita Edwardi Regis*, where she describes some physical aspects and personality traits of her brothers Harold and Tostig, the detail is limited. It has proved impossible to add anything further beyond speculation. Later portraits are highly romanticised, and all images are representations rather than true likenesses. The coins of Harold Godwinson, for example, show him with long hair, moustache, and trimmed beard, depicting how he wanted his image to be shown rather than necessarily a close facsimile. I have placed more emphasis on aspects of character that might be gathered to some extent from our knowledge of their actions and responses to certain situations.

Personal names in Anglo-Saxon England often lead to some confusion. Old English names were often formed of two elements or syllables (dithematic) or a simple uncompounded word (monothematic). Where there are two similarly named individuals, I have tried to distinguish one from the other by giving additional detail. Other rules have been applied where necessary. The first concerns the spelling of Godwin. He has been named by both primary and secondary sources as both 'Godwin' or 'Godwine', and they are both perfectly acceptable. I have adopted 'Godwin' throughout, and likewise the generic term 'Godwinsons' rather than 'Godwins' for the family unit. Individuals with differently spelt personal names have also been given their alternately used name where relevant, but only when first named. These are cross-referenced in the index, an example being Tostig's less-used spelling of 'Tosti'. Another rule applies to epithets. The Norwegian king Harald Sigurdsson is more widely known as Harald 'Hardrada' (translated as 'hard ruler'), and I have used this rather than his patronym of Sigurdsson, although they are interchangeable. Similarly, Harold Cnutsson is better known as Harold 'Harefoot' (reputedly because of his hunting abilities).

Both Hardrada and Harefoot are used as their primary identifier, which is particularly useful in Harefoot's case so that there is less chance of confusing him with either Harold Godwinson or Harald 'Hardrada'.

A few of the regularly referenced names need some explanation. The first concerns Godwin's eldest son, Swegn. There are several ways that his name has been spelt across the sources. It was a common name in Scandinavia and among Scandinavian settlers in England. There are four individuals with that name, including Godwin's son, who feature prominently in this text, so to avoid confusion I have provided them with different spellings. Beyond Swegn Godwinson, Cnut's father (Forkbeard) has been spelt 'Sweyn'; Godwin's nephew and later king of Denmark, Estrithsson, has been spelt 'Swein'; and finally, Cnut's son (Cnutsson) given the spelling Svein. Two other names should be mentioned. Godwin's eldest daughter's Old English name was Eadgyth or Gytha, but she is more familiarly known as Edith, the Norman equivalent of her name, which she adopted after her marriage to Edward the Confessor. I have therefore in all references beyond chapter three used 'Edith' for clarity. Finally, a brief word on Emma of Normandy. Some English sources gave her the name 'Ælfgifu', the Anglo-Saxon equivalent of her name, but she is more commonly recognised by her Norman name of 'Emma' so I have used that preference throughout.

The chroniclers sometimes used different methods to calculate the calendar year. Several systems were adopted. The first of these alternative dates for the year change was the Annunciation on 25 March, the date on which the Christian Church believed the angel Gabriel told Mary of her conception, and the beginning of the year in the Julian Calendar. The second was the Indiction, when property was assessed for tax in the Roman world; in Rome this was 1 September, and in Byzantium 24 September. Another was the birth of Christ on 25 December using the Old English Metrical Calendar. The 1 January date was the Feast of the Circumcision, the date commonly used in Roman civil custom. This has meant that the year dates in some primary source texts are wrong, as they did not all correlate to the twelve-month cycle beginning 1 January. Some events occurring between September and the end of December were given the following year. Contrarily, some events before 25 March became part of the previous year. Consensus has been reached among historians to address these anomalies in nearly all such cases, so all year entries in the text have been adjusted to the modern twelve-month calendar. Another dating issue concerns the switch after 1582 (from 1752 in Great Britain) from the Julian calendar to the Gregorian calendar, as introduced by Pope Gregory XIII. The Julian calendar had calculated too many leap years, working on a year as 365.25 days, whereas the Gregorian calendar had corrected it to the more accurate 365.242 days per year. This meant a realignment in 1752 forwards of eleven days. So, for example, the Battle of Hastings was fought in terms of the re-calculated modern calendar date on 25 October, but to maintain the convention accepted by all historians, dates quoted in primary sources pre-1582 (1752) have been adhered to, meaning that Hastings remains as 14 October despite the later calendar adjustment.

Much of the landscape and physical geography of England has altered significantly in the millennium that has passed since the events detailed in this book, and this should be borne in mind. In terms of the landscape changes, this is particularly relevant when considering the Sussex coastline during the Norman invasion of 1066. The coast around Pevensey, Hastings, and Rye has changed beyond all recognition since then due to significant material deposition and changes in tidal flows and groundwater levels in the intervening centuries. These physical and topographical changes have been recognised and considered when looking at the events surrounding the Norman invasion and the battle that followed, and therefore form an important part of the discussion as to where events took place.

Finally, structural evidence for the eleventh century is limited. There are fewer examples of surviving original sites and archaeological evidence than we would wish for. Most Anglo-Saxon structures were of wooden construction, and those in stone, such as Waltham Abbey or the original Anglo-Saxon Westminster Abbey, were demolished, built over, or significantly changed within a generation or two of the Norman Conquest. I have visited all the key sites and locations in England connected to the Godwinsons, together with other locations that witnessed significant events during this period. All images used in the illustration section are my own unless noted otherwise. In terms of place names, I have used the accepted modern English name for all the towns and locations within the text, both in England and elsewhere, because while it may be authentic to use eleventh-century Old English, Scandinavian or Norman French definitions this can cause unnecessary ambiguity.

A Note on Primary Sources

Firstly, what is understood when we refer to a 'primary source'? It is a source of information that can be found in manuscripts, chronicles, charters, and other documents, verified as being created during, and contemporary with, the period being considered. A primary source equally applies to surviving archaeology, artefacts, and illustrations, although in this book these are secondary in importance to the texts, with the notable exception of the *Bayeux Tapestry*. Primary sources are critical to understanding the eleventh-century history considered in this book. Their quantity, quality, and usefulness to academics, historians, archaeologists, and other disciplines is in providing a window into the events and the lives of people fundamental to historical research and the interpretation of the past. From these sources come the textual and physical evidence that enables continued debate through secondary sources.

Several primary sources do not keep to the letter of the above rule, but there are valid reasons for allowing some leeway beyond these confines. Only a portion of the key sources run parallel to the lifetimes of Godwin and his family. However, the academic community accepts some flexibility. Many texts come instead from the mid-twelfth century or thereafter, from writers that had access to earlier texts or to detail which had been passed by word of mouth, coming under the umbrella of verifiable primary sources. Mostly, these earlier texts have not survived to the present day but were still extant when transposed in the twelfth century or later.

In general terms, any original text is still considered a 'primary source' if it contains material gathered by word of mouth or from writings taken from contemporary sources traceable to the matters being described, and where this detail has been copied or reproduced from that original material. A primary text may not have been written at the time an event took place, but it reproduces detail contemporary to that event. For the timeframe of our text (approximately *circa* 990s to *circa* 1080s), there are about thirty primary source documents key to archival research and crucial for understanding the era.

It is important to recognise the level of reliability and credibility of each principal authority, based not simply on when it was produced but on the background of the writer or chronicler, the circumstances in which they were writing, and how the patronage for their writing encouraged or affected their input. Credibility is helped by the frequency with which an event or incident is recorded within the sources but is not a failsafe guarantee of truth or accuracy. Although similar detail may be replicated across several documents, their detail may have come from perhaps just a single source document. Furthermore, it should not be assumed all major works were produced with the universal intent of telling the facts alone and nothing further. Medieval writers had their agenda, and historical reporting in the medieval period did not exist simply to preserve historical detail but was also possessed with a moral function.[1]

We often assume all medieval chroniclers were historians, but it needs to be appreciated their intent was not always to act as a recorder of factual events. Some were commissioned to write works to promote a specific individual, family, nation state, or viewpoint, to act as a voice for the Church or a member of the nobility, or to give their interpretation for entertainment and gossip. Praising an individual to gain favour was not uncommon, irrespective of whether deserved, and criticism of others could be equally slanted. From this amalgam, modern historians are left to define what should be highlighted or excluded, and what documents are likely to include reliable facts or can be treated less reverently. For this book, I have tried to research as many principal and secondary sources as possible to arrive at my interpretation. Where some matters still engender arguments, such as the involvement of Godwin in the ætheling Alfred's death in 1036, or Harold's oath to William of Normandy in 1064, conclusions have been arrived at based on my own assessment of the known detail. Not all historians or readers may agree with these conclusions, but that is the nature of secondary analysis and ongoing discussion.

The dates within the text have been taken from a combination of primary sources, and where specific dates are replicated by several sources, these are accepted as having greater authenticity. Some year entries in some versions of the *Anglo-Saxon Chronicle* (abbreviated as the '*ASC*') were assigned wrong dates and these errors were copied by later scribes within their works. These have been corrected when identified. Errors occurred when scribes misunderstood or inaccurately read earlier texts or miscalculated dates when duplicating and copying detail years afterwards into their works.

As mentioned in the introduction, dates have been adjusted where necessary to fit our present-day year calendar beginning 1 January.

A further comment needs to be made about the accuracy of elementary texts. Contemporary opinion in the form of a primary source may be nuanced. They have the advantage of being concurrent to the things they describe, but, as has been observed, 'may be prejudiced by love or dislike, may misunderstand, may even be incapable of understanding'.[2] Works were often designed for homiletic or hagiographical purposes alone, so accuracy was not always the main priority. Successful propaganda or plain bias within only a few documents, perhaps described as 'inaccuracies' or 'misinformation', can move us away from a more rational assessment. Vital as these contributions are in the historical record, being economical with the facts can, unfortunately, invalidate some contributions. However, in the strictest sense, the distribution of these primary texts was so limited in their lifetimes that they cannot be labelled as successful propaganda tools as we would understand it in the modern world. The *Gesta Guillelmi* of William of Poitiers, for example, was only circulated in three or four copies.[3] They did not have the means in the eleventh century for these details to be opened for debate.[4] They had greater relevance to their restricted group of contemporaries, but it is later academics that are better able to critique their input, compare their content with alternative sources and evaluate their trustworthiness.

The key primary sources that have been utilised in this work are summarised below. They have provided later generations with detail or discussion appropriate to the period through which the fortunes of the Godwinsons rose and fell. This is not designed to be an exhaustive list, but an overview of the more important primary documents used during my research. Charters aside, there are about thirty sources that form the backbone of the original material.

The major English primary text is the *Anglo-Saxon Chronicle* (hereafter abbreviated as the *ASC*) and there are several surviving versions (given the letters A to F), compiled in different religious houses: Winchester (A), Abingdon (B, C), Worcester (D), Peterborough (E) and Canterbury (F).[5] Repetition is common as scribes often copied entries word for word from other versions. Versions C and D are invariably more hostile towards the Godwinsons, whereas versions A and E are the closest we get to a partisan view.[6] Many of the writers from the twelfth century took their inspiration – and some detail – from the *ASC*.[7]

Charters provide effective and important information during the reigns of Cnut and Edward (the Confessor) about the king's movements, their favoured men, snapshots of the relative status and prominence of individuals; plus, along with the *Domesday Book*, considerable detail about who owned what. From the succession of Cnut in 1016 to the death of Harold

Godwinson in 1066 there are between seventy and eighty surviving royal charters, suspected forgeries included. The *Prosopography of Anglo-Saxon England* website contains the database of charters and many of them are included among the documents gathered in volume I of *English Historical Documents*. The *Prosopography* also contains a separate database of the *Domesday Book* entries and estate distribution.

Two of the prime English sources contemporary to the Godwinsons are the *Encomium Emmae Reginae* (Panegyric of Queen Emma), and the *Vita Edwardi Regis* (The Life of King Edward). The former was commissioned by Emma, the widow of Æthelred II (the Unready) and later Cnut, around 1042 while in exile in Flanders. The scribe's name remains anonymous but he is understood to have been a monk from the abbey at St Bertin. The latter work was commissioned by Godwin's daughter Edith (aka Eadgyth) Godwinsdottir ahead of the Conquest and completed in 1067. This too has been credited to an unknown monk from St Bertin, although in recent years some academics have supported the likelihood it was a monk named Folcard.[8] These two texts are principally the diaries of the two most influential women of the era. The *Encomium* was ostensibly a biography of Cnut and their children at the expense of Emma's first husband and their sons, and is key in commentating on developments between 1036 and 1042.[9] The *Vita* bridges the gap through the dramatic actions of 1066, but it began as a chronicle of Edith's marriage to Edward and her family before being overtaken by events. The tone changes as it records the issues surrounding the Norman invasion.[10]

A string of Anglo-Norman clerical chroniclers appeared in the early twelfth century. John of Worcester's *Chronicon ex Chronicus* (Extended Chronicles) was a continuation and extension of the earlier work of a monk called Florence of Worcester, and Florence and not John was formerly often credited with much of the content. A cleric from Canterbury named Eadmer produced his *Historia Novorum in Anglia* (A New History of England) in the 1120s. It was primarily about ecclesiastical affairs and events beginning in 1066 through to the twelfth century, and Eadmer offers comment not provided elsewhere about the Norman kings. A less useful authority for our purposes regarding the Godwinsons is Symeon of Durham, a monk who wrote in the early twelfth century and who took much detail from earlier works. His *Libellus de Exordio atque Procursu istius, hoc est Dunelmensis, Ecclesie* (The Little Book on the Origins and Progress of this Church, that is of Durham) and *Historia regum Anglorum et Dacorum* (History of the English Kings' Conduct) are combined in an omnibus entitled *Symeonis Monachi Opera Omnia* (Complete works of Symeon of Durham). The most prolific chronicler on that period was the monk William of Malmesbury. His major histories covering the eleventh century are the *Gesta Regum*

Anglorum (Deeds of the English Kings) and *Gesta Pontificum Anglorum* (Deeds of the English Bishops). Finally, we have Henry of Huntingdon and his work the *Historia Anglorum* (History of England). A contemporary of William of Malmesbury, Henry was secular clergy not monastic, but he was a gifted scholar and included more of a story-telling theme than most of his contemporaries.

Another contemporary of John of Worcester and William of Malmesbury was Orderic Vitalis, who had a Norman father and English mother. Orderic was sent to a Norman abbey when aged eleven, where he was given his name 'Vitalis', chosen from an earlier Christian martyr. His multi-volume *Historia Ecclesiastica* (Church History) is one of the essentially important chronicles of the Anglo-Norman age, although part of his content was drawn from the earlier writings of the two Normans William of Jumièges and William of Poitiers. Still, Orderic did amend much of the detail taken from Poitiers. The two main eleventh-century texts from Normandy are the aforementioned William of Poitiers' *Gesta Guillelmi* (Deeds of William) and William of Jumièges' *Gesta Normannorum Ducum* (Deeds of the Norman Dukes). Both were direct contemporaries, and these works were completed soon after the Conquest, but in setting out to legitimise the Norman invasion of England they are partisan to a greater or lesser extent.[11] Poitiers had been a chaplain of William of Normandy, and the *Gesta Guillelmi* was a biography of the duke.[12] Jumièges, a monk, concluded his work in 1070. Here again, he writes from a purely Norman viewpoint. Additional entries in the *Gesta Normannorum* were added by Orderic Vitalis and then Robert of Torigni, another Norman monk, during the twelfth century.

Three other Norman texts are important. The first of these is the *Carmen de Hastingae Proelio* (Song of the Battle of Hastings), from 1067 and attributed to Bishop Guy of Amiens from Ponthieu. It was composed in a poetic form but gives detail not available within other works. The second is the twelfth-century *Roman de Rou* (History of the Norman People) of Robert Wace, written in Old Norman verse. Wace was a Norman poet turned canon, and, like the *Carmen*, his work includes detail not found elsewhere. The third, contemporary with Orderic Vitalis, was by Geffrei Gaimar, a poet probably born in England from Norman parentage. His *L'Estoire des Engleis* (The History of the English) was written in rhyming couplets and took its content from various sources, including the *ASC*. To these can be added the *La Estoire De Saint Aedward le Rei* (Lives of Edward the Confessor), an anonymous work written in the thirteenth century in verse style in French.

Mention should be made of documents from later in the twelfth century and beyond that have been beneficial in piecing together aspects missing from the larger works. The first is *The Chronicle of Battle Abbey*, written by an anonymous monk in 1175. It primarily concerns the background to the foundation of the abbey and naturally supports the Battle of Hastings as taking place on the abbey site, although it was created primarily to defend its autonomy when it came under threat a century after the battle. Two texts originate from Waltham Abbey: the *Vita Haroldi* (Life of Harold), written anonymously, and the *Waltham Chronicle*, composed by a canon at Waltham. They both contain detail about Harold Godwinson's life, death, and burial. Finally, there are a handful of later English texts from the thirteenth and fourteenth centuries which provide affirmation of some eleventh-century events but are perhaps more susceptible to inaccuracies. These include William of Newburgh's *Historia Rerum Anglicarum* (History of English Affairs), Roger of Howden's *Chronicon*, Roger of Wendover's *Flores Historiarum* (Flowers of History), and Matthew Paris's *Chronica Majora* (Major Chronicles).

The Anglo-Saxon/English, Norman and Anglo-Norman works have been supplemented with other primary sources from Britain, Scandinavia, and the Continent. Additional British sources deserving mentions are the *Annales Cambriae* (Annals of Wales) and the *Annals of Ulster*, and these provide an additional record of affairs in Wales and Ireland contemporary with the Godwinsons. The writings of Adam of Bremen, in the *Gesta Hammaburgensis Ecclesiae Pontificum* (Deeds of Bishops of the Hamburg Church), similarly provide good detail on the secular activity on the Continent not available elsewhere. Scandinavian sources are not as prolific as would be hoped; there was not the tradition of writing and recording things, as seen elsewhere across Europe, but an oral tradition instead. There are two notable exceptions: a view of Danish history in the *Gesta Danorum*, written by Saxon Grammaticus in 1185, and in the early thirteenth century the *Heimskringla*, a collection of Norwegian and Icelandic sagas assembled by Snorri Sturluson. These have mixed value, but the *Heimskringla*, with its allegories, provides useful detail when evaluating the Norse invasion of 1066.

Finally, we come to the two volumes known as the *Domesday Book* survey, compiled in 1087 from data collected during a nationwide survey of 1086, in which the Anglo-Norman king William I had requested that all the towns, villages and estates throughout England supply information for tax assessment about their land, property, workers, and livestock. It is helpful because it enables us to see who held certain estates both before and after 1066. The survey provides good information on the land owned by the Godwinsons on the eve of the invasion, but it was not impartial in recording ownership, and the book's compilers were instructed to deny Harold Godwinson his rightful title of 'King' when referring to him.[13]

The last invaluable primary source for piecing together the facts involving Harold Godwinson and William of Normandy in 1064, and the events of

1066, is the *Bayeux Tapestry*, the best-recognised set of illustrations from the Middle Ages. It comprises about seventy separate scenes, beginning with Edward the Confessor and Harold Godwinson in 1064 ahead of the latter's trip to Normandy, and ends with the aftermath of the Battle of Hastings. The tapestry, or embroidery as it should be called, was commissioned in the 1070s. It was originally thought to have been manufactured in Normandy, but historians now concur that it was more likely produced by English seamstresses in Kent, under the supervision of Bishop Odo of Bayeux, William's half-brother. More recently, some have named Eustace of Boulogne as being its sponsor after reassessing the imagery and subtext of some scenes.[14]

In summary, this discussion has introduced readers to the chief primary sources that they will see references to within the central text, and variously listed in the enclosed 'notes' section. They provide the basis of the material within many secondary sources.

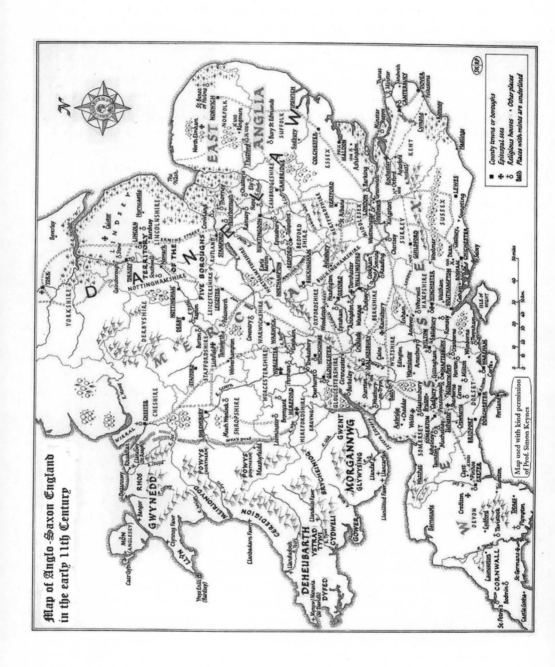

Map of Anglo-Saxon England in the early 11th Century

1

Wulfnoth Cild and the Danish Conquest

Godwin of Wessex was born towards the end of the tenth century, at the cusp of a new millennium. He and his dynastic house were to live through a period of dramatic change. The new century would witness the successful invasion of England by two foreign powers, initially the Danes (1013–16) and then the Normans (1066), and in the life of Godwin's wife Gytha and his children, the Norman invasion would mark the end of over five centuries of Anglo-Saxon hegemony across England. Godwin was a young man when the first of those successful invasions began, ushering in Cnut and a generation of Anglo-Danish kings, concluding a war between Anglo-Saxons and Danes that had followed Danish raids going back decades. However, before we look at Godwin's lifetime and career, we should first try to uncover evidence of his antecedents, the founders of the Godwinson dynasty. Historians have confidently identified the Godwinson family history one generation back from Godwin to a Sussex thegn named Wulfnoth Cild. We will look at Wulfnoth in due course, but it is theoretically possible to move back at least one further generation while accepting that we are in the field of speculation.

There are two interesting lines of enquiry as to Godwin's grandfather, both concerning men of distinguished status with the name Æthelmaer. The first, as suggested by some historians, was Æthelmaer Cild (the Stout), an ealdorman known to have operated between 1005 and 1015, albeit by that time an old man.[1] This ealdorman had other sons named Æthelweard and Æthelnoth, potentially the brothers of Wulfnoth Cild. Æthelnoth was to become chaplain to Cnut post-1016 before becoming archbishop at Canterbury in November 1020. Meanwhile Æthelweard, an ealdorman, was to figure near the top of the witness lists of Cnut's early charters alongside the young Godwin; this is seemingly the same ealdorman who conceded authority in the south-west to Cnut's father Sweyn Forkbeard during 1013. These promotions under Cnut give a positive argument for a dynastic connection with their theoretical nephew Godwin. Æthelmaer Cild's own antecedents can perhaps be traced back through Æthelweard the Historian, the brother of Ælfgifu, the wife and queen of King Eadwig (r. 955–59). From Ælfgifu, the line can be traced back through further generations to King Æthelred I (r. 865–71), brother of Alfred the Great.[2] With this hypothesis we are identifying a blood link between Godwin and the old West Saxon royal house. However, some doubt must be raised concerning the kinship connection of Wulfnoth Cild with Æthelnoth and Æthelweard when we recognise that their known background has links to matters in Western Wessex whereas Wulfnoth Cild's known links are to Sussex.

The second Æthelmaer is a less likely candidate for being Godwin's grandfather. This Æthelmaer was reputedly, as proposed by the chronicler John of Worcester, a relative of ealdorman Eadric Streona.[3] Several academics have supported this hypothesis, and because of its underlying source of origin it is worth a mention, although the connection remains dubious. Eadric Streona was infamous for implementing and overseeing the court coups d'état and the faction assassinations that took place under Æthelred II's reign in the early years of the eleventh century, and Streona switched sides more than once during the English and Danish warfare between Edmund II Ironside and Cnut in 1016. He had progressed to become the king's senior advisor by 1006 and thereafter married Æthelred's daughter Eadgyth. The appellation 'Streona' was added by later clerical writers, translated as 'The Acquisitive', because of his appropriation of Church lands.[4] Knowledge of Godwin's early political career shows that he was opposed to Streona's dynastic house, and Wulfnoth Cild, as will be seen below, was outlawed following a direct altercation in 1009 involving Streona's brother Beorhtric. For that reason alone, a family tie between Godwin and Streona is tenuous. The powerbase of Streona and his brothers lay in Mercia, not Wessex, and on a practical level Wulfnoth was the same age if not older than this other Æthelmaer, so any father-son relationship between them can reasonably be dismissed.

Wulfnoth Cild was a prominent Wessex nobleman during the reign of Æthelred II, a senior thegn who probably owned several large estates in Sussex. The nomenclature of 'Cild' translates as 'child' but was an Old English title given to someone of high rank, although it seems that he was not accredited as an ealdorman. The *ASC* confirms his familial relationship with Godwin, naming 'Wulfnoth the South Saxon' as being 'father of earl Godwin'.[5] In accepting this relationship we should therefore think of Godwin's full name as being 'Godwin Wulfnothsson'. There are connections which support their kinship. Several years after Wulfnoth Cild disappears from the record one of his former estates was passed down to Godwin by the ætheling Æthelstan, the eldest heir of Æthelred II, within his will. This strongly suggests that Æthelstan had known Wulfnoth Cild and knew of the familial affiliation, and by the transfer of this estate Godwin was being acknowledged as the son of Wulfnoth and was belatedly receiving part of his inheritance.

Godwin later named his youngest son Wulfnoth, which by itself is not conclusive evidence he was Wulfnoth Cild's heir but does reinforce the likely connection. Nevertheless, not all historians support this supposition. The text later patronised by Godwin's daughter Edith, the *Vita Edwardi Regis*, makes no mention of her grandfather's noble standing.[6] Instead, it is claimed that Edith seems to imply that her father was not from a noble background and that he only achieved his lofty status when serving Cnut, noting he was 'among the new nobles of the conquered kingdom attached to the king's (i.e. Cnut's) side'.[7] This entry can be interpreted in more than one way, and may simply refer to Godwin achieving his earldom rather than being a pointed reference to his earlier background. It arguably praises his achievements rather than undermines them. More relevantly, it makes no sense for Edith to demean her own noble pedigree and heritage by disparaging the upbringing of her father.[8] Instead, we might regard this in the context of when this particular *Vita* entry was written post-1066. It was intended to gain favour with the new Norman regime by showing her disapproval of the earlier actions of her family during a later period when the reputation of all the Godwinsons, primarily her brother Harold, was openly derided by the Normans.

We find a Wulfnoth witnessing several royal charters between 986 and 1005, but it is unclear if this is our Wulfnoth Cild.[9] His year of birth is unclear, but based on estimates of Godwin's year of birth, discussed below, it is reasonable to deduce Wulfnoth Cild was perhaps born during the 970s and had married Godwin's unknown and unnamed mother by the mid-990s. The first explicit reference to Wulfnoth appears in two versions of the *ASC* for the year 1009, where he is defined as 'Prince Wulfnoth' and 'the nobleman Wulfnoth'.[10] Using this description acknowledges he was an important figure, possibly holding the position of king's thegn. As Godwin would later name his youngest son after Wulfnoth, we can speculate that one of his daughters, namely Eadgyth (aka Edith), Gunhild or perhaps Ælfgifu, was given his mother's name.

The name Godwin is Old English and translates as 'friend of God' or 'good friend'. In researching the *Prosopography of Anglo-Saxon England* database, we discover it was a popular name, and during his career there were over thirty contemporaries of the same name found within various separate texts, and nearly three hundred references to men named Godwin/Godwine within the *Domesday Book*. Even including errors of identification and some duplication this is still a staggering number to hold the name. Perhaps many of these contemporaries were given the name as a mark of respect for our Godwin, and the name was particularly popular in eastern

Wessex.[11] On estimating Godwin's age on his death in 1053, we can speculate that he was probably aged somewhere between fifty and sixty, so was born sometime between 992 and 1002. A few historians consider that Godwin was alive, albeit an infant, when the Dane Sweyn Forkbeard undertook his initial invasion of southern England around 994.[12] The lack of suitable source detail restricts precision, but most historians have calculated a more accurate birth date within the years 996 to 999 based on later events in Godwin's life, such as his promotion to earl, his marriage, and the births of his eldest children. Whether Godwin had any siblings is unclear. There is a tradition of a younger brother or brother-in-law named Ælfwig, gathered from a Victorian study of monastic abbots compiled from a subsequently lost document.[13] In 1063 this Ælfwig was to become the abbot at the New Minster in Winchester and afterwards joined Harold Godwinson at the battle of Hastings. The evidence for a dynastic link is hazy, but if Ælfwig was Godwin's younger sibling, he would have been at least in his late fifties by 1066. The connection is fragile, and if it relates to Godwin, we would expect him to be more prominent much sooner.

Nothing of Godwin's childhood and youth is established. In later centuries, he was portrayed as having emerged from peasant stock. One version of this low-status background emerges in the writer Walter Map's twelfth-century work *Di Nugis Curialium*, which recounts the tale of Æthelred II once losing his way whilst hunting in midwinter and being given shelter by a shepherd. Godwin, the shepherd's boy, tended the king's horse and made the king welcome, and in return, so the tale goes, Æthelred adopted Godwin and subsequently made him an earl.[14] This seems an extraordinarily generous reward, but it makes a good story. Another text, the Scandinavian *Knytlinga Saga*, speaks of Godwin being the son of a Wiltshire swineherd who helped Cnut's kinsman Ulf Thorgilsson, the brother of Godwin's future wife Gytha, recover after the battle of Sherston in 1016.[15] These stories have suspicious similarities, perhaps each originating later in Anglo-Norman circles to further disparage the Godwinsons' dynastic origins. Both versions gained popularity in the Victorian era as 'rags to riches' stories but are now largely dismissed as purely allegorical.

However, by accepting the paternity of Wulfnoth Cild we are accepting that Godwin had been born into a wealthy lifestyle through his father's position and connections, and in turn this would facilitate him making his own personal connections into adulthood. This privileged background would have assured him of a good education, and access to learning a variety of skills that he would employ effectively and adroitly in the years ahead. During Godwin's formative years he saw a sequence of Danish incursions into England during the reign of Æthelred and was perhaps aware through his father of the divided interests that flourished among various factions close to the royal court. Wulfnoth would, by design or otherwise, become embroiled in these political developments. Consequently, Godwin's youth was severely impacted in 1009 by his father's exiling, the details of which are discussed below.

As already noted, Wulfnoth Cild appears in the entries of two versions of the *ASC* in 1009.[16] The chronicle entries relate a significant event, a large Danish raiding army preparing to invade southern England under the leadership of Thorkell (aka Thorkill) the Tall. This was the latest of several serious Danish raids of increased strength and frequency over the previous fifteen years. The English king Æthelred II could not plan an effective and sustained military resistance, and instead often offered tribute payments to the Danes to suspend their attacks, familiarly identified as *Danegeld*. Further discord was caused by Æthelred's purges among the nobility, which in 1006 had seen several prominent ealdormen and thegns replaced with sycophantic devotees. The Mercian ealdorman Eadric Streona had become entrenched as Æthelred's favoured advisor by this date, and was heavily involved in these purges, removing rivals by assassination in some cases. While internal politics dominated, the response to invading Danes remained uncoordinated, and as told in the *ASC* for 1009 the English fyrd was unable to force the raiding armies to battle. The chronicler William of Malmesbury noted that the grand councils 'rarely or never agreed on a sensible course, for they discussed their private quarrels much more than necessary public action'.[17]

Nevertheless, in 1008 Æthelred had ordered the construction of a large navy to counteract further Danish invasions in the south-east. The *ASC* tells us that 'there were more of them (ships) than there had ever earlier been in England in the days of any king'.[18] The ships were based at the primary English naval base at Sandwich in Kent, on the Wantsum Channel next to Thanet, protecting both the Dover Strait and the Thames Estuary. The following year Wulfnoth Cild was named as joint commander of this fleet alongside Eadric Streona's brother Beorhtric. It appears from subsequent events that Wulfnoth was an experienced seaman, whereas Beorhtric's appointment looks to have come through Streona's persuasiveness at court.

Even before Thorkell's fleet arrived in late summer 1009 the English position had imploded. Perhaps for personal rivalry or to promote his own credentials as fleet commander, Beorhtric accused Wulfnoth of a serious misdemeanour, possibly treason. The chronicler John of Worcester later cast Beorhtric's character as similar to that of his brother Eadric Streona, describing him as 'a slippery man, ambitious and arrogant'.[19] This incident was perhaps one element of the factional political divide that had emerged at the royal court after the recent court purges and the previous mishandling of the military response. Streona and his supporters, favoured by the king, were seemingly at odds with a faction that were loyal to the royal æthelings Æthelstan and Edmund (Ironside), Æthelred II's eldest sons. Perhaps this primarily impacted the English strategy against Danish incursions, but deeper political differences between the king and his sons had likely been triggered by the earlier court purges. Wulfnoth Cild looks to have been a supporter of the æthelings, as suggested by Godwin's later mention in the will of the ætheling Æthelstan in 1014.

Whatever the rights or wrongs concerning Beorhtric's accusation, Æthelred believed Wulfnoth had a case to answer, although John of Worcester informs us that Wulfnoth was unjustly accused.[20] Knowing that he would perhaps not receive a fair hearing, Wulfnoth chose instead to take flight and hastily sailed from Sandwich with a flotilla of twenty vessels.[21] Most of these were presumably ships originating from ports in Sussex that were loyal to him, although the majority remained loyal to the king, with the *ASC* noting that Wulfnoth 'raided everywhere along the south coast, and wrought every kind of harm'.[22] All of this infers that Wulfnoth Cild was guilty of something, but the manner of his response seems curious. Being an important noble from Sussex, why did he conduct raids that directly impacted his own region and would antagonise his vassals? Beorhtric seized his opportunity to shine and took eighty ships from the royal fleet and went in pursuit of Wulfnoth down the English Channel.[23] However, displaying his lack of seamanship, Beorhtric was caught out by a sudden change in the weather. While Wulfnoth had taken his small flotilla inshore ahead of a brewing storm, Beorhtric's squadron was hit by strong winds. Many of his ships were sunk while the rest were severely damaged and blown ashore. On hearing of Beorhtric's misfortune, Wulfnoth then attacked the remaining vessels and 'came immediately and burned the ships'.[24]

Having overseen the destruction of a substantial percentage of the English fleet just before it would be needed to face the Danes, Beorhtric was summarily removed from his position. However, after briefly appearing at centre stage Wulfnoth Cild hereafter disappears from the primary record. He probably chose self-exile, realising that with Streona having Æthelred's ear it would be fruitless to seek a pardon. If he was innocent beforehand, the wilful destruction of the royal ships after the storm, no doubt an act of personal retribution against Beorhtric, placed him beyond any hope of restitution with Æthelred. Maybe the young Godwin briefly went into exile alongside his father, or perhaps he had been left at one of the family estates in Sussex in Wulfnoth Cild's haste to escape punishment. It is plausible that Godwin hereafter passed into the care of the ætheling Æthelstan's household, if not in 1009 then certainly before 1014, and it is this that saved him from the ultimate retribution for the deeds of his father. At the king's authorisation, Godwin was nevertheless deprived of his inheritance and his entitlement to his father's former position and estates.

Godwin would later be fast-tracked into the Anglo-Danish court of Cnut in 1017. It is suggested this may have been because his father had joined with Thorkell the Tall's Danish fleet in 1009 after the exiling.[25] This is plausible, but nothing more. Irrespective of his father's movements and allegiances, Godwin cannot have joined him. His appearance in the aforementioned will of Æthelstan, drafted just before the ætheling's death on 25 June 1014, strongly implies that Godwin's loyalties lay with the English at that juncture.[26] Æthelstan would not have included a grant to Godwin if he had previously acted alongside the Danes against English interests. The will assigned an estate at Compton in Sussex to Godwin, an estate previously in the possession of Wulfnoth Cild.[27] This acknowledges that Wulfnoth had already lost his endowments and was still in disgrace. Pardons were not unheard of, but it is more than likely he was already dead. Godwin was in England and of a suitable age by 1014 to receive the gift of one of Wulfnoth's former estates, all of which had likely been divided up in 1009–10.[28] This confirms as well as anything that Godwin's loyalty had remained with the Anglo-Saxon royal house, for had he transferred his allegiance to the Danes in the interim the estate would not have been returned to the family.

By the time of Æthelstan's death, the whole of England had been in a new turmoil. There had been almost continuous warfare with the Danish armies of invasion between 1009 and 1013 led by Thorkell the Tall and Sweyn Forkbeard. By the spring of 1013, Æthelred II had resorted to further payments of *Danegeld* and had employed Thorkell and his fleet as mercenaries to protect London against Thorkell's Danish compatriot Forkbeard's army. That stratagem was doomed to failure, and when the money ran out Thorkell withdrew, allowing Sweyn Forkbeard and his son Cnut to conquer all English resistance by the autumn of 1013. Before the end of that year Æthelred, with his second wife Emma of Normandy and their youngest children, sailed for Normandy and the protection of Emma's brother Duke Richard II. It was probably during this period, between the autumn and early winter of 1013, while the Danes were recruiting English allies and accepting oaths of fealty and demanding hostages across much of the country, that Cnut married his hand-fast wife Ælfgifu of Northampton, daughter of the deceased ealdorman Ælfhelm of Deiran Northumbria (York). Ælfhelm had been murdered by men working for Eadric Streona on the king's instructions in 1006, so the union of Ælfgifu to Cnut is understandable. At a personal level Ælfgifu had valid reasons to support those who opposed Æthelred. She was also related to the nobleman Siferth, who would himself be murdered on the king's instructions in 1015, so the house looks to have previously been supportive to those opposed to Æthelred.

In December, the Anglo-Saxon Witan of senior secular nobles and ecclesiastics acknowledged Sweyn Forkbeard as king of England. A formal ceremony took place on Christmas Day 1013, a date seemingly chosen deliberately to symbolise Sweyn's earlier conversion to Christianity back in Denmark. This was probably performed in one of the senior religious houses in the north Midlands, perhaps Lichfield, close to his main base at Gainsborough on the River Trent, as it is far from clear that Sweyn had fully established himself in London and the south-east beyond receiving formal oaths. However, Sweyn Forkbeard's reign in England was short-lived. On 2 February 1014, he suddenly died, purportedly after falling from his horse at Gainsborough.[29]

The English Witan immediately summoned Æthelred back from Normandy, but he had so little trust that he first sent his ten-year-old son Edward to England to represent him in negotiations. Perhaps Æthelred, prompted by Emma, first demanded an assurance that their boys would be accepted as first in line to succeed him over and above the claim of his older sons by his first wife, Ælfgifu of York. This may be why the boy Edward had been sent as his emissary, and it is likely that Duke Richard II of Normandy, Emma's brother, was influential in ensuring that Edward was promoted as the prime heir on Æthelred's return. With renewed promises given to the Witan – ones he would find it challenging to keep – Æthelred and Emma came back to England.

His initial act was to collect taxes to pay £21,000 to a Danish raiding army at Greenwich.[30] These men were under the command of Thorkell the Tall, and it seems clear his mercenary fleet had accompanied Æthelred back to England to ensure that London did not fall to Cnut before the English king re-established himself. With his father dead, Cnut had assumed control of the Danish army at Gainsborough; however, before he could plan his next move, the re-energised Æthelred had summoned a large English fyrd and launched a campaign towards Gainsborough into Lindsey (Lincolnshire) just after Easter. As the English army pillaged the region that had most strongly supported the Danes, Cnut was forced to abandon his base. The Danish fleet withdrew to the North Sea, but before leaving for Denmark to regroup Cnut landed at Sandwich and, in an act of revenge, 'put ashore the hostages that were granted to his father, and cut off their hands and ears and noses'.[31]

This situation brings us back full circle to June 1014 and the death of Æthelstan, the then heir to the throne. As suggested by his appearance in the will, Godwin must have already been mixing in higher circles, perhaps as a vassal of either Æthelstan or Edmund (Ironside). The will mentioned Æthelstan's father, grandfather, and foster mother, but not his mother Ælfgifu of York or his stepmother Emma or her sons Edward and Alfred.[32] Ælfgifu had likely died some years previously. Furthermore, the will also encompassed provision for three northern thegns: Morcar, Siferth and Thurbrand. Their inclusion is significant, because it highlights ongoing differences between the royal æthelings and their father.[33] Morcar and Siferth would be assassinated by agents of Eadric Streona in 1015 working for Æthelred, and Thurbrand would later be killed in an ongoing Northumbrian blood-feud between his people and those of Uhtred the Bold, a supporter of Edmund.[34] Divisions inside the royal court resurfaced during 1015, which tells us that the restored monarch had learnt nothing from the lessons of 1006–13 and the successes of Sweyn Forkbeard. England remained divided and open for a new Danish campaign. It would appear in 1015, and Cnut would lead it.

From Godwin's viewpoint, we can imagine he saw Æthelred II and the house of Eadric Streona as being fully accountable for his loss of inheritance. He had therefore turned in favour of the æthelings' supporters, those who appear to have been against Streona's politics. Perhaps we can speculate that Godwin had already transferred his vassalage to Edmund at this stage, based on his former connection with the deceased Æthelstan. Edmund, as the eldest surviving of the royal æthelings, now openly led the faction opposed to the strategies of Streona that had dominated his father's internal policies.

On Siferth's assassination in 1015 the king had placed the nobleman's widow Ealdgyth into captivity at Malmesbury Abbey, but in open defiance to his father Edmund released her, returned her to Northumbria, and then married her. John of Worcester dates this to the last two weeks of August 1015.[35] Edmund's actions seem designed to help repair the damage already caused by the assassination and to reunite the royal house with the Northumbrian elite, and through this marriage Edmund gained the submission of Siferth and Morcar's former followers. This decision to rebel indicates that Edmund was already aware that his father was intending to bypass him in favour of Edward in the succession. Nevertheless, in acting against Æthelred's wishes, whatever its merits, Edmund had widened further the already evident gulf between them.

Developments now accelerated. Sweyn Forkbeard had been replaced in Denmark by Cnut's brother Harold (as King Harold II), and in the late summer of 1015 Cnut reappeared off the coast of England with a new Danish invasion armada of more than 200 ships which included a large contingent of Polish mercenaries. The fleet moved along the Channel and into Poole harbour and raided unhindered across Dorset, Wiltshire, and Somerset.[36] The English failed to respond quickly or adequately to the threat. Æthelred had taken ill and retired to his estate at Cosham near Portsmouth while the Danes pillaged Wessex. Edmund meanwhile raised an army in the north to challenge the invaders, and on behalf of the king Eadric Streona finally took to the field. The two English fyrds met somewhere in the south Midlands, but before they had engaged with Cnut, as recorded by the *ASC*, 'the ealdorman (Eadric) wanted to betray the ætheling (Edmund), and therefore they parted without a fight, and retreated from their enemies'.[37] It is difficult to know how to interpret this entry. Perhaps they failed to agree on a strategy, or possibly Edmund became aware that Eadric was untrustworthy or was still ill-prepared to fight Cnut. Suffice to say that Edmund's army was likely too weak to fight Cnut without support.

Immediately after separating from Edmund, Streona returned south and took command of forty ships from the fleet on the pretext of blockading Cnut's armada inside Poole harbour. Maybe this had been agreed at his meeting with Edmund. However, on reaching Poole, where the Danes had set up their winter encampment, Streona betrayed his promises, not for the last time, and submitted himself, the ships, and his men to Cnut. In early January 1016, with Streona now alongside him, Cnut crossed the River Thames near Cricklade and plundered extensively further north into Warwickshire.[38] Trying to piece together events in these early months of 1016 is difficult. The *ASC* cryptically noted that 'when it was made known to the king that one who should have been of help to him wanted to betray him, he (Æthelred) left the army and turned back to London'.[39] Mention of betrayal would point to Eadric Streona, and maybe Æthelred had finally seen the light. However, the *ASC* scribes have not been restrained in describing Streona's negative traits in other entries so why not name him here? Perhaps the chronicler was instead referring to Edmund if the relationship between father and son had broken beyond repair. It should be remembered that Æthelred had resolved that Edmund and his other sons fathered with Ælfgifu of York were to be superseded in the succession by his sons with Emma, and from Edmund's perspective Æthelred's conduct since his return had been no better than before. While the king retired to London, Edmund had proceeded to gather forces before turning south, perhaps with the premise of this time unifying his forces with the London garrison.

The prime sources are a little confused, but it appears Æthelred was at first reticent to lead the southern English fyrd. Possibly there was another disagreement on the required course of action. At this impasse, Edmund rapidly returned north again and allied his forces with ealdorman Uhtred (the Bold) of Bernician Northumbria. Edmund and Uhtred then marched their forces into Staffordshire and Cheshire, plundering the estates and settlements owned by Eadric Streona. The English allies and the Cnut–Streona alliance that had also moved into the Midlands failed to clash. While the English had advanced into the north-west Midlands, Cnut advanced his army to the east of them and on to York, presumably intending to attract more support from a region with strong Scandinavian affiliations. This manoeuvre threatened a Danish advance further north and, planned or otherwise, it forced Uhtred to move his forces back to Bernicia to cover the threat. Unwisely, as it transpired, Uhtred then agreed to negotiate. This proved fateful because Cnut, or more likely Streona, had already employed Uhtred's blood feud rival Thurbrand to have Uhtred and his entourage killed during a meeting called to negotiate while under a guarantee of protection. Uhtred and his men were surrounded and murdered, with the *ASC* version C adding that his disposal was made 'on the advice of Ealdorman Eadric (Streona)'.[40]

Godwin does not feature before 1017–18, and we are left to speculate his movements. There is a distinct possibility that he was already part of Edmund's entourage, albeit not yet a commanding figure, during the fighting that was about to play out in 1016. Emma of Normandy's *Encomium Emmae Regina* refers to her husband Cnut's later favouring of Godwin because 'he loved those whom he had heard to have fought previously for Edmund faithfully without deceit'.[41] This supports the argument that Godwin was already fighting alongside Edmund. It also supports the rational case to explain why Godwin appears to have been fast-tracked into a position of authority by Cnut shortly after he succeeded as king, something which was unlikely to have happened if Godwin had not already been a trusted member of the Anglo-Saxon hierarchy.

Moving south, Edmund reached London safely and was besieged there by Cnut, who had been joined by Thorkell the Tall, before Easter (7 April). Æthelred II was already seriously ill, and possibly had been for some time, and a fortnight afterwards he died on 23 April.[42] He was buried in the original St Paul's Cathedral, and his tomb survived until the building was destroyed during the Great Fire of London in 1666.[43] Edmund (thereafter to be given the epithet 'Ironside') was sworn in as King Edmund II by the Witan council at London.

By the summer, it was clear Cnut could not force London to submit. He had constructed a ditch to the south of London Bridge so he could drag his warships west of the bridge and had created a rampart and ditch to ensure complete encirclement, but still he failed to breach the defences. As noted by the *ASC*, 'no one could get in or out (of London)', and despite the Danes having 'regularly attacked the town', the defenders 'resolutely withstood them'.[44] Perhaps because the siege was beginning to take hold, Edmund had already left London and crossed into central Wessex. Leaving a small besieging force behind, Cnut went in pursuit. However, Edmund had time to gather new forces and the two armies clashed in Penselwood Forest in Somerset, probably during the June of 1016. The battle site lies north of the modern A303 road, 2 miles east of present-day Wincanton. A more precise location may be near the Iron Age hillfort known as Kenwalch's Castle, now tree-covered and bisected by Pen Hill Road, a mile or so north of Penselwood village. John of Worcester recorded that 'he (Edmund) gave them (the Danes) battle, won, and put them to flight'.[45] More likely the encounter proved inconclusive. While Edmund gathered yet more fresh troops in Wiltshire, the Danes received their own fresh reserves and were joined there by Eadric Streona.

A greater battle took place after midsummer at Sherston in Wiltshire. John of Worcester again gives the best detail and writes of Edmund's leadership during the fighting, although he also notes that men from Hampshire and Wiltshire fought for the Danes.[46] These were perhaps the men Streona had recruited after first allying with Cnut in Dorset. The *Encomium Emmae* claims that Thorkell, and not Cnut, led the Danish forces at Sherston, and may also have led them earlier at Penselwood.[47] We should suppose that, having been his wife, Emma's input here is reliable about Cnut's absence. The battlefield's whereabouts in relation to the village of Sherston are not precisely known, but it is a good assumption that it was somewhere on or close to the Roman Fosse Way, which runs on a south-west-to-north-east alignment about a mile and a half to the east of the village. The armies had likely approached each other along the Fosse Way. The *ASC* scribe states that the Danish raiding army broke off the fight.[48] We have no details of the fighting, but we are entitled to claim this as a victory for Edmund, as the Danish army withdrew from further engagement in the West Country and retired back towards London.

Godwin and his father were later indirectly linked to Sherston, not in a description of the battle but in association with his family origins. The reference, as previously noted, comes from the mid-thirteenth-century Icelandic saga about Cnut, the *Knytlinga Saga,* in which it tells of the Danish Jarl Ulf Thorgilsson escaping from Sherston and being befriended soon after by the swineherd Wulfnoth and his son Godwin. The tale continues, and for helping Ulf, Godwin was rewarded subsequently with Cnut's patronage.[49] Godwin was later to marry Ulf's sister Gytha, which was probably the event that prompted the story. As already mentioned, this tale is drawn from the allegory of Godwin being of lowly stock, replacing the shepherd in Walter Map's *Di Nugis Curialium* with a swineherd, and transposing Æthelred II's patronage with Cnut's.[50] It is stretching the imagination to accept that within three years Godwin was transposed from swineherd/shepherd to earl of Wessex. However, the association of Godwin with Sherston may perhaps contain a kernel of truth, in that Godwin may have fought as a young man there alongside Edmund.

After the triumph at Sherston, Edmund pursued the Danes back east. Manoeuvring north of the Danish siege lines around London, he surprised the besiegers and drove them to their ships at Brentford.[51] However, some English drowned while pursuing the Danes across the River Thames, and Edmund was forced to withdraw also. He was finding it challenging to raise sufficient new levies after the casualties suffered at Penselwood and Sherston, and now Brentford, and despite his successes, he was obliged to return west to recruit more men. The Danish siege of London resumed while Cnut took his fleet into the Thames Estuary and along the River Orwell in Suffolk, pillaging across a wide area before returning and sailing his fleet up the River Medway into Kent. Cnut may have thought Edmund's forces were spent, but the English king came back and attacked again, catching the Danish army at Otford, near present-day Sevenoaks, and pursued them eastward, slaying many, through Aylesford north of Maidstone and on to the Isle of Sheppey.[52]

Now came a moment that altered Edmund's and England's fortunes. After Otford, Eadric Streona reassessed his options, deserted the Danes, and swore a new oath to support Edmund. This is proof that Edmund now looked likely to win the war and expel the Danes for good. Why Edmund accepted Streona's oath is difficult to comprehend; it seems illogical from what we know of Streona's character up to that point. It may have been a question of needs must, with the English king requiring the extra fighting men from Mercia that Streona could provide.

With Streona alongside, Edmund pursued Cnut across the Thames and into Essex. He caught up with Cnut and gave battle on 18 October 1016 at a place named Assandun (meaning 'ass's hill'). There are two viable locations for the battleground. The first is in northern Essex at Ashdon, about 4 miles north-east of Saffron Walden. Those supporting Ashdon point to the archaeological evidence of an earlier eleventh-century stone church, a spot now occupied by the fourteenth-century All Saints Church, which has been suggested as the church Cnut later established in 1020 to commemorate the battle. It has been argued that the Danes had sailed up the River Stour and then entered the River Granta and were caught while returning to their ships by Edmund, who had moved his army via the Roman Ermine Street and Icknield Way.[53] Critics of this location have argued that it is too far north for Cnut to have brought his fleet inland; it was 50 river miles from the Thames.

The second location for Assandun is at Ashingdon 'hill' or 'mount', which is named by the primary sources, the *ASC*, John of Worcester, and within the *Encomium Emmae*.[54] It supports the idea that the Danes had entered the River Crouch or the River Stour. Ashingdon is 2 miles south of the Crouch, about 3 miles north of present-day Rochford, leading to a scenario in which the Danes were trapped between Edmund and the Stour. Assandun has been defined as taking place between Ashingdon and the village of Canewdon, with Edmund's forces attacking eastward towards Canewdon. The sources tell us that after initial early successes by the English, Edmund's centre and left wing were enveloped by the Danes. Eadric Streona's Mercian forces on the right wing had delayed their attack or had fled the field. John of Worcester praises Edmund's fighting qualities anew, but tells us it was Streona's betrayal that cost the English victory, recording that just when the Danes were wavering Streona 'took flight, as he had earlier promised Cnut, with the section of the army under his command'.[55] Up to that point the English had had the best of it, but Streona's move, which may indeed have been pre-planned, turned the tide and the Danes were victorious. Many Anglo-Saxon nobles were killed, including ealdormen Ælfric of Hampshire and Ulfcytel (aka Ulfketel) Snilling of East Anglia and Bishop Eadnoth of Dorchester-on-Thames.[56]

After he had established himself, Cnut ordered a minster to be built on the battlefield to commemorate his achievement. As with All Saints Church at the alternate location, the present-day St Andrew's Church at Ashingdon is believed to be on the site of the original minster that Cnut is said to have founded afterwards in 1020. Most historians prefer this Ashingdon site out of the two favoured options, both for its better primary text support and its geographical setting. Following the defeat at Assandun, Edmund again returned to the West Country to recover his resources. However, he was followed by Cnut and a meeting was arranged between them on an isle called Alney (or Ola) on the River Severn in Gloucestershire near Deerhurst. Deerhurst was the home of St Mary's Priory Church, an important early Anglo-Saxon site with which Edmund had previous connections, and here the two leaders agreed to divide the kingdom. Edmund was to control Wessex and Cnut Mercia, apparently including London. The Danes were given additional tribute to ensure the peace would hold.[57] The tribute payment suggests that Edmund had lost the initiative after Assandun, although the situation regarding London is unclear. The garrison and citizens had resisted Cnut over two sieges beforehand, and his later actions would indicate that he was still not assured of their immediate loyalty. London may have remained within Edmund's control, or perhaps was designated a neutral zone.

This agreement was unlikely to have survived for long, but it proved to be in force for only a few weeks. On St Andrew's Day, 30 November, six weeks after Assandun, Edmund Ironside died, possibly the result of a wound infection or illness following recent events.[58] John of Worcester recorded that Ironside died in London, which seems improbable, while Henry of Huntingdon names instead Oxford, although both may be inaccurate.[59] Edmund's body was taken to Glastonbury Abbey and buried close to the tomb of his grandfather King Edgar. Some primary sources later delved deeper into the cause of Edmund's death. A more troublesome version revolves around an assassination, supposedly delivered by a knife from below while he was answering a call of nature.[60] Henry of Huntingdon relates how Edmund was 'treacherously killed' by 'the son of Ealdorman Eadric (Streona) ... by his father's plan'.[61] The twelfth-century writer Geffrei Gaimar in his prose on the history of the English, his *Estoire des Engleis*, writes that Edmund was killed by Streona with an arrow from below.[62]

The story of this ignominious end may be nothing beyond later anti-Danish propaganda, but several sources repeat it and place Streona squarely behind the murder. It cannot be entirely dismissed. Upon Edmund's death, the English Witan nominated Cnut as his successor across all England. Emma and her children may have lingered in England after Æthelred had died, but likely crossed to Normandy as soon as news was received of Edmund Ironside's death. It is plausible she had remained in England, but Edward, and presumably Alfred with him, had crossed no later than December, as there is a record of Edward taking an oath at the abbey of St Peter's in Ghent, Flanders.[63]

We have largely ignored Godwin while narrating the circumstances around Cnut's invasion and the warfare between Edmund and the Danes, and that is because he remains absent from the primary sources. Whether he was with Edmund at Assandun and then part of his entourage at the River Severn and Deerhurst remains speculative. It would be nice to consider he had become a close advisor and possibly a friend of the king, but he was probably not in Edmund's inner circle and he was still relatively young. An alternate argument has been put forward by some historians that, as Godwin was to become one of Cnut's closest advisors during 1017–18, he must have joined the Danes in the warfare of 1016. This cannot be dismissed entirely – we have no primary evidence either way – but it relies on hindsight. Godwin had no prior reason to join the Danes in 1016 while an English king sat on the throne, so to interpret his motives ahead of Edmund's death as being pro-Danish because of later vassalage to Cnut is not a rational argument.

Genealogy Chart of the House of Godwin

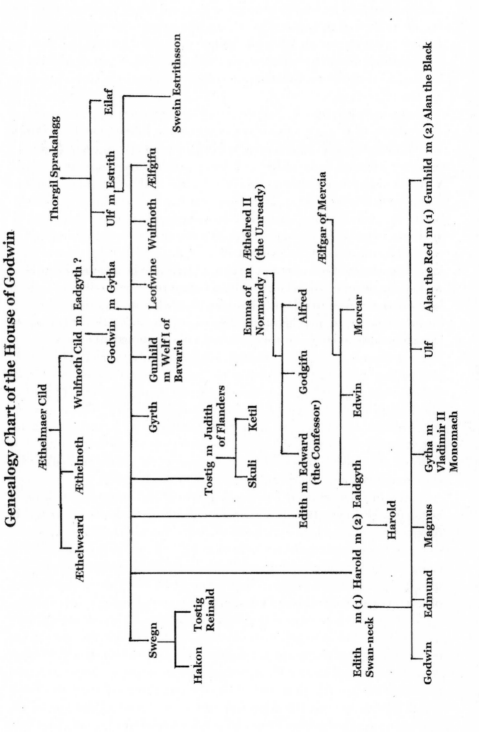

2

Godwin's Rise to Power

After Edmund Ironside's death the English Witan accepted Cnut as king of all England, and Archbishop Lyfing conducted a coronation service in London in the first few weeks of 1017. However, Cnut's relationship with London's citizens was less than amicable, and he was to impose a heavy tax on the settlement. London had been Æthelred II's preferred primary residence but not Cnut's, at least not initially. He located his court at Winchester, and further embellished the city as his 'capital' in his early years on the throne, including maintaining the treasury there and improving the major churches to reflect his earlier conversion to Christianity.[1] This preference for Winchester would change in time. London was better situated for communications, notably with the Continent, and it was Cnut rather than Edward (the Confessor) who first developed a royal palace at Westminster close to the existing monastery.[2]

Cnut's brother, Harold Sweynson (Harold II), continued as king in Denmark. However, Harold's premature death the following year would require Cnut to raise heavy taxes in England to finance a military expedition to retain his dynastic authority in Danish-held regions of Scandinavia. The cause of Harold's death while still in his early twenties is unknown. The question of a potential inherited medical problem which shortened the lives of several of Sweyn Forkbeard's descendants is considered in a later chapter.

Godwin was to emerge at the Anglo-Danish court a year after Cnut's accession, and we shall return to Godwin shortly, but for now we need to build the picture of the measures Cnut took to establish Danish rule. Military command was paramount. He introduced the professional housecarls (aka huscarls), the 'household troops', as a standing elite military force. These would in time become the dominant arm of the fyrd and the core of the retinues of the elite nobles. Cnut divided government of England into four spheres, loosely based on the four largest old Anglo-Saxon kingdoms, namely Wessex, Mercia, Northumbria (comprising Deira and Bernicia), and East Anglia. This placed the administration and military responsibilities of each of these regions in the hands of an earl. Cnut initially took control of Wessex, East Anglia went to Thorkell the Tall and Northumbria to Eric Hákonarson (aka Eric or Yric of Hlathir).[3] Eadric Streona was appointed to Mercia, seemingly part of the terms agreed with Cnut beforehand for betraying Edmund Ironside and re-joining the Danes. Not all of Mercia went to Streona. Eilaf (aka Ecglaf), the brother of Godwin's future wife Gytha, was allocated Gloucestershire, Ranig was given Herefordshire, and Hakon Ericsson (son of Eric Hákonarson) received Worcestershire.[4]

In the early months of 1017 Cnut began to cull the Anglo-Saxon ealdormen and thegns whom he considered possible threats to his position. These included Northman, oldest son and heir of the Mercian ealdorman Leofwine; Æthelweard, son of ealdorman Æthelmaer Cild; and Beorhtric, offspring of Ælfheah of Devon.[5] Æthelweard, if the link to Æthelmaer Cild discussed previously is accepted, was Wulfnoth's Cild's brother, which, as proposed, made him Godwin's uncle. John of Worcester links the purges to those nobles formerly closest with Edmund Ironside, but specifically those who witnessed the agreement with Cnut at Alney on the River Severn and knew of the provisions supposedly granted by Cnut for Edmund's surviving family to rule Wessex after his death.[6] Cnut, however, seems to have had no intention of keeping that commitment. At face value, John's comment suggests that Godwin was either not present at Alney or was considered no threat to the new regime. These purges included the hunting down and killing of the ætheling Eadwig (aka Eadwy), Edmund Ironside's last surviving brother and the fifth and youngest son of Æthelred and Ælfgifu of York. In the initial weeks following his brother Edmund's death Eadwig had remained on the loose, but there had been reconciliation with Cnut over the winter of 1016/17. Some historians have suggested that after giving assurances to Cnut Eadwig had then attempted a rebellion, which had failed, and it was this that forced Cnut to kill him.[7] The chronicler William of Malmesbury elaborates on Eadwig's exile, writing that Eadwig had 'returned surreptitiously to England, died while in hiding, and was buried at Tavistock'.[8]

As part of his father's compromise with the northern English aristocracy during the earlier warfare of 1013, the young Cnut had made a political marriage, as touched on beforehand, with Ælfgifu of Northampton, the daughter of the previously influential but deceased ealdorman Ælfhelm. Cnut had taken Ælfgifu back to Denmark in 1014 and their first son, Svein (Cnutsson), was born there. Their second son, Harold Cnutsson (thereafter to be given the appellation Harefoot), came two years later, and it was Harold that would be involved in the Anglo-Danish succession crisis, as

King Harold I, twenty years later. In July 1017, without repudiating his hand-fast wife Ælfgifu, Cnut took as his second wife Æthelred II's widow Emma of Normandy.[9] This was ostensibly a political alliance. It was also a way of placating the English by returning their former widowed queen to prominence. As advocated by William of Malmesbury, it would have also persuaded Emma's father Duke Richard I of Normandy to not advance the claims of his grandchildren, the English æthelings Edward and Alfred, in the knowledge that male heirs from the union of his daughter with Cnut would be next in line for the English succession.[10] The union could have been agreed months beforehand if Emma had lingered in London over the winter of 1016/17, and Continental sources infer that London did not surrender to Cnut until the marriage was negotiated.[11] Some historians see Emma as being held a 'prisoner' of the Danish king and having no alternative but to accept a marriage.[12] Nevertheless, Cnut's refusal to repudiate his previous marriage to Ælfgifu of Northampton would store up future problems.

Emma had three children from her first marriage: Edward, born 1003–04; Alfred, born 1005; and a girl named Godgifu (aka Goda), probably born in between the two boys. Emma was already in her early thirties by 1017, Cnut several years younger. Whether she was forced into this marriage is a moot point; she seems to have coveted returning to her role as queen, and it is clear thereafter that she had stronger feelings for Cnut than she ever had for Æthelred. For Cnut, union with the widow of a former king helped validate and legitimise his position. Emma's children by Æthelred remained behind in Normandy, which was sensible as Cnut would surely have had them killed. However, it perhaps illustrates in full hindsight that her relationship with Edward and Alfred meant less to her than her new husband and position.

Edward would have had no inkling of his mother's intentions. A charter from Ghent in Flanders at Christmas 1016 in which he avowed that the property lost to the Danes would be restored when he returned as king implies that he knew nothing of Emma's plans.[13] This may have been the first instance but not the last where Edward would feel betrayed by his mother. The marriage came in the understanding that any male children from their union would become heirs to England, over and above any claims made by Edward or Alfred. Potentially children from Cnut and Emma's union would also inherit Cnut's Anglo-Scandinavian empire, but if Cnut and Emma did not produce a male heir there was the additional assurance that the succession would pass to his heirs from his earlier marriage. Their first child, the only boy as it transpired, was Harthacnut (aka Hardecnut), born during 1018, but the line of progression would ultimately prove to be more complicated. Cnut's sons Svein and Harold (Harefoot) from his earlier marriage to Ælfgifu would play a part after their father's death, particularly Harold. So too would Emma's sons with Æthelred, although the likelihood of Edward or Alfred laying claim to the English throne probably seemed a distant possibility in 1017.

Cnut next looked to dispose of Edmund Ironside's two young boys, Edmund and Edward, from Ironside's marriage to Eadgyth. They were still infants by 1017–18, little more than babies, but while they remained alive there was potential that those wishing to reinstate the West Saxon line would gather around their cause. Cnut had to be seen not to be directly involved in their disposal, and Emma may have encouraged him in this action.[14] A plan was devised to send them to 'safety' to Sweden, with secondary secret instructions to have them killed. Various primary sources confirm the æthelings were sent to the Swedish king Olof Skötkonung to be put to death.[15] However, the plan backfired. As noted by William of Malmesbury, Olof 'spared their lives, and they later took refuge with the king of the Huns (Hungary)'.[16] The chronicler was only half right. As discussed again in a later chapter, recent research shows the orphans first travelled from Sweden to the court of the Russian king Yaroslav I (the Wise), and many years would pass before they arrived in Hungary.[17] Edmund was to die in 1054, but the youngest ætheling, Edward (subsequently known as Edward the Exile), would make a dramatic return to England in 1057.

Cnut's final act of 1017, when matters had settled, was to dispose of Eadric Streona, displaying a ruthlessness that Streona would have ironically appreciated. This was an example of Cnut's logic that someone who could betray their king, as Streona had done to Edmund Ironside, could equally one day do the same to him, and therefore had to be removed. William of Malmesbury writes in some length about Streona's demise, barely concealing his pleasure and detailing the imagined conversation between them at Cnut's court. Malmesbury narrates that Streona told Cnut, 'First I abandoned Edmund for you, and then also put him to death out of loyalty to you.' Cnut responds, 'Then you too will deserve to die if you are guilty of high treason against God and myself by killing your own lord and a brother who was in alliance with me. Thy blood be upon thy head; for thy mouth hath testified against thee.'[18] This implies Streona had arranged Edmund's murder, and was a piece of text the chronicler seems to have enjoyed writing. The Mercian ealdorman was reportedly strangled, and 'thrown out of the window into the Thames, thus paying the due penalty for his perfidy'.[19] The *Encomium Emmae Reginae*, commissioned by Emma after Cnut's death long before Malmesbury's work, tells a different version in which Cnut tells Eric Hákonarson (aka Eric of Hlathir) to 'pay this man (Streona) what we owe him; that is to say, kill him, lest he play us false', upon which Eric immediately beheaded Streona.[20] By implication, these versions absolve Cnut of involvement in Edmund's death, and tell of a level of respect he had held for his former adversary. Nevertheless, that aside, the reality was that Streona was no longer of use to Cnut and was a convenient scapegoat.

The rise of Godwin in the Anglo-Danish court of Cnut is more surprising by its swiftness and suggests that he was already a significant figure during Edmund's reign. Some argue that to achieve such a promotion he must have previously given oaths to the Danes. Perhaps this argument is reinforced if we acknowledge the kinship links of Wulfnoth Cild to Æthelmaer Cild and Godwin's 'uncles' Æthelnoth and Æthelweard, for it is known that both Æthelmaer Cild and Æthelweard had yielded peacefully to Cnut's father Sweyn Forkbeard in the warfare of 1013. The prominence of Æthelmaer, Æthelnoth, and Æthelweard as men who cooperated with the Danes implies, if we trust the dynastic affiliation, that Godwin had similarly given oaths after his father's exile. The link to these men remains open to interpretation, but it is noticeable that in Godwin's later life there is no obvious friendship or obvious connection with Æthelnoth that we would expect to find if they were nephew and uncle. There is the connection Æthelweard had with the ætheling Eadwig, and by association with Godwin, if as debated Godwin had acted alongside Eadwig's brothers Æthelstan and Edmund. The association is thin, and therefore the relationship these men had to Wulfnoth Cild must remain unclear. Æthelweard was subsequently removed by Cnut at Easter, 17 April 1020.[21]

Godwin comes across later in his career as an opportunist, but this does not necessarily mean that he was servile or sycophantic. There is no hint in any of the primary sources that he acted in the style of an Eadric Streona or alienated the Anglo-Saxon thegns in Wessex who formerly supported the West Saxon royal house. Godwin was perhaps a realist, prepared to recognize the new administration once further resistance proved useless. All the nobles were involved in pursuing their own agendas. This was often a high-risk strategy, but Godwin was apparently more prudent and was able to do it better than the rest.[22] Godwin's career, not Streona's, seems to represent the normal state of affairs. Members of the nobility were often opportunists, but there was a sense of honour which is perhaps difficult to grasp in a modern context. Where we see a breakdown of friendship it was usually through family allegiances and personal feuds rather than a leaning towards 'everyone for themselves'. Men like Streona were the exception, not the norm.

The trust Godwin was to receive from Cnut was partly a consequence of his previous loyalty to the former regime. He must have played a highly effective political game at this juncture, truthful enough not to deny his former close connections to the Anglo-Saxon æthelings, but willing to show his full acceptance of the current regime, in a manner that impressed Cnut more so than the sycophantic approach displayed by others. Nevertheless, some historians see him differently, speculating that his rapid promotion was because his father Wulfnoth Cild had married a Danish woman and had transferred his allegiance to Sweyn Forkbeard and Cnut during the Danish wars of 1012–16.[23] However, there is no evidence Godwin's unknown mother was Danish, and equally no evidence Godwin's father had supported the Danes after his exiling. In contrast, Godwin's connection with the æthelings pre-1017 implies he only transferred his allegiance to Cnut after the death of Edmund.

The disdain with which Cnut treated those who flattered him is presented in the allegorical account of the Danish king defying the tide, a story familiar to most children. The twelfth-century chronicler Henry of Huntingdon was the principal source accountable for it becoming a popular legend, telling us how Cnut had placed his chair on the seashore and insisted that the tide not rise.[24] It was repeated by Geffrei Gaimar in some detail, with the incident taking place at Westminster and Cnut trying to stop the Thames rising.[25] The incident as detailed may be pure fiction, but it is emblematic. It's meaning has been frequently misinterpreted. It was not a display of Cnut's arrogance or vanity, as often described, but rather a rebuke aimed at his courtiers to demonstrate his humility. Its original context has been lost, but we should see it as a symbolic facet of Cnut's character, his determination not to surround himself with flatterers but to seek instead court advisors prepared to speak openly whether good or bad. At some stage Godwin must have come to Cnut's attention as someone who fitted that category. We can never know for certain, but perhaps Godwin was prepared, as an advisor, to risk contradicting the new Danish monarch. On a practical level Cnut needed links to the former regime during the early transition to Danish rule to ensure the English factions would more readily accept his new administration. Godwin was seemingly the man chosen to fill an important role.

The tale of Cnut and the tide has associations with Bosham, a large, safe tidal harbour incorporating Chidham and Thorney Island, 4 miles south-west of Chichester. Bosham is mentioned in the Venerable Bede's *The Ecclesiastical History of the English People*.[26] It is the location most closely identified with Godwin and his family. It was the site of the drowning in the mill-race of Cnut's eight-year-old daughter, the remains of whom are believed to be those first discovered during excavations at Bosham's Holy Trinity church in 1865 and assessed again in the twentieth century.[27] A memorial tablet for the child, originally placed in 1906 but moved in 1954 to lie over the original grave, can be seen today. Holy Trinity is claimed to be the oldest surviving site of Christianity in Sussex, dating originally from the seventh century. Much of the present-day church contains sections from the early eleventh century. These include the lower sections of the tower and part of the chancel walls which were added by the Godwinsons, although the chancel arch is late eleventh century. The spire is a fifteenth-century construction. A royal hall in stone, as depicted in the *Bayeux Tapestry*, is said to have been sited just north of the church, but there has been no major archaeological research so far. The drowning of Cnut's daughter is traditionally dated to 1020–21, by which time Godwin was an earl. Identifying the mother of the deceased child leads to an interesting hypothesis about Godwin's promotion and his future wife Gytha, and this is looked at towards the end of this chapter. Perhaps we can speculate that Cnut owned the estate or had already granted it to Godwin and was visiting him when the girl drowned. It is plausible that Bosham had previously been held by Godwin's father Wulfnoth Cild, as several estates in the south-west corner of Sussex can be linked to the Godwinsons.

Initially, Godwin was not part of Cnut's inner circle, but he soon features strongly during the latter part of 1018. Danes naturally figure highly in Cnut's early charters, but there are a few prominent Anglo-Saxons alongside Godwin during 1018–19. Aside from the Danes Thorkell the Tall, Eric Hákonarson, Eilaf (aka Ecglaf) and Hakon Ericsson, English ealdormen such as Leofwine, Æthelric and Æthelweard also feature. Once the primary threats to his rule had been resolved, Cnut appears to have worked hard to accommodate many of the English nobility into his Anglo-Danish administration. One fundamental change was that the former Anglo-Saxon title of 'ealdorman' was henceforth replaced with the title of 'earl'. The earls represented a larger region than the ealdormanry had but performed a similar function in terms of regional administration. Godwin would on his promotion be known as 'earl'.

In 1018 Cnut rendered a tax across England 'that was in all seventy-two thousand pounds', plus another 'ten-and-a-half thousand pounds' from London.[28] This was an unprecedented tax of one pound on each hide, amounting to nearly 100 per cent of the total economic income from 1017.[29] It was basically to pay the overdue wages of many Danish warriors and the fleet, but also to pay for additional recruits for Cnut's new campaign in Denmark planned for 1019 following the news that his brother King Harold II of Denmark had died suddenly. Cnut may have singled out London for a heavy tax, perhaps in punishment for the problems the London garrison and its citizens had caused him in the recent warfare.[30] To collect these funds Cnut needed the cooperation of the established Anglo-Saxon administrators and collectors, so from an early stage he was keen to engender English support. Godwin may have been one of those charged with overseeing the gathering of taxes across much of the south. Cnut's first Danish campaign likely began during 1019 and stretched into the following year, where he led the Danes against the Wends (Slavs of the southern Baltic), who had posed a threat to southern Denmark.[31]

Before that, in 1018, Cnut had called a council at Oxford, possibly soon after the tax impositions. A law code was composed for him by Archbishop Wulfstan (Lupus) of York, drawing on earlier legislation and an adaption of

Æthelred II's Enham code of 1008. In it was the declaration that all English and Danes were to be considered equal, and it reiterated the laws of King Edgar (r. 959–975) as the basis for a new understanding. A further, lengthier code was drafted, again by Wulfstan of York, after a second meeting at Winchester. These codes were a further reiteration and extension, again tied to Edgar's codes, and are the most extensive record of laws surviving from the Anglo-Saxon period.[32] They set out how justice was to be administered and by whom, and dealt with punishments for perjury and adultery, but noticeably are concerned with recognising the importance of the Church and adoption of Christian dogma. Clearly Cnut was adapting himself into what he saw as a model monarch, drawing a line under his recent purges and marking his intent to rule henceforth as a just and fair king. Under Wulfstan's tutelage, Cnut learnt the rudiments of what it meant to be a good Christian king, further legitimising his rule.

Cnut's letter to the English people written after his 1019 Danish campaign claimed that the expedition, and hence the tax collections, had been necessary to avoid a potential later invasion from Denmark.[33] The chronicler Henry of Huntingdon says that Cnut's army comprised both English and Danes, and a major battle took place at an unknown location in Denmark. Henry writes that Godwin was there, adding that 'the English earl led the army in a night attack on the enemy without the king's (Cnut's) knowledge ... he fell upon them unawares, slaughtered and routed them'.[34] When Cnut drew up his battle lines the following morning he found an already beaten enemy, and 'he henceforth esteemed the English as highly as the Danes'.[35] The *ASC* in contrast does not mention Godwin's prominent involvement, indeed the chronicle omits reference to Godwin for most of Cnut's reign. However, the narrative may rest on an earlier source researched by Henry of Huntingdon that carried some level of reliability. Cnut was to conduct several campaigns in Scandinavia over the next decade, and Godwin was present in at least two of them. The timing of this first campaign and Godwin's rapid promotion thereafter seem to coincide with him performing well on the battlefield. Of the seven identified charters issued by Cnut during the first two years of his reign Godwin witnessed five of them, but in the last two of these, which are dated to 1019, he appears higher in the lists than any of the senior Danes and all the other senior Anglo-Saxons.[36] This climb to become the principal witness implies that he had played a prominent part in the campaign of 1019.

Textual evidence suggests Cnut divided day-to-day administration of Wessex into two spheres.[37] Æthelweard, the man we have potentially identified as Godwin's uncle, looks to have already been overseeing the Wessex shires west of Hampshire, whereas a charter dated no later than 1019 acknowledges that Godwin had been awarded the earldom of central Wessex including Sussex, Surrey, and Hampshire.[38] Some historians have argued, based on his background in Sussex, that Godwin assumed authority there even earlier.[39] This appears to have been the reward for his loyal service, whether military or organisational, on campaign or at court, and he received lands to go with his title, lands from which wealth could be derived. For example, Godwin's initial appointment as earl had seen him gain, either through grants or transfers, ownership of several valuable estates including Aldermaston in Berkshire and Over Wallop in Hampshire. Through his extended authority further west, new large estates such as Moretonhampstead in Devon and Puddletown in Dorset were assigned; and finally, when later being awarded Kent, estates there included Fordwich and Dover.[40]

Æthelweard was declared an outlaw in 1020, creating a further opening, and Godwin's surge to power gathered pace. Dorset and Berkshire likely came under his remit at that stage, likewise Æthelweard's old shires in western Wessex, plus Cornwall, by 1023.[41] Impressive as his rise was, Godwin was not averse to emphasising his own importance. Accentuating entitlement and wealth were part and parcel of status. When he became rich, he patronised an Icelandic poet (a skald) to promote and publicise his achievements, calling attention to his accomplishments.[42] It was likely from the distribution of such poetry that the legend of his progress from swineherd to earl, as told in the Icelandic *Knytlinga Saga*, had originated. It was part of the drama of 'rags to riches' which, rather than demeaning his reputation, could in contrast be used to emphasise his achievements.

Godwin's progress can be assessed through Cnut's charters, and they form an important primary source, so this would be a suitable moment to consider their function within the royal administration. There were two commonly used forms of charter: the diploma and the writ, including wills. The term 'charter' is adopted to identify a diploma, a single parchment. They were typically granting rights or privileges from the king, mostly in the form of land and estates, to secular individuals, clerics, or religious houses.[43] They gave to the beneficiary legal possession, and freedom from certain obligations to the king. As they were composed by clergy attached to the royal court, they were almost without exception in Latin. Their most striking features for historians are where they were produced, and through the list of witnesses signing the document the composition of royal court councils and the status of individuals at court. Witnesses signed below royalty in order of their rank; senior ecclesiastics signed above senior secular nobility, and the lesser clergy and thegnage below them. Charters bore no authentication, and even the signatures/crosses of the witnesses were added by the scribe responsible for the text.[44] Writs, generally written in Old English, were shorter documents and far fewer, bearing evidence of their authenticity and authority by having a two-sided seal attached. They were an instruction, an address, to a named group or official, commonly made at a shire or hundred court, and therefore did not require witness ratification.[45]

During 1020 Cnut revisited the scene of his victory over Edmund Ironside at Ashingdon (Assandun) and dedicated the founding of a church on the site. In the same year he is recorded as visiting Edmund's tomb at Glastonbury, both actions perhaps triggered by rising political tensions and a need for him to openly and publicly display his contriteness for Edmund's demise.[46] Aside from the minster at Ashingdon other churches followed, including Corhampton in Hampshire, which is the best-preserved church from the Anglo-Saxon period in southern England.[47] The years 1020–21 mark the divide perhaps when Cnut ceased to be a king ruling by force and ruled henceforth in the guise of a typical Anglo-Saxon king. He is seen to endorse the English Church at a personal and wider level and adopt English institutions and practices and promote equally the citizens whether they were Danish or English, putting the welfare of England at the centre of his North Sea empire. From detail taken from the *Domesday Book*, Danish names appeared beyond the regions previously associated with Scandinavian influences.

There are no surviving charters issued by Cnut during 1020–21. This coincides with a disagreement with his old ally Thorkell the Tall, which led to Thorkell's exiling back to Denmark at Martinmas (11 November) in 1021.[48] After this exiling a further opportunity arose for Godwin. Thorkell's earldom of East Anglia required reassignment, so while Cnut took a greater interest in controlling that region, we can speculate that it was now that Godwin was granted extended authority over all of Wessex. Cnut no longer needed a large body of housecarls to maintain control, and his reduction of the fleet and standing army reveals this. His transfer back to Canterbury during this period of the remains of Archbishop Ælfheah, killed by Thorkell's Vikings in 1012, is a demonstration of his commitment to the country and the Christian Church that he intended to rule England peacefully. There would not be the mass replacement of the elite landowners through appropriation but by patronage instead. Likewise, no need to construct fortifications to hold the population in subservience or devastate the countryside, in marked contrast to the Norman invasion of England a half-century later. Unlike William of Normandy's invasion, Cnut was better placed to understand his English subjects in both speech and custom.[49]

It remains debatable, but possibly Godwin was given the title of earl as early as 1018. Some historians place it around 1020–21 instead, and one or two argue for it being after Godwin had acted as regent in England during Cnut's third Scandinavian campaign of 1026–27.[50] The charter witness lists would suggest one of the earlier dates. Godwin was already signing as second or third in the secular lists behind Thorkell and Eric of Hlathir by 1019, and it is hard to imagine he would have been permitted such prominence if he was not already in command of his own earldom. After Thorkell's exiling Godwin reached the top of the witness lists in 1023, so we can justifiably dismiss arguments for his earldom coming after that date.

Godwin was to marry the Danish noblewoman Gytha Thorgilsdottir, the sister of Cnut's brother-in-law Ulf. She was the offspring of Thorgil (aka Thorkel) Sprakälagg. Folklore surrounds Thorgil's background, although the assumption remains he was a respected warrior. However, on the topic of Gytha the chronicler William of Malmesbury confuses his sources. He informs us that Godwin first married an unnamed sister of Cnut who had been involved in the slave trade. They had had a boy who at a young age was riding 'a horse given him by his grandfather, when the animal plunged him into the Thames ... and he was drowned', with his mother then being 'struck by lightning, and so paid the penalty for her cruel acts'. Malmesbury records a second marriage to another spouse, 'of whose origin I am ignorant', with whom Godwin later had his children.[51] No other prime source has a similar narrative, and this second spouse presumably refers to Gytha. It is possible Godwin had already been married, and this wife had died before he then met Gytha. Malmesbury confuses the dead wife as being Cnut's sister, and his entry moralistically links the fate of the drowning boy and the lightning-struck woman to her participation in the slave trade.

Some historians have taken this as evidence that Gytha was active in trading slaves. However, it is far from clear that Malmesbury's accusation should be directed towards her. That any of the Godwinsons involved themselves in the slave trade cannot be proved one way or the other. However, it cannot be disputed that Godwin and Gytha would have had slaves within their household, as did all those among the wealthy. In that respect they were typical of their class. Slavery was a fact of life, an accepted part of society across the known medieval world. Peasants taken in warfare invariably became slaves elsewhere, and the Vikings are particularly noted for exploiting this trade.

Godwin's climb up the ladder was further boosted by his union with Gytha, Ulf's sibling and a kinswoman of Cnut, and a case has been made for Godwin's earldom being recognised around the time of this marriage. This seems a rational assumption. Two Continental writers, Adam of Bremen and Saxo Grammaticus, acknowledge Gytha's kinship with Cnut, with Adam telling us he was told directly by Gytha's nephew Swein Estrithsson (Ulf's son) that 'Canute, the King of the Danes gave his sister-in-law to Godwin'.[52] Grammaticus meanwhile, writing a century after Adam, wrongly names Gytha as Swein Estrithsson's sister and not his aunt, but reinforces the idea that Cnut saw it as a political union that aided his kingship, made 'in the hope of bringing the two nations (England and Denmark) together in love and kinship'.[53]

It is reasonable that Cnut saw the positives in promoting his most-trusted senior Anglo-Saxon noble into a union with a member of his wider family. However, which came first? Was the betrothal arranged because of Godwin's rapid rise within Cnut's inner circle, a recognition of his new standing; or was it the reverse, did the marriage to a kinswoman of Cnut give a boost to Godwin's position at the royal court? Did it follow Cnut's return to Denmark in 1019, where Godwin may have accompanied him and shown his military acumen? Weighing up the clues, the initial scenario seems more logical, endorsed by a successful campaign in Denmark. Godwin was considered suitable husband material for Gytha specifically because he had already achieved a certain relevance, and perhaps a personal understanding or friendship with her kinsman Cnut.

The *Vita Edwardi*, commissioned later by Godwin and Gytha's daughter Edith (Eadgyth), names Gytha as being Cnut's sister, not Ulf's, and this has often been quoted in various texts.[54] You would think Edith ought to know her own mother's heritage. However, it has been suggested that this discrepancy likely originates from a misspelling of the genitive in earlier texts of the use of the Latin word *sororum*, which if out of context can mean either sister or sister-in-law. The implication is that Gytha could be the sister of either Cnut or Ulf, but her sibling link to Cnut can reasonably be dismissed. Adam of Bremen is a reliable source, writing when Gytha was alive, and had taken his detail of her being Cnut's sister-in-law directly from her nephew Swein Estrithsson. Furthermore, it also suited Edith in later life to link her mother to Cnut rather than to Ulf, who had been disgraced and killed by Cnut in 1026 thirty years or more before Edith began dictating the *Vita*.

Godwin and Gytha's marriage was a political arrangement between Anglo-Saxon and Dane, but we cannot dismiss the idea that they were also romantically attached. Their first meeting may have come from her father Thorgil having brought her to England with her brothers Ulf and Eilaf (aka Ecglaf) Thorgilsson soon after Cnut's accession. Alternately, perhaps Godwin had first met Gytha when accompanying Cnut during the Danish campaign of 1019. As sister to Ulf and Eilaf, both of whom would feature prominently during Cnut's early reign, Gytha was as close to the new royal court as any, and Godwin could not have hoped to achieve a better match to advance his career. Her brothers had accompanied Cnut on his campaign of 1016 and Ulf had married Cnut's sister Estrid (aka Estrith) Sweinsdottir the same year.[55] In trying to establish their marriage year several options remain valid. Many prominent historians support the premise that it came during 1019–20 in the aftermath of the discussed campaign.[56] The year 1020 seems to be a reasonable estimate. This would place Godwin somewhere between the ages of twenty-one and twenty-four. Like Godwin, Gytha's birth date can merely be estimated. She was possibly of a similar age to her new husband, perhaps born during 997–98, which would make her about twenty-two in 1020. This would have been relatively old for the norms of the period.

An even later date during 1022–23 has likewise been offered as a date for the marriage based on political developments when Cnut was reconciled in Denmark with Thorkell the Tall. The reconciliation included Thorkell being created earl of Denmark and guardian for Cnut's third son, his first with Emma, the young Harthacnut.[57] Godwin may have accompanied Cnut, and if so the marriage to Gytha may have been in Denmark assuming this is the journey quoted in the *Vita Edwardi Regis* when the writer remarked that 'Godwin was his (Cnut's) inseparable companion on the whole journey'.[58] Thorkell's position was short-lived as he was to expire within a year, and he was replaced by Ulf Thorgilsson, Gytha's brother, both as regent and Harthacnut's guardian. This coincides with Godwin's move to top spot in the charter witness lists in 1023.[59] However, as was pointed out above, Godwin had already established himself by 1018–19 and the arguments for his marriage taking place no later than 1020 seem a better estimate when looking at the birth of their first child.

While discussing Godwin and Gytha's marriage it is worth further conjecture why Cnut had reason to support both the marriage and Godwin's elevation. The matter revolves around the identity of the child drowned in the mill stream at Bosham mentioned earlier. The girl referred to as Cnut's daughter was drowned around the year 1020–21 aged eight. That meant that she was not his first wife's Ælfgifu of Northampton's child, because Ælfgifu and Cnut had not married until late in 1013, and their first child Svein came the following year. The premise is therefore that the child was illegitimate and the mother unidentified. There is, however, another possibility surrounding the child's identity which is worthy of conjecture despite no hard evidence. It would explain the link between Cnut, Gytha and Godwin, and endorses another reason for Godwin's favoured position at Cnut's court.

The argument for debate is that the drowned girl was perhaps the illegitimate offspring of Cnut and Gytha. This scenario stands or falls on Gytha's estimated age by 1013, the date the child was born. If Gytha was born before 1001 she could theoretically be the mother. During this period, many girls reached sexual maturation by the age of twelve. Perhaps we can conjecture that Godwin had agreed to take both Gytha and her illegitimate daughter in agreement with Cnut sometime before 1020, and by doing so cemented his position as Cnut's trusted vassal. The girl's unfortunate death could have occurred just before or after Godwin and Gytha's marriage; either scenario fits the premise. It would perhaps explain why Cnut's daughter died at Bosham, an estate that was later synonymous with the ownership of the Godwinsons and may already have been owned by Godwin. Once again, we need to acknowledge that this is speculation. However, before condemning it out of hand we should consider Godwin and Gytha's eldest son Swegn's subsequent claims that he was not the offspring of Godwin but the son of Cnut.[60] Is it coincidental that Swegn carried the same name as Cnut's father? His claim, discussed in a later chapter, has been viewed as the rantings of a wayward son, but perhaps it could have some foundation if we acknowledge the premise of an ongoing relationship between Cnut and Gytha that only ended when she married Godwin. Are we exaggerating this too far by linking Godwin and Gytha's marriage and Swegn's birth to Godwin's meteoric rise within the Anglo-Danish king's court?

3

Establishing a Dynasty

Godwin and Gytha's marriage was not considered relevant enough for their contemporaries to record, but this was nothing exceptional for the times. However, it was likely a lavish ceremony befitting their social standing and wealth. Godwin was already an earl at Cnut's court and Gytha, through her brother Ulf's union, was intricately connected to the royal Danish dynasty. The wedding further enhanced Godwin's status. Adam of Bremen noted that it was one of a series of marriages arranged by Cnut to bind the English to his kingship.[1] Within twelve months of the marriage, their first child, Swegn, was born. As introduced in the previous chapter, Swegn was later to claim when he had reached his maturity that Cnut, and not Godwin, was his father.[2] Whether Swegn first made this claim while Cnut was still alive cannot be known (Cnut died in 1035), but we shall return to this again later.

Historians generally agree that the couple had a minimum of eight offspring, six boys and two girls, but sound arguments have been made for a third daughter and there are suggestions of another girl and another boy who did not survive to adulthood. It is plausible Gytha had one or two children that did not survive beyond infancy, which was not an unfamiliar occurrence in the Middle Ages. Gytha was certainly still of childbearing age around 1040 when their last known child, Wulfnoth, was born, which might imply Gytha was indeed born sometime after the turn of the millennium. Of the seven confirmed offspring after Swegn they were, in the sequence of their estimated births: Harold, Eadgyth (aka Edith or Gytha), Tostig (aka Tosti), Gyrth, Gunhild (aka Gunnhilda), Leofwine, and Wulfnoth. A level of speculation is necessary when assessing when they were born. A few historians have placed Edith's birth ahead of Harold, while some others have set it after Tostig. Precise dates are not available from the sources, and there is a general neglect of any detail. This is perhaps to be expected; only a few individuals from Anglo-Saxon history have their year of birth recorded.

Estimates can be established for the birth dates of the children based on an assessment of later events, such as Edith's marriage, the early appearance of the Godwinson sons within the charter lists, or when they were appointed to their earldoms. A reasonable assessment acknowledges that Harold followed Swegn in 1023–24. Edith is almost always listed before Tostig in the sequence. There was perhaps a gap of two or three years between them, so we can estimate that Edith was born around 1025–26, and Tostig no later than 1027–28. After Tostig came another boy, Gyrth, then the second daughter, Gunhild, and the fifth son, Leofwine, these three following between the years 1031 and 1037. The youngest son, the last of the eight acknowledged children, was Wulfnoth, born around 1040.[3] A third girl, named Ælfgifu (aka Ælfgiva), is quoted in some secondary sources, and there is reasonable cause to consider her the ninth confirmed child. Ælfgifu Godwinsdottir was possibly the woman linked to a betrothal in Normandy related to the events of 1064 described in chapter twelve. She might be the woman who curiously appears in a scene in the *Bayeux Tapestry*, the inference clearly understood by contemporaries but not fully grasped by later generations and modern historians.[4] If we accept Ælfgifu as Gytha's third daughter, her birth might be placed just before or after Wulfnoth. Finally, but rarely, additional mention is made of another boy named Ælfgar, and another girl named Eadgiva. Hard evidence for these two children has eluded historians so far, and it is plausible that they perished while still young children.

It is noticeable the four eldest boys were given names of Scandinavian origin. Early medieval naming practices were linked to familial, social, or cultural ties, and by choosing these names Godwin and Gytha were highlighting their patron–client connection with the Anglo-Danish throne, and Gytha's Danish heritage.[5] With that regard, the name Swegn, Old Norse for 'young man', was perhaps given in respect of Cnut's father Sweyn Forkbeard, and Harold, of Norse-Germanic origin composed of the elements for 'army' and 'rule', was perhaps named after Cnut's elder brother Harold (aka Harald) Sweynson. Tostig and Gyrth were similarly Norse-Germanic names, with Tostig meaning 'well-known nobleman' and Gyrth 'to gird with sword'.

Unlike Godwin, a familiar name for the period, none of these names had been commonly seen in England before the early eleventh century. There are only two other examples of individuals named Harold in English texts before the 1020s, and no earlier examples for either Tostig/Tosti or Gyrth.[6] The two youngest boys, Leofwine and Wulfnoth, were old Anglo-Saxon names, the former meaning 'dear friend', and the latter a combination of the elements for 'wolf' and 'boldness'. We have no precedent for the name Leofwine among the parents' kin groups or close associates. However, it was a commonly used name across all the English kingdoms since the tenth century, so perhaps the boy was called after a relative of Godwin's father or grandfather. Wulfnoth is perhaps easier to understand, presumably in memory of Godwin's father, Wulfnoth Cild. It is perhaps significant that Leofwine and Wulfnoth were born and named after Cnut's death in 1035, which suggests that Godwin no longer needed to respect his former patron–client connection with the Danish king when naming his youngest sons.

Eldest daughter Eadgyth's (Edith) name was derived from two components of Old English, the initial part meaning 'riches' or 'blessed' (Ead) and the second 'battle' or 'fight' (Gyth). She may have been named after a grandmother – her father's unnamed mother – or was simply called 'Gytha' after her own mother. She was not referred to by her Old English name by later primary sources and is now simply referred to as Edith, the Norman form for Eadgyth. Her family would have known her as Eadgyth, or perhaps Gytha, but it was after her union to Edward (the Confessor) in 1045 that she adopted the use of the Norman Edith in preference to Eadgyth. Within her later commissioned text *Vita Edwardi Regis*, she does not refer to her Anglo-Saxon name falling into neglect. Historians refer to her as 'Edith' in virtually all modern references. The second daughter's name, Gunhild, was derived from Old Norse and composed of the elements for 'battle' and 'fight'. Cnut's mother is referred to in the *Heimskringla* Scandinavian sagas as Gunnhild, and Cnut's sister was similarly named, so this may have been the inspiration behind Godwin and Gytha choosing the name.[7] Finally, Ælfgifu, if we accept her as their third daughter, comprised two components of Old English meaning 'elf' and 'gift'.

Little or nothing is known about the upbringings of the Godwinson children. No external biographer emerges to give us an insight into their lives. Edith's *Vita Edwardi* noted that her parents provided her and her siblings with an education 'which would make them useful to future rulers'.[8] Much of their study would have been close to the royal court or religious houses, mixing with others of similar stature. Edith spent time at the convent school at Wilton Abbey, perhaps based there for much of the year, and Gunhild probably likewise. Beyond her native tongue Edith could reputedly speak three other languages – Danish, Norman French and Latin – and Gunhild similarly spoke Danish and Latin. Danish came naturally from having a Danish mother, and the Latin from time spent at Wilton, but Edith's Norman French was likely gained later in life only after her marriage. Similarly, all the other Godwinson children would have spoken a combination of English and Danish within the household when growing up, and there were comparable elements between the two languages.

Most of the population could neither read nor write and it was known for some senior nobles to be equally illiterate by choice, relying instead on their clerks and priests. Furthermore, the level of teaching was erratic and varied from region to region. It is highly unlikely that the Godwinson children were themselves illiterate. A man of Godwin's status would have ensured that all his children received the best education available. We do not have specific details from contemporary texts but can glean information from accepted general practices among the elite during the late Anglo-Saxon age. Perhaps the boys were sent for additional learning to Canterbury or the New Minster school in Winchester for a time and provided with the best education in the classics.

As they matured their close association with the Church brought them into contact with some of the best scholars of their time, and the visits made to Rome by Harold, Tostig and Gyrth in their later life suggest they were already highly educated. Edith's ability after her marriage to manage the domestic side of Edward's court at a young age indicates that she had been given a good grounding by her mother and others in estate management. The boys meanwhile would have been taught military strategy and the art of leadership, perhaps at times by Godwin himself, alongside riding and fighting with assorted weaponry at an appropriate age. The later exploits of Swegn, Harold, and Tostig tells us they were trained well in the art of warfare, the latter two having an aptitude in strategy and military tactics. We can assume that the younger brothers were similarly trained in these arts.

In the first years of Cnut's reign, Godwin was the most prominent Anglo-Saxon at court. His signature first turns up in a charter as early as 1018.[9] Up to and including 1022, he appears in nine of the eleven surviving charters issued by Cnut in that period. In six of those he signed in second or third place in the list of secular witnesses.[10] When considering that he was surrounded by men that had been alongside Cnut when he had won the English throne, Godwin's rise at court was already astounding. He had broken into the Danish dominance, supplanting the ageing Earl Leofwine of Mercia as the most trusted senior Anglo-Saxon. Thorkell the Tall and Eric of Hlathir were close to Cnut, as was Gytha's brother Eilaf (aka Ecglaf); but other Danes such as Eric of Hlathir's son Hakon Ericsson and jarls Ranig, Thorth and Tovi were also prominent. However, notable as Godwin was, other Anglo-Saxons joined him. These included Leofwine and a minister named Ælfgar, who had been at Æthelred IIs court, and other ministers such as Ælfric, Ælfwine and Odda who were newly appointed by Cnut and appear in a handful of witness lists in the early 1020s.

That the ageing Earl (formerly Ealdorman) Leofwine had remained in position is perhaps surprising, and conceivably this is because there was a possible kinship link between his family and Cnut's hand-fast wife Ælfgifu of Northampton.[11] Nevertheless, while Leofwine had accepted the Danish succession, his son Northman had openly supported the ætheling Eadwig after Edmund Ironside's death and had been eliminated in the purges. This tells us that Cnut was prepared to accept Leofwine's oath of loyalty knowing that he carried with him the Anglo-Saxon support of Mercia, in much the same way that the appointment of Godwin carried with it the support of the Wessex nobility. The trust that Cnut had in Godwin is acknowledged in the *Encomium Emmae Reginae*, where it was recorded it was 'the case that he (Cnut) loved those whom he had heard to have fought previously for Edmund faithfully without deceit'.[12] By 1023, with Thorkell back in Denmark, Godwin headed the secular witness lists in the charters. From that moment he signs above all the Danes, his brother-in-law Eilaf, Eric of Hlathir and Hakon Ericsson. Godwin was to retain that position for the rest of Cnut's tenure as king.

Cnut had embraced Christianity, a move not followed by all his key supporters. Preserving the critical infrastructure involved maintaining the status quo in the Church, and a review of his early charters reveals he found it convenient to maintain the old churchmen in situ. These included Archbishop Lyfing at Canterbury, Archbishop Wulfstan (aka Lupus) at York, and Bishop Ælfsige at Winchester. However, Wulfstan had hitherto held York and Worcester in plurality under Æthelred II and agreed to pass the Worcester diocese to Leofsige, while a new appointment, another Godwin, was named as bishop at Rochester. There were simply no Danish candidates for ecclesiastic vacancies. When Lyfing died in 1020 Cnut replaced him with Æthelnoth, who had been the king's chaplain; this is the Æthelnoth possibly identified as Godwin's uncle previously.[13] It is plausible that Æthelnoth achieved his position because of a kinship connection with Godwin, or, if we wish to turn the argument around, Godwin's status benefitted from his connection with Æthelnoth.

Chronicle entries after 1023 concern Cnut's campaigns back in Scandinavia and his pilgrimage to Rome, but beyond these events, disappointingly there are no entries of major significance during the remaining twelve years of his reign. We are left in the dark as to the development of Godwin's career. For example, *ASC* version A carries no entries at all between 1023 and 1030, version C has no records between 1024 and 1027, and version D includes only one entry (Bishop Ælfric's visit to Rome) between 1025 and 1027.[14] However, before that semi-interlude in the historical record, the *ASC* version D gives us a detailed record of the event in 1023 when Cnut assembled the Church leaders to conduct the ritual transfer of Archbishop Ælfheah's body from London for reburial at Canterbury. Ælfheah had been murdered back in April 1012 at Greenwich by Viking warriors under Thorkell the Tall, although Thorkell had not directly ordered it.

The translation of the archbishop was another sign of the Danish king showing his Christian zeal and further contriteness for the earlier actions of his Danish army of invasion. The entire event was conducted with grand ceremony and looks to have taken more than a week. From St Paul's Minster on 8 June 1023 Archbishop Æthelnoth and Bishop Beorhtwine of Wells and several other bishops and earls gathered, including no doubt Godwin, as Ælfheah's remains were conveyed across to Southwark and on to Rochester. On 10 June Queen Emma and her five-year-old son Harthacnut joined the cortege, and the following day the archbishop's remains arrived at Canterbury. On 15 June, they all gathered to witness his reburial on the north side of the altar at Christ Church.[15] This was an announcement to wider society that Cnut needed exculpation and forgiveness from the Church for Ælfheah's murder at the hand of Danes, and a display of his commitment to the Anglo-Saxon Church and his subjects. As earl of Wessex, Godwin would have been present at this ceremony, with Gytha alongside him.

Cnut struggled to maintain full authority over his North Sea empire, which comprised England, Denmark, and Norway. However, it is worthwhile stressing that the territory controlled by Denmark in the early eleventh century was larger than its recognised modern borders. To the south, it extended about 35 miles to the River Eider from its present border with Germany and northwards Denmark held jurisdiction over the provinces of Skåne, Halland and Blekinge, now in southern Sweden.[16] The situation between Denmark, Sweden and Norway was often volatile. Thorkell the Tall had been acting as regent in Denmark for Cnut after they had resolved their differences, but by 1025 Thorkell had died. He was replaced by Cnut's brother-in-law, Gytha's brother, Ulf Thorgilsson. There were two key incidents in Scandinavia in 1026 which have become intertwined, and the primary sources are incomplete or confusing. Godwin's two brothers-in-law, Ulf and Eilaf were central to events. During 1026 Ulf tried to convince those Danish jarls discontent at Cnut's continued absence from Denmark to elect the king's young son Harthacnut (aged eight) as their new Danish ruler. Harthacnut had earlier been sent to Denmark under Ulf and Eilaf's care. This move was a ruse by Ulf, supported by his brother, to ensure he could act as regent for the boy, effectively controlling Danish domestic policy.

In parallel came the news that the formerly exiled Olaf Haraldsson of Norway had returned and had joined forces with the Swedish king Anund Jakob against Denmark. Cnut had already responded to news of what Ulf had planned, and a large Anglo-Danish fleet under his command had already crossed the North Sea. Ulf and Eilaf had escaped interrogation and looked to join the alliance of Olaf and Anund in some capacity. Cnut's immediate attention was directed to dealing with the enemy fleet that lay in anchor at the mouth of the Helge River (aka the Holy River) in Skåne, a province then under Danish authority, but now present-day Nyehusen in southern Sweden.

The *Heimskringla* of Snorri Sturluson relates that Olaf and Anund had lain a trap for Cnut by building a dam a few miles upstream on the Helge and had then withdrawn into the Baltic Sea on first sight of Cnut's fleet. Too late to engage that day, Cnut moored his vessels near the mouth of the Helge, and Snorri relates that the allies released their upstream dam, capsizing several of Cnut's ships and drowning many men.[17] Despite this setback the Anglo-Danish fleet engaged the enemy the following day, and because of Cnut's greater numbers Olaf and Anund were forced to withdraw. Ulf and Eilaf were subsequently pardoned, but the reconciliation proved temporary, and Ulf only survived to the Christmas of 1026. The *Heimskringla* wrote of an argument between him and Cnut after a game of chess, and Ulf was murdered the following day inside Trinity Church at Roskilde on Zealand.[18]

This seems indicative of how serious the concept of loyalty was to Cnut, more so than his ties of kinship. In the context of Godwin's rise inside Cnut's court Godwin's loyalty to the king may have been his strongest asset. The Dane seems to have held Godwin in the highest regard and valued his ability in warfare and his skill as a diplomatic advisor. They were of a similar age, with Cnut perhaps three or four years older. The *Vita Edwardi* commissioned later by Edith, although biased, was nevertheless contemporary to Godwin's lifetime, and it describes her father, as per the words of Cnut, as being 'the most cautious in counsel and the most active in war'.[19] Most historians are comfortable in accepting, as noted, that Godwin had accompanied Cnut on his initial expedition back to Scandinavia in 1019, where Godwin had shown his bravery and resourcefulness on the battlefield. He likely accompanied him also on the 1023 campaign. What is difficult to measure is Godwin's involvement in subsequent expeditions, particularly if we accept that during Cnut's absences from England, he had grown to rely upon Godwin to act as regent.

William of Malmesbury places Godwin alongside Cnut at the battle of the River Helge (Holy River) in 1026.[20] The Norman writer Gaimar adds that Godwin killed the King of Sweden (Anund) there.[21] However, these primary source entries are unconvincing. Malmesbury's assertion that Godwin led Cnut's English forces in 1026, where the English were 'encouraged by Earl Godwin ... to display their courage' and 'by completing their victory secured the earldom for their leader', is hard to accept.[22] The chronicler has probably conflated the campaign of 1026 with one of the earlier expeditions (1019 or 1023), as we cannot be expected to believe that Godwin was only awarded his earldom several years after becoming the top signatory of the king's charters. Gaimar's entry that Godwin killed Anund is pure invention. Anund lived and remained king of Sweden until 1050.

After dealing with Scandinavia in 1026 Cnut led a campaign in late 1027 into Scotland to suppress King Malcolm II. This campaign likely followed Cnut's earlier visit to Rome that year to attend the Holy Roman Emperor Conrad II's succession on 26 March. Malcolm had also attended the ceremony, and maybe he had snubbed Cnut's claims to overlordship of Scotland whilst there, hence the campaign. Little is known about this expedition, but it was at least successful in its basic intent as Cnut obtained from Malcolm a promise of peace and friendship.[23]

Throughout Cnut's tenure, Godwin accumulated landholdings across most of southern England. It is self-evident that through his links with Sussex he owned many estates in that shire. However, assessing his first association with Kent is more problematic. Later in life, Godwin forged close connections with that former kingdom, and his combined estates in the south-eastern shires recorded in the *Domesday Book* far exceeded his other holdings in Hampshire and Surrey and the West Country. Kent was likely incorporated fully into Godwin's sphere of control sometime between 1026 and 1028 when Cnut was actively occupied elsewhere, in Scandinavia and Scotland and his visit to Rome.

The historical record for the events of 1027, and for the year 1031, have become confused within the primary sources, and perhaps partially transposed. The key issue seems to concern the dating of Cnut's trip to Rome mentioned above. Historians have suggested that evidence points to Cnut being in Scotland in 1031, not in 1027, where he received the submission of Malcolm II and lesser rulers named Iehmarc (aka Echmarcach), from the Western Isles, and Maelbeth.[24] This Maelbeth almost certainly refers to Macbeth, who was to become King of Scotland in 1040. We shall return to this 1027 *versus* 1031 debate shortly. However, in 1028–29 Cnut was to undertake what would be his last offensive in Scandinavia to subdue the Norwegians, and Godwin seems to have acted as regent in England for the time when Cnut was overseas.[25] In 1029 a council was held at Nidaros (subsequently renamed Trondheim) in Norway, in which Cnut proposed the government he wished to operate across Denmark and Norway. Hakon Ericsson, the heir of Earl Eric Hákonarson (aka Eric or Yric of Hlathir) and the king's brother-in-law through his marriage to Cnut's sister Gytha Sweynsdottir, held the regency over Norway, and the twelve-year-old Harthacnut was proclaimed King of Denmark.[26] This situation lasted for less than a year.

Meanwhile, the primary sources disappoint. All versions of the *ASC* active at that period except for version C (Abingdon) refer merely to one event specifically concerning Cnut's activities between his return to England in 1029 and his death in 1035.[27] This one event is Cnut's journey to Rome, which the chronicle has dated to 1031, and this brings us back to the debate regarding the years 1027 and 1031. Henry of Huntingdon, William of Malmesbury, and John of Worcester all include their detail of a single trip by Cnut to Rome taking place in 1031, which illustrates that they, writing nearly a century afterwards, were unaware of the chronological error in the *ASC* and had duplicated it.[29] It is plausible that Cnut made two trips to Rome, but if we are restricted to a single visit then it came in 1027. The reliable date we have is that Cnut attended the coronation, conducted by Pope John XIX, of Conrad II as Emperor of the Holy Roman Empire, which we have established took place on 26 March 1027 and not 1031.[28] The incongruity seems to emanate from a confusion by the chroniclers over two significant battles in Scandinavia, the battle of the Helge in 1026 and the battle of Stiklestad in 1030. Scribes knew that Cnut's Rome trip took place a year after a famous battle, but unfortunately they wrongly linked it to Stiklestad not the Helge.[30] It suggests the *ASC* entry was not added to the chronicles during Cnut's reign or even soon afterward, but much later, hence the cause of the initial dating error.

William of Malmesbury and John of Worcester include hefty entries in their works detailing in full Cnut's letter to the Church leaders, nobles, and all the people of England, written after his return from Rome.[31] Seemingly Cnut had had something of an epiphany there. In this letter, he vowed to amend his ways, 'to rule justly and devoutly ... to observe equitable justice in all matters', and to ensure 'impartial justice may be enjoyed by all, noble and common, rich and poor'.[32] This was a man far removed from the warrior who had mutilated hostages in the Anglo-Danish wars eleven years earlier. This message was effectively a plea for renewed loyalty from the English in acknowledgement of his frequent absences from the kingdom. However, his spiritual realignment came with a practical side, because while on the Continent Cnut had also negotiated trade concessions for English merchants.[33] Detail of Godwin's activities during this period are regrettably missing, although we can assume that he was effectively acting as regent and was the most important figure in England during the king's absences.

In contrast to the shortage of chronicle entries, there are a dozen extant charters issued by Cnut between the years 1026–35, all but one of them after 1030.[34] Even accepting the dubious validity of a few, they enable us to monitor the transfer of power within Cnut's inner circle. Looking at the wider question of charters throughout the regime, it can be seen with good justification that gaps in the sequence fit the periods when Cnut was absent from England for one reason or another. By 1030 most of his old Danish allies at court had perished or retired. Among these was Hakon Ericsson, who had been given authority by Cnut to act as governor in Norway in 1028 but had drowned in a shipwreck in the Pentland Firth in 1030.[35] Hakon's drowning was seized upon by Olaf Haraldsson II as a chance to recover Norway from the Danes, but Olaf was killed at the battle of Stiklestad. To cement the Danish victory and to re-establish full authority across Norway,

Cnut despatched his hand-fast wife Ælfgifu of Northampton and their young son Svein Cnutsson there to rule as regents. However, the new laws they brought in were in some ways stricter than those applying in Denmark – for example, no man could leave the country without their joint approval.

Between 1030 and 1032 Ælfgifu imposed fresh forms of taxation and penalties for violence in keeping with Cnut's administration in England, but unlike the English the Norwegians were not as easily focused on compliance. These measures encouraged renewed Norse resistance, and by 1033–34 Olaf's son Magnus was called back from exile and gathered Norwegian support to challenge Danish rule once again.[36] In 1034 Magnus led an uprising and Ælfgifu and Svein were forced to flee. Svein transferred to Denmark and Ælfgifu returned to England. Svein was to die only months later, but crucially it seems Cnut had already conceded all Danish claims to Norway by 1035. This, probably above any other evidence, confirms that Cnut must have already been seriously ill, likely terminally, some months before his death. With Cnut too sick to lead a new campaign in 1034, and with no suitable commander to send in his stead, Norway was lost. Godwin springs to mind here but realistically it seems highly unlikely that he could have gained enough support or the vassalage of native Danes, let alone Norwegians, in sufficient numbers to defeat Magnus. In any case, if the king's health was already deteriorating Godwin was best positioned to remain and oversee matters in England.

In the last years of Cnut's reign, a new group of nobles had replaced the old guard, although Godwin remained pre-eminent. The Anglo-Dane Osgot (aka Osgod) Clapa had become a regular charter witness by 1033, as had jarl Tovi, and the jarl Thorth was still an occasional witness. Siward of Northumbria, a Dane who probably arrived in England during one of Cnut's Scandinavian campaigns, appears in a single charter in 1033, but he would thereafter, along with Godwin and Leofric, become part of the triumvirate of important earls during the 1040s.[37] A decade lies between the removal of Eric Hákonarson, the former Earl of Northumbria, and the appearance of Siward, during which Northumbria may have been controlled by Hakon Ericsson up to his drowning in 1030 and thereafter from Bamburgh by the Anglo-Saxon Ealdred II. For the other Anglo-Saxon elements, Earl Leofwine of Mercia had died by 1024, but Ælfgar and Ælfwine continued as occasional signatories, and in 1032 Leofric, the son of Leofwine, signs regularly and prominently immediately below Godwin.

By this period, the Godwinson dynasty was firmly established. From assessing the estates that had transferred to Godwin and Gytha during the 1020s they were already, through his ambition and drive and her initial connections to Cnut, the wealthiest among the elite. Nothing specific is known of their business ventures, but it can be assumed that Godwin had trade links to the Continent and there were also links to Ireland. The later assistance that the Irish would give to the Godwinson family during both the 1050s and 1060s suggests a long-term association. The origin of this Irish connection could be linked directly to Gytha and the import and export trade links she established with Dublin. Several sources hint at her direct connection with the Dublin slave trade, which, along with other commodities, formed a lucrative means of income.[38]

Through lack of primary detail, we are forced to move quickly through Cnut's final years. There are three chronicle entries between 1032 and 1034, and all concern Church matters. The *ASC* keeps us well informed of deaths amongst the senior clergy, namely those of Ælfsige of Winchester (succeeded by Ælfwine) in 1032, Leofsige of Worcester (succeeded by Beorhtheah) and Merewith of Wells in 1033, and Æthelric of Dorchester-on-Thames in 1034.[39] In 1032 Cnut is seen issuing a grant to Glastonbury Abbey, the site of Edmund Ironside's tomb, which guaranteed the abbey's rights and customs without interference. This was acknowledgement perhaps of Cnut's remorse and continued guilt over involvement in Edmund's murder sixteen years earlier.[40] Not unexpectedly, the sources are silent on Godwin and Gytha and their young family. By 1034 Gytha had likely just had or was pregnant with her sixth child, Gunhild.

Relations with Normandy may have been strained in the last months of Cnut's tenure, and this likely encouraged Duke Robert of Normandy to look towards the succession claims of Edward and Alfred, the two English æthelings in his care. For Cnut's part he seems to have played a diplomatic balancing act with Normandy over several years in the knowledge that the Norman dukes were hoping or planning to assist in placing either of Emma's sons on the English throne ahead of Cnut's Anglo-Danish sons. Maybe as early as Richard II's or Richard III's dukedom Cnut had gifted the estate at Rameslie in Sussex to the Norman ducal abbey of Fécamp. This would prove significant in later decades.

By 1034–05 Duke Robert was purportedly ready to launch an invasion fleet, perhaps the result of a disagreement between Cnut and Robert that went back to when Duke Richard II, Robert's father, had agreed that his son would marry Cnut's recently widowed sister Estrith. The marriage either did not take place or Robert, as noted by the Norman scribe Rodulfus Glaber, had repudiated Estrith soon afterwards.[41] Perhaps Robert was looking for an excuse to launch an invasion on behalf of his aunt's two Anglo-Norman æthelings. A Norman invasion fleet sailed from Fécamp early in 1935 but bad weather diverted it westward to Jersey. Some of these ships were utilised later by the ætheling Edward the following year, but Duke Robert was to die soon after his failed invasion in the last months of 1035 whilst on a pilgrimage to Jerusalem.

Notwithstanding the diplomatic issues with Emma's Norman kin, Cnut maintained good relations with Europe elsewhere. One of his last diplomatic acts was to betroth his and Emma's daughter Gunhilda (not to be confused with Godwin's daughter Gunhild), to Henry, the heir of Conrad II, the Holy Roman Emperor. Denmark may have been threatened by military action from Conrad, and to safeguard Jutland from German interests a political marriage was an expedient way of ensuring peace.[42] The marriage came in 1036 after Cnut's death, and Gunhilda's husband would become Emperor Henry III in 1046, although Gunhilda would die young in 1039 from malaria caught while accompanying Henry on a campaign in southern Italy.[43]

Cnut died on 12 November 1035 at Shaftesbury aged about forty.[44] His body was conveyed to Winchester and buried in the Old Minster alongside the remains of the old Anglo-Saxon kings, Ecgberht, Æthelwulf, Eadred, Eadwig and Æthelred II. Burial inside the Old Minster had undoubtedly been stipulated, so Cnut could associate himself for posterity alongside the line of Anglo-Saxon kings and not as a Danish usurper. His approaching death may not have been entirely unexpected, as hinted at above. The Scandinavian text *Knytlinga Saga* tells us he died of an illness related to jaundice, contracted that summer. Maybe he had been unwell for some time. One of the last charters Cnut issued in 1035, with Godwin signing at the head of the secular witnesses and Leofric of Mercia second, concerned a grant to Sherborne Abbey. Research on the phrasing of this document acknowledges that Cnut was by then seriously ill and had apparently accepted he would not live much longer.[45] Godwin had already likely been delegated further responsibilities over several years, and we can assume he had a significant role at the royal court during the last months of Cnut's reign. Cnut's failure to confirm a successor and ensure his legacy would have profound implications. Earl Godwin was to play an important pivotal role, and not an enviable one, during the next uncertain phase as Cnut's two widows, Ælfgifu of Northampton and Emma of Normandy, fought for supremacy and the succession claims of their respective sons.

CNUT'S CHARTERS 1018 to 1035 – LIST OF SECULAR WITNESSES

CHARTER NO. (SAWYER)	950	951	952	953	954	955	956	958	980	984	977	959	960	961	962	963	971	964	979	967	968	969	970	972	974	975	976
YEAR	1018	1018	1018	1018	1019	1019	1019	1022	1022	1022	1023	1023	1023	1024	1026	1031	1031	1032	1032	1033	1033	1033	1033	1033	1035	1035	1035
ÆLFGAR	10			10	15		12						9		11	6	6				8	6				17	
ÆLFGEAT					15	15								15							9				9		
ÆLFRIC	9				23		11								18						12				6	9	
ÆLFWINE							9	13	14											3			3				4
ÆTHELMAER					24	14			8			8	18		10						10				13		
ASLAC	8			8		9																10					
BEORHTRIC	4			16	14	16						9	19	14													
EILAF (Earl)	3			4	7	5	4	2	4	3	3	2	2	2													
ERIC of HLATHIR (Earl)	2		2	2	5	3	2	1	1	1	2	4	3														
GODWIN (Earl)	2		6	5	8	2	3		2	2	1	1	1	1	1	1	1	1	1	1	1	1	1	1	1	1	1
HÁKON (Earl)					2		6		5	5		4	3	3	2	2											
LEOFRIC				14	14				18	5	18	10	7		13												
LEOFRIC (Earl)																2	2	2	2	2	22	2	2	2	2	2	2
LEOFSIGE				20	20				17				19			10	7										
LEOFWINE (Earl)				3		5			6	6	4																
ODDA	11			11	16										9	7	4	2	2	2	19	4	2	2	15	2	2
ORDGAR				12									9	7	8	5	5				20	9	9	9			
OSGOD CLAPA (Earl)															7	5		8		5	5	5	9	3	16	6	3
RANIG (Earl)	4			6	9							5			4	4	3								4		
SIGEWEARD						17								20							11				10		
THORKELL (Earl)	1	1	2	1	1	1	1											3									
THORTH	7			7		10			9			5	10	4	8	6	9	9		6	9	4			6		
THURKIL						13			10					8				16		7	7						5
TOVI	9		9		12							11		10	6	6	12	7	4	4	6	7	7		7		5

Note 1) Numbers denote the position that individual signed within the secular witness lists

Note 2) Only individuals that signed a minimum of five charters are listed

Note 3) Table compiled from data gathered from Prosopography of Anglo-Saxon England database (www.pase.ac.uk)

4

Godwin and the Anglo-Danish Succession, 1035–1036

Godwin had become a major landowner through a combination of royal grants and growing importance. Much of the land that would be accumulated before his death was already in his possession by 1035. The *Domesday Book*, compiled in 1086–87, indicates a huge volume of estates still under Godwin's name as of 1066, although these would of course have previously transferred to his wife, his children, or to favoured vassals, years earlier on his death. By assessing the land that Godwin would have held in 1035 and continued to accumulate during the reign of Edward (the Confessor) there is a surprising distribution. Bearing in mind that the *Domesday Book* compilers were open to errors, the survey still shows that land was held across twenty shires. As would be imagined, Godwin held more estates in Sussex – several dozen – than anywhere else. He also had significant holdings in Hampshire and Kent, and across western Wessex in general in lesser numbers. However, elsewhere there are unexpected statistics. Godwin held only a handful of estates in Surrey and Berkshire, but approximately 130 combined, albeit relatively small holdings, across Lincolnshire, Norfolk, and Suffolk.[1]

Of the estates listed in the survey which still named Godwin as the holder, the largest according to fiscal income were Folkestone and Hoo (near Rochester) in Kent, Hurstpierpoint (north of Brighton), Willingdon (near Eastbourne), Bosham and Singleton in Sussex, with the latter two only 7 miles apart. Other lucrative estates included Witley (near Godalming) in Surrey, Saltwood (near Hythe) in Kent, Chalton in Hampshire, and Stoughton and Westbourne in Sussex.[2] These last three, like Bosham and Singleton, are all a handful of miles from Chichester. What is of interest here is that Compton, the estate that Godwin inherited from Wulfnoth Cild, sits between Chalton and Stoughton, which indicates that this corner of Sussex close to the Hampshire border was perhaps the epicentre of the original dynastic wealth of Wulfnoth Cild.

In the weeks that followed Cnut's death, his two widows pushed the credentials of their sons among the Witan and the senior nobility. Historians have accepted that Emma was a formidable woman for her times, adroit at playing the political games necessary to succeed in a male-dominated environment. Emma was promoting Harthacnut, her only son by Cnut. However, her rival Ælfgifu of Northampton was perhaps just as ruthlessly opportunistic. Reports of her using bribery and lobbying among the nobility came to the notice of Harthacnut's sister Gunhilda in Germany from a source within the court of her father-in-law Emperor Conrad II.[3] Ælfgifu's eldest son by Cnut, Svein Cnutsson, had died in Denmark months before his father, so she was now backing her second son Harold (Harefoot). The appellation 'Harefoot' came from his supposed speed and ability at hunting, although the oldest surviving reference to it appears in the *Liber Eliensis* of Ely in the early twelfth century.[4]

The Church had refused to recognise Ælfgifu's hand-fast marriage to Cnut on moral grounds, naming her a concubine. That principle enabled the clergy to approve Cnut's marriage to Emma without breaking their ethical codes or insisting he first divorce Ælfgifu. Nonetheless, there is no evidence Cnut ever refuted his first marriage. The ecclesiastic community placed Harthacnut's legality over that of Harold Harefoot, but with Cnut not having named his preferred successor it was ultimately both secular and clerical members of the Witan that needed to reach a majority judgment. A month after the king's death a council was called at Oxford.[5] The clergy were heavily represented, but their preferred choice, Harthacnut, was barely seventeen. Furthermore, he was still in Denmark spearheading renewed attempts to recover Danish control in Norway and would likely remain there for an indeterminate period.

Ælfgifu and Harefoot therefore had one advantage: Harefoot was in England and available to take immediate control. Opinion remained divided, but as remarked by the *ASC* version E, the Mercian Earl Leofric and 'almost all the thegns north of the Thames, and the men of the fleet in London, chose Harold (Harefoot) as regent of all England'.[6] Support for Harefoot would have come also from Siward in York and Ealdred II, the heir of Uhtred, in Bernicia. Not all concurred, notably Godwin and some others in the south. In simplistic terms the alternate camps highlighted the political rivalry between the two dominant earls Leofric and Godwin. On this occasion Leofric's faction persevered and it was decided by majority that Harefoot was to act as regent while the country awaited Harthacnut's return.[7] Nevertheless, Harthacnut was at this stage still seen as the legitimate successor to the throne.

Behind this agreement was an ongoing diplomatic war between the two widows and their supporters to achieve dominance within the Witan. There was compromise, but the rumblings of discontent continued. Godwin is said to have argued in favour of Emma's son Harthacnut, to ensure the continuity of a single king ruling both England and Denmark and preserving Cnut's North Sea empire. Emma's offspring had a better legal entitlement to the throne and was supported morally by the Church. It was agreed she would remain resident in Winchester with those housecarls (huscarls) previously loyal to Cnut and hold Wessex in hand for the arrival of Harthacnut. She used this opportunity to commandeer the royal regalia and treasury held at Winchester to make it inaccessible to anyone else. The *ASC* names Godwin as 'their (Emma and Harthacnut's) most loyal man', and clearly at this point Emma and Godwin were acting in unison.[8] Henry of Huntingdon notes the Oxford meeting acknowledged that Emma and the former king's household should have care of Wessex and Godwin would be their leader in military affairs.[9] For at least several months after Cnut's death Godwin remained dutiful to his Anglo-Norman widow and the Anglo-Danish succession of her son.

If Harthacnut had returned to England at this point, there is reason to believe that Harefoot would have stepped down as regent, and Leofric, Siward and others would have accepted Harthacnut as monarch. However, the longer he remained overseas, the more precarious the arrangement was for Emma and the more support for Harefoot grew. Emma had perhaps underestimated the backing her rival Ælfgifu of Northampton had north of the Thames, as endorsed by the chroniclers Symeon of Durham and Adam of Bremen.[10] Harefoot also had the backing of London but, perhaps more importantly if there was to be military involvement, the fleet moored at London/Greenwich. Leofric's support probably rested on a kinship link to Ælfgifu. Perhaps with a realisation that Godwin had heretofore dominated the royal court, this was an opportunity for Leofric and others to obtain greater relevance and to reposition themselves whilst curbing Godwin's aspirations. However, was there a greater incentive for supporting Harefoot that revolved around the situation in Scandinavia? If Harthacnut succeeded to the throne, he was more likely to drain English resources to bolster an ongoing war to recover Norway, whereas Harefoot was much less predisposed to commit to a new Scandinavian campaign. To gain their backing, Ælfgifu may have already pledged to the Mercian and northern nobility that her son would not intervene in Scandinavia.

Some historians have remarked that Harthacnut always showed a greater commitment to Denmark than England; he spent most of his life there. If this was clear in 1036, it may have swung opinion away from him.[11] In contrast, Godwin could have been attracted to Emma's cause and Harthacnut's claims for the opposite reason, hoping to restore Cnut's lost empire and supply military aid to Denmark under Harthacnut's kingship. We should not forget his wife Gytha was Danish and would have urged her husband to aid her native country in the wars with Norway.

Cnut's intentions regarding his successor are unclear. The German chronicler Adam of Bremen wrote in his *Gesta Hammaburgensis Ecclesiae Pontificum* (Deeds of Bishops of the Hamburg Church) that Cnut had wanted his son Svein Cnutsson to take over Norway, Harthacnut to reign in Denmark, and Harefoot to rule England.[12] By selecting Harefoot for England, Cnut would have been seriously jeopardising Emma's position and placing her under the rule of her stepson and the influence of her rival Ælfgifu of Northampton. This scenario would come to pass in due course, and Emma was indeed compromised. Elsewhere, the Norman writer William of Jumièges later claimed that during Cnut's illness he had promised Duke Robert I of Normandy that the English æthelings at the Norman court since 1016 (Edward and Alfred) were to be given half his kingdom at his demise.[13] This claim was used to reinforce the validity of Robert planning an invasion of England in 1035 when it was clear the throne would go to either Harthacnut or Harefoot, but the Norman fleet never crossed the Channel.

Of the two primary candidates, there were complications over Harefoot's legal and ethical status caused by his mother's hand-fast marriage to Cnut, and furthermore, Cnut had probably not envisaged Harthacnut remaining in Denmark. However, Cnut's earlier understanding with Emma was that their male heirs would invalidate the claims of any offspring born from his union with Ælfgifu of Northampton and similarly would override the claims of Emma's children by Æthelred II. Emma was to hold this commitment to the eighth degree. She virtually disregarded Edward and Alfred for over eighteen years while they remained in Normandy. At the root of this was her relationship with Cnut; beyond their understanding on the succession, there seems to have been a general affection between them that had been missing in Emma's marriage to Æthelred.

Before Christmas 1035, after Harold Harefoot was given the regency, coins were struck in both his and Harthacnut's names, Harefoot north of the River Thames and, in his absence, Harthacnut south of it. However, there were anomalies. York, Lincoln, and Stamford struck some coins in Harthacnut's name and many southern mints, including London, Oxford, Cambridge, Bristol, Dover, Exeter, Salisbury, Southwark, and Wallingford, struck coins for both.[14] The situation was uncertain, but evidence that coin production had ceased in Winchester coincides with Harefoot's decision at this stage to seize the royal treasury. Versions A and C of the *ASC* infer that Harold had already sent soldiers to Winchester to seize Emma's money and possessions left by his father. John of Worcester notes that Harold then 'began to reign as if the rightful heir, not, however, as powerfully as Cnut because

Harthacnut, the heir with the stronger claim, was awaited'.[15] Harefoot was undoubtedly urged on by Ælfgifu, but the chances of matters escalating rested on the response of Godwin. However, the earl seems to have stepped aside peacefully and did not interfere. The treasury in Winchester was not Emma's personal wealth, and as regent, Harefoot was entitled to gain access to it.[16] However, there were additional motives. Emma could have used the treasury to promote Harthacnut's cause over his, but that option was now closed.

Harold Harefoot's actions are understandable, and we can guess Emma's response, but perhaps the surprise is that we know so little of Godwin's position post-Oxford. At that meeting, he had supported Emma but had concurred with the majority to accept Harefoot as regent until Harthacnut's return. However, despite being named by Henry of Huntingdon as acting for Emma and the deceased king as her military leader, Godwin had allowed Harefoot's men to seize the treasury unchallenged.[17] Was Godwin being pragmatic and avoiding unnecessary conflict, or had he already identified the way things were likely to develop and, without Emma being aware, switched to Harefoot's camp? It may have already been evident that Harthacnut would not be arriving for some time, perhaps many months, if he arrived at all. In the weeks and months that followed this bare fact began to harden. With this knowledge it seems logical and sensible that Godwin should stabilise his position and align himself with the majority, supporting the one man in England able to assume the kingship there and then.

As Harthacnut's absence continued matters became more confrontational between the two camps. Emma ramped up the assertions against Harold Harefoot's legitimacy. As noted in the *ASC* versions C and D, 'Some men said of Harold (Harefoot) that he was the son of King Cnut and Ælfgifu … but to many men it seemed quite unbelievable.'[18] In her *Encomium Emmae Reginae*, written years later, Emma's encomiast asserts that not only was Ælfgifu a concubine, meaning her offspring had no valid attachment to the throne, but she was not even Harefoot's mother. It was noted 'as a matter of fact, the assertion of very many people … that the same Harold was secretly taken from a servant who was in childbed, and put in the chamber of the concubine (i.e. Ælfgifu), and this can be believed as the more truthful account'.[19] John of Worcester later elaborates, and tells us that neither Svein nor Harefoot came from the union between Cnut and Ælfgifu and that Harefoot's claim 'to be the son of King Cnut by Ælfgifu … is quite untrue, for some say he was the son of a certain cobbler'.[20]

The matter can never be validated one way or the other, but it should be recognized that Emma's spin was a success. It is her version of events and not Ælfgifu's that has survived for posterity, and conclusions can be drawn from that. Propaganda against Harefoot orchestrated by Emma probably began even when his father was alive, as he was away from Cnut's court for much of the time during his youth, brought up and educated at his mother's estate in Northampton.[21] Despairing of Harthacnut ever arriving, Emma turned instead to her homeland of Normandy. She contacted her sons Edward and Alfred as to their interest in the English succession, urging them to make their challenge for the throne. She had switched from Harthacnut, her plan A, to Edward or Alfred, her plan B. Edward was by then aged around thirty-two and Alfred a few years younger. As æthelings, they had valid legal claims. Their renewed motivation would be sparked by a letter they each received from their mother in the spring of 1036, and within weeks both had responded, prepared plans, and undertook to sail to England separately.

These letters have become the subject of a conspiracy theory involving Harefoot that has caused much debate among historians. The claims centre around whether Emma sent the messages or whether they were forged in her name by Harefoot or Ælfgifu. The *Encomium Emmae Reginae* goes into detail about the source of the original letters, and from the version Emma gives us it is clear she attempted to shift blame onto Harefoot for what later occurred. Her Flemish scribe in the *Encomium* related what happened, apparently repeating word for word the messages sent to Edward and Alfred.[22] Let us presuppose they were from Emma. The letters criticised the rule and actions of Harefoot and urged the æthelings to return to England expediently while the opportunity still existed to replace the usurper. It was a final desperate measure to maintain her position and ensure that a son of hers – it seems she did not mind which – attained the English throne. The question of the originator of the letters will be looked at again below, but without the letters it is unlikely they would have undertaken any expedition in 1036.

Edward garnered support from the Norman court, but Duke Robert I of Normandy had died the previous year and his eight-year-old son William I (the young Conqueror to be) had succeeded him. Support for Edward came not from the boy duke but from his father's former supporters who had bankrolled Robert's earlier attempt to raise a fleet.[24] Meanwhile, Alfred had obtained some backing from Flanders but could not raise sufficient mercenaries.[25] Instead, he travelled to Boulogne, where his sister Godgifu had recently married her second husband, Count Eustace II of Boulogne. There is every indication that Godgifu's brothers had arranged the marriage as a means of persuading Eustace to back their coming enterprises to England. At Boulogne Alfred recruited cheaper but possibly less professional soldiery. John of Worcester noted later that Alfred had 600 men.[26] Versions C and D of the *ASC* recorded the arrival of the ætheling Alfred into England, although not Edward, while version E fails to mention either of them, and John of Worcester's chronicle includes detail gathered from other sources.[23] The evidence hints that both brothers were prepared for a military encounter. The æthelings' appearance on English shores would prove ruinous, particularly for Alfred. From the available evidence, their attempts, which appear to have been coordinated in the beginning, were inept.

Dealing with Edward first, Norman sources say he left for England ahead of Alfred in the autumn of 1036, numbers unknown. William of Jumièges and William of Poitiers both record that he sailed from Normandy with forty ships 'filled with armed men' and arrived at Southampton Water.[27] His Norman recruits were likely experienced soldiers, and his arrival in the Solent tells us he aimed to make for Winchester and liaise with Emma. William of Poitiers states that Edward's plan was nothing less than seizing the throne, but soon after his soldiers had disembarked they were intercepted by the Hampshire fyrd, and an engagement was fought close to the Solent. This was a remarkably rapid response by the fyrd and may suggest Godwin or one of his senior thegns had gained intelligence of Edward's intent and the timing of his landing. William of Jumièges writes of victory for Edward in the encounter, noting he 'came on land and swiftly sent a considerable part of their number to their death', but adds, 'As a victor he (Edward) and his men then returned to their ships.'[28] Edward's force re-embarked and sailed back to Normandy. Jumièges entry hides the truth of it, which is that the ætheling had suffered a defeat. Why not carry on to Winchester if a victory had been gained? His withdrawal implies his forces had come off worse, or that he had further news that a larger English army, perhaps led by Godwin, was gathering. Jumièges tells us Edward had accepted that he could not get into the kingdom without a larger army.[29] The Norman writer Wace adds that Edward disembarked at Barfleur on returning to Normandy.[30]

Alfred seems to have formed similar plans to get to Winchester, as noted by the *ASC*, perhaps hoping to liaise with his brother.[31] However, their movements were poorly coordinated and maybe they were acting independently to their own agendas. William of Poitiers records that Alfred sailed from Wissant (10 miles south of Calais) and landed at Dover, seeking 'his father's sceptre' – in other words, the throne of England.[28] One primary source states Alfred arrived with a 'mighty force of vessels ... at Sandwich', while a further source records that his contingent was considerably greater than this brother's.[32] John of Worcester adds that they brought with them many Norman knights.[33] There may have been several hundred experienced soldiers in Alfred's party, a substantial fighting force. He must surely have foreseen some degree of confrontation, but the initial response from Harefoot, and from Godwin as Earl of Wessex, is a little confusing. It appears, unlike the preparedness in Hampshire, a landing had not been predicted in Kent. Alfred marched his army unchallenged from Kent westward across the North Downs. His aim was likewise to reach Winchester and his mother, perhaps to unite with his brother, but unknown to Alfred Edward's attempt had already failed. Why Alfred was not confronted sooner is puzzling. Maybe Godwin had been occupied in dealing with the threat posed by Edward or the plan had been to waylay Alfred in Surrey.

The sources pick up the story of a meeting between Godwin and Alfred near Guildford. It is fair to assume Emma had not advised Godwin of her arrangements with her sons, and if so the relationship between the dowager queen and the earl must have become strained by this juncture. Godwin was likely as surprised as anyone when first made aware that the æthelings had landed in England. From Godwin's standpoint, there was no advantage in him supporting Emma's initiative, and maybe he even believed Alfred had arrived without her prior knowledge. Either way, he found himself in a difficult position, but his first focus was on defending his earldom.

Tradition has it that Godwin met Alfred at Guildown, the track leading westward up onto the downs out of Guildford beyond the crossing point of the River Wey. *ASC* version D writes that Alfred wanted to visit his mother in Winchester but was intercepted by Godwin because 'those who wielded great power in this land would not allow that', and 'he (Godwin) had him set in captivity, and he also drove off his companions'.[34] Godwin may have had instructions to perhaps delay him while Harefoot assembled forces in London. Henry of Huntingdon acknowledges Godwin's concern about the magnitude of Alfred's army and suggests this was why he acted, and John of Worcester notes that Godwin 'detained Alfred ... as he (Harold Harefoot) had commanded'.[35] However, we know there was no initial confrontation, so Alfred looks to have met Godwin freely and accepted hospitality from the earl. He may have believed that Godwin was still acting in his and his mother's interests. In fact, Godwin may have told him such. Is it plausible that Emma still had faith that he would support her sons? Nonetheless, in the context of the recent armed confrontation with Edward's forces it seems more likely that Godwin had already decided that in the interests of the kingdom he would prevent Alfred from reaching Winchester. At best, Godwin would likely have urged Alfred to withdraw to avoid further bloodshed.

William of Poitiers writes that 'Earl Godwin received him (Alfred) with nefarious guile and betrayed him through wicked treachery' while openly appearing to honour him.[36] Alfred's men were separated into small groups, and Godwin assigned them into houses across Guildford for the night. If Godwin had previously given oaths to Harefoot, maybe he was playing for time, detaining his guests whilst awaiting the appearance of Harefoot's men. In the early hours, Godwin men – or perhaps Harefoot's soldiers, depending on your viewpoint – moved through the settlement, disarming and restraining the ætheling and his soldiers as they slept. In the morning, Alfred's men were separated, and the *ASC* tells of them being killed, maimed, blinded, or sold into captivity.[37] John of Worcester refers to torturing and scalping and the cutting off of hands and feet, the most graphic of the various reports, and estimates that 600 men were killed.[38]

Godwin is then said to have handed the ætheling over to Harold Harefoot, and Harefoot ordered the rest of Alfred's companions to be beheaded and for Alfred's eyes to be put out.[39] The writers Geffrei Gaimar and Wace and the *Encomium* add that one man in ten of Alfred's soldiers was killed, but that there were so many they were again divided up and only every tenth man from that number was spared.[40] Perhaps less than fifty remained alive. So heinous was this act that the *ASC* version C scribe wrote a ten-line alliterative verse on the incident which included the lines, 'No more horrible deed was done in this country / since the Danes came and made peace here.'[41] On face value, this acknowledges that Alfred must have brought with him substantial numbers, but it should be recognised that Harefoot and Godwin would have been very concerned about the size of this foreign army and the possibility of others joining them.

The traditional tale is that many of the captives were first taken up into the downs leading west out of Guildford and summarily executed. Gaimar names it as Geldesdon Hill (Guildown).[42] In the eleventh century, the route east to west followed what is now Guildford High Street down to the River Wey fording point and then west via the road known now as The Mount in Guildford, which led up to join the ridge of the Hogs Back (modern A31). In 1929, a burial site was discovered on the ridge during work undertaken in the rear garden of a house on Guildown Avenue, which runs parallel to the south of The Mount. Further excavations by archaeologists identified a large Anglo-Saxon cemetery, and after extensive work, over 200 separate individuals were catalogued.[43] This is believed to be only part of a much larger cemetery utilised over several centuries on this site, most of which remains undisturbed.

Despite some initial evidence to the contrary, the hypothesis was developed that all the identified burials were connected to the 1036 Guildford massacre, and some secondary authorities have further elaborated that version. However, the consensus from the accumulated research is that this location served several functions. It had been a community burial site and a location for executions and burials of miscreants over a long period. Osteologists and archaeologists have assessed that many of the unearthed remains can be linked to the mid-eleventh century, further determining that a large percentage of them could have been part of Alfred's 1036 army. From their positioning in the graves, many appear to have been bound when killed, and the 1930s surveys speculated that their bone structures, specifically their skulls and leg bones, coincided with those familiarly found on the other side of the Channel (i.e. Boulogne/Normandy).[44] This interpretation is open to speculation until further research on the skeletal remains is conducted.

Abingdon's version (C) of the *ASC* is more hostile of Godwin than other sources because, as pointed out by some academics, Abingdon Abbey had had two Norman abbots either side of the Conquest.[45] The first was a kinsman of Emma and Alfred, and the second had been at Jumièges and doubtless knew Robert of Jumièges (aka Champart), who was to be a later adversary of the Godwin family during 1048–52. Norman chroniclers took clues from version C and almost revelled in descriptions of Godwin's deceit, with Wace writing that Godwin 'committed treason, following in the footsteps of Judas' and had 'betrayed the son of his natural lord and the heir to the domain'.[46] William of Malmesbury describes Godwin's involvement as being spread by 'rumour-mongers' but this does not stop him telling us that 'through treachery of his compatriots and of Godwin especially (Alfred) was blinded at Gillingham and sent from there to the monastery of Ely'.[47]

The frustration for historians is that we do not know Godwin's intent. However, it was not an accidental meeting but designed for a purpose, and opinion is divided over whether Godwin had been caught out himself by Harefoot's arrival. There is no way of knowing whether he operated freely or on Harefoot's instructions. It is plausible Godwin planned to act as a peacemaker, maybe to try and persuade Alfred to return to Wissant peacefully, but that Harefoot had tracked Alfred and had then moved against them at Guildford with no warning to Godwin.[48] Later events acknowledge, as hinted at previously, that Godwin had likely already accepted Harefoot's lordship and was no longer 'Emma's man'.[49] Knowledge that Emma had changed her primary allegiance from Harthacnut to her sons by Æthelred could have similarly altered Godwin's political stance.

It was clear by the autumn of 1036 that Harefoot was in the ascendant and Emma had lost influence, leaving Godwin in a difficult position. Possibly Godwin's true intent can be gleaned from his responses to similar critical moments later in his life. He was usually pragmatic, preferring to negotiate before fighting. If he was guilty of the capture and massacre of Alfred's men, he was likely led by the logic of acting swiftly to avoid a greater conflict and a potential protracted new war for the English throne. Alternately, Harefoot may have arrived unexpectedly, and Godwin was powerless to oppose him. Finally, to play devil's advocate, the issue may have revolved around the question of Godwin's earlier loyalty to Cnut, the man who had given him his opportunity and earldom. We can reasonably argue that Godwin had automatically transferred his loyalty to Cnut's heirs, rather than to the Anglo-Norman offspring of Æthelred II (the Unready), the man who had evicted his father from England a generation earlier. Godwin cannot be cleared of all suspicion, and he could easily have functioned independently and strongly to show his support for Harefoot. In his defence, he may have initially met Alfred on good terms and only acted when realising the ætheling intended ultimately to seize the throne. The potential for civil war was back in focus. In that situation, his ultimate responsibility was to defend his earldom and prevent civil war, as it had thus far been prevented between the factions supporting either Harefoot or Harthacnut.

Subsequently, the strongest criticism against Godwin comes from Norman writers, as seen, and these are clearly biased. Emma was later reticent to name Godwin as being answerable for murdering Alfred, and she put the blame squarely on Harefoot. Her entry in the *Encomium*, written several years afterwards, defends Godwin's reputation by telling us that the earl 'met him and took him under his protection, and forthwith became his soldier by averment under oath' before 'diverting him from London'.[50] This implies that she knew that Godwin met Alfred as an ally and was trying to keep the ætheling away from Harefoot, but had been caught out by developments. She writes that after Godwin had settled Alfred and his soldiers into quarters, Harefoot turned up unexpectedly and removed them from the earl's care.[51] That Emma would still believe this years later is a convincing argument for Godwin's innocence, although the matter remains open for debate.

From Guildford, the ætheling Alfred was shipped via the River Wey and River Thames on to Ely in East Anglia, away from London and Godwin's Wessex. This location was presumably selected to prevent knowledge of the massacre leaking out among the senior nobility and tells us it was likely a unilateral decision by Harefoot. If Harefoot had not conducted affairs at Guildford he was certainly conducting them by this stage. Either on his arrival at Ely or beforehand, Alfred was blinded. The *Encomium* scribe details graphically how he was tortured, held down, and blinded, Emma telling her encomiast to be as graphic as possible to further defame Harefoot's reputation.[52] Some sources describe Alfred being delivered to Ely, while others describe him first being found in the nearby marshes. Either way, the intent had probably been to keep him incarcerated and out of the way at Ely, but the blinding had been botched and proved fatal. Alfred was placed in the care of the monks after his mutilation but died from his injuries. He was buried at the west end of Ely Abbey.[53] Horrific as Alfred's demise was, it was common medieval practice for failed pretenders to the throne who had threatened the established administration to be deprived of their sight and not killed. This way, the king had no death on his hands but his rival's claim was nullified. However, there may be another gruesome reason Alfred was blinded. Ælfgifu of Northampton, Harefoot's mother, had seen the blinding of her own brothers three decades earlier on the orders of Alfred's father Æthelred II, so she may have thought it sweet justice that Emma's offspring should be treated the same.

We can return now to reassess the infamous letters that had brought Emma's sons to England. After the above events, Emma distanced herself from any responsibility for her sons having crossed the Channel. In hindsight, it had been a grave error of judgement and she intended to avoid being held even partly responsible. The section in the *Encomium* concerning the original letter is designed to relieve her of any involvement, and she states that Harefoot had forged the message as if from her.[54] Could or would Harefoot issue a letter in Emma's name? Was it logical to draw the æthelings out of Normandy to seize them and pre-empt a possible threat? It is plausible, and many historians accept it. If Harefoot was behind the forgery, the plan was risky but worked out exactly as hoped. The counter-argument is that Harefoot would not want to entice two more claimants over to England when he was still trying to establish his entitlement over and above Harthacnut.[55]

Most academics agree that Emma was the likeliest source of the letters, and logic would suggest this.[56] This conclusion still applies even if we accept that Harefoot could theoretically have authenticated the message with Emma's seal, which he could have taken during his raid on Winchester several months earlier.[57] The wording of the note nonetheless strongly implies it was from Emma, not Harefoot. One sentence highlights her growing frustration: 'I wonder what plan you are adopting, since you are aware that the delay arising from your procrastination is becoming from day to day a support to the usurper of your rule.'[58] This wording seems far too personal for a forgery.

Furthermore, her additional plea that 'one of you' (i.e. Edward or Alfred) seek to take the throne implies additional intrigue.[59] Emma well knew that Edward was the 'rightful' heir over and above his younger brother and the message seems designed to force Edward to act to avoid the risk of Alfred usurping his claim. The manipulative content smacks too much of Emma's hand to be the work of another. Her denial in the *Encomium*, it should be remembered, came later when Harthacnut was on the throne and Emma was desperate to claim that he had always been her favoured choice. Neither son took the letter as anything but genuine. Even if Harefoot had duplicated Emma's seal, she surely factored in a code of some sort, some extra identification in her correspondence, which would have told them beyond doubt that the message was from her and not a falsification from elsewhere.

5

Godwin and the Anglo-Danish Succession, 1037–1042

Harold Harefoot's succession to the English throne (as King Harold I) is noted in the regnal lists as taking place on 12 November 1035, the day Cnut died.[1] However, as already considered, in the first instance he was named as regent north of the Thames, then assumed authority across all of England during 1036, before being finally and formally crowned in 1037. When Emma's sons landed in England, Harefoot was already installed as monarch with the Witan's majority approval. This likely included Godwin's adherence. Coin examples extant from late 1036 are evidence that Harefoot had been recognised as ruler not just north of the Thames but across Wessex, and that his coins were being minted not only in Winchester but more widely.[2] The *ASC* acknowledges that in 1037, 'Here Harold (Harefoot) was everywhere chosen as king, and Harthacnut forsaken because he was too long in Denmark'.[3] The chronicle scribe was working on his calendar year beginning 1 September (as noted in the introduction) so this was more likely sometime between September and December 1036. In endorsing Harefoot the Witan had chosen the candidate with an English mother (Ælfgifu of Northampton) not a Norman one. Harefoot had held the support of Earl Leofric of Mercia and others north of London for some time, and now had Godwin's backing. What the nobility desired was stability.

Harefoot was still young, barely twenty, and detail of him is somewhat obscure. It is highly probable his mother Ælfgifu, Emma's rival, played an important role, and effectively acted as regent, certainly for the initial period of his reign.[4] She could have been behind his action to deal uncompromisingly with the ætheling Alfred, and likely was also involved in his next move. Soon after Alfred's disposal Harefoot led a contingent of soldiers to Winchester and deprived Emma of Cnut's treasury, ensuring that if she plotted again with Edward there would be no risk of them using the royal exchequer to recruit more mercenaries. Godwin's inability or unwillingness to intervene tells us he had already shifted his allegiance, irrespective of whatever standpoint historians take over events at Guildford. Emma's involvement in the recent landings was widely suspected, and probably justifiably so. Godwin, if he had not done so beforehand, would have had little option but to distance himself from any earlier allegiance to her and place himself behind Harefoot.

In seizing the royal treasury, Harefoot also removed the coronation insignia of crown and sceptre from Winchester with a view to ratifying his rule at both a secular and ecclesiastic level. He requested Archbishop Æthelnoth, at Canterbury since 1020 and a regular signatory of Cnut's charters, to consecrate and crown him using the regalia.[5] The *Encomium Emmae Reginae* scribe later elaborates that Æthelnoth had allegedly self-contentedly responded to Harefoot 'that while the sons of Queen Emma lived he would approve or consecrate no other man as king', refusing also to permit any prelate to similarly use the regalia on Harefoot.[6] How are we to assess Godwin and Emma's relationship after these events? Emma may have felt betrayed, but there is a greater argument that overall Godwin had more reason to feel aggrieved. As discussed previously, she had likely kept him in the dark about her plans with her sons which led to Godwin facing a large force of foreign soldiers inside Wessex. If Godwin knew of Emma's letters, he could perhaps use that against her in the years ahead.[7] It should be remembered Emma denied her involvement. When Emma commissioned the *Encomium*, she put the blame for Alfred's death squarely on the then deceased Harefoot and, as noted beforehand, apportioned no retrospective blame on Godwin.

Harefoot's position solidified over the winter of 1036/7. Another key event had been the death the previous year of his elder brother Svein Cnutsson in Denmark.[8] Svein, like Harthacnut, had not been able to leave Denmark, but his death had encouraged Magnus I of Norway, recently arrived from exile, to reignite the Norse–Danish war. By doing so Magnus had through necessity detained Harthacnut in Denmark, and Emma seems to have already given up on Harthacnut returning to England any time soon. Despite her undoubted status, Emma now faced an uncertain future.

Archbishop Æthelnoth at Canterbury died in October 1038, although the royal priest Eadsige had previously taken over many of the archbishop's duties. His semi-retirement may have been due to ill health but may also be linked to his earlier refusal to allow Harefoot access to the royal regalia or to allow another bishop to conduct the coronation service. Eadsige was more accommodating towards Harefoot. The new king's inauguration came in January or February 1037. As payback, the new king ignored Æthelnoth and

Canterbury and his coronation service took place either at York or London, performed by Ælfric Puttoc, Archbishop of York.

During the reigns of her two husbands (Æthelred II and Cnut) Emma had witnessed more than thirty charters over a thirty-three-year period. She was the most influential woman of the eleventh century, surpassing Edith Godwinsdottir's later role, in terms of documented recognition of her position and influence. However, by 1037 she had become politically isolated, and with the removal of the royal treasury and the realignment of Godwin, her grasp on power had gone. She would resurrect her position of influence upon the eventual arrival of Harthacnut in 1040 but as things stood in 1037, having avoided detention when Harefoot had raided Winchester, she would soon be forced into exile. After his coronation, Harefoot moved decisively. The *ASC* records dramatically that she 'was driven out without any mercy to face the raging winter'.[9] This was probably before March 1037, but perhaps Emma had already chosen self-exile rather than place herself at the mercy of her rival Ælfgifu and her son. She did not leave penniless; a woman of her resourcefulness would have ensured she had transferred what funds she could ahead of this foreseen eventuality.

Emma sailed to Flanders, where she was given a property in Bruges by Count Baldwin V.[10] The interest here is that she chose Flanders rather than Normandy; as the sister and aunt respectively of the former dukes Richard II and Robert I, and great-aunt to the young new duke William (later the Conqueror), Normandy would seem more logical. It is probably safe to say that her relationship with Edward, now back in Normandy, was not at this stage positive, and he may have blamed her for initiating the events that had led to his brother's demise. There were problems across the Channel, too. William of Malmesbury recorded that 'there was no safety for her in Normandy', with 'her brother and nephews being now dead'.[11] Normandy was indeed experiencing a period of anarchy. The nine-year-old William had been duke for less than eighteen months by the middle of 1037, and his position was precarious. To survive potential assassination, he had needed the assistance of King Henry I of France and his uncle Robert, Archbishop of Rouen, alongside a group of loyal supporters. On the death of the archbishop in March 1037 the boy duke was placed in the care of Alan of Brittany, and the situation would remain volatile for several years. The Norman chroniclers William of Poitiers and William of Jumièges later made much play of the connection William (the Conqueror) had with his great-aunt (Emma) and Edward during this period. However, this was an exaggeration, as in reality he was still a boy under the control of others, and both age and circumstance make it clear that there was no close relationship with either Emma or Edward at any stage.

Harefoot was to be on the throne of England until March 1040, but documentary evidence is sparse and there are no surviving royal charters.

Any that were issued were likely destroyed soon afterward by his successor. He does appear as the primary witness in a charter issued by Lyfing, Bishop of Worcester.[12] Lyfing had been one of Harefoot's most loyal supporters and had received the bishopric through the king's influence.[13] It is noteworthy that Lyfing was to become one of Godwin's closest associates, and this 1038 charter sees Godwin signing first among the secular witnesses and above Earl Leofric. This implies and recognises that Godwin had become accepted and was fully immersed within Harefoot's inner circle.

Harefoot's temperament to rule is open to debate, but some historians suggest the real power behind the throne was his mother Ælfgifu.[14] His legacy and reputation suffered in the propaganda war of words after his death and the Church was similarly critical according to the sources. This negativity continued into the later Middle Ages. Among the general slurs was talk of him having rejected Christianity, one of the strongest accusations any churchman could hurl at any individual; Harthacnut would be likewise criticised by the clergy, although perhaps not as strongly or frequently. William of Malmesbury expands this theme by writing that in Harefoot's reign the citizens of London 'had by now almost adopted barbarian ways'.[15] That Malmesbury wrote in such strong terms four generations later acknowledges that the legacy of Harefoot's reign was seen negatively. The motive behind Emma's slanderous accusations about Harefoot's parentage within the *Encomium* are obvious: they were designed purely to ruin his reputation and entitlement to the throne in favour of her own son.[16]

Perhaps Harefoot was not a good ruler; we cannot be clear. Nevertheless, this may only prove that the later propaganda against him had been extraordinarily successful. At what point do we dispute the source detail and how much has been deliberately twisted to suit a viewpoint? However, condemnation was not universal. Mention of his good character appears in contemporary work from the scriptorium at Crowland Abbey, where he is said to have presented Crowland with his silk coronation robe and diverse gifts.[17] He is also favourably remembered by the abbeys at Glastonbury and Ramsbury.[18] Throughout his reign support remained consistent north of the Thames. In Mercia, Earl Leofric's brother Eadwine (aka Edwin) had likewise supported him before being killed in battle in 1039 by the Welsh near Welshpool. This again suggests some kinship connection between the Mercian dynasty and Ælfgifu of Northampton which had guaranteed their loyalty.[19] Loyalty for Harefoot in Northumbria under Earl Ealdred II (up to 1038) and thereafter Eadwulf III (aka Eadulf) may have been equally strong because in 1041 Eadwulf was to be killed following instructions from Harthacnut.

In the autumn of 1039, Emma summoned Edward and then Harthacnut to her residency in Bruges. Emma's recollection in her *Encomium* was that Edward was unable or unwilling to make a further attempt to seize the English throne.[20] Harthacnut had just reached a peace agreement with the Norwegian king Magnus I to end the war with Denmark. (The terms of this agreement had potential implications not only in Scandinavia but also England, and these are explored in a later chapter.) Harthacnut agreed with his mother that the moment was now right to challenge Harefoot's rule. Mercenaries were sought and ships commissioned for a hostile takeover of the English throne, and over the winter of 1039/40 Harthacnut assembled an invasion fleet in Denmark.[21] The question was where in England he would find support. Harefoot was recognised throughout as king, from Wessex to Northumbria, and none of the earls were likely to change their allegiance now, including Earl Godwin.

However, fate was to intervene, and warfare was avoided. Just ahead of Harthacnut's fleet setting sail that summer news came that Harefoot had died at Oxford on 17 March 1040. He had, according to the *ASC*, reigned for 'four years and sixteen weeks', which was calculated from the death of his father not from his coronation date.[22] He may have been ill for several weeks, and his last moments were attended by Bishop Lyfing, which is proof he had not rejected Christianity. Harefoot was taken for burial at the church at Westminster, on the riverside at Thorney, rather than for burial alongside his father in the Old Minster at Winchester.[23] Presumably Westminster had been his wish, but we cannot reject the idea that Bishop Ælfwine of Winchester had refused to accept the king's body for burial in his church. The allegiance of the bishop, in situ at Winchester since 1032, had, openly or otherwise, likely remained with Emma. A later charter of Harthacnut's dated 1042 donated land in Hampshire to Ælfwine, which all but confirms this.[24]

Harefoot had died aged only twenty-three or twenty-four. When linked with the non-violent deaths of both his father Cnut (aged about forty) and his half-brother Harthacnut (aged about twenty-four), it has been suggested that some form of a hereditary paternal disease was the cause, passed down through Cnut's line.[25] Other examples of non-violent deaths with blood ties to Cnut include Harefoot's brother Svein Cnutsson, aged only twenty-three, and Gunhilda, Cnut and Emma's daughter, aged eighteen. These appear to be more than coincidental and perhaps point to a familial disorder.

The matter of the succession was back on the table sooner than many had wanted or expected. Two candidates had strong blood ties to the royal line, Harthacnut and Edward, but only one of them desired the throne. Swein Estrithsson, Harthacnut's cousin, had a much weaker claim. In any case, Swein would seem to have settled for being offered control of Denmark when Harthacnut was looking to take the English throne. Peace had broken out in Scandinavia and Harthacnut was planning to return to England, and of course, Emma was now throwing her full support behind him and not Edward. From his later reticence in 1042, we know that Edward was not pushing his own claims.

It is unlikely, but possible, that Harefoot had a young heir. Mention has been made that he had married a woman named Ælfgifu, possibly a hand-fast marriage, and she had produced a son named Ælfwine.[26] If true, the child could have been no older than eight when his father died. Not only was he too young to succeed, but he was also illegitimate; he would have had little or no support and would be unlikely to survive in the political arena once Emma had retrieved her position. The story goes that the youth became a monk, where he is mentioned in the charters of the Abbey of Saint Foy in Conques in southern France.[27] Ælfgifu of Northampton did not remain long in England after Harefoot's death. In a complete turn of fortune, she did what Emma had done three years earlier and took herself into exile. She disappears from the historical record here, and perhaps took her grandchild with her into exile, maybe to Francia, before Harthacnut and Emma returned to England.

However, Harthacnut's succession was not assured and may still have needed military enforcement. He had sailed from Denmark to Flanders with ten ships over the winter of 1039/40 as a preliminary move, but the door to England had swung open on news of Harefoot's death. In England, the Witan had quickly gathered and agreed to offer the throne to Harthacnut. Godwin seems to have accepted this decision, though perhaps with some trepidation bearing in mind his earlier involvement in Alfred's demise and support for Harefoot against Emma. The decision was probably unanimous and, being a skilled diplomat, Godwin may have seen the advantage that could be achieved by being among the first to nominate Harthacnut. He was likely already repositioning himself for the return of Emma and the problem this might pose for his future status.

The Witan sent messages for Harthacnut to come and claim the throne, but despite the open offer he was taking no chances. Keeping to his original plan, he assembled a fleet of sixty-two warships. No doubt his mother had warned him that all the earls who had supported Harefoot, Godwin included, may still resist him. There was no guarantee of a peaceful coronation, but no opposition materialised. In truth, there was little alternative option open to the Witan and the earls. Harthacnut's fleet 'came to Sandwich, 7 days before midsummer (17 June) and he was immediately received by both the English and the Danes'.[28] It was the first time he had set foot on English soil since his father was alive, perhaps since he was a young boy. He was aware Kent, as part of Wessex, was under Godwin's jurisdiction, and Emma would have already explained Godwin's earlier political stance. However, Godwin was pragmatic if nothing else and welcomed Harthacnut, as did the senior earls

Leofric of Mercia and Siward of Deiran Northumbria (York), and all the senior secular and ecclesiastical leaders.

Swayed to some extent by his mother – although we should keep her influence in proportion – Harthacnut had within his first few days back ordered that the corpse of his predecessor be exhumed. William of Malmesbury states that several men encouraged Harthacnut on this course, Ælfric Puttoc, Archbishop of York, principal among them.[29] Ælfric had acted in Harefoot's coronation, so presumably he was hoping to display his newfound loyalty, which he further displayed by accusing Bishop Lyfing of Worcester of having been involved in Alfred's murder in 1036.[30] Ælfric's desire to add Lyfing's see at Worcester to his own York archbishopric was no doubt his prime motivation; in fact, he briefly held the diocese afterwards but had to release it within a year.

As part of his own atonement for crowning Harefoot, Ælfric Puttoc was one of several men sent by Harthacnut to exhume the corpse, buried four months previously. As recorded by John of Worcester, the party included Stor, master of the royal household, Eadric, the steward, Thrond, the executioner, and finally Earl Godwin.[31] Godwin's inclusion in this unsavoury act was presumably Emma's idea. The erstwhile king's corpse was then beheaded, and his remains were thrown into the adjacent River Thames at Westminster. The remains were later reputedly gathered by a fisherman in his nets and carried for secret burial to the Danish cemetery in London at St Clement Danes in the Strand.[32] The church was rebuilt by the Normans and has seen several other rebuilds since, but Harefoot's grave was probably destroyed during the first rebuild.

The summons for Godwin to attend the proceedings was a punishment, and he may have even been required to assist hands-on with the gruesome duty.[33] However, this was not the end of what appears to have been a ritual humiliation. Godwin was forced to swear his innocence regarding Alfred's capture, mutilation, and death, and swear another oath that Harefoot was behind Alfred's murder.[34] This was all high drama and theatre, but the intent, likely orchestrated by Emma, was to put Godwin in his place, force him to display his vassalage openly and remind him he was expendable. The death of Alfred seems to crop up in the texts regularly, and the assumption is it remained a deep issue with Emma long after the event, and, as the sources imply, with Edward also.

However, Godwin went further in ensuring he would endure as a central figure in the revised administration and preserve his earldom. He presented the new monarch with a large and elaborate warship. This ship had a beak of gold and contained eighty soldiers, each of whom came with two sixteen-ounce gold bracelets, a gilded helmet, a Danish axe, and an iron spear.[35] This alone shows the wealth available to Godwin mid-way through his career. (He was to give a similar warship and crew, perhaps even more extravagant a ship and crew, to Edward two years later.) Godwin likely saw the gift as a means towards gaining Harthacnut's favour, but it could be interpreted as admitting guilt in the Guildford incident.[36] By presenting such a valuable gift it can be viewed as a form of *wergild*, a payment which a perpetrator of a crime had to pay to a victim or their kinsmen. The level of *wergild* compensation to be paid was based on the victim's status. Here, the implication is that the value of the warship and crew Godwin gave to Harthacnut probably equated to the *wergild* value for a royal ætheling.

For Godwin, the critical moment had passed. Satisfied with his open display of vassalage and subjugation to her son, Emma would have known, even if her son did not, that they needed Godwin's backing just as much as they needed that of the other senior earls. They could not afford the risk of removing him. Although Earl Leofric of Mercia and others had accepted vassalage to Harthacnut, it should be recalled that they had supported Harefoot during 1036, more so initially than Godwin. Removal of any of the senior earls at this point could have jeopardised the fledgeling accession, but without Godwin, the most powerful noble in England, Harthacnut's position would be compromised. Godwin was still perhaps to reach the summit of his career, but already by 1040 he was a commanding figure. Wessex was one of the two richest regions of England (the other was East Anglia), and the earldom controlled the primary and shortest route to the Continent and remained the most influential region politically and militarily. In his role as Earl of Wessex Godwin similarly controlled the vassalage of many of the wealthiest thegns in England.

However, one senior noble who was expendable was Earl Eadwulf III in Bamburgh in Bernicia, who had replaced his brother Ealdred II in 1038 after Ealdred's murder. Eadwulf had been amongst Harefoot's foremost supporters and had recently restored Bernician Northumbrian control in Cumbria against a Scottish invasion led by King Duncan I. As part of uniting Bernicia and Deira, Earl Siward of Deira had married Eadwulf's sister Ælfflæd. Siward was to have two sons. The first, Osbeorn, was from a previously unknown relationship, but the second, Waltheof, was Ælfflaed's child. However, much in the vein of how Eadwulf's father Uhtred the Bold had been betrayed and murdered in 1016, the same was to happen to him in 1041. Harthacnut saw Eadwulf as a threat, someone to be removed. After promises of safe conduct from the king ahead of a planned meeting, Eadwulf was intercepted and murdered. The *ASC* accuses Harthacnut of plotting it, naming him as 'a pledge-breaker', and of having ordered Eadwulf's murder.[37] It is Symeon of Durham, the chronicler most familiar with events inside Northumbria, that implicates Siward in the assasination.[38] Siward's involvement in the murder of his own brother-in-law seems coldly calculated, but from his perspective it proved his loyalty to the new monarch, with the additional reward of absorbing Bernicia into his Deiran sphere and assuming control over all of Northumbria.

Harthacnut's tenure, more so perhaps than his predecessor's, would not be a success. He proved to be unpopular, showing too much immaturity and naivety in his decision making, and according to one source he 'did nothing worthy of royal power'.[39] One of his major widescale actions in 1041, with echoes of Cnut in 1017, was to impose heavy taxes and raid the royal treasury to pay off the large fleet and the warriors he had brought across the Channel the preceding year. The amount was so great that 'scarcely anyone could pay it'.[40] A figure of £21,099 is quoted, plus another £11,048 paid for thirty-two ships.[41] This primary source detail is a little ambiguous, but it can perhaps be explained by identifying that the larger figure refers to payment to the warriors released from their oaths along with half of the original fleet that then dispersed, while the second figure refers to the standing fleet that he intended to maintain as operational. It has been reasoned that an extrapolation of the amount needed to pay off the Danish warriors puts their number at over 2,000.[42] Only a handful of charters from Harthacnut have survived, but we can speculate that much of this extra taxation was used to garner support from the existing establishment as well as to give favours to housecarls who had sailed with him a year earlier.

During this round of tax collecting an incident took place at Worcester on 4 May 1041 wherein two of the king's housecarls, Feader and Thurstan, were slain while collecting taxes. As recorded by John of Worcester, the two housecarls had first sought safety inside a tower in the monastery before being slain.[43] Harthacnut's response was not immediate, but he assembled most of his housecarls and summoned his senior nobles and their retinues to travel to Worcester in the autumn. This included not only Godwin of Wessex, Leofric of Mercia and Siward of Northumbria, but also the regional ealdormen Thored (aka Thuri) and Hrani, the latter formerly one of Cnut's closest associates.[44] They arrived at Worcester on 12 November, several weeks after the summer harvest had been gathered, plausibly to cause maximum damage and distress. On Harthacnut's orders many citizens were killed, much of the town burnt down, and the cathedral damaged during four days of plunder. Leaving Worcester, they then pillaged a large area of the shire. Godwin, alongside the others, is unlikely to have taken pleasure from this, and as Worcestershire lay in his Mercian earldom and was the home of his ancestral tribe the Hwicce, it would have been particularly distasteful for Leofric. Nevertheless, Leofric did not disobey the royal order and this can be contrasted with Godwin's response when he was faced with a similar conundrum in Kent in 1051, looked at in a later chapter, whether to obey the monarch or to defend the rights of his vassals.

Harthacnut appears in eight surviving charters, four he issued and four as a witness. Of those he witnessed, one (S983) was a charter from Cnut he witnessed as a youth before leaving for Denmark, and three were leases of land from Bishop Lyfing of Worcester to Bishop Æthelric of Durham.[45] Perhaps this is evidence of Lyfing being penalised further for having been one of Harefoot's chief supporters amongst the clergy. Of the four known charters by Harthacnut, one may be forged (S995), but in the three more reliable documents Godwin appears first in all the secular witness lists, and Leofric second in the two he signed. The maintaining of Godwin's name at the head of the secular signatories demonstrates that whatever difficulties there had been in the early weeks of Harthacnut's reign Godwin was soon re-established as the key senior noble. Siward appears third in all three. Emma witnesses all of them immediately below her son.[46] Other Danes such as Tovi, Thuri and Ordgar were prominent, having survived from the reign of Cnut and through the period of Harefoot's reign. This acknowledges that Harthacnut did not take excessive reprisals against all those who had acted alongside the previous regime. Harthacnut is not known to have married, and Emma's position in the lists endorses that. It is a sign of her having recovered her full status, possibly with more influence at her son's court than she had held under Cnut's reign.

Towards the end of 1041, Harthacnut called for his stepbrother Edward to leave Normandy and settle back in England at the royal court. It is unclear if they had met beforehand; their paths could have crossed in Bruges when visiting their mother. Emma was likely behind the invitation, and Edward's arrival in England is the last entry within Emma's *Encomium*.[47] Some historians hint at a more complicated scenario. A work called the *Quadripartitus* originating from Winchester in the early twelfth century refers to a meeting in 1041 between Edward and an assembly of nobles on the Hurst spit in the Solent, during which Edward was made to swear he would uphold Cnut's laws.[48] Whether this was part of a plan to oust Harthacnut from the throne prematurely is unclear, but it would seem to have been an event in which Harthacnut was not involved, or indeed Emma. Edward may have already been nominated as Harthacnut's heir but talk of a coup is perhaps implausible. Emma would certainly have remained supportive of Harthacnut, and Godwin likewise at this stage, with Emma's priority being to ensure that Edward would succeed only on the death of Harthacnut.

Edward was blood tied to the old royal line of Æthelred II (the Unready), but the question also remains whether he was willing to accept the role of potential successor. He may have left Normandy primarily because the duchy was still in a state of anarchy, with the young Duke William's position still far from secure. Edward's Old English vernacular may have become rusty, and his more natural tongue would have likely been Norman French. His mother Emma had presumably taught him some skill in languages when he was a child, but he had been away from England and regular exposure to the language for a quarter of a century.

Harthacnut's partnerships are a closed book. He was possibly unable to father any children, and there is no mention of a wife, even a handfast wife or a concubine. This leads us to the question of who would succeed him. It would prove to be Edward, but we are left with the unusual situation that a king in his early twenties was about to nominate an unmarried man in his mid to late thirties, and seemingly a career bachelor to that date, as his successor. This seems illogical when securing the succession was so important, not just to England but to the future relationships with Denmark, Norway, and the Continental powers. The conclusion is perhaps that the king thought he yet had plenty of time to produce a natural heir, although some historians have argued that there had already been warning signs of Harthacnut's poor constitution, or of a serious illness, which was likely to shorten his life. This may well be the case and explains the decision to recall Edward back across the Channel as surety.[49]

At around the same date the king's cousin Swein Estrithsson (aka Estridsson), the offspring of Ulf Thorgilsson and Cnut's sister Estrith (Estrid) Sweynsdottir, was likewise summoned from Denmark to England. Swein, through his kinship with Gytha Thorgilsdottir, was thereby also Godwin's nephew.[50] The future succession may have been discussed; Swein was a potential candidate, being a grandson of Sweyn Forkbeard and nephew of Cnut. However, the major debate concerned the renewed warfare between Denmark and Norway, and the transfer of authority in Denmark from Harthacnut. Swein was charged with protecting Denmark from Norwegian dominance, and he was supplied with a fleet of ships by his cousin, likely some of those that Harthacnut had employed the previous year.

Harthacnut would be dead in less than a year. His death while still young was to continue the unfortunate Cnut family trait noted previously, perhaps a paternally inherited weakness. It came while he was attending the wedding of his father's old favourite Earl Tovi the Proud and his much younger bride Gytha, daughter of Osgod Clapa (aka Osgot Clapa), at Lambeth on 8 June 1042. Harthacnut, as recorded by the *ASC* scribe, 'died as he stood at his drink, and he suddenly fell to the earth with an awful convulsion … and he spoke no word afterwards'.[51] He was taken to Winchester Old Minster for burial, where he was laid alongside his father. None of the primary sources gives a cause of death, although heart attack or stroke is often suggested. Poisoning is possible but unproven and perhaps too dramatic, although the mention of a 'convulsion' leaves it open-ended and he was not a popular king. He may have been frequently unwell, and his earlier agreement with Magnus the Good of Norway concerning the English and Danish succession described elsewhere may have been made in the knowledge that he could not or would not produce an heir.[52]

In summarising Harthacnut's brief reign, the suggestion is that he was a lesser king than Harold Harefoot and not worthy of comparison to his father. Reviewing the main English sources, neither of Cnut's two successors receive positive input from the scribes. This did not stop the Norman sources praising Harthacnut over and above Harefoot, however, with William of Poitiers writing that 'this man (Harthacnut) was more like his mother's family, and did not rule by cruelty as his father and brother had done'.[53] This summary seems almost the opposite of reality, but Poitiers' words were not aimed at praising Harthacnut per se, rather given more readily because he was the son of Emma, the woman of Norman descent associated with the ducal dynasty. It suited the Norman chroniclers writing in the post-Conquest period to praise the man who had enabled Edward to position himself in line for the English throne, by association further validating the position of Duke William for the English succession.

It is plausible that the half-brothers Harthacnut and Edward had become friends in the brief time they knew each other, despite their personalities appearing to be on different ends of the spectrum. However, hindsight tells us that both displayed a quick temper, irrational behaviour, and indecisiveness, which would have been considered signs of weakness by their contemporaries. Conversely, if we see Edward as a more aggressive and less passive character, he may have resented his half-brother's time on the throne. The most damning indictments of Harthacnut's reign come from Edward's early years on the throne, and Edward may have promoted these. Justified as these criticisms may have been it also seems to contradict our image of Harthacnut and Edward being close friends, and points to a deeper undercurrent in their relationship. For Edward, this may simply have been a retrospective way of damaging his mother. Even though she was probably fundamental to his recall, she surely had not foreseen him having to succeed to the throne so quickly.

There would be potential cause for concern amongst the Witan on Harthacnut's death, but Godwin was particularly well placed to be influential. He knew Emma probably better than anyone, and they likely had a mutual respect despite not always seeing eye to eye. He had friends in the Church, including Archbishop Eadsige at Canterbury and Bishop Lyfing of Worcester, both of whom he had known since the regime of Cnut. He had formed a good working rapport with Leofric of Mercia, and it was Godwin who remained as the senior royal advisor under Harthacnut and Godwin who was the best situated to work alongside Edward and Emma. Ahead of Edward's confirmation by the Witan, Godwin did what he appears to have been good at and adapted to the situation at hand. Perhaps once more taking the most politically astute course, he and his friend Bishop Lyfing pushed for Edward's immediate succession. It is notable that, as recorded by John of Worcester, it was 'mainly by the exertions of Earl Godwin and (Bishop) Lyfing' that Edward ascended the throne.[54]

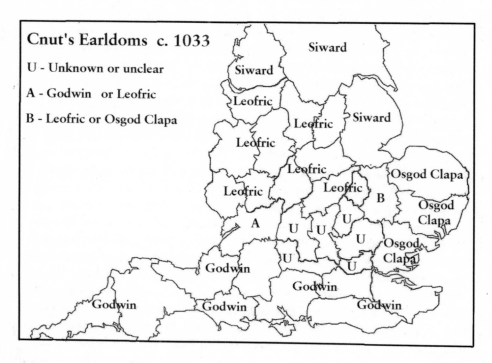

Cnut's Earldoms c. 1033

U - Unknown or unclear

A - Godwin or Leofric

B - Leofric or Osgod Clapa

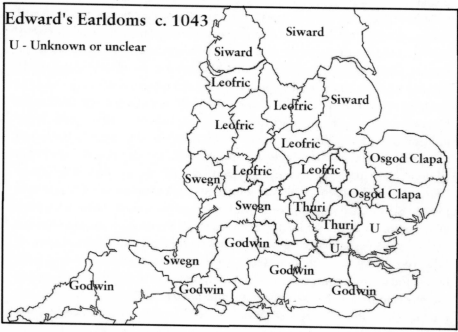

Edward's Earldoms c. 1043

U - Unknown or unclear

6

Politics, Queen Edith, and the Rise of the Godwinsons

Edward (afterwards to be known as 'the Confessor') was elected as king in June 1042, but there was some delay before his consecration, which took place in the Old Minster in Winchester on Easter Sunday, 3 April 1043.[1] The delay of about nine months was not particularly excessive in comparison to other comparable Anglo-Saxon transfers of power. However, Edward had chosen Easter for its significance in the calendar and to send a message about his future reign. Furthermore, the previous autumn had brought with it a famine, and it is likely the ceremony was primarily delayed until the worst effects of the famine had passed. The location for the ceremony, Winchester, the capital of Alfred the Great, still held significance. It not only had an association with the old West Saxon royal line, but it was the home of Edward's mother and the resting place, in the Old Minster, of his father and stepbrother. The city was under the care of Godwin as Earl of Wessex. Archbishop Eadsige of Canterbury performed the coronation ordo, in unison with Archbishop Ælfric Puttoc from York, with almost all the bishops of England in attendance.[2] Ælfric's byname of 'Puttoc' was derived from the Old English *pyttel*, meaning 'kite'. This nickname was not a complimentary one and can also be translated as 'buzzard', denoting a man of dubious character.[3] The Bishop of Winchester, Ælfwine, although not named in the sources, was presumably also present, and along with Lyfing at Worcester he would become one of Edward's strongest supporters among the clergy. Perhaps Edward's succession had not been straightforward, but there was no obvious alternative. As noted by the German chronicler Adam of Bremen, the English look to have already recognised Edward as the royal heir at the first signs of Harthacnut's failing health.[4] Edward's inauguration marked the end of the twenty-six-year tenure of the Danish kings in England and a return to the old bloodline of the Anglo-Saxon house of Wessex.

An important attendee at the ceremony was Harthacnut's cousin Swein Estrithsson. Adam of Bremen suggests that Swein saw himself as a potential successor and that Edward later agreed to Swein's nomination to succeed him, even if Edward were to have sons of his own.[5] The Danish scribe Saxo Grammaticus in his late twelfth-century work *Gesta Danorum* makes the same claim.[6] This perhaps illustrates a pattern of events that Edward was to repeat. Nevertheless, the claim can be refuted here for several reasons. Edward had no entitlement or authority to offer the English throne under the existing legislation, and the Witan never seriously contemplated Swein's candidacy. Godwin would have preferred Swein's candidacy before 1042, one suspects, but not once Edward had been installed as monarch. Godwin had already invested time and energy into securing his position at the new king's court.

Reaction to Edward was mixed. William of Malmesbury's *Gesta Regum Anglorum* is scathing of Edward's abilities but not of his later reign, noting, 'The simplicity of his character made him hardly fit to govern, but he was devoted to God, and therefore guided by him.' Malmesbury records that during Edward's regime there was no civil strife or foreign war, and that ' at home and abroad all was peace and quiet, a result all the more surprising in that he was so gentle, and could not bring himself to utter a harsh word against even the lowest of mankind'.[7] This is not an entirely accurate assessment, but it suggests Edward was willing to concur easily to any advice given from strong and influential characters at the royal court – and there was none more persuasive than Earl Godwin of Wessex.

Moving back a little, Malmesbury further implies that Edward had been uncertain about accepting the vacant throne, recording that Edward had asked Godwin for advice and for his help in returning to Normandy before the inauguration. Malmesbury delights in describing the conversation between Godwin and Edward, whereby Godwin advised, 'There is nothing in the way if you are willing to trust me, my authority carries very great weight in England, and in the side which I incline to, fortune smiles. If you have my support, no one will dare oppose you, and conversely. Agree with me therefore for true friendship between us, undiminished honours for my sons, and my daughter's hand. As a result, you will soon see yourself as king.'[8] This highlights succinctly Godwin's standing in 1042–43, and not without a certain indication of arrogance.

Nevertheless, there is no reason to suppose that Godwin was in any sense a kingmaker, as all the senior earls and the Witan had still needed to verify Edward's appointment.[9] Godwin must have seen new opportunities opening to him under Edward not evident previously under Harthacnut. In these circumstances persuading Edward to take the throne would have benefitted Godwin in several ways, increasing his importance even further and making him almost indispensable at the royal court. Perhaps there was a realisation by the earl and by Emma that by working together they would both benefit. Godwin likely exploited Edward's hesitancy, the *Gesta Regum* noting that Godwin 'loaded him with copious promises', telling him that 'as the son of Æthelred and grandson of Edgar, the kingdom was his by right'.[10]

However, we should look at things from Edward's perspective. Whereas Cnut had the military strength of his Scandinavian empire to support his early days on the English throne, Edward, in contrast, had no such independent power base.[11] Support from Normandy was no longer an option, and he needed to quickly attach himself to one or more of the key men in England. Godwin, as the long-standing earl in Wessex, with stronger ties with London, was the sensible choice. It was practicable and logical for the new king to ally himself to the Godwinsons and promote their standing even further, thereby securing the loyalty of the house most capable of upholding and supporting his position.

Edith, Edward's future wife, tells us in the *Vita Edwardi* that her father was so keen to champion Edward's claim that he sent bishops over to Normandy to collect Edward.[12] Unless Edward had been visiting Normandy when Harthacnut died this cannot be accurate, as we have seen that he was already in England. From what we know of his career Godwin must have been a persuasive and forceful figure, someone able to influence two men as different as Cnut and Edward. He seems to have bent Edward to his will, particularly in the early years of the reign. William of Malmesbury, not one of Godwin's best advocates, noted that 'some people followed his (Godwin's) authority, some had been won over by gifts', but that 'a few who resisted beyond what was fair and just received a black mark at the time and later were banished from England'.[13] To display his loyalty, Godwin repeated what he had done with Harthacnut by presenting Edward with a fully manned warship. Both these acts were politically motivated, although the first was more an act of appeasement, a *wergild* payment perhaps to atone for Godwin's part in the events of 1036. The writer Gaimar is explicit that Edward directly accused Godwin of Alfred's murder, and the earl had to swear an oath that he had played no part.[14] However, by 1042–43 the situation had changed. Godwin was acting from a position of greater authority and no doubt confidence. The gift may have had an element of atonement, but it displayed Godwin's confidence, wealth and importance; here was a man whose words the king should heed. The warship was reputedly larger than the previous one given to Harthacnut; Godwin was taking no chances of being outmanoeuvred by any of the other senior nobility. The vessel was fitted out for 120 warriors, the prow decorated with a golden-winged dragon and the stern with a golden lion.[15] This appears to have equated to two full crews, with each man provided with a helmet, hauberk, sword, shield and axe.

Godwin next put his energy and skill into furthering the careers of his eldest children. Initially, this involved his firstborn, Swegn, and his eldest daughter, Edith, then the next eldest, Harold. How much persuasion Godwin needed is difficult to assess, but Swegn Godwinson was looked on with favour by Edward and by late 1043 he had already received an earldom which included the Mercian shires of Herefordshire and Gloucestershire and the West Saxon shires of Somerset, Oxfordshire and Berkshire. Presumably, Earl Leofric of Mercia would not have looked favourably on Swegn's appointment in Herefordshire. By 1044 Swegn had signed his first royal charter, and over the next twenty-four months or so he would sign another thirteen, many of them for transactions outside his main sphere of influence.[16]

Despite living on the Continent for about twenty-five years, the new king may have had a grasp of Old English, likely refreshed since his recall by Harthacnut and his mother. The early witness lists in Edward's charters show surprising continuity between him and Cnut. Many individuals who witnessed documents for Cnut and through Harold Harefoot and Harthacnut's reigns survived into Edward's first years. Until a vacancy occurred by natural causes there was no reason to change Church personnel, but Edward also left well alone major changes amongst the thegnage and officials at court. Research has identified that of the nine thegns to sign Edward's initial charter of 1042 six had been Cnut's men and two were Harthacnut's.[17] Danes and Anglo-Danes remained prominent, men such as Osgod Clapa, Thuri and Ordgar. Osgod and Thuri also retained their earldoms in Edward's initial phase, and Ordgar was notable for remaining prominent at the royal court through to 1050. Of the ten most frequently named thegns who commonly witnessed charters between 1042 and 1046, seven had survived from Cnut's time and only one was newly introduced by Edward.[18]

More widely, the reliance Edward placed on Godwin in the early stages of his tenure may have led to him harbouring a resentment that would not surface fully until much later. This showed itself in some of Edward's policies once he was established, seeking a closer connection with the other senior earls, particularly Leofric of Mercia. Leofric may have played a more important role at court than is often appreciated, which could have neutralised Godwin's influence to some extent. William of Malmesbury acknowledges that there must have been an initial variance between the major players, and writes that 'the generous support of Leofric ... was his (Edward's) defence against the hostility of Godwin'.[19] This implies that the dangers of Godwin monopolising the king's ear were understood.

Several historians have criticised Edward's attitude, with one succinctly observing that if he had willingly given Godwin even greater authority he was a fool, and if he had not approved of the outcome he was not in full control of his kingdom.[20] This argument has traction. Godwin had an advantage through his role as Earl of Wessex, giving him privileged access to the royal court at Winchester, where it can be assumed Edward spent much time when not at his other favoured palaces at Westminster and Gloucester. Judging by the charter witness lists he was a permanent fixture. In the first twenty-four months of Edward's reign, seven extant charters have been identified, and Godwin signed all of them as the senior secular witness.[21]

Godwin's capacity to gain Edward's trust, or should we say compliance, was perhaps partially down to his rapport with the dowager queen Emma. The key to their relationship post-1042 may go back to the events of 1036 and the letter Emma is said to have sent to the æthelings. The *Encomium* she commissioned later distances herself from controversy, but Godwin's knowledge of the letter, if he knew of it, could easily lead to her being implicated if he had spoken out.[22] We can speculate that Godwin may have gleaned details of the letter when hosting Alfred at Guildford. She had presumably convinced Edward that the letter was faked by Harefoot, as claimed in the *Encomium*, but Godwin may have known differently. There was, therefore, mutual self-interest between the earl and the dowager queen that served them both to cooperate.

Emma's sway at the royal court at this juncture remains open for debate. William of Malmesbury throws some light on her relationship with Edward, although the detail comes near the end of her life rather than soon after Edward's succession. He writes that 'long had she mocked her offspring's years of need' and that 'she never contributed anything out of her own resources, passing down the hatred of the father to the child; for she had loved Cnut more while he was alive and dwelt more on his praises after his death'.[23] This acknowledges that Emma had loved her second husband, Cnut, but had loathed her first, Æthelred II, and her earlier actions had confirmed that her favoured son was Harthacnut. Emma appears to have misunderstood Edward, but from his perspective there appears to be a clear dislike of her that had likely festered since his brother's death, and possibly can be traced back even further to her abandonment of him and his brother in 1017. Only when he was established did this anger fully materialise.

Edward moved against his mother in mid-November 1043. Perhaps as some historians suggest he suspected that she was now involved in further plotting with Magnus of Norway.[24] This would seem both illogical and implausible on her part. Notwithstanding the reasons behind it, Edward summoned his senior earls Godwin, Leofric and Siward with their retinues and rode from Gloucester to Winchester, surprising Emma in her residence of God Begot Manor. The *ASC* version D recorded he 'robbed her of all the treasures which she owned ... because earlier she was very hard on the king her son, in that she did less for him than he wanted before he became king, and also afterwards'.[25] Edward required the treasury, although the primary intent seems to have been to humiliate his mother and restrict her ability to interfere in his affairs. John of Worcester adds that Emma had been 'extremely harsh to him', but after taking the gold, silver and valuables, Edward 'commanded that an adequate supply of necessities be ministered to her, and ordered her to live there quietly'.[26] Part of Emma's wealth had come from the tax concessions she had been gifted through possession of God Begot, given to her originally by Æthelred II.

As Earl of Wessex, Godwin may have had conflicting interests in this royal quarrel, and specifically on the impact within Winchester, but faced with the support the king had received from Leofric and Siward, Godwin probably decided that once again pragmatism was his best approach. Emma was meanwhile experiencing déjà vu. Harefoot's men had done the same thing several years earlier before she had fled to Flanders. The Winchester treasury would have held a large sum, considering the former harsh taxation regime of Harthacnut, and Emma had likely accumulated considerable additional personal wealth on the back of this. How much was inside the treasury in 1043 is not known, but Henry of Huntingdon claimed that at the death of William I (the Conqueror) in 1087 the silver alone within the royal coffers amounted to £60,000.[27]

The recently appointed Bishop Stigand of Elmham in East Anglia, a future Archbishop of Canterbury and a man central to the Godwinsons in the years ahead, may have shared in Emma's temporary humiliation. As her chaplain and chief advisor, Stigand was similarly deprived of some of his wealth.[28] Nevertheless, Edward was to reinstate him within a few months.

Having satisfied himself with belittling his mother, Edward did not dispossess her of all authority; at least not completely or for long. She had witnessed the earliest of Edward's extant charters below Eadsige, Archbishop of Canterbury, and another in early 1043, and after the Winchester incident Emma was soon restored and witnessed three more charters during 1044 and another in 1045. In half of these documents, she witnesses second only to Edward, and moving forward briefly to the last of them she was to sign jointly with, but above, Edith Godwinsdottir, her son's new queen.[29]

In the summer of 1044, Edward banished Cnut's younger sister Gunhild (Gunhilda), along with her two sons Hemming and Thorkell.[30] Gunhild is not to be confused with Cnut's daughter of the same name who had died prematurely in 1038, although the chronicler Symeon of Durham confused matters by naming Gunhild as Cnut's niece and not his sister.[31] Gunhild and her sons travelled to Bruges, a familiar place of sanctuary for Anglo-Danes, before moving on to Denmark. Why she was banished is unclear. Some academics have argued that along with the additional exiling of Osgod Clapa thereafter, this was part of a policy to remove those who had backed

Swein Estrithsson's potential claims to the throne and was part of an anti-Dane policy in general.[32] This argument is questionable once we factor in that Edward was to promote Swein's brother Beorn to an earldom along with other Danish kinsmen during this same period. However, it should be remembered that Beorn, like Swein, was a nephew of Godwin and Gytha, and his later promotion was perhaps another illustration of Godwin's capacity to influence the king.

Godwin and Gytha were both active in donating gifts to religious establishments during this period, These are thought to include donations at Winchester, Sherborne, Southwark and Shaftesbury, and Godwin has most notably has been connected with the churches of St Olave's in Chichester and St Mary in Castro at Dover. Gytha was connected to several foundations in western and central Wessex. Among them, she is associated with the Church of St Olave's in present-day Fore Street in Exeter, and credited with founding St Nectan's Church at Hartland in the far west of Devon, where a stained-glass window installed in the 1930s depicts Gytha within the present-day late medieval structure. Part of the nave at the present St Olave's in Exeter may date from the 1040s or 1050s. The main Godwinson residence at Exeter is believed to have been adjacent to the original church to the south.[33]

During his career under Edward, as under Cnut, Godwin was to tie his fortunes closely to several senior churchmen. These included Lyfing and Eadsige (the latter as Archbishop of Canterbury), and the future archbishops Stigand and Ealdred. Lyfing had been a protégé of Godwin and had accompanied Cnut on his visit to Rome. After being restored to the bishopric at Worcester he continued to work with Godwin until his death in March 1046.[34] There was a mutual benefit in retaining a close understanding with these men. In return for Godwin supporting their houses and personal promotions, and acting as arbiter in Church matters, they could repay him by transferring Church land, more formally provide the backing of the Church, and bolster him at court.

Eadsige had replaced Archbishop Æthelnoth in November 1038 but had become ill soon after receiving his pallium in 1040, and during 1043 he successfully appealed to the king to accept Abbot Siward of Abingdon as his coadjutor at Canterbury rather than go through the normal channels for a successor.[35] Abbot Siward later fell ill himself, and Eadsige returned to his post in 1048. As with his original appointment he needed Godwin's support, and in return the earl was rewarded with grants of Church property. Possibly linked to arrangements between the archbishop, the abbot and Godwin was the earlier transfer from Æthelnoth of the 'third penny' of the taxes for Kent to Godwin. The 'third penny' was a legal entitlement based on who administered the shire. In this case, it allowed Godwin to claim one-third of the tax revenue for administration costs and protection of Kent. Questions would be asked later about the legality of such transfers to blacken Godwin's name, but the 'third penny' entitlement was not uncommon, and the king and other nobles had the same entitlement across other shires, as Godwin himself had across Wessex.

During 1044, Godwin secured the betrothal of his eldest daughter, Edith, to the king. This was no minor achievement. A betrothal to foreign nobility by the king, preferably to the daughter of royalty in the case of an ætheling, would have been the normal course of events to secure a foreign alliance. For Edith, a more likely predicted betrothal may have been with a nobleman from Flanders, Germany or Francia, or perhaps the son of an English noble. There are countless examples, and Edward's sister Godgifu had made two Continental marriages, first to Drogo of Mantes and then Eustace of Boulogne. A royal match was, therefore, a major triumph for Godwin but was perhaps less than Edward should have aspired to. The union did not bring him a useful political alliance. In contrast, it served Godwin well. His family was to be directly connected to the throne of England, adding to his dynasty's dominance inside the royal court, not to mention the private royal bedchamber. Edith's marriage cemented the king tightly to the Godwinsons.

Edward had passed the age of forty and Edith was nearly two decades younger, but the age gap was not unusual for the period. The union may have been something Godwin had been working on since Edward became monarch. The wedding took place on 23 January 1045 in Winchester's Old Minster.[36] During the ceremony, Edith was anointed and delivered with a ring and crown, with an explicit reference to the imposition of hands.[37] By this ritual she was recognised as queen by both Church and State. Separate from the marriage ceremony, she was defined as being consecrated a queen, not simply the spouse of a king.[38]

How are we to view Godwin in all this? We do not have enough detail of his personality to reach an undisputed conclusion. Historians place themselves in two camps. One argument is that Godwin was a ruthless operator, meticulously and constantly planning everything to gain greater power for himself and his family whenever and wherever he could. In this scenario, Edward is portrayed almost as feeble-minded, a willing victim who conceded authority to Godwin to remove some of the burden of kingship from his own shoulders. The alternate argument portrays Godwin in a better light. A man of honour and intellect who accepted the extra responsibilities that fell to him and his household in duty to the king, his earldom and the country. It was probably a combination of both arguments, with Godwin simply doing what others would have done given the same circumstances. As previously seen, Godwin had frequently worked things to his advantage with his most powerful and difficult contemporaries. This tells us he was a persuasive speaker, skilled in bringing others around to his viewpoint or convincing them he could be relied on as their strongest advocate.

Nevertheless, whichever image of Godwin you prefer, Edith's marriage to Edward had raised the stakes. The only thing needed to surpass this now was a royal child, an heir to Edward.

Trying to describe Edith's qualities and personality traits from this distance is, as with many other historical figures, difficult and potentially imprecise. Historians must make judgements on what may be valid, and within that is the challenge of the reliability of primary source detail. For Edith, the *Vita Edwardi*, which she commissioned, gives some clues. Her encomiast writes that she actively practised discretion, was as generous as her husband, excelled in painting, needlework, poetry and prose, and was widely read. He further adds that she was exceptionally beautiful and virtuous.[39] For her scribe to describe her as beautiful and virtuous is not particularly surprising, so the claim must remain open. Besides her native tongue, she spoke fluent French, Irish and Danish, the latter her mother's language, and all the Godwinson children would have spoken English and Danish. Edith's knowledge of Norman French must have come primarily from her new spouse and the other Normans Edward had brought to England. Edith was willing and able to support Edward and bridge any potential culture gaps from his time in Normandy. She is reported to have employed a Norman chambermaid as her constant companion, perhaps initially as a translator.

Edith commissioned the *Vita* sometime between 1067 and 1075, and it was intended to celebrate not only Edward but the deeds of her father and brothers. The work rejected self-modesty, noting that 'the maiden (Edith) is so beloved, proved to be good and wise, that she can have no opposition since nothing ought to be said of her but good'.[40] The mid-twelfth-century Norman chronicler Wace describes Edith as 'a beautiful maiden', perhaps copying from the *Vita* itself, but continues further on the question of the marriage consummation and the royal relationship, noting that 'people said that he (Edward) had not lain with her (Edith) carnally or known her carnally. But no one ever saw this, and there was no dispute between them.'[41] Ultimately, it is impossible to know. Most details about the marriage came either from Edith herself or from less reliable Anglo-Norman sources many years afterwards.

Henry of Huntingdon notes that Edward married Edith 'for the protection of his kingdom', which implies that he saw the union as the most politically astute choice.[42] William of Malmesbury's *Gesta Regum Anglorum* writes that Edith was a woman schooled in the liberal arts, but 'she had a bad judgement in worldly matters', and 'if you were astonished by her learning, you would at the same time feel a certain lack of intellectual humility and of personal beauty'.[43] This contrasts with other sources. Regarding Edward and Edith, Malmesbury informs us that 'the king's policy with her was neither to keep her at a distance from his bed nor to know her as a man would; whether he did this out of hatred for her family, which he prudently concealed to suit the time, or whether from a love of chastity, I have not discovered for certain. One thing is very widely reported, that he never broke the rule of chastity by sleeping with any woman'.[44] When this was being written in the 1120s there were by then increasing calls in hindsight to have Edward canonised as a saint.[45] Edward's sainthood finally came in 1161, which led to him being awarded the title of 'Confessor', a title given to a holy person having maintained a virtuous existence. Apart from a belated development, it was an affirmation of his apparent chastity. As seen within this history, Edward's virtuousness is open to debate, and it seems his canonization was politically driven at a period when Westminster Abbey was striving to increase its importance.

We are left with several reasons why Edward and Edith remained childless, any of which may explain why. He may have prevailed as a virgin and remained celibate, and the possibility he was homosexual or impotent cannot be dismissed. His only marriage came well beyond a reasonable age for a nobleman to seek a partner. Edith, being much younger than him, was of childbearing age for most of their marriage but she may have been barren and unable to give birth. They would not be the first or last royal couple unable to provide an heir, but if we are forced to name the likeliest cause for Edith's childlessness it would seem to point towards Edward. Their immediate contemporaries skirted around the matter, for no other reason than it would have highlighted problems concerning the succession. As Edward aged, the problem came more to the fore, and perhaps he always knew he could not, or would not, provide a successor. For Godwin, Edith's barren marriage was a disaster, as the heralded prospect of a Godwinson succeeding to the throne of England slowly unravelled as the years passed.

Comparisons are considered in later chapters as to the overall wealth the Godwinsons held compared to the king. By the late 1040s, Godwin alone held estates valued at £5,159 compared to Edward's £3,605.[46] However, this was purely land values. The king could still rely on the *heregeld*, which averaged 2 shillings a hide, plus two-thirds of the profits gained from fines at the courts. The high point of Godwin's career may have come in 1045–46 after Harold Godwinson's appointment to the earldom of East Anglia. Harold was aged about twenty-two, his promotion perhaps coming within weeks of his sister's wedding. The earldom covered the shires of Essex, Suffolk, Norfolk and Cambridgeshire. The award of an earldom brought with it estates and wealth, and it gave Harold a powerbase independent from his father.[47] He appears eleven times as earl within Edward's charters between 1045 and 1050.[48] Harold's elevation likewise meant that he was entitled to a third of the royal profits from customs duties and court fines. The customs duties must have been lucrative as the trading ports of East Anglia, among them Ipswich, Norwich, Maldon, Colchester and Dunwich, carried much of the imports and exports of the entire country.

Perhaps it was during 1045–46, if we consider the age of their eldest child, that Harold first met Edith (aka Eadgyth) Swanneshals (aka Swan-neck or The Fair). Edith was heiress to extensive estates in Essex, Suffolk and Cambridgeshire, and so their initial meeting likely came shortly after Harold had received the earldom of East Anglia. Their union is much debated, but it was a common-law (hand-fast) partnership which lasted until Harold's death. The sanctity of the relationship would remain formally unrecognised by the Church, and this enabled Harold to marry his 'second' wife Ealdgyth in 1065–66, the offspring of Ælfgar, while keeping his association with Edith and without breaking any ethical or ideological rules. However, unlike many partnerships, Harold and Edith's was not for temporary political advancement; their association was long, and apparently a love match.

They would have six children – boys Godwin, Edmund, Magnus and Ulf, and daughters Gytha and Gunhild – between the years 1046 and 1058. Some historians have suggested that Ulf was not Edith Swan-neck's but was the second boy from Harold's marriage to Ealdgyth.[49] The eldest two boys have Anglo-Saxon names, the first clearly named after his grandfather. It is true that Edmund was not an uncommon name but giving the second boy that name suggests a potential connection with Edmund Ironside through Godwin, as considered previously. The youngest sons, Magnus, and Ulf, received Scandinavian names, implying recognition of their grandmother Gytha's Danish origins, or alternately that Edith Swan-neck's roots were Scandinavian. The eldest three were all born between 1047 and 1051, with Ulf appearing at least several years later. The eldest girl, Gytha, named after her grandmother, was born perhaps in 1053–54, and Gunhild, so named because Harold's sister Gunhild may have been his favourite sister, came a few years later.

Returning now to Edward's kingship, all his surviving charters relate to estates and grants in the south or south Midlands, thereby acknowledging that he did not venture any further north than Worcestershire, a fact generally accepted by historians. Edward's reticence to venture north or much beyond his favoured sites of Westminster, Winchester and Gloucester as he grew older would enable the Godwinsons to become even more indispensable during the late 1050s and early 1060s. As with other Anglo-Saxon charter lists, Edward's surviving charters contain several likely forgeries, although they continue to encourage debate.[50] Nevertheless, there are at least twenty reliable charters issued between 1043 and 1050, and Godwin appears first in the secular witness lists in all of them. Similarly, Earl Leofric is a constant attendee, and Siward of Northumbria is present in all but four. At a personal level, the relationship between Godwin and Leofric must have been one of mutual respect, not one of bitter rivalry. There is no evidence of enmity between them, despite Godwin's dynasty prospering better than Leofric's.[51]

The appearance and relevance of the other Godwinsons within the charters contain several surprises. The eldest son, Swegn, regularly witnesses fourth on the lists among the secular signatories up to 1046. Harold first appears in 1043 immediately below his father, higher than expected, and likewise, the next son, Tostig, signs further down the lists in that same charter, which casts some doubt on its authenticity.[52] Their prominence in 1043 does not equate to their known career paths. Harold's earldom came in 1045, after which he was a frequent signatory of the king's charters. Tostig's career path took longer to emerge. He appears in the lists from 1048 onwards, usually signing sixth or seventh among the secular witnesses, although it would be several more years before he was given his own earldom.[53] The next eldest son, Gyrth, if we omit the likely forgeries, is absent from the charter lists until Edward's second decade as monarch, but interestingly his younger brother Leofwine appears in three charters between 1048 and 1050. Gyrth was perhaps four years older than Leofwine and should be more prominent than his younger sibling. This cannot be explained and calls into question the validity of some lists, as Leofwine was little more than eleven or twelve in 1048.[54] Finally, their cousin Beorn Estrithsson signs several charters after he is appointed earl in 1045.

Edith Godwinsdottir also appears in the dubious charter of 1043 referred above, two years before her marriage, which reinforces the likelihood it is a forgery. After her marriage (January 1045) she becomes a regular witness over the next two years, appearing below Emma in a charter of 1045 they both witnessed.[55] Again, this raises questions of authenticity. Emma ceased witnessing charters in 1045, probably due to another breakdown in her relationship with Edward, one in which he finally and effectively banished her from court. Perhaps this significant rift between son and mother was linked to Edward's marriage to Edith, to which Emma may have strongly objected in the knowledge that it would indisputably reinforce the Godwinson domination inside the royal court. Nonetheless, Godwin may have acted as mediator between Edward and Emma. Defining the relationship between the Earl of Wessex and the dowager queen post-1042 remains a conundrum, but the suspicion is that any previous friendship between them had already cooled significantly following the reign of Harold Harefoot.

Like Emma, Edith disappears from the witness lists after 1046 but reappears again in 1052. Maybe we can speculate that Edward was already tired of her less than two years into the marriage.

The next phase of Edward's reign up to 1050 saw him having to deal with the potential menace of a Norwegian invasion and the diplomatic accord between England and Denmark. The first noticeable cracks began to emerge in the king's relationship with Godwin, originating from their different viewpoints on the Danish question. Swein Estrithsson, Godwin's nephew, had been at war with King Magnus I of Norway, the illegitimate child of

Olaf II, since at least 1043.[56] Godwin had urged Edward to dispatch ships to support Swein but had been repeatedly rebuffed. Magnus had nullified Swein in Denmark by 1045–46, and following this, questions whether England should send military support to Swein were resurrected. Furthermore, a more serious problem soon emerged when rumours were received that Magnus was planning to invade England.

The notion that Magnus felt empowered to invade England seems hard to grasp, but he believed he had an entitlement to the English throne. The claim originated in the agreement he made with Harthacnut several years earlier during the previous peace negotiations in which they purportedly agreed that the first of them to die would be succeeded by the other across both Denmark and Norway.[57] Harthacnut had predeceased Magnus, so the Norwegian had claimed his entitlement to Denmark. However, Magnus also interpreted this earlier concord with Harthacnut to include the throne of England. This extended entitlement has been dismissed by most historians, and the original agreement with Harthacnut is itself suspect. Nevertheless, an invasion of England seems to have been a real enough threat for several months, if not longer.

Maybe Edward now regretted his decision not to support Swein when first urged by Godwin. To this must be added the rather bizarre suggestion that Emma had been prepared to support Magnus against Edward because of Swein's kinship with Godwin. If true, clearly Emma's relationship with both her son and the earl had collapsed by 1046 if not before, betraying perhaps her resentment for Godwin's earlier prominent role when she was deprived of her wealth.[58] That she would choose to support a Norwegian invasion nonetheless seems incredible. Her relationship with Edward may have fractured beyond repair, but it is hard to imagine Emma believed giving support in any shape or form to Magnus would benefit her own situation.

Nerves at the royal court were not helped by a large raiding fleet of Vikings, led by Lothen and Yrling, sailing from their base in Flanders in 1048 and pillaging parts of north-east Kent.[59] That incident, combined with the fear of a Norse invasion, persuaded Edward to assemble on standby 'a very strong fleet at the port of Sandwich against Magnus ... who was intending to invade England'.[60] The Norwegian offensive did not materialise that summer, and in the following year the return of Harald Sigurdsson (aka Hardrada, 'Old Norse for 'hard ruler') to Scandinavia changed Magnus's priorities. It emerged Harald Hardrada intended to seize both Norway and Denmark from Magnus, but his initial action was to ally himself with Swein Estrithsson. A stalemate forced Magnus to share the Norwegian throne with Hardrada, although he kept Denmark for himself.

Swein's alliance with Hardrada lapsed once the latter had gained a share of the Norwegian throne, and early in 1047 Swein again sent delegates to England requesting help to oust Magnus from Denmark. There was still considerable Anglo-Danish mawkishness throughout England. It had only been five years since the line of Anglo-Danish kings had ended, and many of the nobility, such as Siward in Northumbria, remained overtly Danish in both blood and sentiment. A glance at the names in Edward's charters during this period confirms that Danish influences remained strong, and the Witan council still included many men of Danish or Anglo-Danish extraction. Nonetheless, Edward had already embarked on a policy to reconfigure his court and dilute these influences, a policy not overtly anti-Danish but more subtle, designed rather to show that a powerful king ruled England and to deter Scandinavian thoughts of invasion.[61]

One of the major Danish political casualties, aside from Cnut's sister Gunhild mentioned previously, was Osgod Clapa (the byname means 'coarse' in Old English). Osgod, formerly Earl of East Anglia, had been outlawed in 1046.[62] He was an established figure who had been signing charters for the Anglo-Danish kings since 1026, appearing frequently in Cnut's charters and in three of Harthacnut's. His exiling followed a disagreement at the royal court and continued the process of reducing Anglo-Danish influences. The likelihood is that Osgod had fallen foul of Edward and Godwin after objecting over-zealously to Harold Godwinson replacing him as earl in East Anglia.[63] This would not be the last time that the promotion of a Godwinson would lead to the banishment of an established but potential rival to the dynasty. Osgod Clapa was to emerge again in 1048 in a bid to gain some revenge for his displacement.

Edward had recently committed English resources to play a peripheral role in a Holy Roman Empire military alliance, which included Swein Estrithsson, as part of an ongoing Continental war over control of Lotharingia, primarily in opposition to Flanders and France. Edward may have been concerned about the threat from Norway, but despite being part of the same alliance alongside Swein he still declined to send aid to him. Meanwhile, Godwin maintained his case for sending support to his nephew, with John of Worcester noting that the earl had argued 'the king ... might safely send him (Swein) at least fifty ships with their complement of soldiers'.[64] Nevertheless, Earl Leofric and other senior nobles disagreed, not wishing to see England become involved in the warfare in Scandinavia. Edward was demonstrating an ability to ignore Godwin's pleas. Godwin, on the other hand, had personal ties with Denmark. He had given vassalage to Cnut and the Anglo-Danish regime since 1017 and had a long-standing empathy for the Danes. He owed his position to that regime. His wife Gytha was full-blood Danish, his children half-Danish, and the four eldest boys given Scandinavian names. For want of a better description, Godwin had become an Anglo-Dane with Anglo-Saxon roots.

Swein could not break Denmark free from Norse control, which would probably have been the case even if Godwin had persuaded Edward to send help. The *ASC* noted that Magnus 'had a great power in ships'.[65] Swein was briefly driven out of Denmark, the Danes forced to pay tribute to Norway. However, within a matter of months, on 25 October 1047, Magnus of Norway died. Accounts vary, but it seems he probably succumbed to disease or illness, not a war-wound.[66] Harald Hardrada assumed full control of Norway and Swein, almost by default, inherited the Danish throne. It appears Magnus knew he did not have long to live and had decreed that Swein be allowed to rule Denmark. The warfare, this time between Swein and Hardrada, would resume in a year or so, and in time Hardrada would resurrect Magnus's earlier claims to the English succession. It was the further embellishment of this contention that would see Hardrada invade England in 1066.

With the threat from Norway having dissipated, Edward's attention moved to the request from the Holy Roman Emperor Henry III to deploy the English navy to help limit the movements of Baldwin of Flanders along the Channel. This was part of the ongoing dispute between the empire and Flanders and its allies concerning the region of Lotharingia. Baldwin was supported by King Henry I of France and William of Normandy while the emperor was supported by Geoffrey Martel of Anjou and Swein of Denmark.[67] Edward seems to have followed a policy of non-intervention as best he could without unduly aggravating any party, but following Henry III's request, he placed the fleet and ship-army on standby at Sandwich in 1049. This coincided with the reappearance of the exiled Osgod Clapa at the head of a large flotilla, and with the movements of Swegn Godwinson in 1049 that we shall deal with in chapter seven.

Godwin's dominant position with the king was less assured as the new decade approached. Little is evident from Edward's actions alone, but some would argue that Edward held reasons for despising Godwin.[68] This remains open to examination. Although Godwin had by oath disowned any involvement in the death of Edward's brother Alfred in 1036, Edward had likely always thought him in some way culpable. Nevertheless, Edward owed Godwin much. The earl's support for Edward's nomination had been crucial, and his backing of Edward at that moment had probably convinced those who had otherwise been doubtful about the nomination. However, several years into his reign, with the king and his earls having worked together to stabilise the kingdom after the Harefoot–Harthacnut era, Edward may have had space to reflect and reassess. As previously argued, perhaps he held some resentment for having been persuaded to marry the eldest Godwinson daughter, and, perverse as it may seem, resented Godwin not only for persuading him to marry a wife he did not want but for the earl's influence in the fundamental decision to accept the throne in the first place.

7

Swegn, the Black Sheep

Swegn Godwinson, the eldest child of Godwin and Gytha, was to prove to be a volatile character and something of a 'black sheep' within the family. His temperament looks to have been almost the opposite of his father's, more impulsive, less rational, and Swegn stands apart from his siblings in almost every aspect of his personality. Among the Godwinsons, only Tostig's character appears to come anywhere near to Swegn's, although Tostig was a model of equability in comparison. Whereas his father and brother Harold acted confidently in most matters, the image we have of Swegn is one of arrogance. There is no obvious explanation for it unless we conclude that Godwin overindulged his firstborn and allowed him leeway not given to his other children.

As hinted at in chapter three, a scandal seemingly erupted within the Godwinson fold over Swegn's claims that King Cnut, and not Godwin, was his real father. These accusations are disclosed by the monk Hemming of Worcester in his *Cartulary*, which was written about thirty to forty years after Godwin and Swegn's deaths. Unlike some other contemporary texts, the *Cartulary* was primarily intended as a historical chronicle and record, although Hemming remains the only primary source that refers to the issue.[1] The original source used by Hemming remains unclear and may have been word of mouth, but the seed for the accusation appears to originate soon after Cnut's death when Swegn had reached maturity. Gytha responded to her son's claim with incredulity and anger. This must have been a widely known claim at the time because Gytha swore on oath to a gathering of the wives of the Wessex nobility that she and Godwin were Swegn's natural parents. Hemming noted that Swegn's original accusation was directed solely to his paternal line, not his maternal line, so it is puzzling why Gytha should feel the need to swear confirmation that she was his natural mother.

What initiated Swegn's claims? Some suggest he was motivated through arrogance or vanity in linking himself to royalty, thereby claiming to be throneworthy.[2] But is there more to it than that? The potential for an earlier relationship between Cnut and Gytha has already been speculated. The *Cartulary* records that Swegn repeated his allegation after he had become an earl (post-1043).[3] Based on his later exploits, this is not out of character, and perhaps the story has been embellished specifically because of his later reputation. Godwin continued to support and defend his son later in life when many might have done otherwise. Maybe questions over Swegn's parentage cannot be completely rejected, although ultimately there may be no basis for the story other than anti-Godwin rhetoric. Nevertheless, if the story was intended to discredit the Godwinsons it seems odd that Swegn and not Harold was the target for such retrospective propaganda.

Godwin was able to promote his eldest son into Edward's royal court within months of the coronation, before beginning his project to tie the king to his eldest daughter Edith. Swegn was awarded his first earldom in 1043, when still in his early twenties. Perhaps to the chagrin of some senior nobility, such as Leofric and Odda, with prior interests in parts of the region, Swegn was allocated authority over the shires of Gloucestershire, Herefordshire, Oxfordshire, Berkshire and Somerset.[4] Leofric, with his connection with the Hwicce tribal heritage in the territory bordering Wales, would have been particularly irritated. Herefordshire and Gloucestershire came with the knowledge that the border with Wales was often difficult to control. However, the extent of the earldom is perhaps surprising, and it appears Godwin had transferred his authority in Somerset and Berkshire as a way of further promoting Swegn's standing. Swegn first emerges in a charter of 1043, where he signs fifth in the list of secular witnesses.[5] Over the next three years, he would sign a further fifteen, most of them immediately below his father and the earls Leofric and Siward. His disappearance from the lists coincides with events that transpired in 1046, as looked at below.

Swegn's early few years as earl passed uneventfully, although it can be assumed he would have had problems in dealing with Welsh raiders. This was a constant problem. The border was a combat zone, and the English carried out frequent military campaigns into Wales to counteract the raiding activities of the Welsh. However, the matter was not restricted to Englishmen fighting Welshmen. Within Wales, there were two main protagonists that by the 1040s controlled all the country. In the north was Gruffydd ap Llywelyn, King of Powys and Gwynedd, and in the south Gruffydd ap Rhydderch, King of Deheubarth, a catch-all definition that included the kingdoms of Dyfed, Seisyllwg, Brycheiniog, Glywysing and Gwent. In 1046, in response to increased raiding into Herefordshire by Gruffydd ap Rhydderch, Swegn allied himself with Gruffydd ap Llywelyn.[6] Both had an interest in curbing

Rhydderch's activities. It proved to be a successful campaign, but on returning Swegn committed his first compulsive act that seriously damaged his position and the interests of his family.

While travelling back through Herefordshire, Swegn requested that Eadgifu, Abbess of Leominster, be brought to him. He then 'kept her as long as it suited him, and afterwards let her travel home'.[7] Hemming of Worcester recorded that Eadgifu was held for more than a year and was only returned to her abbey when Archbishop Eadsige and Bishop Lyfing threatened to excommunicate Swegn.[8] Swegn's response was to raid estates in Worcestershire owned by Lyfing.[9] Without disputing the basic story of the abduction, the dating within sources cannot be accurate. Lyfing died in March 1046, and the Welsh campaign had probably been in late 1045, which the chronicler transposed to 1046 if working on a calendar change at the beginning of September (see Introduction). It is more likely Eadgifu was held for several weeks at most.

John of Worcester claimed that Swegn wanted to marry Eadgifu, and perhaps the abduction was a means of forcing her into marriage, thereby enabling Swegn to gain control of Leominster's vast and wealthy estate.[10] However, was this Swegn's primary motivation? In trying to make sense of this it would appear he already knew Eadgifu and had perhaps developed a romantic attachment to her. Possibly he had previously but unsuccessfully petitioned marriage to the abbess, so had decided to take matters into his own hands.[11] Swegn was likely unmarried beforehand, or indeed afterwards; there is no mention of any named hand-fast wife or concubine. Despite this, he is credited with having fathered two sons, Hakon and Tostig Reinald (aka Ranig). Some have suggested these boys were born to the abbess, but it seems more likely they were mothered by an unnamed concubine sometime before 1046. The boy Hakon would later be one of the two hostages – the other was Wulfnoth Godwinson – sent to William of Normandy following the crisis that enveloped the Godwinsons during 1051–52. Interestingly, the name Hakon was also the name of Cnut's nephew who had been Earl of Worcester during the 1020s, and it has been advocated that Abbess Eadgifu was related to the former earl. Eadgifu's kinship affiliation to Cnut may be a correct supposition and might further explain Swegn's wish to tie himself to the abbess to reinforce his status.[12]

Indignant as contemporary ecclesiastics and later clerical chroniclers may have been, there were no serious sanctions taken against Swegn. Some would argue with justification that it was commonplace during the Middle Ages for the nobility to abuse their position. However, the sources are silent as to Edward's viewpoint, and the fact he took no subsequent action and the threat of excommunication proved hollow might imply that the abbess's abduction was not as brutal or as firmly against her wishes as portrayed. The unknown factor remains whether there was a romantic attachment between Swegn and Eadgifu. He may simply have acted without forethought, and, as noted by the *ASC*, 'afterwards let her travel home'.[13] However, the episode illuminates his impulsive nature, a misreading of the norms of the day with no comprehension of the future or wider consequences. Whatever the truth, Swegn had gone against convention, but it is not clear what stance his father chose. We would like to think Godwin rebuked his son and forced him to give recompense payments to the abbess and the abbey. However, as would be witnessed in later episodes, Godwin seemed to be willing to forgive Swegn for almost anything. Maybe Swegn, as the first child, was his father's favourite.

From what we know, Swegn Godwinson was not forcefully or formally exiled, but travelled to Count Baldwin V's court in Flanders over the winter of 1046/47. It was said he 'had left England ... because he was not permitted to marry Eadgifu'.[14] This self-exile suggests that the aforementioned incident was serious and Swegn may have belatedly realized the error of his ways. Perhaps the Church had petitioned the king, or Godwin had finally acted to deal more harshly with his son. Swegn's movements over the following year are a little vague. The *ASC* noted that he lived in Bruges all winter and 'then towards summer went out'.[15] This detail is hardly illuminating, but it must refer to his known arrival in Denmark. During 1047 Swegn travelled to assist his namesake cousin Swein Estrithsson in the Danish war against the Norse and Magnus I (the Good) Olafsson. It has been speculated he had gone on instructions from Godwin, who had previously been denied the chance to send the Danes some English assistance.[16] This is perfectly feasible, and would put a temporary distance between Swegn and the royal court and assist Swein Estrithsson without openly going against the king's wishes.

As noted in the previous chapter, Magnus of Norway was to die on 25 October 1047, and Swegn Godwinson likely stayed in Denmark in support of his cousin against the new threat from Harald Hardrada.[17] The following year he travelled back to Flanders, perhaps supporting Baldwin V's conflict with Emperor Henry III. Swegn's brother Harold, and their cousin Beorn Estrithsson, had benefited in his absence. Beorn's friendship with Harold looks to have been strong. He had lived in England for much of his life and was a regular at Edward's court, a witness to several royal charters between 1045 and 1049, signing ahead of the younger Godwinson brothers.[18] During 1048, while Swegn was still in Flanders, his five-shire earldom was reassigned. Harold Godwinson was assigned Herefordshire and Gloucestershire, and Beorn given Oxfordshire, while Godwin probably resumed control of Somerset and Berkshire.

Despite Swegn Godwinson's waywardness, Godwin remained as powerful as ever. His dominance is sometimes accredited to Edward's weak character, and those seeking to find some easy explanation point to Edward's blood ties with Æthelred II. Was there a weakness in the royal line that Edward had inherited? To accept this would be to disparage not only Edward and his father but also consequently Godwin's abilities. The relationship between Edward and Godwin waxed and waned. It should be remembered that on Harthacnut's death Edward had been friendless in England and had spent over twenty years in the Norman court learning Norman ways. In 1042 he had needed a powerful ally to establish himself. His relationship with his mother was volatile, so who better than Godwin, the most powerful of the earls and holder of the prime earldom of Wessex? Furthermore, there is no indication that the promotion of Godwin's children during this period seriously adversely affected royal policy or that Edward was not controlling affairs. Godwin and his house, perhaps none more so than Edith, had prospered under Edward, but their relationship looks to have been mutually beneficial and not detrimental to king or country. Renewed consideration of Edward and his reign by historians has seen his rapport with Godwin as being much more nuanced than the image sometimes given of Godwin dominating the royal court.

Throughout 1048 and the following winter Godwin must have been constantly petitioning Edward to pardon his eldest son. Whether summoned by Edward or because Godwin had convinced him to come back and fall on the king's mercy, Swegn was back in England by 1049. John of Worcester writes that he arrived with eight ships.[19] This coincided with a further visit to England of Swein Estrithsson, pleading once again for English help, and perhaps they had initially travelled together. It further coincided with high activity in the Channel that spring and summer related to the ongoing conflict over Lotharingia. As already considered, the Holy Roman Emperor Henry III had requested Edward to assemble a fleet at Sandwich in preparedness to assist in the sea war against Baldwin V of Flanders and Henry I of France. Furthermore, to complicate matters the exiled Osgod Clapa crossed the Channel from Bruges soon afterwards with a fleet of thirty-nine vessels to raid into East Anglia, attacking his former earldom, which was now in the possession of Harold Godwinson.[20] The fleet at Sandwich may have moved against Osgod; in any case, his pirating was curtailed when all but a handful of his vessels were lost during a storm.[21] John of Worcester informs us that the greater part of his fleet made for Essex, 'but on their return, a cruel storm caught them, and drowned all except two (ships) which were captured across the seas'.[22] Osgod took his wife and six surviving ships and retreated to Denmark, and takes no further part in the historiography.

We are fortunate that versions C, D, and E of the *ASC* all provide good detail on aspects of Swegn's re-emergence in the spring of 1049. Having left Flanders, he landed at the household estate at Bosham, no doubt hoping for the support of his family in his pursuit of a pardon from the king. However, Godwin was not there. He had earlier been summoned by Edward to command ships to guard the Channel against any movement from Baldwin of Flanders, and Harold and Tostig were likewise on similar duties. However, trying to analyse Swegn's next move is problematic. Version E of the chronicle tells us that Swegn 'made peace with the king', and he was promised 'that he would be entitled to all those things which he formerly possessed'.[23] This cannot be accurate. From the events that transpired, there was no possible circumstance in which he had met Edward at this point to be given such a promise. Granting his wish at this stage was not straightforward because his earldom had already been divided between his brother Harold and his cousin Beorn.

Through amalgamating the various primary source details, it looks like Swegn first set out for London before hearing that neither Godwin nor Edward would be there.[24] The king was possibly en route to Sandwich to oversee the naval manoeuvres and somewhere en route Swegn was informed that he could not expect clemency and was granted four days' safe-conduct to leave England. Perhaps Edward had learnt that Swegn, in his recent absence, had been acting alongside Baldwin. Seeing his father as his only hope of being able to persuade the king, Swegn determined to find him and so returned to his ships at Bosham.[25] Meantime, a large contingent of the English fleet, with Godwin, Harold, Tostig and Beorn Estrithsson prominent in command, had sailed from Sandwich along the coast of Kent and Sussex to counteract potential naval activity from Flanders.

However, a turn in the weather separated the ships and forced the forty-two vessels commanded by Godwin and Beorn to seek shelter in Pevensey Bay.[26] This was the same storm that, further east, was about to sink most of Osgod Clapa's flotilla off the coast of Essex. At Bosham, Swegn received news that his father was at Pevensey, so, leaving his ships in Bosham harbour to avoid the storm, he rode the 60 miles to meet with Godwin. Whether they eventually met is unclear. Godwin may have refused to assist his son in his plea to the king, but the likelihood is, based on what followed, that Godwin had already put out to sea again by the time Swegn reached Pevensey and the two did not meet. Nevertheless, Beorn was still onshore, and Swegn turned to his cousin to implore him to accompany him cross-country to Sandwich to help plead with the king. Beorn was persuaded, and John of Worcester adds that, with no reason to feel endangered, Beorn left Pevensey with only three companions.[27]

On leaving Pevensey, instead of riding to Sandwich, Swegn decided they should first return to Bosham, on the premise that he was concerned that his ship mercenaries would desert him if he delayed longer.[28] By the time they arrived at Bosham the plan seems to have changed, although the detail within the *ASC* seems a little confusing.[29] What had happened during the journey? Perhaps Beorn had confirmed he would plead on Swegn's behalf but had similarly informed him that neither he nor Harold had any intention of returning the shires they had been allocated from Swegn's former earldom. No doubt angered by this, Swegn may have decided a better option was to take his cousin hostage, perhaps as a bargaining tool. His men seized Beorn, bound him, and carried him onto their ship.[30] Swegn then sailed his flotilla westward along the Channel. Version E of the *ASC* records he landed in Axmouth, several miles west of Lyme Regis, while versions C and D, the source used by John of Worcester, noted that he landed instead at Dartmouth.[31] Swegn's precise plan is unclear, but by the time his ship reached Devon he had decided to kill his cousin.

Beorn Estrithsson's body was hastily buried 'in a certain church', unnamed by the sources, and Swegn's ships then took sail.[32] His brother Harold, and possibly his father, were already in pursuit. Harold traced his brother's movements and Beorn's makeshift grave was found and his corpse recovered. The scribes noted that Beorn was conveyed to the Old Minster at Winchester and buried alongside his uncle King Cnut, with *ASC* versions C and D adding that Harold himself fetched Beorn back for burial.[33] A trial against Swegn was held in his absence at the court of the housecarls, which implies that Beorn had an honourable status with the royal guard. The king declared Swegn a *nithing*, meaning in Old English a wretch, villain or outlaw, which was the ultimate rejection, an example of how the concept of 'honour' was still valued in Anglo-Scandinavian society.[34]

Swegn meanwhile avoided his pursuers and headed back east, but on reaching Sussex six vessels and crew from his original eight had already deserted him. News of Beorn's murder spread fast. Two of the six vessels that had deserted Swegn were captured at Hastings and their crews killed while his two remaining ships crossed to Flanders. His nephew's murder no doubt angered Godwin but it also placed him in a difficult situation with Edward and potentially with Beorn's brother Swein Estrithsson; moreover, it crucially tested the unity of the Godwinson family. Beorn's assassination prompted another reshuffle from an angry Edward. Leofric of Mercia and Odda of Deerhurst were each offered some additional authority, as was Edward's nephew Ralph of Mantes (aka Ralph the Timid), the offspring of the king's sister Godgifu. Ralph had arrived in England soon after Edward and may have already been given some responsibility for the East Midlands. Godwin and Harold may have been forced to surrender some estates in recompense and recognition of their kinship with the outlawed Swegn. Edward would have been wary of reallocating shires to any of the Godwinsons, although his response remains ambiguous.

These events were undoubtedly dramatic, but it is perhaps a reminder of the volatile nature of politics and the relationships between lords and vassals in Anglo-Saxon England that in due course a staggering volte-face by the king was to follow. Swegn would not simply be pardoned by Edward several months later but would also be given back most of his former earldom. No doubt Godwin's continued pleas to the king were behind this decision, and he also enrolled Bishop Ealdred of Worcester in the plan to reintegrate Swegn, but it appears to be a baffling outcome nonetheless, and perhaps other forces than Godwin may have been urging the king to restore Swegn. Looking ahead to 1051 in what was to be a confrontation between the king and Godwin, some historians have suggested Edward, with his new advisor Robert of Jumièges (Champart), was already working towards deliberately giving Swegn enough rope with which to hang himself, and by doing so purposely bringing on a more acute conflict with the whole Godwinson dynasty, including his wife Edith.[35]

Ealdred, a friend of Godwin and thus partly through the earl's recommendation, had replaced the deceased Lyfing at Worcester during 1046. While returning from a mission to Rome in 1049 it was Ealdred who had met Swegn in Flanders and been influential in his recall. The bishop appears to have obtained a vow from Swegn to undertake a pilgrimage as repentance for his sins, a journey he would begin in 1052, and in return, Ealdred had offered to speak on Swegn's behalf to the king. The bishop may have had a more pressing incentive. In July 1049, the shires of Gloucestershire and Herefordshire had been invaded by the Welsh, possibly Worcestershire too, so with his bishopric threatened Ealdred may have seen Swegn's restoration, in the knowledge of Swegn's earlier military exploits across the Welsh border, as beneficial towards the security of the region.[36]

Godwin's best weapon with Edward was his diplomatic skill. Henry of Huntingdon noted that Swegn 'came to an agreement with the king on the surety of his father Godwin'.[37] There is accumulated evidence that Godwin must have been a persuasive personality, but to successfully retrieve Swegn's position seems astonishing. Was there money exchanged between the earl and the king as part of the arrangement to smooth matters? If so, the sources are silent. At a familial level, the evidence implies that Swegn was his father's favourite son and that Godwin on more than one occasion favoured him to the detriment of his dynastic interests and all-round family unity. Did Godwin see something of his younger self in his eldest child, or, playing devil's advocate, was it overcompensation to allay rumours over Swegn's parentage? The disharmony within the Godwinson family must have been dramatic. Harold and Beorn were not just cousins but close friends, and Godwin's efforts to get Swegn pardoned likely went against the wishes of several members of the family.

Swegn Godwinson's full rehabilitation is evidenced in a charter of 1050, whereby he witnesses the document in fourth place above Harold, Tostig and Edward's nephew Earl Ralph.[38] It is unclear how much of his earldom or which shires were reinstated. Contrary to the shire reallocation after Swegn's first exiling, Harold did not object to some land ownership distribution to accommodate his brother. This suggests that Harold had received compensation elsewhere previously. He had likely kept Herefordshire, gained during Swegn's first exiling, and was presented, along with Ralph of Mantes, redistribution of Beorn's former holdings in Hertfordshire.[39] It is also an illustration of how the Godwinsons could close ranks under the guidance of the family patriarch. They would do the same in the crisis that unfolded in 1051.

The underlying trend at court had shifted by 1050. Swegn Godwinson's accumulated misdeeds may have diminished Godwin's standing. In 1050 and into 1051 Edward decommissioned a large section of the royal fleet, and with that came the abolishment of the *heregeld* tax that was associated with the navy. Responsibility for the naval defence was instead given to the Cinque ports (Dover, Hythe, Hastings, New Romney and Sandwich) in exchange for privileges.[40] The Godwinsons had been prominent in leading the fleet, and disbanding it took away more of Edward's reliance on them.[41] The dominance of the Anglo-Danish faction, of which Godwin and his household were embodiments, was waning.

Edward had previously exiled prominent Danes who had been important political figures under Cnut. He had also invited to court men from Normandy and its surrounds, those he had known from his time there, and given them important roles at court or in the Church. One of the first, a Norman named Robert Champart (of Jumièges), was notable among them. He had been given the bishopric of London in 1044 in preference to Godwin's candidate, and a mutual loathing between bishop and earl had developed in the intervening period. The changing attitude of the king is witnessed in his newfound interest in the appointment of senior clerics as 1050 approached, candidates that went against Godwin's advice, seemingly deliberately. In September 1049, Edward had assigned one of his chaplains, another Norman named Ulf, to the important bishopric of Dorchester-on-Thames to replace the deceased Eadnoth.

On 29 October 1050, on the death of Archbishop Eadsige of Canterbury, Edward nominated Robert Champart as Eadsige's replacement, preferring to move Champart to Canterbury rather than promote an English candidate.[42] The monks of Canterbury had wanted Eadsige replaced by Ælric (aka Æthelric), one of their fraternity. Godwin had been called in to support their choice in his role as Earl of Wessex, and there is the possibility, as suggested by the *Vita Edwardi*, that Ælric was related to the Godwinsons.[43] It was indisputably the monarch's prerogative to appoint an archbishop, but the Canterbury community proceeded anyway to elect Ælric per canon law and then asked for Godwin's support.[44] Godwin seems to have made an issue of this but the king refused to be moved and Champart was confirmed to the archbishopric. Who held the archbishopric at Canterbury, and what their political leaning was, had become part of the prevailing power politics. In hindsight, Champart's appointment proved to be another sign of a developing strain on the ongoing relationship between the king and Godwin, but even so, it was not yet apparent that Edward was likely already holding thoughts of moving against his senior earl more directly in 1051.

On 22 January 1051, Archbishop Ælfric of York died. In a further snub to Godwin, Edward bypassed Godwin's friend Bishop Ealdred of Worcester and gave the York post to Cynesige, another of his royal chaplains.[45] Taken on their own, this and the earlier decisions do not appear significant but when put together a pattern emerges. Edward was pushing his prerogative, something he had not pursued as vigorously beforehand in domestic matters. From Godwin's perspective, and despite the fact Cynesige was Anglo-Saxon, not Norman, he may have seen recent events in more simple terms: a gradual but continuous weakening of not only his power but more generally of the English and Anglo-Danish former dominance in the royal court. William of Malmesbury accepts that some of Edward's appointments were linked to his previous life in Normandy. Robert Champart was the most pronounced of these, recognising the friendship the two men had built up while Edward was in exile at the Norman court and while Champart was a monk at Jumièges.[46] This commonality was to be expected if Edward missed aspects of his life in Normandy, perhaps even the ability to speak Norman French naturally with others. We usually think of Edward as archetypal Anglo-Saxon English, but we need reminding he had previously set foot in England only once within a twenty-five-year period (1016–1041).

Sources vary, but it took until mid-Lent 1051 (early March) before Edward confirmed Robert Champart as archbishop. This four-month delay was likely because the nomination was not universally supported, and Godwin was likely prominent among the dissenters. Following this, Edward nominated Spearhavoc (aka Sparrowhawk), then Abbot of Abingdon, as Champart's replacement at London.[47] This seems to have been a concession by the king aimed at appeasing Godwin, to counterbalance the failed nomination of Ælric. The fallout that developed from Spearhavoc's appointment gives us the first clear sign, rather than just a suspicion, that Godwin and the new archbishop were at odds. Robert Champart had likely already replaced Godwin as first in line to the monarch's ear before his promotion to Canterbury, but he dominated the king's advisors thereafter. It cannot be denied he did not hesitate to use this to his advantage at the royal court, the *Gesta Pontificum* of William of Malmesbury adding that Champart was active in 'deposing some and elevating others, just as he wished and pleased'.[48]

Soon after his nomination Champart collected his pallium from Pope Leo IX and was back in England by the end of June 1051 for the feast of St Peter.[49] Spearhavoc then approached him to receive his blessing and his formal ordination at London, but Champart refused, claiming that the pope had forbidden the bishopric to be assigned to Spearhavoc.[50] This went against the king's previous instructions, but illustrates the confidence, some would say arrogance, that the new archbishop was exhibiting. There is no evidence that the pope had refused to confirm Spearhavoc, but Edward accepted Champart's word. However, there may have been a more obvious reason for denying Spearhavoc the bishopric. While abbot at Abingdon, Spearhavoc had formed a friendship with the Godwinsons, so Champart's motivation was to oppose Godwin's preference.[51] There was a stalemate; Spearhavoc took his post in London without recognition from Champart, and Edward remained on the fence.

Spearhavoc's position was to become untenable later in 1051 and he was expelled from London and England, the timing not unrelated to the Godwinsons dramatic fall from grace detailed in later chapters. However, Spearhavoc did not go empty-handed, taking with him sacks of valuables from the London diocese and gold and gems that had originally been designated to further embellish Edward's crown. His access to these jewels seems implausible until it is recognised that Spearhavoc was also a renowned illustrator, goldsmith and worker of precious metals. He therefore had access to the royal collection and his artisan skills had possibly first brought him into contact with Godwin, Edward and Queen Edith.[52] He was replaced at London by William, another Norman recommended by Champart, who had been acting as the king's priest.

The question of Edward's encouragement of foreign churchmen, nobles and advisors over to England is a topic often discussed by academics. As time passed the influence of some of these men had, and would have, profoundly impacted court dynamics and the king's decision-making. Edward's initial intention seems to have been to bring to England a few favoured friends from his time in Normandy. This is perhaps understandable; he had lived there most of his life. He had arrived a virtual stranger in his own country during 1041, and after his estrangement from his mother Emma, Godwin had filled the vacuum. The situation was now different.

It has been estimated that by 1050 four in ten of the king's court clerks were foreigners. Not all these recent arrivals were Norman; some had come from Flanders, Brittany and Lotharingia, such as the Breton Ralph the Staller and Bishop Herman, who was awarded the Ramsbury bishopric in 1045.[53] Edward's nephew Ralph was the only foreign nobleman to be given an earldom and there are no obvious French or Norman names among the king's senior thegns and reeves.[54] Nevertheless, as noted below, in the secular community there were already some significant foreigners. On a wider scale, the debate continues whether Edward was deliberately building up a sizeable foreign presence inside England. However, if that had been his intent, surely he would have brought over many more and given them more leading roles than he ultimately did. A search of the primary sources reveals only a few dozen that held positions of authority among the hundreds of native Anglo-Saxons of equal standing at this period.

However, one notable exception was Robert FitzWimarc, a Norman-Breton who was a kinsman of both Duke William and Edward. He had been awarded a site 6 miles north of Bishop's Stortford at Clavering in Essex; conspicuously, several sites were also granted to Norman nobles strategically close to the Welsh border.[55] It has been suggested Edward was carefully establishing a 'Norman colony' in the region.[56] Several sites that were to evolve into what we would familiarly recognise as fortified castles are located there, such as Richard's Castle 3 miles' south-west of Ludlow, awarded to a Norman named Richard FitzScrob. This castle was one of only a handful built in the motte-and-bailey style in England before the Norman Conquest. Some historians have referenced that the orientation and location of FitzScrob's castle point to it being better suited to defend attacks from the east (England) and not from Wales, suggesting other motives for its construction.[57] Nevertheless, having visited the site, this conclusion seems hard to acknowledge.

In overall consideration, it cannot be denied that a significant Norman presence in the shape of Edward's nephew Ralph, FitzScrob, Osbern Pentecost, a castellan named Hugh, and others was centred strategically in Herefordshire and Shropshire close to Wales. However, these were not primary sites English nobles would have chosen as desirable locations and had Edward planned anything more permanent and divisive he would surely have allocated his Norman friends some estates in the south-east, closer to London and the shortest sea routes to Normandy. Many more were needed if he intended anything more sinister. Furthermore, it should not be imagined that Godwin, Leofric and the other senior nobles within the Witan and the Anglo-Saxon establishment would have easily allowed him such leeway. A long-term plan for Edward establishing Norman pre-eminence among the nobility seems improbable. It is an argument that rests primarily not on the evidence as it stood *circa* 1050, but on knowledge in hindsight of the events of 1066.

8

Crisis and Exile

By 1051 the relationship between Edward and Godwin had evidently deteriorated. From the events that were about to follow, it would seem Edward was not overly disturbed by this state of affairs, but something had festered with him. While the king had recently cooperated with Henry III of the Holy Roman Empire in Germany and his allies in the English Channel against Baldwin V of Flanders and Henry I of France over their Lotharingia dispute, the Godwinsons in contrast had remained favourable to Baldwin. Swegn Godwinson had stayed in Flanders during this period, possibly fighting alongside Baldwin's forces. Furthermore, over the summer of 1051 Tostig Godwinson was betrothed to Baldwin's stepsister Judith, the daughter of Baldwin IV and his second wife Eleanor of Normandy. Baldwin perhaps hoped this union to one of the Godwinsons would gain him favour with Edward.[1] Eleanor, as the daughter of Duke Richard II, was also William of Normandy's aunt, so by his marriage to her daughter Judith, Tostig had linked himself in kinship to William. This kinship link between Tostig and William may have had some relevance in the events of 1065–66 to be considered later.

Flanders had conceded to Henry III in the Lotharingia wars by 1051, but Tostig's marriage potentially undermined Edward's previous stance and his alliance with Henry III, and placed the Godwinsons at odds with his foreign policy. The decisive event that led to the critical fracture between king and earl arrived in the shape of Count Eustace II of Boulogne in the late summer of 1051. He and Edward had formerly been brothers-in-law through Eustace's earlier marriage in 1047 to the king's sister, Godgifu. Eustace had been excommunicated by Pope Leo IX for his marriage to Godgifu. It had been her second marriage, but she had died in 1049, the same year that Eustace had succeeded his father (Count Eustace I) in Boulogne. Boulogne and Flanders were adjacent, and the politics in the region remained unpredictable after the recent conflict.

Eustace of Boulogne also had something in common with Duke William of Normandy, because William's betrothal in 1049 to Matilda of Flanders, the daughter of Baldwin V, had also been forbidden by Leo IX, and both had ignored the papal edicts.[2] Normandy had been a minor partner in alliance with France and Flanders in the recent wars over Lotharingia. Eustace's marriage of 1047 had moved Boulogne closer politically to both England and Normandy, as Godgifu was not just Edward's sister but, through her mother, had been niece to Richard II of Normandy and was therefore connected to Duke William. With the Continent still shuffling for position following the war, Eustace may have seen this as a good time to reinforce his friendship with his former brother-in-law. The purpose of Eustace's visit has been lost in the detail. His deceased wife had formerly held estates in England, so perhaps he had arrived to discuss the retention of those. It could have been connected, as discussed below, to the attempt to transfer supervision of the castle (burh) at Dover, or the preliminaries of trying to reach a more formal alliance with Edward.

Eustace arrived in England in early September 1051 to meet Edward. There is no separate record in the sources of him crossing the Channel either before or after 1051 until taking part in the Norman invasion of 1066 as one of William of Normandy's allies. Coincidence or otherwise, his arrival came only a couple of months after Archbishop Champart (Robert of Jumièges) had returned from collecting his pallium in Rome. Champart had been formally sworn in as archbishop on 29 June. The possibility of the archbishop breaking his return journey at Duke William's court is discussed later, but perhaps he had then visited Boulogne, and if so, it could be linked to the count's appearance in England shortly afterwards. Eustace had sailed from Wissant, 10 miles down the coast from Calais. The chronicler John of Worcester acknowledges he landed at Canterbury, by way of the River Stour, while the *ASC* version D and William of Malmesbury name his disembarkation point as Dover.[3]

We can hypothesise that Eustace had no regard or liking for the Godwinsons. Godgifu, when married to him, had probably told him how Godwin had been responsible for the death of her brother Alfred. Men from Boulogne had accompanied Alfred over to England in 1036 and many if not all of them had been massacred at Guildford. Tostig's recent marriage to Judith of Flanders may have forced Eustace to reconsider the dynamics between himself, Normandy and England, because Judith was the aunt of Matilda of Flanders, who had recently been betrothed to William of Normandy. A combination of developments had likely brought Eustace to England, but what was to take place afterwards suggests that a plan of sorts may have been conjured between him and Edward that would strengthen Edward's position over Godwin and assist Eustace at the same time.

There are various accounts of what took place over the following days and weeks, but a summation of events can be assembled from versions D and E of the *ASC*, William of Malmesbury's *Gesta Regum Anglorum* and John of Worcester's *Chronicon* (Chronicle).[4]

The story begins and revolves around Eustace's actions in Kent. Most historians follow version E of the *ASC*, namely that Eustace had met with Edward and was on his return journey when an 'incident' took place in Dover.[5] However, according to John of Worcester, Eustace sought out Edward at Gloucester a day or two after the 'incident', which suggests they had not met beforehand.[6] In summary, Eustace's party had eaten in Canterbury and were making their way to Dover.[7] He had perhaps visited Canterbury to meet with Robert Champart after leaving Edward. It has been suggested, in the knowledge of later developments, that Champart was party to plans designed to provoke Godwin and remove him from his position of authority, or at the very least to curtail his power.[8]

As if Eustace knew to expect trouble, the *ASC* records that 'when he was some miles or more this side of Dover, he put on his mail coat, and all his companions, and went to Dover'.[9] This implies pre-meditated action. Eustace's advance guard had gone ahead to arrange lodgings when 'one of his men came and wanted to lodge at the home of a certain householder against his will, and wounded the householder, and the householder killed the other'.[10] John of Worcester records the householder was killed first.[11] Whichever it was, when Eustace and his entourage arrived they killed the townsman and a further twenty citizens, possibly in the burh on the cliff top. In response, the townspeople killed ten of Eustace's soldiers before, outnumbered, he was forced to leave. William of Malmesbury embroiders the tale, noting that only Eustace and one other escaped, with difficulty, and John of Worcester and version D of the *ASC* add that he made straight for Edward at Gloucester.[12]

This isolated event was to affect Godwin and his family beyond their initial expectation. If it was deliberately designed to create a pretext for Edward to challenge Godwin's standing in Wessex, it would succeed spectacularly. However, Dover may have had further specific significance for Eustace. Although the concept seems nonsensical from Edward's perspective there could be some credence to support the suggestion that with the English king's backing Eustace intended to establish a permanent garrison of his own inside the hilltop burh at Dover.[13] The burh was strategically positioned directly across the Channel from Eustace's ports at Boulogne and Calais, so the idea of him wishing to control Dover is not as far-fetched as it might appear. His long-term interest in Dover's burh seems to have persisted in later years. Despite being one of William of Normandy's most important associates in the invasion of 1066 and playing an important part in the Battle of Hastings,

Eustace later allied himself in 1067 with the men of Kent and attempted but failed to try to capture Dover from William's half-brother Odo of Bayeux.[14]

Eustace's activity at Dover seems to have had Edward's approval, or at least his blind eye, and by design or otherwise, Godwin was rapidly placed in an unenviable position. On reaching Gloucester Eustace relayed his version of the events to Edward. The scribe for the *ASC* version E notes he 'gave a one-sided account of how they had fared', and that it was 'more the townsman's fault than his; but it was not so'.[15] William of Malmesbury later described Eustace as being 'an advocate for his own side', which would seem obvious.[16]

Godwin was summoned to attend the king at Gloucester and was commanded, in his role as Earl of Wessex, to deal severely with the residents of Dover for attacking Eustace and his retinue. Godwin was reticent to take immediate reprisals until he had heard all sides of the story, and the *ASC* acknowledges that 'the earl would not agree to the incursion because it was abhorrent to him to injure his own province'.[17] William of Malmesbury praised Godwin's response, noting that 'Godwin … being a more clear-headed man, perceived that one ought not to pronounce a verdict after hearing the charges of one side only'.[18] Malmesbury then continued: 'Besides which, his (Godwin's) reply seemed much more consistent with the administration of justice; the leaders of that stronghold ought to be calmly charged with sedition in the king's court, and if they could clear themselves, they should leave the court unscathed; if they could not, they should make satisfaction to the king … and to the count to whom they had done harm, either financially or physically.'[19] This is one of the most illuminating views into Godwin's character found among the primary sources, showing him to be rational and objective.

Advance knowledge of Eustace's plans or not, the king's demand to Godwin seems obdurate. Godwin's options were to refuse the king's command and risk the consequences or punish the townspeople of Dover without a fair hearing. Dover was not only under Godwin's jurisdiction as earl, but it was one of his major estates, and he had recently founded the church of St Mary in Castro inside the burh at the top of the cliffs.[20] Godwin would choose to risk Edward's ire rather than betray his vassals and the townspeople. This says much about him. It would have been easier to concede to the king's demands. Perhaps he underestimated Edward's new resolve, but we must also assume he was still oblivious to any hint of being manipulated.

Having refused the king, Godwin was in danger of outlawing himself. Edward summoned the Witan to meet at Gloucester around 8 September, the Feast of St Mary, so all could hear details of the events in Kent and the earl's refusal to punish the citizens of Dover. Godwin set out for Gloucester and en route was joined by Swegn and Harold along with their retinues. John of Worcester records that Godwin 'mustered an innumerable army from his whole earldom … his eldest son Swegn from his … and his other son

Harold from his earldom'.[21] William of Malmesbury puts forward a fatuous explanation that Godwin had only mustered troops to counteract Welsh incursions into Gloucestershire, but adds that Leofric and Siward and all the nobility were gathering at Gloucester, and Godwin, 'knowing they were under suspicion did not think it safe to come without armed protection'.[22]

The Godwinsons halted 15 miles south-east of Gloucester at Beverstone, formerly an estate owned by Swegn but now under Harold's lordship.[23] The estate was a mile or more north of present-day Beverston village, close to Chavenage Green, the hundred meeting place south of Longtree.[24] From there, Godwin sent messages to Edward that Eustace and his men should be 'given into their hands'.[25] There is no mention of Tostig, Gyrth or Leofwine in these reports. That is not to say that one or more of them was not alongside their father, but they did not hold earldoms in 1051 and would have been more restricted in gathering men in numbers to support their father and brothers.

Edward had already urged earls Leofric and Siward, and likely also his nephew Ralph of Mantes, to muster their troops at Gloucester before the Godwinsons entered the shire. John of Worcester tells us that messages were 'sent in haste to the Earls Leofric … and Siward … whom the king asked to hasten to him … with all those they could muster'.[26] The *ASC* scribe writes that Godwin and his sons had been informed that the king would take measures against them.[27] There then developed a stand-off.

It was likely anger that had led Godwin's response so far, particularly if the knowledge that Eustace had planned to seize Dover had become clear. Swegn had likely urged his father to take immediate steps while the more astute Harold had advised calm. John of Worcester says Godwin demanded 'Count Eustace and his associates as well as both the Normans and the men of Boulogne who held the castle on the cliff at Canterbury' be handed over to him.[28] John's wording on this issue has perhaps been overlooked by some historians.[29] He incorrectly names Canterbury, not Dover, but the key point is that he exerts that both Normans and Eustace's soldiers were in command of the burh and still occupied it. Edward seems prepared to consider attacking Godwin, but Leofric and 'certain others' were advising him it would be 'a great folly that they should embark on a war with their compatriots'.[30] Godwin meanwhile told his forces 'not to take the initiative … but they should not retreat without defending themselves'.[31] A message sent to Beverston advising Godwin to 'leave off all wrong-doing' finally ended the stand-off, and the king called for a second meeting to be held at London to address the issue. The Godwinsons made a tactical withdrawal.[32]

A conflict had been avoided, but the matter remained far from over. Godwin's response had left Edward angry, although the Godwinsons' show of military strength was likely not planned to go beyond that. For a man who had previously shown such astute diplomacy on many occasions beforehand, this was not Godwin's finest hour. Nevertheless, it is difficult to see what other course had been open to him without a serious loss of face. The codes of the day gave him an obligation to protect his people in return for their loyalty. If he had complied with Edward's orders many of his tenants would have been arrested and executed without a fair trial. Such news would have spread throughout Wessex and undermined his position.

Negotiations outside Gloucester may have included a hostage transfer.[33] On Godwin's part, this was likely the moment that his youngest son Wulfnoth, aged around ten, and Swegn's son Hakon, perhaps a few years younger, were exchanged. The significance of these two noble hostages would play an important role well beyond Godwin's lifetime. Back in London Edward delivered the summons for Godwin and Harold to attend the reconvened council meeting for 24 September 1052.[34] The summons had not included Swegn, so irrespective of handing over Hakon as a hostage it appears Edward's patience had been spent and Swegn had already again been banished. What Godwin expected from the council meeting cannot be known, but in hindsight it looks like he had already lost any chance of redemption even before attending. This was a different Edward, one now showing a determination to damage the Godwinsons irrevocably.

Ahead of the second meeting Edward gave orders that further militia was to be raised north and south of the Thames to assemble at London. Leofric and his Mercian followers had likely remained with the king, as possibly had Siward's. The sources describe it as 'a raiding-army', which suggests many thegns and their vassals, and the call to arms of the thegns in Wessex and East Anglia is significant. As noted by the *ASC*, 'the king asked for all those thegns that the earls (Godwin and Harold) formerly had, and they resigned them all into his hands'.[35] Edward was raising the stakes. His royal summons, being from the highest authority, obligated the Godwinsons to release the thegns under their vassalage and for these thegns to attend the king at London instead. These were probably 'king's thegns', who although sworn to the Godwinsons held their lands directly from the monarch.[36] This reinforced Edward's forces while depriving the Godwinsons of many thegns. While Godwin and Harold seem to have complied, Swegn may have refused to release his thegns to the king's summons, which likely accounts for his ongoing 'probation' being rescinded and him being 'upgraded' once again to the status of outlaw ahead of the London meeting.[37]

When Godwin and Harold arrived at Southwark, across the Thames from London, many of their thegns had failed to accompany them, although the *ASC* version D describes Godwin's force as being 'a great multitude from Wessex'.[38] This seems an exaggeration, for the reasons indicated above. We assume that Tostig, Gyrth and perhaps even Leofwine were alongside their father. However, Swegn was absent, possibly already arranging to sail into exile from Bristol, as would be clear from later events, likely intending to go to Ireland. Aware of the possibility that the council meeting could become a de facto trial of treasonable acts against the king, Godwin asked for safe conduct and an exchange of hostages before agreeing to cross the Thames.

Edward responded by ordering that they come 'with stipulations that they should be unarmed and bring only twelve men with them'.[39] His position had hardened; he was not inclined to negotiate further. Bishop Stigand, acting as the mediator between them, was instructed to tell Godwin he could have his peace and pardon if he could restore to the king his brother Alfred.[40] On hearing this Godwin understood he and his family were unlikely to have a fair hearing and 'took flight when night fell'.[41] The following morning Edward convened his council in Godwin's absence, and the whole Godwinson family were declared outlaws. William of Malmesbury, in his *Gesta Pontificum Anglorum*, says that the calls of treachery came from all at Edward's court, 'but it was Robert (Champart) who blew the loudest trumpet and took the lead in the accusation'.[42] The family were given five days to leave England.[43]

This directive did not include Queen Edith, although she would be forced to leave the royal court. Edward was probably by now regretting his childless marriage. Before her parents and siblings had even left England, Edward repudiated her and confiscated 'the whole of the queen's resources ... to the last penny'.[44] Voices against Edith led by Champart could have been gathering for some time. In her self-appointed post as keeper of the king's household, and possibly also the budget, she had likely clashed with some of the privy councillors and administrators recently brought in by her husband.[45]

Edith was dispatched to the king's half-sister, the abbess at Wherwell in Hampshire, the unnamed youngest daughter of Æthelred II and his first wife Ælfgifu of York.[46] The haste to remove Edith suggests that Edward had been advised to divorce her quickly to enable him to quickly remarry. The Church looked unfavourably upon divorce, but non-consummation or adultery would ensure a legal divorce. Failure to produce an heir was justification enough, and indeed it is plausible Edward and Edith had not consummated their marriage.[47] There was no Anglo-Saxon precedent for a king divorcing on the presupposition that his wife was barren. However, if Edith could be persuaded to take the veil, she would automatically renounce her queenship and it would release Edward to freely divorce and marry again.[48] Nevertheless, Edith did not take holy vows and other ways of securing a divorce were investigated. An accusation of adultery against Edith was considered and suspicion lay with Edith until her death. William of Malmesbury records that she later felt compelled on her deathbed confession to proclaim her innocence of any adultery once again.[49]

Several months later, perhaps no later than the spring of 1052, Edith was given permission to relocate to Wilton Abbey. She had strong connections with Wilton and had received her education at its convent school. Many years later her association with Wilton was strengthened when she had the abbey rebuilt in stone. The final rededication of the new building was to take place during the autumn of 1065. Nothing of the original Anglo-Saxon abbey buildings survive today. The medieval complex was all but destroyed during the dissolution of the monasteries, the building of a Tudor estate on the site and finally when the present Wilton House estate was constructed. The oldest surviving structure is the 'Almonry', which dates to the fourteenth century.[50]

After being supposedly manipulated for years, Edward had broken free of his symbolic shackles by his actions during 1051. He had earlier removed his mother in similar circumstances. In accepting this premise, we are painting Edward as previously weak, someone easily influenced and easily persuaded. However, is that the correct interpretation? More recently, historians have seen Edward and Godwin's relationship as more nuanced.[51] In examples of their disagreements before 1051 such as the appointment of bishops, foreign policy in relation to Flanders, Boulogne and Normandy, or support or otherwise for Swein Estrithsson in Denmark, Edward had not deferred to Godwin. Similarly, he had previously outlawed Swegn Godwinson despite, we presume, Godwin's pleas for his son's pardon. The truth may be that he was simply re-establishing his authority, having realised that his wedding to Edith had been forced on him when he was vulnerable. If he was looking to change his marital circumstances it was necessary to first diminish his father-in-law's influence. The opportunity to create a rift which he could claim was justified had come through his kinsman Eustace. Nevertheless, none of this should underplay the idea that perhaps Edward still also held a deep-seated grudge against Godwin due to the circumstances of his brother's death.[52]

Leaving Southwark, the Godwinson men travelled urgently to Bosham (Thorney), their favoured estate near Chichester, where they joined the womenfolk.[53] Swegn was likely already at Bosham. They had been given five days' grace to leave England. However, the speed with which they left English shores suggests to us they had made plans in advance for such an eventuality and had already gathered significant portable wealth to take with them. A ship was prepared, into which 'they hastily put as much gold and silver and precious things as she could carry'.[54] Ignoring the grace period, Archbishop Robert Champart reputedly sent a large force to apprehend the Godwinsons; but Godwin and Gytha, together with Tostig, Swegn, Gyrth and Tostig's wife Judith of Flanders, had already taken ship for Flanders when Champart's men arrived at Bosham.[55]

Reference to Judith and Tostig is of interest because the *Vita Edwardi* names Tostig's marriage as taking place in October, after the confrontation with the king.[56] An October marriage would have taken place after the Godwinsons reached Flanders, and Judith was unlikely to have been in England in

September. Perhaps we can extend this further, and surmise that Tostig was already in Flanders before his wedding, at the time of the exiling, which would explain why there is no reference to him either at Gloucester or London.

Meanwhile, Harold and Leofwine made for Bristol, probably with a few dozen of their retinue, with a plan to sail to Ireland using a vessel that had been equipped beforehand by Swegn. As suggested above, Swegn had originally intended it for his own exile purposes but had joined his family at Bosham instead. The youngest son, Wulfnoth, being held as a hostage in London, had no opportunity to flee with his siblings. The second daughter, Gunhild, is not named, but she had likely remained undisturbed in the nunnery she had joined a few years beforehand, probably at Wilton.

On the king's instructions, perhaps still within the grace period Edward had originally given, Bishop Ealdred of Worcester had been sent with a force to waylay Harold and Leofwine, but the *ASC* notes that 'they could not, or they would not' intercept the exiles.[57] Ealdred was sympathetic to the Godwinsons and had allowed them to continue unhindered. Harold and Leofwine sailed on to Dublin. The *Vita* records that they were received by Diarmait mac Máel na mBó, the king of the province of Leinster, but this is not entirely accurate. In fact, in 1051 the king in Dublin was Echmarcach, and it was only the following year that Diarmait took control of Dublin after expelling Echmarcach.[58] There were long-standing trading links between Bristol and Dublin, and it should be assumed previous favourable links between the Godwinson family and Diarmait. Their flight had not been random, they knew they would be welcomed there, and Dublin was an ideal base to buy ships and hire mercenary warriors across eastern Ireland for a potential planned return to England. Queen Edith in the *Vita Edwardi* acknowledges that Ireland was a natural recruiting ground.[59]

Days after the Godwinsons had sailed Edward followed Archbishop Champart's advice and replaced the Godwin-endorsed Spearhavoc as Bishop of London with William, his Norman priest. However, the crucial issue was replacing the Godwinsons and reallocating their earldoms. Edward appointed Odda of Deerhurst as earl over western Wessex, comprising Somerset, Dorset, Devon and Cornwall. Odda had witnessed charters as far back as Æthelred II, plus also charters from Cnut and Harthacnut. He had been a regular witness since Edward's succession, established, loyal to the throne, and able to take control of western Wessex without difficulty. Ælfgar, the thirty-year-old son of Earl Leofric of Mercia, was given Harold's old earldom of East Anglia, including Essex.[60] The shires of Huntingdon and Northamptonshire were traded off to Earl Siward, but the redistribution of Swegn Godwinson's former earldom, which had undergone recent changes and comprised Berkshire, Oxfordshire, Gloucestershire, Herefordshire and Somerset, is less clear.

Somerset was absorbed under Odda's new earldom and perhaps the logical approach was to assign Oxfordshire, Gloucestershire, and Herefordshire to Earl Leofric. They abutted his existing Mercian earldom, which then covered Worcestershire, Warwickshire, Shropshire, Staffordshire, Cheshire and Derbyshire, and would have been a sign of Edward's gratitude for Leofric's firm support during recent events. Herefordshire was likely assigned instead to the king's nephew Ralph of Mantes, possibly with some responsibilities going to the Norman Osbern Pentecost. Osbern had accompanied Edward back to England in 1041, held land in the Midlands, and was an associate, perhaps friend, of Ralph. Ralph was probably also granted control of Bedfordshire, Buckinghamshire, Hertfordshire and Middlesex now, although some historians argue that this did not come until 1053–54. Berkshire looks to have been unassigned and placed instead under royal control. Elsewhere, Kent was perhaps placed under the jurisdiction of the archbishop. Replacing Godwin in the other shires of Wessex, where he had been lord for thirty years, would require diplomacy, and was likely unassigned and placed under immediate royal authority while the king pondered how to manage the region.[61]

Soon after the Godwinsons were exiled version D of the *ASC* tells us that 'Earl William' (Duke William of Normandy) 'came from beyond the sea with a great troop of French (Norman) men, and the king received him and as many of his companions as suited him, and let him go again'.[62] Symeon of Durham and John of Worcester repeat a similar entry and the Norman writers William of Poitiers and Wace embellished it further after the Conquest.[63] The claims are that Edward offered William the English succession during this visit. However, recent scholarly assessment of the *ASC* entry has raised doubts, with some suggesting it was not contemporary to 1051 but was added in the 1080s or later to support William's claims post-1066.[64] As argued by some historians, however, if William did not come to England in person the offer of the throne could have been relayed earlier through the intermediary of Robert Champart, sent to Normandy to pass on the proposal.[65] This would coincide with Champart's journey to Rome to collect his pallium, which was undertaken between Lent (mid-February) and 27 June 1051. As seen already, the archbishop may have jointly visited Normandy and Boulogne on his return from Rome.

Historians have debated for decades the claims concerning William's visit; it is one of the key pillars of his later assertion to the English throne. Edward's mother Emma, being the sister of William's grandfather Duke Richard II, was William's aunt, so as cousins the invite has some credibility. The timing of the purported visit would endorse the argument that Edward sought to secure Norman support to counter the potential future threat of the Godwinsons planning or attempting a return.[66]

The offer of the throne is another matter. Although Edward may have sought Norman pledges of support, he is unlikely to have offered the throne as a bargaining chip. William of Poitiers, the duke's biographer writing just after the Conquest, asserts that Duke William had told him, 'My lord and kinsman King Edward ... made me his heir, on account of the great honours and numerous benefits which I and my ancestors conferred on him.' Poitiers then adds that Edward 'did not do this without the consent of his magnates, but in truth with the advice of Archbishop Stigand, Earl Godwin, Earl Leofric, and Earl Siward, who also confirmed with a handfast oath, that after the death of Edward they would receive me as their lord. He gave me the son and grandson of Godwin as hostages.'[67]

Wace is less specific, but nonetheless agrees with his fellow Norman, noting, 'For the honour of the good family with whom he had been raised, and because of William's valour, he wanted to make him heir to his kingdom.'[68] From a Norman perspective, they had long supported the exiled Edward's entitlement to the English throne over and above Danish claimants. A Norman charter of Duke Robert I, William's father, from the early 1030s includes Edward witnessing as 'Eduuardi Regis' (King Edward); and a later charter for Duke William's confirmation bears a similar subscription for Edward.[69] Edward was grateful to Normandy, William's uncles Richard II and Richard III, and William's father Robert I, for giving him exile, but passing on the English succession to Robert's son surely exceeded any reasonable repayment of a perceived debt.

Despite this contact, the idea there was a long-standing friendship between the cousins during Edward's time in Normandy is misleading and distorted. For several years after the seven-year-old William had become duke in 1035 Normandy was in anarchy, and the boy was kept in power only through the support of his great-uncle Archbishop Robert of Rouen and King Henry I of France. When he returned to England in 1041 Edward was more than twenty-five years older than William, so it is unlikely Edward and William's paths had crossed significantly. The Norman primary source entries were designed to embolden William's entitlement but were aimed for post-1066 Anglo-Norman consumption. This is to be expected, but for that reason, they must be treated with great caution.

A meeting between them is plausible but the accumulated evidence is not convincing. The absence of any Norman source texts prior to the Conquest on this matter suggests there is also no substance behind the claimed promise of the throne. Various historians have observed that Duke William was campaigning against Geoffrey Martel, Count of Anjou, for control of Maine, the region south of Normandy, during late 1051, and would have been unable to cross the Channel at this time. This is a debatable point, but in any case, William had other ongoing issues. His marriage to Matilda of Flanders was still under consideration by Pope Leo IX, which had more to do with the papacy's support for Emperor Henry III and the alliance between Normandy and Flanders than it had with William and Matilda's links through consanguinity of kinship.[70] Not that William was not ambitious. He would have learnt, perhaps even directly through his wife, that the Godwinsons had been exiled from England and were at that moment inside Flanders. Any trip made to see Edward would be in the knowledge that Godwin and his family were absent, a good opportunity for the Norman duke to assess the scale of the disagreement between Edward and his senior earl, and whether there was scope to exploit the situation somehow.

There is no other record of William revisiting England after 1051 when there was ample opportunity to do so. One would think if William had been offered the English throne, he would have made another visit in the fifteen years between 1051 and 1066, even if only to have the promise reinforced. That he did not puts the whole claim in serious question and at worst exposes it as a complete fabrication. Within England, Edward had plenty of opportunities subsequently to formally announce it, and if a promise had been made it would have been publicly acknowledged.[71] He remained silent on the subject.

Poitiers' claims regarding the consent of the English magnates, as noted above, might be more convincing if he had not included Godwin in the list of men who supposedly approved William's nomination. Aside from the unlikely premise that Godwin would have made such an oath, he and his family had already been exiled and he was in Flanders during the autumn of 1051. That being the case, if the Norman chronicler was dealing in facts he should have known that Godwin would have been unable to give any such oath at the time.[72]

In concluding the detail on this period of crisis we should briefly revisit the whereabouts of the hostages Wulfnoth and Hakon. Their subsequent arrival and detention in Normandy is not disputed and was an additional safeguard which put them beyond the reach of the Godwinsons. Their transfer took place between October 1051 and June 1052, during the Godwinson family's period of exile, but there are two possible scenarios. The first rests on accepting that William of Normandy visited England, and that it was then Edward handed over Wulfnoth and Hakon. The second, more likely rendering is that Edward sent them as captives to Normandy in the archbishop's company, as noted earlier.[73] Wace noted that Edward requested William 'look after them until he himself asked for them', then adds that 'it appeared as if he wanted him to hold on to them permanently ... until he could have his kingdom if he died before him'.[74] The offer of the kingdom is again thrown in here, but irrespective of that issue it acknowledges that Edward was intending to use Wulfnoth and Hakon as long-term bargaining chips should Godwin attempt to return. They were the probable reason Harold Godwinson made his fateful trip to Normandy in 1064, which is discussed in chapter twelve. The significance of their imprisonment in Normandy cannot be underestimated.

EDWARD THE CONFESSOR'S CHARTERS 1043 to 1053 – LIST OF SECULAR WITNESSES

CHARTER NO. (SAWYER)	1000	1001	1004	1005	1006	1007	1008	1009	1010	1011	1012 (1)	1012 (2)	1013	1015	1016	1012 (3)	1018	1020	1021	1022	1023	1025
YEAR	1043	1044	1044	1044	1045	1045	1045	1045	1045	1045	1045	1046	1046	1046	1046	1048	1049	1050	1050	1050	1052	1053
AELFGAR	15										10					9	11					
AELFSTAN		12	6	6	12	11	12	12	16	8	11					8	8	7				7
AELFWEARD			16						18							13		16				
BEORHTRIC		9	5	9	9	10	10	10	10	9						13	7	9			8	8
BEORN (Earl)					6	6	5	5								5						
EDITH (Queen)					X	X	X	X	X	X3	X	X	X		X	X						
EMMA (Queen Mother)	X	X		X						X2												
GODWIN (Earl)	1	1	1	1	1	1	1	1	1	1	1	1	1	1	1	1	1	1	1	1	1	1
HAROLD (Earl)	2					5	5	5	5	5	5				2	4	3	3		5	3	4
KARL				13								13	12		11	12						
LEOFRIC (Earl)	3	2	2	2	2	2	2	2	2	2	2	3	2	2	2	2	2	2			2	2
LEOFWINE (Earl)																6	8	11	10	11		12
ODDA (Earl)		7	7	8	9	9	6	7	8	8						10	8					
ORDGAR		5	8	5	6	7	7	8	6	6			3		3	11	10					
ORDWULF		14	14													12	15					
OSGOD CLAPA (Earl)		6	4	5	6	7	8	8	7	5	7		4									
RALPH (Earl)	7																5	5		5	5	5
SWARD (Earl)		4	3	3	3	3	3	3	3	4			3		3	3	4	4			4	3
SWEGN (Earl)	5	4	4	4	4	4	4								13							
THURED	11	11							13		19											
TOFIG																		9	9	9		9
TOSTIG (Earl)	6															7	7	6	7	6	6	6

Note 1) Numbers denote the position that individual signed within the witness lists – the Godwinsons highlighted in bold
Note 2) Only individuals that signed a minimum of four charters are listed
Note 3) Edith signed immediately below the king
Note 4) Table compiled from data gathered from Prosopography of Anglo-Saxon England database (www.pase.ac.uk)

9

Return of the Godwinsons

The expulsion of the Godwinsons sent shockwaves across parts of England, particularly Wessex, but by the spring of 1052 the immediate political storm seems to have passed. Edward acted swiftly to reassign the earldoms. In reallocating them among a broader group, he had reinforced his loyalty base. Nevertheless, it is interesting that at a more grassroots level there is no evidence of a major redistribution of estates among the thegnage. In terms of royal charters during the period of the Godwinson's exile, nothing has survived. It is always possible that documents could have since been lost or destroyed, but if in fact none were issued it is questionable why Edward failed to use the period to his advantage.

With a greater influence from Continental advisors within his inner circle now that the Godwinsons had been removed, Edward's diplomacy was to move closer to alliances with several Continental powers at the expense of the old links with Scandinavia. This had been an ongoing trend for several years but could now be freely extended. He had achieved a closer union with his kinsman Eustace of Boulogne and possibly also with his distant cousin William of Normandy, and no doubt with Henry III, the Holy Roman Emperor and Henry I of France. As Count Baldwin V of Flanders was harbouring Godwin and most of his family presumably Flanders remained outside this sphere.

Initial signs seem to confirm that Edward did not expect Godwin to return. Even with the monies the Godwinsons had taken with them and with some assistance from Baldwin V, they could surely not raise a sufficiently armed fleet to threaten anything beyond a raid. Other exiles had tried and failed to recover their status in the past. Godwin was the most high-profile exile there had been, but whether this would prove advantageous or disadvantageous would need to be tested. In exile at Bruges, the Godwinsons used their wealth to make contacts in the region to gather a mercenary fleet and the men to sail it. However, it would be many months before Godwin could launch his plan to return. The exiled earl may have envisaged returning to England in 1052 if circumstances proved favourable, and Swegn, Tostig and the young Gyrth would have been crucial to their father's morale and planning over the winter. He no doubt hoped that he still retained a strong loyal base among the thegns of Wessex, and perhaps even knew he could rely on such support should he attempt to return, but there was no precedent for such a turnaround of fortune.

Before launching a military operation to reclaim his position Godwin attempted to use his diplomatic skills. Messages were sent to Edward asking for the opportunity to come in peace and clear his name. According to the *Vita Edwardi* envoys were likewise sent to the English court on Godwin's behalf from Baldwin V and King Henry I of France.[1] Henry I may have been concerned over a potential strengthening of the alliance between England and Normandy, so was looking at Godwin's restoration from the wider picture. However, it seems inexplicable that the Godwinsons would expect Edward to take notice of Baldwin, given the king and count's ongoing differences.

Over the winter of 1051 and spring of 1052 Godwin received encouraging messages from agents and traders that there was still strong ground support across Wessex willing to fight for his cause, with many urging him to come back.[2] When the time came to test the waters Godwin would have to do it without his eldest son, however. While at Bruges the temperamental Swegn seems to have had an epiphany. Perhaps honouring his earlier pledge to Bishop Ealdred when he was last pardoned by the king, Swegn had already left his family and Bruges to undertake a pilgrimage to Jerusalem. Maybe he had become a reformed character, with Godwin and Gytha having a hand in his decision.

In the spring of 1052, Edward received the news that his mother Emma (renamed Ælfgifu in Old English) had died at her residence of God Begot Manor in Winchester. She was aged around sixty-seven, but the chronicle scribes disagree over the date, one recording 6 March and another 14 March.[3] Emma had lived her last decade relatively quietly, perhaps spending periods at Nunnaminster (St Mary's Abbey) in Winchester or further afield at Wherwell, Romsey or Wilton. Sources are silent whether she and her son established a new understanding ahead of her death; it is plausible they had never fully settled their differences. She had not witnessed any of Edward's charters since 1045. God Begot Manor was situated on Winchester's High Street just south of the Market Cross, with the rear backing onto St George's Street. Today, the surviving building on the site has seen continuous usage by various retail outlets, but sections of the top floors and the rear of the building are much older, some internal parts claiming to be part of the rebuild undertaken by Emma in 1050.

The manor of God Begot was willed by Emma to the monks of the Old Minster in Winchester, which is where she was taken for burial. She was rested, as per her wishes and with Edward's approval, not with his father and her first husband Æthelred (the Unready), but alongside her second husband, Cnut. Her bones, and those of the others buried there, would in 1093 be transferred to the new Norman cathedral which was consecrated after the demolition of the Old Minster. There would be further upheaval to all the burials inside the cathedral during the English Civil War, including Emma's and Cnut's, and Godwin's also, which is discussed briefly in the final chapter.

Edward would not have been unaware, thanks to traders or his own spies, that Godwin was making plans, and as further word arrived it became clear the king would need to take precautions. The sources record he ordered forty, or perhaps fifty, of his fastest ships to be stationed at Sandwich, ready to intercept a Godwinson fleet.[4] This figure may be an exaggeration. In 1050, Edward had taken the step of dismissing about ten more hired vessels, and as mentioned beforehand, had abolished the *heregeld*, the tax raised to pay for the navy. During a period of peace this was good for the royal treasury and economy in general but it seemingly left only two or three dozen ships still under royal authority to guard the Channel. Ralph and Odda, recently appointed as earls but with no previous experience commanding ships, were given command. Their advancement seems to have occurred because there were no other outstanding candidates, but Odda was a long-standing member of the Witan, and Ralph was Edward's nephew.

The timetable of events in the summer of 1052 is a little confused, and there is debate as to whether Godwin's flotilla sailed for England once or twice. Some sources seem to conflate his efforts into a single attempt but combining all available detail it would seem he set sail twice. The first was primarily designed as a reconnoitre in the south-east, and the second was the major assault, the principal concerted effort. Godwin moved with an unknown number of ships from the estuary of the River Yser on 22 June 1052 and made for Dungeness, adjacent to Romney Marsh.[5] By now, the alert was out; Godwin had barely landed at Dungeness before news came that the royal fleet under Ralph and Odda was moving down the Channel preparing to engage him.

Godwin's ships at this point were likely heavily outnumbered but, as noted by the *ASC* version E, the movement of the royal fleet coincided with a bout of severe weather.[6] Alert to the presence of the fleet and deteriorating conditions at sea, Godwin took his ships west into the safe shelter of Pevensey Bay. Ralph and Odda, unable to locate him and perhaps apprehensive of their seamanship in unusual weather, returned to Sandwich. William of Malmesbury adds that the fleets 'had come to close quarters' but 'the sudden onset of a thick fog confounded their ardour for battle ... making them invisible to each other'.[7] Heavy fog in June would have been an unusual piece of fortune for Godwin, but perhaps Malmesbury's detail originates from a story Ralph and Odda later used when being called upon to justify to Edward their failure to locate and engage Godwin's ships.

With the royal fleet absent, Godwin continued to gather reports from across Sussex and further afield of the potential support available to him before making his way back to Flanders. He would have been encouraged that many thegns and their vassals, including those seamen along the south coast and others as far as Surrey, had pledged to support his reinstatement. The main effort would come just a few weeks later.

The response by Edward to his former senior earl's appearance seems a little agitated and confused. John of Worcester records the king's fleet withdrew back to London via the Wantsum Channel.[8] This seems an extraordinary action. Possibly he was angry with Ralph and Odda and intended to replace them, but even so, why withdraw the whole fleet? Maybe they had told him that Godwin's attempted invasion had failed, and the danger had passed. Conversely, perhaps Edward already feared the worst and was planning to secure the defences around London and Westminster. The *ASC* version E notes the ships were recalled so Edward could appoint new commanders and oarsmen but 'it was delayed so long that the ship-campaign was wholly abandoned'.[9] This hints at poor leadership and a loss of nerve. News may have reached him that support for Godwin was already significant. Ralph and Odda were duly relieved of command, but replacements were not forthcoming. There are signs here already of the problem Edward would soon face. There were not enough men prepared to fight the Godwinsons, and the basis of this may have rested in the belief that they had thought Godwin harshly dealt with beforehand.

Godwin's major attempt came perhaps only a week or two after midsummer. The number of vessels is unknown, but he may have had upward of twenty. His reconnaissance had told him most if not all the ships and crew in the south coast ports would support him, many of them having been decommissioned by Edward when he abolished the *heregeld* tax. However, Godwin initially bypassed Kent and Sussex as part of a planned movement west along the Channel towards the Isle of Wight. During his exile, there were likely regular lines of communication between Godwin and his two sons in Ireland, even accepting the natural time delays in receiving messages.

Harold and Leofwine had over the winter of 1051/52 hired ships and crew across Ireland, aided by the assistance of King Diarmait mac Máel na mBó of Leinster. However, they had left England with fewer resources, and sources tell us they left Ireland with only nine vessels.[10] Based on their known later movements in the south-west, they probably sailed in early July 1052. This was within a week either side of when their father and brothers had launched their supreme effort, which implies that there was some agreed, coordinated plan. However, Harold was acting on his own at the head of this squadron, because Leofwine was aged no older than fifteen or sixteen in 1052. From Dublin, they likely picked up additional mercenaries at Wexford and Waterford – towns, along with Dublin, which had been founded by Norse and had strong Scandinavian influences.

The *ASC* records they then heading up the Bristol Channel, 'near the borders of Somerset and Devon', and landed at Porlock.[11] Why Harold landed in north Somerset is unclear; maybe it was simply to refurbish supplies, or more likely to test local sentiment for the Godwinsons. It is suggested one reason Porlock was chosen was that it lay close to Selworthy, 2 miles inland to the east, an estate that had belonged to Edith before her removal from court.[12] However, Harold and Leofwine would be disappointed, as a large fyrd from Devon and Somerset was quickly gathered to oppose them. That the local militia fought against Harold and Leofwine rather than join them instead has puzzled some historians. However, the thegns in the south-west had extended their vassalage to Odda, their new earl, and besides – something which Harold may not have appreciated – the thegnage of Somerset may have held bad memories of Swegn Godwinson's time as earl over the region.

The encounter may have taken place on the foreshore of Porlock Bay soon after the Godwinsons had disembarked. The *ASC* version D, repeated by John of Worcester, records that the resulting encounter led to victory for Harold and the death of over thirty thegns.[13] The elimination of that many thegns suggests a large fyrd had been assembled, but to defeat them so roundly the Godwinsons must have had a minimum of 400 men within their nine ships. Harold and Leofwine then re-embarked and sailed back west towards and around Land's End, and then moved their flotilla east up the English Channel.[14] The response from Somerset would contrast with the loyalty the family would later receive in the south-east, from Hampshire, Surrey, Sussex and Kent, where Edward had not directly replaced Godwin, and where vassalage and loyalty to him and his family was still upheld by many thegns and their supporters.

Godwin, with Tostig and Gyrth presumably alongside him, had already based himself at the Isle of Wight. Further messages had crossed between Godwin and Harold in the preceding weeks, and Wight seems to have been their planned rendezvous point. However, because of Porlock and possibly other unrecorded difficulties, Harold's schedule had been impacted and his force was late in arriving. Godwin therefore moved on to raid Portland while he waited. Portland was a prime royal estate owned by the king, and Godwin's fleet 'did whatsoever harm they could'.[15] Dorset, like Somerset, had become part of Odda's new earldom in the recent changes, so hitting Portland was making a statement to both Edward and Odda. The people of Dorset do not appear to have resisted, but details of Godwin's latest movements must have reached Edward within days. The king's apparent inactivity would be a feature over the weeks that followed. However, Edward had several weeks earlier seemingly permitted Edith to reallocate from Wherwell Abbey with necessary due ceremony to Wilton Abbey, her old place of education and the location she favoured, as noted in the previous chapter.[16] The timing of this transfer is interesting and could be connected to the strengthening evidence that her family was attempting to restore its position.

Having sailed without further incident to Dorset, Harold and Leofwine met their father at Portland during the second half of August, with the *ASC* scribe adding that 'both made their way eastward until they came to Wight ... and then made their way from there to Pevensey'.[17] Perhaps they diverted briefly to their estate at Bosham, before continuing along the coast, drawing support in ships and men from Hastings, Dungeness, Romney, Hythe, Folkestone and Dover.[18] As had been required under Edward and in previous regimes, these ports had been contracted to perform military service, each to provide a minimum of twenty ships and crews.[19] It was many of these same vessels and crews, disbanded recently by Edward, that were now backing the Godwinsons.

Messengers had been dispatched ahead calling for supporters to gather behind Godwin's banner, and his army and fleet grew as thegns and levies continued to join from Sussex, Kent, Surrey and all along the south-east coast.[20] Eastern Wessex was the region with the greatest degree of support for the Godwinsons, but at Dover it was necessary to take hostages. Aside from being one of Godwin's own estates, Dover was of course the place that had sparked the dispute between the earl and the king when Godwin had refused to punish its townsfolk. The need to take hostages here therefore looks odd, unless perhaps it is proof the town and hilltop burh were now being occupied by the king's men. We could elaborate further and suggest that Edward had permitted Eustace of Boulogne to garrison some men at Dover also after the Godwinsons were exiled, and it was these men who were taken as hostages.

Moving past Deal, the Godwinsons 'came to Sandwich with a streaming raiding-army', where they took more hostages and seized any royal vessels that had remained in port.[21] The main royal squadron had withdrawn to London. Edward apparently remained inactive, but one writer who contradicts other authorities is Henry of Huntingdon, who claims in his work *Historia Anglorum* that Edward's ships had met the Godwinsons fleet as they passed the mouth of the River Stour in the Wantsum Channel.[22] Henry continues to relate that the king was on a ship within the royal squadron and that it was there, and not London, that Edward and Godwin first came to terms. This version of events seems improbable, and it is highly unlikely Edward had accompanied his navy in Kent. There is no record of him ever directly commanding a fleet, or indeed at the head of an English fyrd, and the only surviving example of him perhaps being present on the battlefield relates to his failed attempt to reach Winchester and his immediate withdrawal in 1036.

The consensus from diverse primary sources is that the Godwinson fleet moved from Sandwich through the Wantsum Channel, with their land army keeping pace, entered the Thames Estuary and steered for London. Some vessels diverted to raid the Isle of Sheppey, targeting Milton Regis, another royal estate just north of present-day Sittingbourne, whereupon it was burnt to the ground.[23] This detail is presented in version E (Peterborough) of the *ASC* but omitted from the Canterbury (version F) edition. The raid on Milton Regis has been offered by the scribe as evidence that Godwin was unconcerned about pillaging the shire.[24] This conclusion is a little hasty. As with all large armies of this period, some degree of pillaging on campaign was inevitable. However, it is pertinent that no other settlement is named as being attacked, and it is clear Milton Regis, along with Portland previously, was raided specifically because it belonged to the king.

Throughout these escalating actions Edward gives us the impression of being unmindful of the scale of the problem facing him. His fleet had been withdrawn to protect London, and even when news came of the burning of Milton Regis and of the Godwinson fleet and land army having passed Gravesend he still remained inactive. He had available the London militia and his armed retinue, but more soldiers were needed. It should have been clear that the king needed the militias which could be raised by Leofric, Siward, Ralph, Odda and Ælfgar to assemble without delay. They had been summoned, with the principal sources noting that Edward had, rather belatedly, sent out for more aid, but 'they came very late' or 'were too slow and did not come in time'.[25] The king's nephew Ralph of Mantes had likely responded promptly, but it is difficult to know whether Leofric and others deliberately delayed their response or simply had insufficient time to gather their forces to reach London ahead of Godwin.

It is implied the summons had been issued too late. Siward of Northumbria and his thegns, for example, could not be expected to arrive in a matter of days from the first summons, and it is a fair assumption he was not the only senior noble that had been unable, or perhaps unwilling, to raise an army hastily, move to London, and to fight Godwin. By moving quickly, Godwin had amplified the king's tardiness and placed himself in a powerful position. Perhaps from his many years of working alongside Edward, he had judged correctly that the king was likely to prevaricate when placed under pressure. The difference on this occasion, compared to Gloucester in 1051, was that Godwin's fellow earls do not appear to have been prepared to fight him.[26]

When Godwin's combined army and fleet approached London, the levies of earls Leofric, Siward and possibly Ælfgar may still not have reached Edward. Ralph was probably there, and perhaps Odda too, although in their haste they had likely brought fewer soldiers than Edward would have hoped. This muted response was potentially damaging for Edward, but it epitomised the lack of appetite for civil war among the nobility, and perhaps some empathy for how the Godwinsons had previously been treated. They likely had some empathy for Godwin and his family given the turn events had taken the previous year, had perhaps become wary of Edward's decision-making and the advice he was receiving from new court advisors. The king had demonstrated he could remove the Godwinsons and redistribute their estates with no qualms, and for men like Leofric and Siward, the thought must have been that if he could do that to Godwin then he may look one day to do the same to them.

The Godwinson fleet moved towards Southwark, and with Edward's ships being anchored to the west of London Bridge Godwin waited for the flood tide before passing through the bridge. While awaiting the tide, Godwin had meetings with prominent London citizens and arranged an uncontested passage beyond the bridge. John of Worcester adds that 'he had previously bound himself to (the citizens) with promises of one sort or another'.[27] It was the day of exultation of the Holy Cross (14 September 1052), and it had been 355 days since Godwin had been outlawed when last at Southwark.[28] Support for Edward's position had seemingly already disappeared, but the king had seriously underestimated the depth of loyalty towards the Godwinsons in the south and south-east that had resurfaced once Godwin had set foot in Wessex again.

Once through London Bridge, Godwin's ships fell into formation 'as if they wanted to circle around the king's ships', but the royal fleet showed no signs of forming into position.[29] The Godwinson land army aligned itself along the south bank, and the king's force – which the *ASC* describes as 'a great land army', which seems an exaggeration for reasons previously indicated – prepared to defend the north bank.[30] The stand-off can only be imagined. Godwin had raised the stakes, and Edward was eager not to be forced to back down, but neither had the appetite for further escalation. The sources noted that 'they did not want that this country should be the more greatly laid open to foreign men, should they themselves destroy each other', and 'almost all were loath to fight their kinsmen and fellow countrymen'.[31]

The Anglo-Saxon appetite for compromise was an important factor. These nobles had seen how divisions in the kingdom under Æthelred II had led to invasion and conquest, and since the death of Cnut developments had revealed that the kingdom needed to stand united against other external threats. Edward no doubt longed to see Godwin humiliated, and if necessary challenged and beaten in battle, for having the effrontery to raise an army against him. However, he did not have the necessary military support or indeed the unqualified backing of his earls to undertake action, and leading his forces in battle was not one of Edward's noted qualities. Godwin had not desired conflict, but he had undertaken a convincing and very risky game of bluff. It would not have served him to begin a clash of arms in which no one, particularly his family, would gain. If fighting broke out with Edward's earls, the Godwinsons would never be restored to their lands.

The military strength Godwin had gathered behind him was designed to intimidate Edward and bring him to the negotiating table. Discussions began the following day. The king and Godwin exchanged negotiators, and, as put succinctly by John of Worcester, 'the wiser on both sides restored peace between the king and the earl'.[32] Godwin asked that he and all his kin 'be entitled to all the things which had unjustly been taken from them'.[33] Edward initially prevaricated, so much so that Godwin's followers feared nothing would be agreed and grew agitated to the point where he only calmed them down with difficulty. The *ASC* tells us Godwin and Harold, accompanied by a contingent from their personal retinues, only 'landed' after assurances of their safe conduct. A Witan council was then held at Westminster.[34] Bishop Stigand of Winchester was the most prominent among the mediators, trusted by Edward but also on good terms with the Godwinsons. During the negotiations, more hostages were exchanged, and some historians suggest it was only during this exchange that Wulfnoth and Hakon were handed over, as was noted by the Canterbury scribe Eadmer.[35] This contradicts other sources, and the previously described scenario of the hostage transfer during 1051 remains the favoured likelihood. It would be meaningless to use Hakon as a hostage when his father Swegn Godwinson was at that moment en route to the Holy Land.[36]

An agreement was reached between Edward, the Witan and the Godwinsons after Godwin had been allowed the opportunity to clear himself on oath and to put forward his argument against the earlier charges. He was 'clean granted his earldom as fully and as completely as he ever owned it, and all his sons all what they earlier owned, and his wife and his daughters as fully and as completely as they owned'.[37] William of Malmesbury praised Godwin for his powers of persuasion, adding that 'that aged man, master of language that would move the hearts of his audience, cleared himself successfully of all the charges brought against him'.[38] Edward had not given his pardon easily. He would have been angered that his fleet had failed him and that his earls and chief supporters were unwilling to take up arms when Godwin had directly threatened his security. He would also have been angry at a deeper level. Removing the Godwinsons in 1051 had allowed him perhaps greater freedom, whether real or abstract. It can be imagined that he was initially bitter about welcoming them back; their pardoning brought with it a return to the old status quo, and a certain loss of face.

An indication Edward conceded more than he would have wanted was that he agreed to outlaw, as put by the *ASC*, 'all the French (i.e. Norman) men who earlier promoted illegality and passed unjust judgements and counselled bad counsel in this country'.[39] The scribe for version D of the chronicle freely blames Edward's new group of foreign advisors while avoiding any direct criticism of the king. Nevertheless, Edward did keep some of his Norman companions at court, including Robert the Deacon and his son-in-law Richard, and Robert FitzWimarc, but the list did not include Archbishop Robert Champart. The archbishop had played a significant role in persuading Edward to take a hard line against the earl and his family in 1051.

By September 1052, the tables had turned. Edward's acceptance of Godwin's terms gave Champart and his fellow compatriots little time to react, which suggests that the archbishop had until the last moment expected the king to stay resolutely behind him. In that respect Champart had not understood Edward or the power of the earls, when combined, to affect royal policy. He and his companions were immediately outlawed, John of Worcester adding that these Normans 'had devised evil laws and pronounced unjust judgements and given the king much bad counsel, to the prejudice of the English'.[40] With the situation irreparable, Champart and those closely connected to him quickly packed and left while they had the chance. By all accounts, the archbishop only just evaded capture. Champart, together with William, Bishop of London, and Ulf, Bishop of Lincoln, and their retinues fled via London's east gate, where they 'killed and otherwise injured many young men' before heading for the Essex coastline near Walton-on-the-Naze and sailing for the Continent.[41] Bishop William of London had panicked or had been poorly persuaded to flee with Champart and the others, because he was recalled to England with no recriminations to resume his bishopric a few months later.

The question of Wulfnoth and Hakon's whereabouts resurfaced as soon as the Godwinsons were restored. It is hard to imagine that Wulfnoth's release would not have been at the forefront of his father's negotiations with Edward. The preferred version is that they were already in Normandy, but it is plausible that if they had been detained in London Champart may have taken them with him when his party fled the city. News of the Godwinsons' rehabilitation brought concern to the Normans who had allied themselves against Godwin in 1051. Version E of the *ASC* recorded that some seized horses and headed west towards the castle of Osbern Pentecost at Ewyas Harold in Herefordshire, presumably Osbern among them if he had been at Westminster. Others went north, and shortly afterwards some others, as further noted by John of Worcester, 'surrendered their castles' and were 'allowed by Earl Leofric to pass through his territories in their way to Scotland'.[42] These men would arrive at the court of Macbeth, King of the Scots (Alba). Had they all been Edward's appointees they would have needed to seek his permission and not Leofric's, so presumably these were the Normans who had garrisoned their castles close to the Welsh border without Edward's full knowledge or acceptance. However, it is unclear why these Normans had not first sought to return to Normandy rather than head north, unless we assume they judged themselves to have had no hope of reaching the Channel undetected once the Godwinsons had been restored.

It has been debated that it was in Edward's interests to retain the Godwinson hostages under his indirect control even though he had restored Godwin and Godwin's family to their former positions. With this in mind, some historians have argued that the three separate 'escape' parties described above, with the approval and knowledge of Edward, left London by the west, north and east gates simultaneously as a way of confusing the Godwinsons and preventing them from locating and releasing their kinsmen in time.[43] There is validity to this approach: one last throw by Edward to ensure Godwin did not hold all the cards in their future relationship. Holding the hostages, even if not directly, still gave him a level of authority or persuasion over the Godwinsons should he need to use it.

Meanwhile, after crossing the Channel, Robert Champart headed for the court of Duke William of Normandy at Rouen.[44] If he had taken the hostages with him, as per the scenario above, maybe this was finally when they came into the hands of the duke. From Rouen, Champart then made his way to Rome, where it is said he was able to persuade Pope Leo IX that he had been expelled from his Canterbury diocese illegally and without foundation. Purportedly armed with a letter from Leo proclaiming his innocence and requesting he be restored to Canterbury, Champart, it is said, headed back intending to present the letter to Edward. This cannot be verified; there is no record he presented any papal proclamation.

His claim was, in any case, false, and can be easily dismissed. Anticipating his forced dismissal, he had abandoned his archbishopric by running away to avoid the consequences of Godwin's restoration and a ruling from the king on his position. Even if a papal proclamation had been issued, it is difficult to see how he could be reinstated. Once the Godwinsons had retrieved their former authority and positions, including Edith's place alongside her husband, there was no chance of Champart restoring his career or returning to England in any capacity. He returned instead to his abbey at Jumièges, and likely died shortly afterwards in the spring of 1053, although William of Malmesbury preferred a different ending, writing that the former archbishop died en route back to England with his letter from the pope unopened.[45]

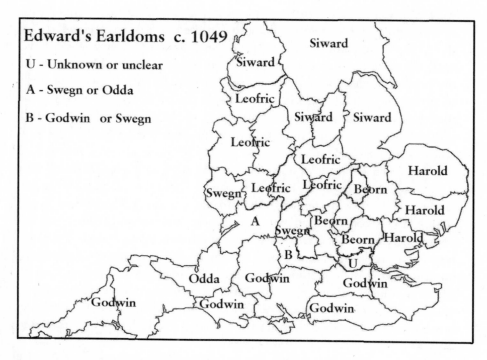

Edward's Earldoms c. 1049

U - Unknown or unclear

A - Swegn or Odda

B - Godwin or Swegn

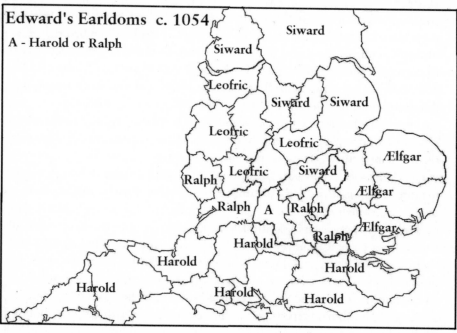

Edward's Earldoms c. 1054

A - Harold or Ralph

10

The Death of Godwin and the Emergence of Tostig

Edward's council reinstated the Godwinson family to their former status, without exception, in the autumn of 1052. The appearance is of the dynasty moving almost seamlessly back into power. Godwin and Harold were restored to their earldoms overnight, and Edith was summoned back to the royal household from her confinement at Wilton Abbey within days. Their return obviously had the greatest impact on those who had gained from the family's exile, primarily Odda in the south-west and Leofric of Mercia's son Ælfgar in East Anglia. All of Wessex, the length and breadth from Kent to Cornwall, was returned to Godwin. This included all the westernmost shires that had been allocated to Odda, although he was compensated by retaining Swegn's former shire of Gloucestershire and perhaps a share of Worcestershire alongside Leofric. Ælfgar's recently acquired earldom in East Anglia was returned to Harold in full, but he received no compensation elsewhere.

It was different for the remaining Godwinson men. The next eldest son, Tostig, would have to wait a few more years for his opportunity, and because of their young age, Gyrth and Leofwine would wait even longer. Edward's nephew Ralph of Mantes held onto Herefordshire, formally at least, and also kept Middlesex and Buckinghamshire. These were not up for reallocation, as neither was a further reshuffle of the remaining shires across Mercia. For Edward, the problem was not a lack of candidates; instead, there were too few earldoms being divided among too many nobles wishing to fill them. Nevertheless, to try to retain a political balance Edward would in the years ahead sub-divide regions of Mercia into smaller units by reallocating various shires. Contrary perhaps to the general view, not all the king's Norman and Continental advisors and nobles had fled or lost their entitlements in 1052. Alongside his nephew Ralph, the Bretons Robert FitzWimarc and Ralph the Staller plus several other Norman or French nobles were to remain in or close to the royal court, including the recently arrived chaplain Osbern FitzOsbern.[1]

In terms of royal charters, there are two surviving documents issued soon after the Godwinsons' restoration and Godwin smoothly continued at the head of the secular witnesses for both these charters.[2] Harold appears just below Earl Leofric, as he had done before the crisis, and Tostig emerges two places below him. Further down the lists, Leofwine appears in the second of these documents, but his prominence and Gyrth's absence is puzzling. His inclusion casts doubt on the validity of this witness list. Gyrth does not appear as a signatory until 1055, and Leofwine was several years younger than his brother. Within the ecclesiastic community a replacement was needed for Robert Champart in immediate terms and Stigand was appointed to the archbishopric at Canterbury while still holding his bishopric at Winchester in plurality. Stigand was a good choice as far as the Godwinsons were concerned. He already had a previously established relationship with Godwin after transferring from Elmham in East Anglia to the Winchester bishopric four years earlier, and their friendship strengthened further because of his successful recent mediation between the Godwinsons and the king. William of Malmesbury, writing from detail drawn from post-Conquest Norman propaganda against Stigand, describes him as 'a prelate with a bad name for ambition and one who sought promotion beyond his due'.[3]

The Godwinsons had other ecclesiastical friends in the shape of Archbishop Cynesige at York and Bishop Ealdred at Worcester. Cynesige in the years ahead would conduct the consecration of Harold's church at Waltham Cross, and Ealdred would later replace him at York while retaining his see at Worcester. In a similar vein to Stigand's plurality at Canterbury and Winchester, Bishop Leofric, educated on the Continent but born in Cornwall, kept the dual sees of Cornwall and Exeter (formerly Crediton); and Herman, a native of Lotharingia, retained the dual sees of Ramsbury and Sherborne. The prevalence for a limited few trusted individuals holding sees in duality would seem to have been a deliberate policy that suited both the king and his senior earls.

There was, however, a spate of deaths by natural causes among the senior clergy before All Saints' Day (1 November 1052). These included Bishop Wulfsige of Lichfield, Abbot Godwin of Winchcombe, and Abbot Æthelweard of Glastonbury.[4] They were joined by Ælfric, brother of Earl Odda, in December. Odda later built a chapel at Deerhurst, near the River Severn in Gloucestershire, for Ælfric's soul. During the seventeenth century, it was absorbed within an adjoining farmhouse, and only during the Victorian era was its original purpose re-established and determined as being 'Odda's Chapel'. The chapel is now under the care of English Heritage and can be visited today. The adjacent St Mary's Church in Deerhurst, part of an earlier monastic priory, visited by Edmund Ironside and Cnut during their negotiations in 1016, was and remained an important religious site for the Mercians from the ninth century onwards.[5]

Swegn Godwinson was absent when his father and family had launched their attempt to recover their former status within the English hierarchy. As seen, he had parted with them at Bruges to undertake a pilgrimage to Jerusalem and the Holy Land some months before Godwin had sailed for England. Ostensibly, this was as an act of penance after his previous misdeeds, reputedly undertaken alone and barefoot. However, the *ASC* recorded that having completed his pilgrimage Swegn 'died while on his way home at Constantinople on Michaelmas Day (29 September, 1052)'.[6] This was coincidentally only a week after the Godwinsons had been restored to their former positions in England. John of Worcester adds more detail, telling us that Swegn died from excessive cold and hunger while passing through the region of Lycia (southern Turkey), and William of Malmesbury added further to it by recording that he 'was ambushed by the Saracens and mortally wounded'.[7]

This was an unfortunate end for the Godwinson 'black sheep', although few beyond his parents and perhaps a few of his siblings would have mourned his passing. In summarising Swegn the contemporary opinion among academics is that he had psychotic tendencies, possessing a wayward and probably violent nature. Mention of Swegn appeared later within Edith's *Vita Edwardi*, where her Flemish encomiast writes of four children of Godwin, whom he allegorises within his prose as 'four streams' that brought honour to the family, while the fifth is a 'gulping monster' that attacked the roots of the parent trunk.[8] While a few disagree over a precise interpretation the majority of academics accept that the writer intended to separate Swegn (the gulping monster) from his brothers Harold, Tostig, Gyrth and Leofwine. Presumably, being her own commissioned work, Edith concurred with the sentiment. Meanwhile, ignorant still that his eldest son had died, Godwin may have remained hopeful that Edward would allow Swegn a pardon after his act of atonement. The report of Swegn's death would not reach England until the spring of 1053.

The earlier realignment of the earldoms during 1047–52, particularly those that affected the security of the border with Wales, seems to have encouraged the Welsh to use the opportunity to expand their raiding. In 1049 Gruffydd ap Rhydderch, King of Deheubarth, and the man that Swegn Godwinson had campaigned against three years earlier, defeated a force led by Bishop Ealdred of Worcester. This had been followed in the early weeks of 1052, while the Godwinsons were in exile, by another major raid led by Gruffydd's brother Rhys ap Rhydderch. Rhys harried as far as Leominster, defeating a significant force led apparently by some of the Normans Edward had appointed to the Welsh border region. For the English, the return of the Godwinsons gave a new unity of purpose, and in his Christmas court of 1052 at Gloucester, the king ordered reprisals against Rhys. The Welsh king was killed in this new English campaign within days at Clyro just west of Hay-on-Wye, and on 5 January 1053 his head was brought to Edward as proof of a successful campaign.[9] Rhys' brother Gruffydd ap Rhydderch was to be killed in 1055 by Gruffydd ap Llywelyn, King of Gwynedd and Powys, making the latter the first sole ruler of all of Wales.

During the last days of 1052, Godwin was taken ill, although he was said to have then fully recovered.[10] By now in his mid-fifties, the stresses and strains of the previous sixteen months had probably taken their toll physically and mentally. In the first few weeks of 1053 he and his family were further rocked when news reached them of Swegn's death. Godwin undoubtedly took this news badly, coming as it did so soon after his illness. He had strived for all his family, but Godwin had perhaps spent the greatest share of his energy in fighting Swegn's corner, clear in his efforts to re-establish Swegn after his periods of exile. We cannot know for certain, but Godwin may simply have favoured his eldest son over and above his other children. That the news of the death contributed to his own demise is conceivable; he was to die only a few weeks later.

Godwin's death is recorded in several primary sources, including entries in the *ASC*, William of Malmesbury's *Gesta Regum Anglorum*, Henry of Huntingdon and John of Worcester, and the late twelfth-century Norman writer Wace in his poem *Roman de Rue*. The *ASC* dates it to 15 April 1053 in the Julian Calendar.[11] Most sources record Godwin dying while at the king's court at Winchester – more of which below – but Henry's *Historia Anglorum* names the location as Windsor.[12] The Norman writer Wace meanwhile names Godwin's demise as taking place at Odiham in Hampshire, and this location is repeated by Richard of Devizes in his translation of the *Winchester Annals*.[13] Most historians accept Winchester as the venue – it is the likelier choice because of its importance in the eleventh century – but the alternative sites are worth reviewing. Edward had an estate at Old Windsor west of London, while Odiham was on the London to Winchester road and equidistant between Winchester and Windsor.[14]

Windsor could claim to be the venue if Godwin's demise came while attending the king's court, but Odiham is not an obvious choice to arrive at, which paradoxically may support it as a candidate. From researching the *Domesday Book* land-ownership records the estate of Odiham before 1066 did not belong to Edward but was in the possession of Earl Harold, so there is every reason to assume that in early 1053 the estate was owned by his father.[15] An area in Odiham south of the High Street known as 'The Bury' has been offered as the location of a former high-status Anglo-Saxon residence, conceivably the hall owned by the Godwinsons.[16]

On the death itself, the *ASC* Version C is perhaps the most succinct, recording that Godwin was at dinner with Edward and Harold and Tostig when he 'suddenly sank down against the footstool, deprived of speech and of all his strength', and was carried into the king's chamber in the hopes he would recover, but remained 'unspeaking and helpless' before dying in three days.[17] John of Worcester was to repeat much of the same, noting that the earl was 'struck down by a sudden and unexpected illness ... but deprived of his strength, he departed this life the following Thursday in wretched pain'.[18] He had collapsed at the Easter Sunday feast on 12 April, likely through suffering a major stroke.

The retelling of Godwin's death became a popular story after the Norman Conquest. However, as time passed details of the way he died become exaggerated in some primary sources, which ties us again to the question of propaganda and the Norman agenda after the Conquest. As addressed in better detail elsewhere, efforts were made under the reign of William I (the Conqueror) to discredit or disregard the reign of his predecessor Harold II (Godwinson), and for good measure this was extended further on occasion to deride the memory of Harold's father. This rendering of the narrative was incorporated in the works of some later Anglo-Norman writers, and William of Malmesbury expanded on the story better than most. He painted a different image to both the *ASC* and his contemporary John of Worcester. Malmesbury sets the fatal dinner scene using full literary licence, with Godwin saying to Edward, 'I notice, your Majesty ... that at every mention of your brother you look at me with a frown on your brow: May God not permit me to swallow this mouthful, if I was ever aware of having done anything designed to endanger him or hurt you', and the earl 'was choked by the food he had just put into his mouth, and turned up his eyes to death'.[19] Malmesbury, being a cleric, connects the specific manner of Godwin's demise to what was effectively a witnessing of 'divine retribution' for his participation in the ætheling Alfred's death seventeen years earlier.

However, the narrative continued to gather momentum and the most elaborate text came from the anonymous author of a thirteenth-century work in Norman French, *The Lives of Edward the Confessor*.[20] It is useful to include much of that text here if merely to show how much embellishment had been added in the interim. The tale goes that while Edward and Godwin were feasting a servant poured the earl some wine, causing him to remark playfully to Edward, 'So brings one brother to the other, help, who was in danger.' Edward then referred suddenly to the death of Alfred: 'So might mine had he been living, if you, earl, had permitted him.' Godwin responded with indignation, saying, 'Thou hast reproached me with the death of Alfred your brother, for which I am not to blame, I will prove it openly, the mockery much troubles me.'

Godwin then took a morsel of bread and before eating it announced, 'If I can enjoy this morsel ... I am not to blame for his death, all at the table will see, so I am either acquit or to blame for it.' In response, Edward blessed the morsel, saying, 'May God grant that the proof be true.' On putting the bread in his mouth Godwin is said to have suddenly become pale, losing breath and speech and slumping down, and as *The Lives of Edward the Confessor* noted, 'By the morsel which sticks fast, dead is the bloody felon.'[21] We can see without further explanation that, now long removed from the original event, the myth had become much more interesting than fact for the medieval readership.

Earl Godwin was buried in the Old Minster at Winchester close to Cnut, Emma and his nephew Beorn.[22] English contemporaries are reported to have mourned his passing in language typically used for high-profile individuals in the medieval period, but in Godwin's case we can accept it at face value. The support that had flocked to him months earlier when he had sought to restore his dynasty illustrates he had the respect of his vassals and the loyalty of the people of his earldom. However, the Norman Conquest ensured that eulogies written for Godwin would not endure without criticism for long, and as Harold's father his reputation and legacy were affected accordingly. He had been Earl of Wessex for more than three decades, second only to the monarch for most of it, and the trusted primary counsellor for two very differently styled monarchs.

Assuredly Godwin produced a will, but it and its details have not survived. For a man of his stature, we can assume that some written instruction had been left for his heirs. From the content of surviving Anglo-Saxon wills from prominent individuals, we can conclude that Godwin handed his sword down to Harold, the sword being a powerful symbol passed from generation to generation. Harold probably received most of Godwin's estates across Wessex, although the Norman policy of removing Harold where possible from the historical record post-1066, as in the listed estates in the *Domesday Book*, has restricted the available evidence.[23] All household members of both genders would have received an inheritance, and most of Godwin's estates appear to have been in Sussex, Kent and Hampshire. A large grouping is noticeable, by quantity if not necessarily by size, on either side of the Hampshire–Sussex border within proximity to Chichester. The largest of his estates by land value included Bosham, Willingdon, Singleton and Hurstpierpoint in Sussex, plus Dover, Hoo and Folkestone in Kent and Chalton in Hampshire.[24] There are several estates which Godwin and Gytha look to have held jointly before his death. Harting in Sussex was a large estate later shown in Gytha's name, but whether it was maintained by her prior to her husband's death is unclear. Gytha's primary income came from land in Dorset, Wiltshire, Somerset and Devon. The majority appear to have been in Devon, but the largest were Aldbourne in Wiltshire and Frampton in Dorset.[25]

Estates later identified to Gytha and her daughter Gunhild Godwinsdottir likely came to them in 1053 at the time of Godwin's death, as did those known to have still been under the lordship of his various sons just before the Conquest. As a sign of her connection with Devon, and with Scandinavia, and probably also to commemorate the memory of her husband, Gytha founded St Olave's Church in Exeter in 1053. The building was dedicated to the former Norwegian king Olaf Haraldsson II, who had been made a saint during the 1030s. There were to be several churches in England devoted to Saint Olaf, including two in London and one in York. It is interesting that Gytha chose to dedicate the church at Exeter to Olaf, as it had been her kinsman King Cnut, sponsor of Godwin's rapid rise, who had forced Olaf to first flee Norway.

Godwin's death naturally required another reshuffle of the earldoms. Harold was transferred from East Anglia to Wessex, which contained the shires controlled by Godwin before 1051, but with the addition of Berkshire and Wiltshire. There would have been pressure on Edward to appoint Tostig, and perhaps Gyrth also, but Harold was not yet the dominant influence his father had been. Ælfgar, son of Leofric, was brought back once again to replace Harold in East Anglia, which satisfied Leofric and the Mercian elements.[26] Perhaps against expectations, Ralph again retained Herefordshire and his shires north of London. Siward was probably granted Northamptonshire and Huntingdonshire under his jurisdiction of Northumbria, a potential short-term arrangement which would see these two shires tied to the Northumbrian earldom until the Conquest. The sources are vague on the redistribution of other regions across much of the Midlands. Harold or Ralph controlled Oxfordshire; Odda likely kept control of Gloucestershire; and Leofric held or retained Leicestershire, Warwickshire and Worcestershire.

Edward may have been given a new lease of life with Godwin no longer around. As a sign perhaps of this fresh energy, he issued a new coin type during 1053. This may not sound significant, but the image on the coin depicted Edward as a warrior king wearing a pointed helmet.[27] This implies a newfound confidence, free of Godwin's shackles. Nevertheless, the image is perhaps an ironic one, because Edward was anything but a warrior king. Queen Edith would hereafter become more influential than ever within the royal household, involved in everything from her husband's wardrobe to his rapport with his earls. Edith and Harold could theoretically work together to guide royal policy, but to what level they would succeed in that naturally depended on Edward.

Historians continue to debate how easily or otherwise Edward was influenced by those around him. He may never have had any clear-cut policies of his own, other than dealing with problems in front of him as they arose. His over-reliance upon those he appointed has been frequently argued, and not just in terms of his relationship with Godwin, and this apparent tendency to be manipulated has been regarded as an obvious weakness. However, the inverse argument could be put that he was astute and shrewd and particularly good at delegating, perhaps even cunningly so. The thesis is that Harold and Edith, along with Tostig later, acted as his trusted helpers for the remaining years of his reign. This idea comes from our knowledge that in his last years he withdrew from the decision-making processes, but an honest assessment is that we cannot be certain how much responsibility for the government administration Edward delegated to the Godwinsons and his other senior earls during the rest of the 1050s. Rather than grudgingly yield authority to them, a different perspective could be he instead happily allowed them to take some of the burdens from his shoulders.[28]

An image of Edith's relationship with her husband seems clearer post-1052 than beforehand, although admittedly most of our information comes via Edith's commissioned work the *Vita Edwardi*. References to Edith's personality within it are open to scrutiny for obvious reasons. Her encomiast tells us she was so modest that, unless invited by Edward, she never sat on a throne at his side but preferred to sit at his feet. Furthermore, she had a significant influence in private over her spouse, ensuring he would always appear in public suitably arrayed and with proper ceremony.[29] Input beyond the *Vita* shows a different Edith; in one example a determined woman, interfering and hard, and possibly bad-tempered.[30] Her involvement in the assassinations that took place during Tostig's later earldom in Northumbria, as claimed by some sources, suggests she could be uncompromising when necessary. The primary sources portray a mellowing of her relationship with Edward, with Edith becoming more like a mother or daughter than a wife. The notion Edward was heavily influenced by his wife is perhaps telling, and it hints at his apparent passivity, but the feeling from Edward's reign post-1053 after Godwin's death is of a king more relaxed with his situation.

Opinion on Edward's foreign policy has been divided. He forged closer unions with the Holy Roman Empire and France, and closer and friendlier ties with Normandy and Boulogne. However, his politics on Scandinavian affairs were protectionist, to refrain from involvement and seemingly to try to loosen further the ties that England had enjoyed with Denmark over previous generations in exchange for closer ones with mainland Europe. This looks to have been his policy for almost all his reign. As observed, he had hitherto refused to support Swein Estrithsson against Norway, while the Godwinsons, with Gytha's Danish connections, had looked first to Scandinavia and not the Continent. Perhaps, as has been suggested, Edward's strategy was nothing more than keeping on good terms with his closer neighbours to discourage Norse aggression.[31] His stance on Denmark meant he would have clashed with the Godwinsons on this, although Harold, for different reasons, was more in tune with Edward's thinking in forging new and stronger links with Europe. This was perhaps the obvious difference between Harold and Godwin, and perhaps why the exchange between Edward and Harold looks to have been less fractious.

Northumbria, a region he never visited, had been one that Edward had had minimal involvement with during the 1040s. Perhaps because of the upheavals in England since 1051, the Scots of Alba under Macbeth had increased their activity south of the border. Earl Siward had requested the king's help, and in 1054 Edward sent men and ships to complement Siward's forces, with orders to take a large invasion force into Scotland.[32] Siward had a personal interest. King Duncan I, his sister Sybil's husband, had been killed by Macbeth in 1040. Duncan's son Malcolm, thereafter to be Malcolm III (aka Canmore) of Alba, had since the age of nine taken exile in England during Macbeth's reign.[33] Edward's plan was possibly to facilitate installing Malcolm on the throne of Scotland, thereby halting cross-border incursions, and it is highly likely that Malcolm, then aged twenty-five, accompanied Siward's army.

Siward clashed with Macbeth somewhere near to Perth or Scone on 27 July 1054, and the *Annals of Ulster* noted that 3,000 Scots and 1,500 English fell in the battle.[34] The traditional site is at Dunsinane Hill, 8 miles north-east of Perth, next to the modern B953 road. William of Malmesbury claimed Macbeth was killed in this battle, although Macbeth escaped the defeat and lived for a further three years. Nevertheless, the encounter was costly for Siward. The fatalities included his eldest son Osbearn and his nephew the young Siward.[35] One of Siward's allies who perished at Dunsinane was a certain Dolfin, and as described in a later chapter, it would be Dolfin's son Ulf that would be assassinated by Tostig Godwinson's agents several years afterwards.

Before March 1055, Earl Siward died. He had contracted dysentery, but, as remarked by Henry of Huntingdon, made sure he was kitted-out in full armour, sword and shield before he died as a mark of retaining his honour.[36] He was buried in the original minster at York, which the *ASC* names as Siward's foundation at Galmanho, now lost. The minster was believed to have been near to Bootham Bar in the present-day city centre.[37] Siward's death posed another potential crisis for Edward. With Siward's heir Osbearn having predeceased him, the remaining son, Waltheof, whom Henry of Huntingdon says was 'still a small boy', was too young to replace his father.[38] Edward needed a replacement he could trust to implement his policies in the north. No doubt with Harold and Edith urging the king, the man he chose was Tostig Godwinson.

For Tostig, with his background in Wessex, assuming authority in Northumbria was not straightforward but there was no suitable local candidate that Edward could trust to keep the peace. There was still a rivalry between the old divisions of Bernicia (Bamburgh) and Deira (York), within the entrenched Northumbrian secular structures, and the stronger Scandinavian influences in the north further complicated matters. In simple terms, Bernicia retained a greater part of its Anglian origin among its hierarchy, whereas Deiran York was much more Anglo-Scandinavian, and indeed the recently deceased Siward, as previously noted, had likely first emerged as part of the contingent that had arrived with Cnut or soon thereafter. Many Northumbrian customs and laws were based on those that had been established at the height of the Danelaw, and York was still dominated by Anglo-Danish protocols.

It is true Tostig was half-Danish and was, therefore, better suited than most outside of the borders of Northumbria, but he was probably naïve to the difficulties he would face in Northumbria in comparison to his family's earldoms in the south. Rejecting the position was not an option; another chance may not occur for years. The early twelfth-century *Gesta Regum Anglorum*, with the advantage of hindsight and knowing Tostig's later fate, noted harshly that 'Tostig was advanced by King Edward ... at the end of which his habitual ferocity roused the Northumbrians to revolt'.[39] Hindsight aside, Tostig's selection marked a change in royal policy, an appointee from the south given an earldom in the north. Edward was probably happy to promote Tostig's nomination; there may well have been a friendship or understanding between them, more so than with any other of the Godwinson brothers, including Harold. Hitherto Edward had relied on Mercia and Northumbria to act as counterbalances to the power of Wessex and the Godwinson family. However, Tostig's appointment to Northumbria unmistakably abandoned that strategy.[40]

Tostig's Northumbrian earldom brought with it the linked Midland districts of Northamptonshire and Huntingdonshire, and it may have been this which caused immediate concern to Earl Ælfgar, who had perhaps hoped that after the death of Siward he could absorb these two shires into his East Anglian earldom. In addition, according to some historians, Ælfgar may have had direct designs on gaining Northumbria for himself via the heritage links of his wife Ælfgifu to the old Northumbrian nobility. This connection is far from clear. Ælfgifu's unnamed mother was reputedly English, hence her daughter's Anglo-Saxon name, but other sources also claim that Ælfgifu was the sister of the Norman William Malet, which if true casts some doubt on any family Northumbrian association.[41] The link with William Malet might suggest that Ælfgar's marriage had been an earlier political arrangement as part of Edward's programme of forging closer links with Normandy.

Matters were to reach a head at a Witan council meeting convened by Edward in London seven days before mid-Lent on 19 March 1055.[42] The primary sources say the hearing was called to consider an accusation or accusations made against Ælfgar. This is plausible – he may have already been outspoken when first learning of Tostig's promotion. Both the *ASC* and John of Worcester record that Tostig had already been selected before the Witan meeting and that 'not much later, King Edward ... outlawed the guiltless Earl Ælfgar, son of Earl Leofric'.[43] However, it could well be that the sources are misplaced, and that it was when Tostig's nomination was formally announced at this council that Ælfgar first spoke out of turn in response to the pronouncement, and accusations and counter-accusations followed from there. One suggestion is that Tostig's faction had anticipated opposition from Ælfgar to Tostig's appointment and had pre-planned a confrontation which was easily triggered by an accusation in front of the king.[44] The exact accusation against Ælfgar is unknown, but he was found guilty of treason and was exiled by consensus.

The principal sources have varying views. Versions C and D of the *ASC*, the chronicles from Abingdon and Worcester, write that Ælfgar 'was outlawed well-nigh without fault', which was the line also taken by John of Worcester.[45] Chronicles E and F, written at Peterborough and Canterbury, differ from this, both noting that when accused of treason 'he admitted this before all the men who were gathered there, although the words shot out against his will'.[46] Reading between the lines, perhaps Ælfgar responded angrily to the initial accusation, making matters worse, and provocation from one or more of the Godwinson brothers, possibly pre-meditated, led to the exiling. The evidence is cloudy, but Gyrth was likely established in East Anglia as Ælfgar's replacement. An undercurrent between the two dynasties had often been present, since perhaps the succession of Harold Harefoot. Ælfgar's exile nonetheless highlights that his father Leofric was now an old man and of much less significance at court, an argument supported by Leofric's absence from the witness lists within the charters after 1053 even though he would live for another thirty months.

Appointing Tostig to Northumbria allowed Edward to bring the region more in line with the rest of his kingdom, and from the outset Tostig would strive to push through adjustments in law and taxation in fulfilment of Edward's brief. Evidence of his methods is limited, but the fact he survived in position for a decade against increasing local unrest is testament to his persistence. Being an outsider from Wessex may have helped him because he was initially regarded as neutral by the rival Northumbrian interests within Bamburgh and York. Tostig managed the balance successfully for several years, which is often overlooked.

Once installed, as recorded in the *Vita Edwardi*, Tostig was as equal in devoutness and generosity to the Church as Edith and Harold, perhaps more so than his brother.[47] Both he and his wife Judith gave their patronage to the Church in Northumbria, although donations were ultimately based on the income received from taxation and diverse means from the general population. Further afield, Tostig's relations with Archbishop Cynesige of York were amicable, and Cynesige, as previously suggested, looks to have forged close ties with the Godwinsons. Just before his death, the archbishop was in attendance in May 1060 at Harold's request to dedicate his foundation of the Abbey of Waltham Holy Cross.[48]

Tostig, perhaps as a way of uniting the Bernician and Deiran factions inside his earldom, adopted a devotion to the old Anglo-Saxon Northumbrian cult of St Cuthbert, and he and Judith became generous benefactors of the church at Durham. Tostig's name was written in gold lettering in the *Liber Vitae* (Book of Life) by the Durham scriptorium, which registered the names of people who had entered a state of spiritual confraternity with the church there.[49] Interestingly, his father Godwin's name had been introduced already in the same register. The community of St Cuthbert comprised wealthy landowners, and it benefitted Tostig to support their cult, which in turn benefitted from his efforts to establish more peaceful and law-abiding conditions.[50] The monk Symeon of Durham observed that Tostig 'held the church of St Cuthbert always in veneration', and his wife was 'a very honest and religious woman who loved St Cuthbert even more than did her husband also gave various ornaments to the saint's church'.[51] Symeon describes the couple gifting to Durham an image of the crucified Christ, St Mary and John the Evangelist clad in gold and silver, although the crucifix would be despoiled during a post-1066 uprising by the kinsmen of the Northumbrian nobleman Gospatric.[52]

Tostig also oversaw the resignation of Bishop Æthelric of Durham after a financial scandal and then supported Edward's choice of Æthelric's brother Æthelwine as the new bishop in 1056.[53] However, this went against the Durham community's right of election, and the earl's previously good relationship with them soured. The monks of Durham are known to have taken part in the 1065 revolt against Tostig. A positive piece of local evidence for Tostig's acceptance in his first decade as earl comes indirectly from the inscription on a sundial at St Gregory's Minster in Kirkdale in North Yorkshire. The inscription commemorates the rebuilding of the church by a prominent nobleman named Orm Gamalson 'in the days of King Edward and the days of earl Tostig'.[54] This reinforces the impression that Northumbria was prosperous and stable under Tostig but also tells us that this nobleman was happy to be associated in posterity with Tostig.[55]

After his exile in 1055, Earl Ælfgar made for Ireland, where he recruited ships and crew. Like the Godwinsons, the Mercian nobility had connections in Ireland and perhaps Ælfgar was taking inspiration from the Godwinsons' earlier exploits. Having gained eighteen ships and their crews to add to his forces Ælfgar then sailed to North Wales and approached Gruffydd ap Llywelyn of Gwynedd for a military alliance, which John of Worcester notes was to help him against Edward.[56] His mercenary force then entered the River Dee and moored at Chester. With Gruffydd alongside him, Ælfgar 'gathered a great army with the Irish men and with the Welsh race', and made for Hereford in the autumn of 1055.[57] Hereford lies on the north bank of the River Wye, and an incentive for attacking it was that it held the largest English mint west of the River Severn. Ralph of Mantes, as earl for the shire, mustered an army and on 24 October, 2 miles west of Hereford north of the river, the two forces clashed.

The primary sources record that both sides had 'a great army', although numbers are unknown. The English launched a cavalry attack – something they were not used to employing – but the attack faltered, and Ralph and his supporters were the first to flee. From this incident, Ralph gained his additional later moniker of 'the Timid'. Ælfgar and Gruffydd pursued their enemy, and although Ralph escaped, 400 to 500 of his soldiers were killed.[58] Archaeologists have proposed that the Norman motte and bailey at Hereford may have been originally constructed in timber by Ralph, although if there was a sizeable castle by 1055, it did not prevent the town's sacking. The allies pillaged Hereford, slew many of the citizens, and 'burned it down … and the famous minster … they stripped and robbed of holy things'.[59]

In response, Edward ordered an army to be assembled at Gloucester, and for its command turned to Harold, his new right-hand man, whom John of Worcester describes as 'the vigorous Earl Harold'.[60] Harold soon pursued the allies back into Wales, and with Ælfgar and Gruffydd dispersed he kept his forces inside the Welsh border as he set about repairing Hereford's defences. Harold strengthened the gates and constructed new broader and deeper outer ramparts and ditches that enclosed the northern circuit around the settlement and extended the perimeter defences south of the River Wye.[61] Meanwhile Ælfgar had retired his forces back towards Chester and his fleet on the River Dee and Gruffydd ap Llywelyn had returned to Gwynedd. Sometime over the winter of 1055/56 a meeting between Harold, Ælfgar and Gruffydd was arranged at a place called 'Billings' or 'Billingsley' in Holme Lacy, an estate owned by Harold 5 miles south-east of Hereford.[62] Harold was given full authority to mediate on behalf of the king, with Bishop Ealdred and the ageing Earl Leofric alongside him. An agreement was concluded, the Welsh forces of Gruffydd were withdrawn, and Ælfgar's mercenaries disbanded and sailed back to Ireland. For his part in this Edward awarded Harold the earldom of Herefordshire, replacing Ralph, and Ealdred of Worcester received the additional diocese at Hereford.[63]

As part of the agreement, Ælfgar was fully reinstated to his earldom of East Anglia, which Gyrth Godwinson, who had occupied it barely six months, had to relinquish. Gyrth's loss of East Anglia was perhaps inevitable once Ælfgar had been pardoned. There was no other earldom that could be considered, including Mercia – not while Ælfgar's father Leofric was still alive. The fear of civil war between Anglo-Saxons remained paramount in the minds of the king and his nobles, and, interestingly, Harold's negotiations prioritised peace over and above Gyrth's holdings. This was a sign perhaps of Harold's mindset, where the kingdom's interests were prioritised above the personal interests of his brother. Some would argue that was good diplomacy, although others might point out that Harold lost nothing personally in sacrificing Gyrth's earldom, on the contrary, he had gained another shire. This approach, with Harold prepared to sacrifice family interests for the wider national interest, is a line he would pursue again in 1065, although that similar approach in the situation his brother Tostig faced would lead to much more serious dramatic consequences.

Meanwhile, trouble with Gruffydd ap Llywelyn continued. In March 1056 Harold's former clerk Leofgar, on Harold's recommendation, had been appointed bishop at Hereford. Three months later, on 16 June, presumably with Harold's approval, the bishop launched an attack against the Welsh at Glasbury-on-Wye, 4 miles south-west of Hay-on-Wye, but his force, including many thegns, was overwhelmed and destroyed.[64] This was part of a much larger, ongoing campaign against the Welsh that is underplayed within the primary sources because it failed to achieve its aims. Versions C and D of the *ASC* say it was 'difficult to describe the hardship, and all the travelling and the campaigning, and the labour and loss of men, and also horses which all the raiding-army of the English suffered'.[65] This probably describes a costly and unsuccessful English initiative, which was concluded only when Harold, Leofric and Ealdred negotiated new terms with Gruffydd, where the Welsh king is said to have 'swore oaths that he would be a loyal and undeceiving under-king to King Edward'.[66] Description of Gruffydd's oath of loyalty to Edward should perhaps, in view of the apparent failure of this English campaign, be better called an agreement to cease hostilities.

11

The Earldoms and the
Search for the Exile

The period from 1054 to 1060 was dominated by two issues. The first was a further major reshuffling of the earldoms and the impact of those changes on the fortunes of the Godwinsons. Siward's passing in 1055 would be followed soon afterwards by Leofric and other significant deaths, as discussed later in this chapter. Combined with further complications from Ælfgar these losses gave scope, following Tostig's elevation, for his brothers Gyrth and Leofwine to be promoted to their own earldoms. In Gyrth's case this was rapid restitution for having only held East Anglia briefly beforehand until Ælfgar's restoration. The second issue revolved around the question of the royal succession, a topic that would never be far from the surface, and the quest to unearth Edmund Ironside's heirs and seek to bring them back to England.

The most significant development, if it succeeded, would be the restoration of Edmund's heirs as preferred successors to the throne. For much of his reign, Edward seems to have been confused about which direction he should take concerning the succession question. He changed his mind, or was persuaded to, several times, and this has fuelled the debate over his real intentions.[1] Edith was still of childbearing age, she was still only aged around thirty, but everyone knew by the mid-1050s that Edward and Edith would not produce an heir. As things stood the king's nephews, his sister Godgifu's sons Ralph of Mantes (who was already at Edward's court) and Walter of Mantes, had potential claims to the throne through the maternal line if the king remained childless. However, during 1054 there was a sudden refocusing in which Edward looked for his successor through paternal blood ties going back to his father Æthelred II (the Unready) and the original Anglo-Saxon House of Wessex.

The report of Cnut sending Edmund Ironside's two infant sons Edmund and Edward to Anund Jakob in Sweden soon after his own succession was perhaps known only by a select few of his immediate contemporaries. However, it later emerged, as considered beforehand, that this move was not made to ensure their protection but with the aim of having them murdered in Sweden. In the eventuality the plan failed, and Anund did not kill the infants. How much Godwin knew of this is unclear, but in accepting his previous loyalty to Edmund we should perhaps assume he was unaware of his new king's murderous intentions. It would seem Cnut himself believed they were dead and only became aware they may not be some years later. Alive or dead, to all intents and purposes the Anglo-Saxon æthelings had disappeared from English history. When, and by what means, during the early 1050s Edward became aware that the æthelings may yet be alive is uncertain. Nevertheless, word seems to have reached him they had left Scandinavia and were now in central Europe and he decided to act.

Most of the primary sources writing on the fate of Ironside's children repeat the tale of their exile to Sweden and then to Hungary. Recent research has identified that the boys had left Sweden during the 1020s.[2] However, contrary to prior assumptions they initially went from Sweden to Russia not to Hungary, as per the version of events related by, among others, the writers Adam of Bremen and Gaimar.[3] Perhaps news that Cnut had discovered they were not dead led to this transfer. They were taken for safety to the court of Yaroslav the Great at Novgorod in Russia. This was not a random destination – they had blood ties there. Their mother Eadgyth, wife of Edmund Ironside, had Swedish connections, but importantly she was the half-sister of Queen Ingergerd, the wife of Yaroslav.[4] Later in 1038, aged about twenty-two and twenty-one, Edmund and Edward then made for Hungary, where they aligned themselves behind Prince Andrew in the civil war there after the death of King Stephen I. They were both to achieve high status in Hungary after Andrew's succession in 1046.

Back in England we can envision that Edward now accepted that the old West Saxon royal line, his stepbrother's children, had the best legal claim to the English succession after him. The Witan, Harold, and the other earls must have conceded this with the king before the search for the æthelings began. If persuaded to come back to England, they would secure the succession and would work in unison with Harold, who was already seen as a strong military leader and the most reliable royal advisor. Gone and forgotten, if it ever existed, was the premise that the Norman duke was Edward's heir designate. When news reached the English court that the æthelings were in Hungary the first serious undertaking to locate them began in 1054 when Edward sent Bishop Ealdred and Abbot Ælfwine of Ramsbury to the court of the Holy Roman Emperor Henry III in Germany. William of Malmesbury recorded that 'King Edward, now advanced in years, having no children of his own ... sent to the king of the Huns, asking him to send Edward (Ironside's son)' so that 'he should succeed to the hereditary throne of England'.[5] Henry III had many years earlier been married to Edward's stepsister Gunhild, although she had died in 1038. Nevertheless, Edward hoped Henry III would aid in negotiations with the Hungarians.

Hungary had sought independence from the Holy Roman Empire, and peace between Emperor Henry III and Andrew I of Hungary had been settled the previous year. This was not the most auspicious moment for the English king to seek out the æthelings. Worse yet, the emperor was not the ideal man to act as an intermediary with Hungary and assist in the enterprise. On arriving in Germany Bishop Ealdred politely coaxed Henry to send an embassy to Hungary, and Ealdred remained in Cologne expediting this for a year before returning home unsuccessful and empty-handed.[6] Henry III had prevaricated and deliberately avoided expediting the matter in the belief – correct, as it turned out – that the æthelings had recently fought for Andrew against his empire. Evidence of his prevarication is clear when considering that according to several sources, including John of Worcester and Symeon of Durham, the ætheling Edward's wife Agatha was purportedly related to Henry. This would have made it relatively easy for the emperor to locate both Edward and Edmund's whereabouts if he had wished to do so.[7]

Despite Ealdred's abortive attempt, the king ordered another expedition to be sent out shortly after the death of Emperor Henry III in October 1056. This implies the English suspected the emperor had avoided helping them and acted again when news of his death was received. Henry's widow Agnes of Poitou (aka of Aquitaine), acting as regent for her young son Henry IV, proved more cooperative.[8] However, the situation in Hungary was worsening again and there was only a brief window of opportunity. Initial news came back that the eldest ætheling Edmund had already died sometime after 1050, so it was a case of locating just Edward (hereafter identified as Edward the Exile).

Although the chronicles are muted, there is good reason to believe that Harold Godwinson was utilised on this second occasion. We know he visited Rome in 1056 and had stopped at St Omer in Flanders on 13 November on his journey back from Italy, because he appears as a witness in a surviving charter of that date from Baldwin V of Flanders.[9] Baldwin was to meet Pope Victor II and Agnes of Poitou at Cologne in the following weeks to conclude a peace agreement between Flanders and the Holy Roman Empire, and from there he proceeded on to Regensburg for the Christmas festivities.[10] It is entirely plausible therefore that Harold travelled with Baldwin to Cologne, and possibly then Regensburg, during which he carried out instructions to negotiate with Agnes and Andrew of Hungary, and with the exiled Edward, to discuss the proposal for the exile to come back to England. In view of the potential for the English king to prevaricate Harold undoubtedly saw positives in the return of the Anglo-Saxon heir of Edmund Ironside.

Some academics have argued that as time passed Edward saw his childlessness as a diplomatic asset which he could use to manipulate those who had an interest in the throne.[11] To negate this potential uncertainty Harold, perhaps in agreement with his sister Queen Edith, had by 1056 likely concluded that any steps to secure an Anglo-Saxon successor was the preferred solution. Nevertheless, persuading the Exile to return may not have been straightforward. He was an infant when last in England and had been away for nearly four decades, and presumably had spoken little or no English in that time. However, with the offer of future position and wealth that came with the succession Edward the Exile agreed to the proposal and he began his journey in the early weeks of 1057, probably escorted by Harold. The scribe for version D of the *ASC* rather unusually added a thirteen-lined poem about the Exile's arrival.[12]

Most historians accept the Exile's wife Agatha and their three children, Edgar, Cristina and Margaret, initially accompanied him.[13] The genealogy of Agatha has been debated. John of Worcester, William of Malmesbury, Orderic Vitalis and Roger Howden among others have all provided different theories as to her family tree with no definitive answer. John, for example, claims she was the niece of Emperor Henry III.[14] As noted above, her antecedence is uncertain, and another theory suggests she had connections to Yaroslav the Great at Novgorod, with whom the æthelings had stayed previously.

The exiled true heir apparent to the West Saxon kings arrived in London in early April 1057. The political earthquake this undoubtedly caused within the royal court and the nobility can hardly be imagined, but in a dramatic and almost unbelievable development he was dead within a few days.[15] The *ASC* scribe noted that Edward the Exile had not even met the king before his untimely death: 'We do not know for what cause it was arranged that he might not see his relative King Edward's (face). Alas! That was a cruel fate.'[16] This is an almost cryptic entry, which seems to imply that he had been deliberately prevented from meeting Edward. William of Malmesbury, so often forthright, thought little of the Exile, writing that he 'was a man of no energy in action and no personal integrity'.[17] This opinion seems curious, and a particularly harsh critique of a man whom no one in England had seen beforehand and who had arrived in the country barely days before dying. How Malmesbury arrived at his assessment is therefore puzzling.

Edward the Exile was given a burial at London's major church, St Pauls Minster, the building that was housing the tomb of his grandfather Æthelred II. The manner and timing of Edward the Exile's death needs further consideration because to die within a week of arriving back in England points to suspicious circumstances. Historians are in two camps: some see his death as being unfortunate but nothing untoward, perhaps caused by

1. Compton, West Sussex, the estate formerly owned by Godwin's father Wulfnoth Cild and which passed to Godwin in 1014. (Images from author's collection unless otherwise stated)

2. Fosse Way near Sherston, Gloucestershire; it was in this area that Edmund Ironside fought the Danes in 1016.

3. Bosham, West Sussex, the former Godwinson family estate. The harbour with the Holy Trinity church is in the background.

4. Guildown near Guildford, Surrey. This is the route leading up to the Hog's Back, near the site where the troops of the ætheling Alfred were reputedly assassinated in 1036.

5. St Mary's at Stoughton, West Sussex. The church was originally built in 1050 on a Godwinson estate.

6. Sandwich and the River Stour, Kent; pictured is the site of the key Anglo-Saxon naval base guarding the English Channel and the Thames Estuary.

7. Chavenage Green near Beverston, Gloucestershire. This was the site of the local hundred close to where Godwin and his sons gathered their forces during the crisis of 1051.

8. St Mary in Castro, Dover, the church inside Godwin's estate of Dover Castle.

9. Wherwell, Hampshire, where Queen Edith was despatched by King Edward during the 1051 crisis.

10. Porlock Bay, Somerset, where Harold and Leofwine landed during the Godwinson campaign of 1052.

11. Odiham High Street, Hampshire, the site of a Godwinson estate and possible location of Godwin's death in 1053.

12. Rhuddlan Castle and the River Clwyd, Denbighshire. This Norman castle is close to the former location of Gruffydd ap Llewelyn's palace, scene of Harold Godwinson's raid of 1063. (Image courtesy of A. J. Marshall under Creative Commons)

13. Harold entering Holy Trinity Church at Bosham (left) with the hall at Bosham adjacent (right). (Courtesy of the City of Bayeux)

14. Harold taking the famous oath on the holy relics in 1064 under the instruction of William of Normandy. (Courtesy of the City of Bayeux)

15. Britford, Wiltshire, in the vicinity of the royal vill where news first reached Edward and Tostig of the northern rebellion.

16. Harold Godwinson's coronation (as King Harold II of England) on 6 January 1066 at Westminster Abbey. (Courtesy of City of Bayeux)

17. A silver penny of Harold II. Obverse reads 'HAROLD REX ANG' (King Harold of England) and the reverse 'PINUS ON PILTI', the moneyer from Wilton, with 'PAX' (peace) across the centre. (Image courtesy of Classic Numismatic Group [www.cngcoins.com])

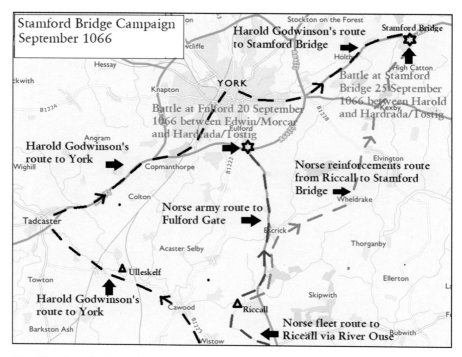

18. The Stamford Bridge campaign, September 1066, after the landing of the Norse fleet.

19. The Ouse at Riccall, North Yorkshire, near the landing site of Harald Hardrada's fleet.

20. The memorial stone and plinth with wall plaque in central Stamford Bridge, North Yorkshire, commemorating the battle of 25 September 1066.

21. The memorial stone and plaque at Battle Flats in Stamford Bridge, the main site of the fighting.

22. Dives Estuary, Normandy, where William of Normandy first assembled his invasion fleet in 1066. (Image courtesy of Sylenius under Creative Commons)

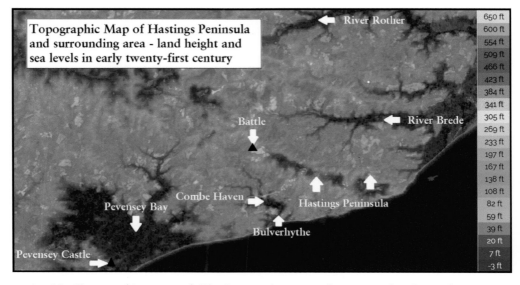

23. Topographic map of Hastings and surrounding area showing colour-coded elevation above present sea levels. (Basic background map courtesy of https://en-gb.topographic-map.com)

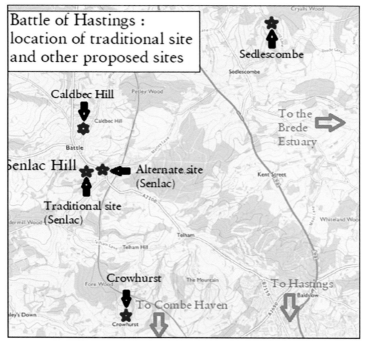

24. The traditional site of the Battle of Hastings and other proposed locations for the battle.

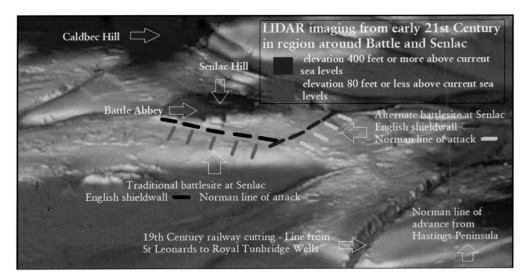

Caldbec Hill

LIDAR imaging from early 21st Century
in region around Battle and Senlac

elevation 400 feet or more above current
sea levels

elevation 80 feet or less above current sea
levels

Senlac Hill

Battle Abbey

Alternate battlesite at Senlac
English shieldwall
Norman line of attack

Traditional battlesite at Senlac
English shieldwall   Norman line of attack

Norman line of
advance from
Hastings Peninsula

19th Century railway cutting - Line from
St Leonards to Royal Tunbridge Wells

25. LIDAR (Light Detection and Ranging) image of Senlac Hill and surrounding
area highlighting elevations above sea level, with the traditional and alternative
alignments of the Norman attack and English shieldwall marked. (Base image
courtesy of http://anglosaxon.archeurope.info)

26. Battle Abbey grounds, East Sussex. This view shows the traditional battlefield
looking north towards the abbey ruins.

27. Battle, East Sussex, looking down the slope of Lower Lake Road from its junction with Upper Lake Road and Marley Lane to the east of Battle Abbey, centre of the proposed alternate battle site at Senlac Hill.

28. Caldbec Hill, Battle, East Sussex, looking from the summit of the proposed alternate battle site north towards the possible location of the Malfosse.

29. At Sedlescombe, East Sussex, looking north up Hurst Lane east of Sedlescombe at the proposed alternate battle site.

30. River Brede, East Sussex, near Winchelsea. This was a major waterway in the eleventh century.

31. Crowhurst, East Sussex, looking south from Forewood Lane in Crowhurst at the proposed alternate battle site.

32. The death of King Harold II, the figure to the left with the arrow in his eye, and the figure to the right falling to the ground and being despatched by a Norman knight. (Courtesy of City of Bayeux)

33. Marker stone in Battle Abbey at the original position of the church altar, where King Harold is said to have fallen.

34. The stone plinth and marker stone in the grounds of Waltham Abbey, Essex, claiming to mark the last resting place of King Harold.

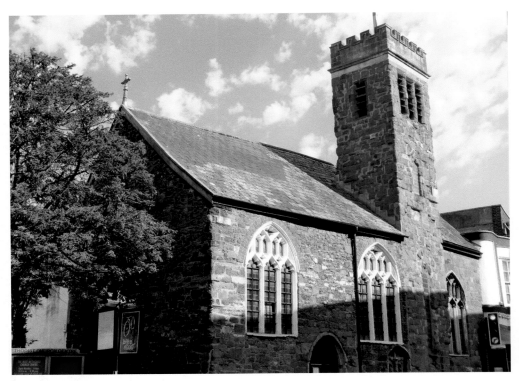

35. St Olave's Church in Exeter, Devon. The present-day church sits on the site of the original structure founded by Gytha on the death of Godwin in 1053.

36. View from Bleadon Hill, Somerset, looking south into the valley of the River Axe, close to the location of the battle of 1068 fought at Bleadon by Harold's sons Godwin, Edmund and Magnus.

illness because of his long journey, while others regard it as dubious and potentially indicating murder. Fatal illness is plausible, but if he had been ill beforehand, it is unlikely he would have agreed to travel. Death from natural causes is the straightforward option, but the timing is extremely coincidental under the circumstances, and the argument for murder remains persuasive. A scribe for the *ASC* supplemented the earlier above entry of 1057 regarding the Exile with an additional eight-line piece after 1066, which cryptically hinted at foul play.[18] That this was added after the Conquest is significant. It perhaps tells us that the chroniclers had either been unwilling to commit this to writing during the previous regime, implying they had delayed their input because they were wary, or had received new knowledge that the Exile did not die from natural causes.

The Danish writer Saxo Grammaticus was to claim that Harold Godwinson had arranged the killing of Edward the Exile, although his sources for that conclusion are imprecise.[19] Several historians have suggested the Exile was poisoned, and a few place Harold Godwinson firmly in the frame. He potentially had the most to lose by the Exile's arrival and the most to gain by his removal.[20] This cannot be argued against; Harold had the motive. Maybe he was considering how things would play out upon King Edward's death and was already reassessing his prospects. Ambiguity remains as to how the exiled ætheling's arrival would impact his standing and that of his family. The Godwinsons may have lost considerable influence when the time would come for Edward the Exile to succeed to the throne. In laying suspicion upon Harold, we come to the question of when he may have first thought of himself as a potential royal successor. Furthermore, can we completely dismiss Queen Edith from the shortlist of possible suspects who might have plotted for the Exile's prompt removal from the equation? If one or more of the Godwinsons was involved, it would suggest Edward the Exile and his offspring were much more of an immediate concern to them than the likelihood of any viable claim to the throne coming from either Normandy or Scandinavia.

Nonetheless, there are some flaws in naming Harold number one suspect. If he did escort Edward the Exile back to England, then why not arrange for his 'accidental' death before crossing the Channel? It would have been suspicious but would have led to less risk of a political backlash in England. In addition, why be involved in the discussions to bring the ætheling back if Harold planned to have him assassinated? It would have been easier to claim negotiations had failed and for Harold to explain to Edward that the plan to return his stepbrother had been thwarted. Lastly, if Harold or his agents did poison the Exile, why allow his son Edgar to survive? Edgar was in England for nearly eight years before King Edward died, and Harold would surely have had opportunities to remove him over that period had he wished.

It has been argued that Harold might have welcomed the initiative to bring back the Exile, as by introducing a new candidate with no existing domestic powerbase he and his brothers could more easily set the framework of the next rule, and use it to their advantage.[21] If that were the case, perhaps Harold had plans to ingratiate himself with the new heir to the throne much like his father had done under Cnut. Some historians therefore argue that Harold may have initially suggested the plan to Edward, and that point may be reinforced by noting it was Ealdred, a close friend of the Godwinsons, who had first been sent to the Continent to find the æthelings, and that Harold had personally led the second, successful search.[22] Ultimately, we can perhaps eliminate Harold as a suspect. He was ambitious, but perhaps too clever to risk any suspicion falling on him which could jeopardise his prospects as they stood in 1056. We should not presume that because he later succeeded to the throne he was already plotting to take it a decade earlier.

Can we look elsewhere for foul play? If Edward had planned to give his stepbrother immediate influence at court, then several other candidates could be named as suspects. As hinted at above, maybe Edith, and perhaps Tostig also, had conspired to ensure the Exile would not establish himself in England. It remains unlikely, but it should not be forgotten that Edith and Tostig were to act together a few years later to assassinate three of his enemies in his earldom of Northumbria. Edith may have thought her influence at court could be threatened by the Exile. Certainly during the period of the return of the Exile and the banishment of Earl Ælfgar she and her senior brothers had already used their almost exclusive proximity to the king to their greatest advantage.

Furthermore, if we work on the premise that Edward had previously offered the throne to William of Normandy, then the Norman duke may be another candidate for wanting the Exile removed. He would have been concerned the English king was now looking to install Ironside's offspring as heir apparent.[23] It is theoretically possible that William was behind it, using his Norman contacts inside England. For William to assert his claim to the throne against Earl Harold when the time came was one thing, but it was another thing entirely to dispute the claims of the legal descendant of the heroic Anglo-Saxon king Edmund Ironside with direct blood ties to the English succession.[24]

Edward the Exile left behind his wife Agatha, his son Edgar and two daughters, Cristina, and Margaret. Edgar was aged six in 1057 and would be effectively adopted by Edward and Edith and looked on as Edward's successor. He appears later as 'Edgar Clito' (*Clito* was the Latin nominative form for ætheling) below the king and queen in an entry in the *Liber Vitae* of the New Minster in Winchester.[25] His sisters were several years older and were given a good convent education in the manner of royal princesses. Post Norman Conquest, Agatha and her daughters fled to Scotland, and as discussed later Margaret would eventually marry the Scottish king Malcolm III, while Cristina became the abbess at Romsey Abbey.

Returning now to the earldoms, Earl Odda, aged over seventy, had abandoned his secular properties to become a monk, but on 31 August 1056 he died and was buried at the abbey at Pershore.[26] Harold Godwinson was given control of his south-west Midlands earldom. A year later Earl Leofric of Mercia also died. The *ASC* recorded his demise on 31 August but John of Worcester dates it to 30 October 1057. John added that Leofric had died at Bromley, which was King's Bromley in Staffordshire and not the Bromley in Kent.[27] Aged in his mid-sixties, Leofric had been the last survivor of the established senior nobility that had ushered England from Anglo-Danish rule back to Anglo-Saxon rule in 1042 on the demise of Harthacnut.

Leofric's body was taken for burial to the monastery at Coventry, a building which he had founded and endowed. His second wife, Godgifu, would survive beyond 1066, but she is better known as Godiva, largely through her legendary ride naked around Coventry as described by the early thirteenth-century writer Roger of Wendover, supposedly done to force her husband to reduce taxation in the settlement.[28] Both Leofric and Godgifu had been generous to the Church. Besides Coventry, they had endowed other religious houses, including Leominster, Much Wenlock, Chester, Stow in Lincolnshire (Lindsey), Worcester and Evesham.[29] Per the *Domesday Book*, Godgifu retained many estates and remained wealthy after her husband's death, much like Gytha's situation after Godwin's death.[30] Leofric's son Ælfgar was to succeed him, but from assessing their ages he was likely the product of his father's first marriage to his unknown first wife rather than Godgifu's son. Finally, following Odda and Leofric, as recorded in the *ASC* for 21 December 1057, the king's nephew Earl Ralph of Mantes also died and was buried at Peterborough.[31] Ralph left behind one child, a boy named Harold, placed into the care of Queen Edith. Some historians have suggested that the boy was named after Harold Godwinson, with whom Ralph is said to have been on good terms.

The earldom of Mercia had already seen its south-western shires redistributed several times over the preceding decade. Ælfgar inherited from his father an earldom which comprised only eight or nine shires, but in the process he would lose East Anglia. The vacuum left behind by the passing of Odda and Ralph, and Ælfgar's appointment to Mercia, allowed or perhaps forced Edward to make further critical decisions. Historians cannot agree on the precise realignment, and there are disagreements over how Ralph's shires were reassigned and some of the other transfers.[32] This is partially explained in that some earls owned significant land in regions which were governed by other earls, and in respect of Gyrth and Leofwine there are no charters to help us confirm precisely when they received their earldoms.

Leofwine took over Ralph's old territories of Hertfordshire and Buckinghamshire, and Gyrth was given East Anglia, which excluded Essex, and possibly Oxfordshire, probably confirmed during Edward's Christmas court. Middlesex could have been handed over to either Harold, Gyrth or Leofwine early in 1058, but changed hands again a year or two later. Likewise, Essex and Bedfordshire were shuffled among the Godwinsons in the same period. Some ambiguity remains, but the holdings of the Godwinson brothers as of mid-1058 can be summed up as below.

Harold	Kent, Sussex, Surrey, Hampshire, Berkshire, Wiltshire, Dorset, Devon, Cornwall, Somerset, Gloucestershire, and Herefordshire
Tostig	Northumbria – comprising Yorkshire, Northumberland, Lincolnshire, Lancashire, and Cumbria (perhaps also Northamptonshire, Huntingdonshire and *Nottinghamshire)
Gyrth	Cambridgeshire, Norfolk, Suffolk, and Bedfordshire (subsequently also **Oxfordshire)
Leofwine	Middlesex, Buckinghamshire, and Hertfordshire (perhaps also ***Essex)

* Tostig held Nottinghamshire by 1060, if not by 1058
** Gyrth held Oxfordshire during Ælfgar's second period of exile and after Ælfgar's death, but possibly first held it at the beginning of 1058
*** Leofwine probably held Essex from 1058, although Harold or Gyrth or both may have had joint responsibility alongside him

The king had limited options. Ralph and Odda had left no suitable heirs, and Siward's surviving son, Waltheof, was still too young to assume any authority. Ælfgar had three sons – Burgheard, Edwin (aka Eadwine) and Morcar – but only Burgheard was mature enough in 1057–58 to be considered for an earldom. The Godwinsons, and we assume Queen Edith also, had likely worked against Burgheard's promotion to their own advantage, thereby fuelling additional resentment in Ælfgar. Little is known about Burgheard except for a journey he made to Rome in 1061 and his death directly after it.[33] Beyond the immediate candidates, Edward was unlikely to promote men such as Ralph the Staller or Robert FitzWimarc, even though they had been at court since the 1040s and had survived the cull of foreigners in 1052–53.[34] Ralph was half-Breton and Robert was Norman, and despite being Edward's trusted men they were never an option when the younger Godwinson brothers were now established enough to take up the roles.

As he had done during 1055, Ælfgar responded badly in 1058 to the latest shire redistribution. He looks to have genuine reasons to feel aggrieved. Whereas he had retained his father's remaining Mercian shires he had not recovered those shires which Mercia had previously lost. Furthermore, Burgheard had been overlooked while the Godwinsons had picked up several more shires between them. They now controlled all the other earldoms across England apart from Ælfgar's reduced Mercian shires. Perhaps, as might be expected, Ælfgar rebelled soon after the reshuffle and was exiled again. It is probably safe to say that he had voiced resentment at the promotions of Gyrth and Leofwine and the transfer of Gloucestershire and Herefordshire to Harold, made in preference to his son Burgheard.

The *ASC* D noted simply that 'here Earl Ælfgar was expelled, but he soon came back again with violence, through the help of Gruffydd'.[35] The scribe writes of this coinciding with the arrival of a raiding ship army from Norway, but complains 'it is too tedious to tell how it all happened'.[36] This record is intriguing, but we are left to guess what took place. John of Worcester refers not merely to Ælfgar joining Gruffydd ap Llywelyn again but of them combining to support a newly arrived Norwegian fleet. A Welsh–Norwegian alliance is supported by another source, the *Annales Cambriae*, which describes a large-scale invasion from the Irish Sea.[37] The Welsh chronicles named the Norse leader as Magnus, but King Magnus I of Norway had died in 1047, so this man's identity is unclear. Many historians accept this was probably Magnus Haraldsson, the heir of Harald Sigurdsson (Hardrada). Hardrada's son would survive to become Magnus II of Norway in the last months of 1066. However, this Magnus was a boy no older than nine or ten by 1058, because Hardrada's marriage to the boy's eventual mother, Tora Torsbergdattar, had only taken place in 1048.

Having allied himself anew with Gruffydd, it was presumably here that Ælfgar gave his only daughter Ealdgyth as wife to the Welsh king.[38] Gruffydd and Ealdgyth would afterwards have a daughter named Nest, but in later years Ealdgyth would marry Harold Godwinson. A political alliance with Gruffydd, who had formerly been king in Gwynedd and Powys but by 1057 had united all of Wales under his kingship, had positive outcomes for Mercia. The Mercian earldom was the first to be affected by any Welsh invasion across Offa's Dyke or Norse–Irish fleet via the rivers Mersey or Dee, so a Welsh alliance gave Ælfgar some assurances that the Welsh king would not raid Mercian territory. The Norse invasion petered out into insignificance, but it is not clear how far Ælfgar and his Welsh allies infiltrated into England on this occasion. Gruffydd may have been unwilling to commit too many of his forces south and eastwards if there remained a potential Norse threat in the Irish Sea. The campaign dissolved more quickly than Ælfgar's earlier rebellion, and within months, although the primary sources are silent, Ælfgar negotiated with Edward and was reinstated to his earldom.

The pardon itself is somewhat surprising, but it presumably was part of the peace deal negotiated to avoid more warfare with Gruffydd ap Llywelyn. Harold, and perhaps Tostig, may already have loomed large in constructing English policies, although the quality of their relationship with Ælfgar remains undisclosed. The events of 1058 suggest that Edward was making a conscious decision to step away from direct responsibility for wider strategy. He may not have planned for this transformation, but his ongoing withdrawal from political life is evidenced in the *Vita Edwardi*. The encomiast noted that 'with the kingdom made safe on all sides by these nobles (i.e. the sons of Godwin) ... Edward passed his life in security and peace'.[39] This follows a theme discussed elsewhere. Evidently the king was happy to delegate. However, it has been argued that rather than concede authority passively Edward had chosen to allow the Godwinsons to build up their wealth and power so that they would take better care of his.[40]

We should now return to the charter witness lists. There is a period of over five years, from the last months of 1053 to the early weeks of 1059, where only one of Edward's charters has survived.[41] This contrasts his first decade, where there are twenty-eight known charters issued between 1043 and 1050, with all but a handful considered genuine. The fall-off in charter production cannot be fully explained, but it may reflect a period of growing political instability caused by the changeover among the earldoms. The period 1053–58 saw the deaths of Godwin, Siward, Leofwine, Odda and Ralph, with more than one major reshuffling of the earldoms necessary. In addition, there had been the exiling of Ælfgar twice, the search for and death of Edward the Exile, plus potential and real invasion threats from Norway, Scotland and Wales. Always under the surface was the question of the succession. After the latest reshuffle, Harold remained the senior secular signatory after Edward. Between 1059 and 1062 there are eight charters, and he signs in first place in all of them. Tostig also signs all of them, the majority immediately below Harold. Gyrth is recorded witnessing six, but perhaps surprisingly Leofwine is seen in only four. The most notable aspect of the documents during this period, however, is the re-emergence of Edith in the witness lists after her restoration as queen, in which she signs just below Edward in most of them.[42]

Wealth meant power, so the family's increasing wealth allowed the Godwinsons to enrich their supporters and draw more thegns into their allegiance, strengthening their respective positions and further adding to their accumulated prosperity. The only suitable data available to us comes from the Domesday survey completed in 1087 and presented in the *Domesday Book*, which lists not simply the landowners as they stood in

1086 but who controlled the various estates, their vassals, and the taxable valuation as assessed prior to the 1066 Conquest. The *Domesday Book* was a fiscal record of the economy, primarily assembled to record the maximum collectable tax, not just the worth or income of the land itself. However, it also served the function of defining who owned what for resolving land disputes.[43] It suggests that Earl Harold held lands valued for tax purposes at £2,846 and his vassals held real estate amounting to £836. The other Godwinson family members held lands valued for tax at £2,341 between them, and their vassals an additional £592.[44]

The family figure was based on the situation in 1066 and refers to the combined revenue of Gytha, Gyrth, Leofwine, Edith and Gunhild but not Tostig. By that date, Tostig's endowments had already passed to the descendants of Ælfgar (Edwin and Morcar). Exact figures are not available, but before 1065, before the removal of Tostig, the inclusion of his estates could have meant the Godwinson family combined held land to the value of £6,000–£6,500. From analysing the *Domesday Book* data for 1066, Edwin and Morcar then owned real estate valued for tax at £2,493, so before Tostig's exiling from Northumbria in 1065 the wealth of Leofric's dynasty was much less significant, probably well under £1,500.[45]

Harold, although he was ultimately Edward's vassal, had become the richest man in the kingdom bar the monarch by 1059–60. More than two-thirds of his wealth was concentrated across Wessex and a further 15 per cent within his former earldom – now Gyrth's earldom – of East Anglia. The rest was divided across several shires, including Herefordshire, Gloucestershire, Yorkshire and Lincolnshire. Nevertheless, his wealth should be placed in context. Edward had more land than Harold, with a taxable valuation estimated at £3,840, although, as can be seen above, the combined wealth of the Godwinsons far exceeded that of the king.[46]

Giving a definitive figure for each Godwinson other than Harold is difficult. Our best estimate is through assessing their landholdings as they are recorded in 1066, although this does not reflect the positions between 1058 and 1062. Gyrth and Leofwine now both held estates beyond the boundaries of their new earldoms. Gyrth, for example, held land in several diverse shires beyond East Anglia including in Bedfordshire, Berkshire, Hampshire, Hertfordshire, and Sussex. However, Gyrth's total landholdings were of a lesser value than Leofwine's. Research of landholder values has estimated that Leofwine owned land valued at about £580 while Gyrth's stood at a relatively modest £250.[47] This probably reflects the variance in prosperity among the shires, not a reflection on their abilities. Furthermore, as mentioned above, 15 per cent of Harold's worth was tied into the East Anglian economy, which took a large sum from Gyrth's earldom. Another comparable estimate as to the distribution of wealth around 1063–64 calculates that Edward and Edith held estates valued at £5,900 and could rely on an annual income of £8,000, while Edwin of Mercia's wealth was estimated at £1,300.[48] Further estimates pre-1065 have concluded that the Godwinson family and their vassals combined held income of £8,400 compared to the Ælfgarsons' revenue of £2,700, and the Godwinson holdings equalled the collective total of the seventy wealthiest thegns in England.[49]

The *Domesday Book* contains several references to Harold taking Church land illegally.[50] A similar claim was produced by the clergy against his father. Claims and counterclaims for ownership of real estate between the monarchy, the nobility and the Church were recurring themes throughout the Middle Ages. In Harold's defence, the accusations are not without some anti-Godwinson sentiment, and during the early Anglo-Norman era it was policy to discredit his regime and reputation. Nine of the claims made against Harold referenced in the *Domesday Book* concern estates in the bishopric of Hereford, but this was from a time when he needed to control the region against Welsh aggression in the mid-1050s.[51] Most records during this period were compiled by Church clerks, who could and at times would rework texts and documents that benefitted the religious houses in which they had a vested interest. The instances of forged or amended primary documents are perhaps more widespread than desired, but dubious accumulation of some estates must have taken place, as in all periods.

As noted elsewhere, Harold, Tostig and Edith, and to a lesser extent Godwin before them, gave generously to several religious foundations. For example, beyond his project at Waltham, Harold was a benefactor to the abbeys at Peterborough, Abingdon and Malmesbury and, alongside Tostig, to Durham Cathedral. Harold was first presented with the estate of the Holy Cross at Waltham during the 1040s following the forfeiture of it by the son of Tovi the Proud, the man who had been present at the death of Harthacnut. Tovi's church was so named because it contained a carving of the crucifixion, the 'Holy Cross', which Tovi had discovered at Montacute in Somerset and had moved to Waltham.

Harold adopted the abbey foundation of Waltham as his own, giving it many gifts including vestments formed of cloth of gold, with gold and jewel adornments and other gold and silver ornaments and furnishings.[52] This displayed his genuine spiritual devotion, a concept whose depth is difficult to comprehend fully today; but adorning his foundation was a way of overtly displaying his obvious wealth to one and all, which was practised by all the secular nobility to a varying degree. The adornments inside the church at Waltham were extensive. Evidence of the values involved came during the 1090s when King William II (Rufus) stripped Waltham of many of its Anglo-Saxon treasures and items worth over £6,000 were removed to Caen in Normandy.[53]

Harold completed a major reconstruction of Waltham Church in stone coupled with a secular college. On 3 May 1060 it was consecrated, with the dedication performed by Archbishop Cynesige of York in the presence of the king and queen. Archbishop Stigand of Canterbury, another family friend, could not perform the ceremony because technically his diocese was vacant. Stigand had never been officially deprived of office by the papacy in 1053 when he was appointed to Canterbury, but he had later declined Pope Leo IX's summons to Rome and had been excommunicated.[54] Successive popes, Victor II and Stephen IX, had followed Leo's edict, and it was not until 1062 and Alexander II's papacy that Stigand's archbishopric was recognised in Rome, although some post-1066 Norman sources, but noticeably not the *Bayeux Tapestry*, would continue to claim he was still uncanonically elected.[55]

Archaeological evidence confirms the Waltham design combined styles from across England incorporating Romanesque features from the Continent. The nave was built from east to west, not west to east, which points to the features in the eastern bays of the nave acting as markers for the original position of the nave.[56] Harold's founding of Waltham as a collegiate church was not a monastic reform and perhaps explains why his work there was largely ignored by many later monastic chroniclers. The abbey church's consecration was one of Cynesige's last important acts because he died on 22 December that year. Ealdred of Worcester, a friend of the Godwinsons, replaced him, and both Harold and Tostig had promoted Ealdred's appointment to York.[57]

The *Vita Haroldi* attributes Harold's devotion to Waltham to having been cured there when praying to the Holy Cross after suffering from a temporary paralysis resulting from one of his Welsh campaigns.[58] The *Waltham Chronicle* later added that Harold would visit Waltham to pray on the way from Stamford Bridge to London in 1066 ahead of the Battle of Hastings.[59] Waltham underwent further reconstruction in the twelfth century, and almost none of the fabric of Harold's church survives today. Norman reconstructions and later medieval work obliterated any surviving Anglo-Saxon sections. However, some original stonework was reused and may survive, particularly at the east end of the present building (the Abbey Church of Waltham Holy Cross and St Lawrence).

In terms of the primary source detail, the second decade of Edward's reign lacks the same coverage as his first. The various *ASC* versions, from which several later chroniclers took their key details, are erratic. *ASC* version A (Winchester) has no entries at all between 1053 and 1066, and F (Canterbury) has none between 1052 and 1057, with only one in 1058, following which version F entries cease. Version C (Abingdon) similarly has no entries between 1057 and 1064, and between the years 1059 and 1062 versions D (Worcester) and E (Peterborough) record ecclesiastic events only. As noted earlier, this coincides with a dearth of royal charters. There are no extant charters from Edward for 1054, merely one the following year, and none during the years 1056–58.[60] Primary source material improves between 1059 and 1064, although excluding likely forged documents there are still only a further eight charters identified. It is likely some documents were deliberately destroyed immediately after the Conquest because those that survive give specific attention to transfers of endowments to the Godwinsons.

The Winchester chronicle (version A) was to record its first entry since 1053 in a brief four-line addition in 1066, but then its only other entry after that came in 1070, before similarly closing its pages permanently. The Abingdon chronicle (version C) resurfaced in 1065, but its last entry closes after recording details of the battle at Stamford Bridge in 1066. The events concerning the subsequent Norman invasion are not entered. That this version of the chronicle would end at this precise moment, literally on the eve of the invasion, seems somewhat perverse. The reduced entries across the diverse versions of the chronicle during this period, and the effective closure of three of the versions (A, C and F) on or just before the Conquest, hints at some form of censorship by the new Norman regime. It is hard to imagine, for example, that the Abingdon scribe would have recorded details of Stamford Bridge but then several days later chosen to end his entries and exclude any reference to the events at Hastings.

EDWARD THE CONFESSOR'S CHARTERS 1054 to1065 – LIST OF SECULAR WITNESSES

CHARTER NO. (SAWYER)	1026	1027	1060	1028	1029	1031	1033	1034	1036	1037A	1038	1040	1041	1042	1059
YEAR	1055	1059	1059	1060	1060	1061	1061	1062	1065	1065	1065	1065	1065	1065	1065
AELFGAR (Earl)		2													
AELFGAR						8	6	15						16	
ASGAR	10	3	6	4		6					5	6		8	
BEORHTRIC	11	6	9			7	5	11	6		5			14	
BONDIG				10			12	9				6	7	10	
EDITH (Queen)	X	X	X	X		X	X	X	X		X		X	X	X
EDWIN (Earl)	4											2	2	5	
GODRIC		12	6										14		
GYRTH (Earl)	3	5	5	4		4	4	5	4		3	3	3	3	
HAROLD (Earl)	1	1	1	1		1	1	1	1		1	1	1	1	1
LEOFWINE (Earl)	4	4	4			6		5	4		4	4		4	
RALPH	5	7	7	3		11	11	8	7		7		8	9	
RODBERT		8	8	12		12	10	7			8		9	7	
SWEARD	10													24	
TOSTIG (Earl)	2	3	2	2	2	2	2	3	2		2		12	2	
WIGOD	2	3	2	3				12						11	

Note 1) Numbers denote the position that individual signed within the witness lists

Note 2) Only individuals that signed a minimum of two charters are listed

Note 3) Edith signed immediately below the king

Note 4) Table compiled from data gathered from Prosopography of Anglo-Saxon England database (www.pase.ac.uk)

12

The Norman Connection

During the early spring of 1061 Tostig, his wife Judith, and Gyrth were part of the secular party that accompanied Archbishop Ealdred and bishops Giso and Walter to Rome to collect their palliums from Pope Nicholas II. Tostig and Judith were likely travelling on pilgrimage. Walter, a native of Lotharingia, had been promoted from his former position as Queen Edith's chaplain. Ealdred's nomination had been supported by Tostig and the earl could help sway the pontiff to smooth through Ealdred's pallium, as Ealdred still held the bishopric at Worcester in plurality alongside his new position. This was potentially problematic, as simultaneously holding the sees of Canterbury and Winchester had proved challenging for Stigand with regard to papal approval. The new bishops, Giso of Wells and Walter of Hereford, needed to receive their consecrations directly from Pope Nicholas because Stigand's position at Canterbury remained ambiguous.

Tostig was received at Rome with honour, being seated next to the pope in the synod convened on Easter Day 15 April.[1] Nicholas II was happy to acknowledge Giso and Walter's appointments, but Ealdred's proved more of a problem and his pallium was refused. The papacy, as feared, was concerned Ealdred had been given York while still retaining Worcester. Furthermore, besides already holding Worcester, Ealdred had also been granted the diocese of Hereford, and had additionally held for a while the dioceses of Ramsbury and Winchcombe.[2] The practice of plurality in England was not uncommon, but it should not have been entirely surprising Ealdred ran into difficulties.

Ealdred, as noted in William of Malmesbury's *Gesta Pontificum*, had hoped to influence Nicholas with coin, by 'having put a case more by money than argument that this had been the custom of his predecessors'.[3] However, to make matters worse the pope not only refused to confirm the appointment but he removed Ealdred's episcopal status, with Malmesbury adding that he 'stripped him of all his honours'.[4]

Earl Tostig remained in Rome, ostensibly to try to induce Nicholas to change his mind on Ealdred, while Judith came back to England with their escort and most of their retinue. However, the pope remained unmoved, and soon afterwards Tostig and Ealdred conceded defeat and began their return journey northwards. When only a few miles from Rome their company were attacked by bandits headed by a local aristocrat who had a grievance against the papacy. The *Vita Edwardi* tells an interesting tale of what took place.[5] Riding at the head of Tostig's company was a Northumbrian noble named Gospatric (aka Cospatric), the third son of Uhtred and his wife Sigen and brother of earls Ealdred and Eadwulf. Edith's *Vita* encomiast omits to explain why Gospatric was in the party, but it seems he had been forced to accompany Tostig's group as a hostage to safeguard him causing potential trouble in Northumbria while the earl was absent. These bandits apparently knew that Tostig was within this group, and hoped to seize money but also to capture the earl and the clerics to use as hostages. The story goes that the bandits did not know Tostig by appearance so asked Gospatric, because of his high-status dress, if he was the earl, and Gospatric confessed he was. The party was robbed and Gospatric taken hostage after purportedly giving Tostig a discreet signal to enable the earl to avoid capture. The party had returned the short distance to Rome after the incident, and Gospatric was later released unharmed when it became evident he was not Tostig.[6]

Back in Rome in a state of distress, the company, having lost purportedly £1,000, were treated with humility by Nicholas. Perversely, the incident worked in Ealdred's favour. Tostig was angry at being robbed within the pontiff's jurisdiction, and William of Malmesbury records that 'Tostig also attacked the pope with harsh, insulting words and got from him the decision he wanted. Tostig said that distant peoples would go in little fear of the pope's excommunication ... for when the king of England heard about this, he would justly refuse to pay Peter's pence to Nicholas, especially as he, Tostig, would not fail to emphasise the truth of the news'.[7] In contrition, Nicholas reversed his decision on Ealdred, verifying his pallium, and gave Tostig's party full recompense to pay for their return travel. Sixteen months later Ealdred would transfer responsibility for Worcester to Bishop Wulfstan.

In England, excluding the difficulty with Malcolm III (Canmore) of the Scots described in the next chapter, the period between 1059 and 1062 was one of relative calm for the Godwinsons. However, having just witnessed along with Harold the appointment of Wulfstan to the bishopric at Worcester on 29 August 1062, their rival Ælfgar of Mercia was to die within the year. His appearance as a witness in a charter of 1065 is therefore a later forgery.[8] Neither the *ASC* nor other writers give details, but he likely died before January 1063.[9] The best evidence to support this can be deduced from looking at the Welsh campaign undertaken by Harold and Tostig in mid-late December 1062, where the offensive was directed against Gruffydd ap Llywelyn, Ælfgar's son-in-law. It is inconceivable Ælfgar would have remained outside events if still alive, and when his death became known Gruffydd had seen it as an opportunity to raid into Mercia with impunity.[10] Similarly the English may have thought the moment was ripe for attacking Gruffydd before he had learnt of Ælfgar's death, which explains Harold's rapid cavalry strike at Rhuddlan over the Christmas season, described below.

Ælfgar was survived by two of his three sons, Edwin and Morcar, perhaps aged about eighteen and sixteen respectively in 1062. He was also survived by his wife Ælfgifu, as she is named in the Domesday survey as holding a handful of estates in Leicestershire and elsewhere in 1066. Burgheard, the eldest son, had, as previously mentioned, died in 1061 and was buried at Rheims, north-east of Paris. It is said he had fallen ill on his way back from Rome, where he had accompanied Bishop Wulfwig of Dorchester-on-Thames in a successful journey to get the bishop's pallium. An alternative scenario for Burgheard's death has been put that he died from wounds received as part of Tostig's company that had been attacked by the bandits near Rome.[11] That Burgheard combined his journey to Rome with the Godwinsons' pilgrimage is plausible, but the vagueness of the primary sources may indicate that his death was not altogether without controversy, affecting the future political bearing between the Godwinsons and the Ælfgarsons. Following Burgheard's demise, Edwin, as the eldest surviving son, was to succeed to the earldom of Mercia soon after his father's death, although just when Edward granted him full authority there is unclear as he does not appear in any contemporary texts until 1065.

Our best authorities on the Welsh winter campaign of 1062/63 are the ASC and John of Worcester.[12] Discussions took place at the king's Christmas court at Gloucester in December 1062, where, with his father-in-law Ælfgar no longer a factor, plans were made to eliminate Gruffydd ap Llywelyn. It was agreed that Harold would conduct a guerrilla cavalry raid to the Welsh king's palace at Rhuddlan, which lay on the River Clwyd in Gwynedd, 3 miles upstream from its estuary on the Irish Sea, the lowest crossing-point on the river. Archaeologists believe Gruffydd's hall lay 300 metres south of the remains of the Plantagenet castle ruins in present-day Rhuddlan, on or near the site of the original Anglo-Saxon burh of Edward the Elder.[13]

The plan was undoubtedly Harold Godwinson's. Another extended Welsh campaign could be avoided if Gruffydd could be removed quickly. The Welsh king would not have expected such a manoeuvre, particularly in winter. Taking 'a small troop of horsemen', perhaps only 50 to 100, Harold left Gloucester 'after midwinter'.[14] Moving swiftly over the 120 or so miles to Rhuddlan, Harold caught Gruffydd generally unprepared. Nevertheless, it seems he had learnt of Harold's approach at the last moment. John of Worcester gives the impression it was a close-run thing: 'Gruffydd, having learned in advance of his approach, took flight with his men, embarked on a ship, and just managed to escape.'[15] As recompense for missing the major prize, Harold burnt down Gruffydd's palace and his remaining ships on the River Clwyd before turning back south the same day. *The Vita Edwardi* gives us a ten-line text devoted to the raid, and it must have been widely renowned at the time.[16] Raiding was not unusual, but deploying a small and fast mounted force to launch a surprise attack over that distance was. As a concept it was likely ahead of its time, and displays Harold's abilities as an accomplished military strategist.

Having just failed to capture Gruffydd with his audacious plan, Harold reverted to tried and trusted methods. As agreed by Edward, Harold and Tostig made plans to act together to destroy Gruffydd's powerbase. Time was taken to prepare a full-blown invasion of Gwynedd and Powys in 1063, probably the largest campaign the English were to conduct into Wales during the eleventh century. Towards the end of May, Harold sailed from Bristol with a large flotilla, rounded the coast at Pembroke and headed north, where he raided all along the coast, forcing the lesser Welsh princes to swear allegiance.[17] Using a naval force was key. Anglesey, the acknowledged granary of Gwynedd and the foundation behind the Welsh king's power, was the first primary target.

A land army had headed north in unison with the fleet, whilst Tostig meanwhile led a Northumbrian–Mercian army into north Wales via Chester. This fyrd was recorded as huge, and included a large cavalry contingent, and the devastation it caused was on a wide scale. The Godwinson brothers then combined forces, and John of Worcester writes they 'met with mounted troops ... and began to lay waste that region'.[18] The Welsh chronicler Gerald of Wales gives tribute to Harold's leadership in organising 'lightly clad infantry' that devastated all Wales, with Gerald himself remembering seeing in the late twelfth century some surviving marker stones that Harold had erected during this campaign inscribed with 'Here Harold was victor'.[19]

Many of Gruffydd's supporters submitted and gave oaths, hostages and tributes. Harold's flotilla was guarding the coastal routes to Ireland, so Gruffydd instead headed into the mountains of Snowdonia. The severity of the offensive was maintained and support for Gruffydd evaporated. On 5 August 1063, he was killed by his own men and 'his head was brought to Harold, and the earl took it to the king', along with the figurehead lifted from Gruffydd's ship.[20] The *Annals of Ulster* named Cynan ap Iago as the chief who brought in the Welsh king's head, but Cynan was not given the kingship. Edward entrusted Welsh affairs instead to Gruffydd's stepbrothers,

Bleddyn ap Cynfyn and Rhiwallon ap Cynfyn, in exchange for oaths and tributes.[21] Gruffydd's widow Ealdgyth, Edwin of Mercia's sister, retired to the Mercian court.

The war benefitted Tostig in other ways. Enough plunder was gathered in Wales and taken back to reputedly satisfy all the thegns of Northumbria, although perhaps Tostig kept most of it for himself; developments in 1064–65 would suggest that the Northumbrian thegns remained deeply dissatisfied.[22] One postscript to this Welsh campaign came in the early thirteenth-century hagiography the *Vita Haroldi*, concerning Harold's health, saying he was suddenly struck down by an attack of paralysis after returning from Wales. When medical remedies failed he instead prayed before the Holy Cross crucifix at Waltham and was restored to perfect health.[23] This story, irrespective of any exaggeration, is useful in demonstrating the ideology of the age and Harold's enduring legacy.

Edward had virtually retired from the decision-making processes of his administration by 1063–64, including all military matters in the Welsh wars, his only contribution being to receive the severed head of Gruffydd when the operation had ended.[24] The extent of his administrative delegation to his senior earls remains open to debate. Queen Edith observed in the *Vita Edwardi* that her husband was now devoting his life to prayer and donating gifts to various religious houses or individual clerics combined with his other pastime of hunting. That Edward hunted confirms he was still active, although his constitution was probably never vigorous. He undoubtedly mellowed as he grew older, and by 1064–65 appears to have been reduced to a figurehead who ratified decisions with little input. There is an element in Edward's character that suggests he found it hard to make decisions. The Norman writers portray him otherwise, but Godwin, and then his sons, appear to have used it to their advantage, as had others.

The assumption is that Edward was happy for the weight of office to be taken from his shoulders, and one historian has aptly observed that during his last years he was reduced to what the French called a *roi fainéant*, translated as a 'do-nothing king'.[25] Harold looks to have been operating as the de facto monarch in everything but title by 1064, if not before. He had emerged as a leader of men and established himself as the king's irreplaceable right-hand man. It was known for some time that Edward and Edith would not produce a royal heir, and as would be seen, the position of Edgar, son of the deceased Edward the Exile, remained unclear. Harold seems to have been well placed to be considered as a potential successor to Edward in due course, although as already mentioned his designs towards the throne remain ambiguous.

In the spring or summer of 1064, Harold Godwinson set out from Bosham, apparently intending to cross the English Channel. From the clue in the *Bayeux Tapestry* scene of Harold leaving his Bosham estate, which portrays the sign of Pisces, his journey began in March.[26] The reasons for his journey continue to attract debate, but William of Malmesbury is the only English source to describe the event.[27] Nonetheless, it is referred to in various detail by five Norman sources, and illustrations relating to the trip are included in the *Bayeux Tapestry*.[28] The tapestry, commissioned by William (the Conqueror's) brother-in-law Odo of Bayeux during the 1070s, illustrates events from a Norman perspective. However, academic opinion favours the belief that the tapestry was woven by English seamstresses in Kent, which post-1066 was under Odo's authority.

The basic timeline, as depicted within the tapestry, begins with Edward seemingly giving some instructions to Harold. This has been interpreted as the king telling the earl to go to Normandy to reconfirm the grant of the English throne to Duke William that Edward had reputedly first offered in 1051, or conversely trying to persuade Harold not to travel to Normandy. William of Poitiers acknowledges the first assertion, recording, 'The truth was that Edward had declared his intention of transmitting the whole kingdom of England to his kinsman William duke of Normandy, first through Robert (Champart) archbishop of Canterbury and afterwards through the same Harold (i.e. in 1064), and had with the consent of the English made him heir to all his rights.'[29] The tapestry then depicts Harold riding to the family estate at Bosham, which would have been held by Harold up until his demise, contrary to the *Domesday Book* (1086) record showing that Edward had granted ownership of it to a Norman, Bishop Osbern of Exeter (Osbern FitzOsbern), pre-1066.[30]

That Harold undertook a journey across the Channel has substance, but the question remains why. The first scenario is that Edward sent him to offer William the throne. The second is that Harold wished to persuade the duke to release his brother Wulfnoth Godwinson, still being detained as a hostage; an action the king may have tried to dissuade Harold from pursuing. As argued by many historians, the idea that Edward had ordered Harold to confirm a promise made thirteen years earlier is one of the least credible claims produced by Norman sources. That supposition ignores the relative power of the monarch and his earls, and Harold's standing by 1064.[31] The concept of the earl travelling to Normandy to offer the English succession to William is therefore bizarre.

Nevertheless, the story gained purchase in Normandy. Wace repeats Edward's pledge to William, but adds, 'I (Wace) do not know which is the correct explanation, but we can find both in writing.'[32] Wace interprets the tapestry scene between Edward and Harold differently, tying it to the Wulfnoth scenario and noting that Edward had warned the earl that 'he could be easily tricked there, for the duke was very astute. If he wished to have his hostages back, he should send other messengers.'[33] Wace tells us Edward refused to give permission and forbade Harold from going to Normandy, an instruction Harold ignored. A plan to barter for Wulfnoth and Hakon's release is plausible; as already argued, they had been kept captive by William since 1051–52. However, why did Harold wait more than ten years to attempt to gain their release, and why decide to act in 1064?

William of Malmesbury suggests Harold's Normandy trip was unforeseen, claiming he had taken ship for another purpose and was 'driven there against his will by the violence of the wind, and to protect himself invented a story', namely the journey to negotiate the release of the hostages.[34] Malmesbury tells us that a storm took Harold's ship along the Channel before being driven ashore 'to the county of Ponthieu', which lay to the north of Normandy.[35] The popular version from Norman sources continues with the earl's party taken captive by Count Guy of Ponthieu and forced to accompany Guy to Abbeville and then on to a place named Beaurain to 'get him (Harold) a long way away from the duke (William)', but through an associate Harold 'sent word to the duke in Normandy to inform him of how things had gone'.[36] Beaurain is 70 miles east of Abbeville, but if we accept a source misspelling, an alternative might be the village of Beaurains near Arras, 45 miles northeast of Abbeville.

Wace continues that 'the duke (William) thought if he held Harold, he would be able to take advantage of this', and 'promised and offered the count (Guy) so much, threatened and entreated him so much that Guy handed Harold over and he took possession of him'.[37] That is not the version other Norman chroniclers provide. William of Poitiers and William of Jumièges portray their Norman duke not as someone taking advantage of the situation but as Harold's saviour, the duke having no other ulterior motive in mind. Harold was passed over to William at the town of Eu, lying on the River Somme between Normandy and Ponthieu. Poitiers tells us that William gave Guy 'lands that were both extensive and rich, and adding great gifts of money besides'.[38] William of Malmesbury calls it a ransom, for which Harold was prepared to reimburse William after being freed from captivity.[39] The gifts were indeed generous if William was operating with no other thought in mind than to free Harold from captivity. However, from later developments, his motives proved less altruistic. William gave Harold use of a manor somewhere alongside the River Eaulne north-east of Rouen.[40]

It is worth being reminded that William of Poitiers wrote his *Gesta Guillelmi* (The Deeds of William) only a handful of years after 1066, but he had been William's chaplain and the *Gesta* portrayed his lord in the best light. This raises questions of reliability, although the case made by some historians is that Poitiers' work, and Jumièges' *Gesta Normannorum Ducum* also, are reliable because they are contemporary. This assertion is fraught with problems. Contemporary does not necessarily equate to greater reliability. Other factors play a part, as touched on in the chapter on primary sources, such as patronage, motivation, ties with other influential individuals or groups, and perhaps most importantly for their works, the direct response from Duke William himself. Wace, in contrast to Poitiers and Jumièges, was writing six decades or more after the Conquest, contemporary with William of Malmesbury, John of Worcester and Henry of Huntingdon. Within his writings in his *Roman de Rou*, he had no reason to follow his earlier compatriots' approved versions that had been contemporary to William.

The benefit to William in arranging the release of Harold, someone he had not previously met, became clear in due course. The contention that Harold's trip was to reconfirm the 'offer' of the throne falls at this juncture, as there is no mention by any of the authorities that Harold then relayed Edward's alleged pledge to the duke after being released. If he had done so, why did Poitiers and others omit to mention it, and why, as will be seen below, did William find it necessary to have Harold additionally pledge the English throne upon hidden sacred relics? The original 'offer' was purportedly from Edward; Harold had no authority to promise the English throne to anyone. Furthermore, if he did, freely or otherwise, it was legally worthless under the English constitution. William of Poitiers noted the duke hoped 'to have him a faithful mediator between himself and the English', but unwittingly perhaps through his chosen words Poitiers is acknowledging that there was no previous agenda for Harold reconfirming the English succession on Edward's behalf.[41]

That Harold was treated with due respect at this point is not questioned. However, weeks later Harold was requested or obliged to accompany Duke William's offensive into Brittany that summer and the duke may have required him to accept vassalage. A scene in the *Bayeux Tapestry* shows Harold rescuing two Norman soldiers from quicksand in the estuary of the River Couesnon near Mont Saint-Michel during this campaign.[42] Harold is said to have gained 'approval both for his character and in the field won the duke's affections'.[43] A display of Harold's bravery was useful for William because if Harold had taken vassalage it reflected well on William. Back at the Norman court, so writes William of Malmesbury, 'to commend himself still more, (Harold) voluntarily confirmed to him (William) on oath at that time the castle of Dover, which was in his fief, and after Edward's death the kingdom of England. For this, he was given the hand of William's daughter, who was not yet of age, and the whole of her inheritance.'[44] Wace names her as Adela, the duke's youngest daughter, but this is not possible because historians place Adela's birth no earlier than 1064 and probably post-1066. The chronicler Orderic Vitalis is likely correct in naming the betrothal was instead for William's eldest daughter Adeliza (aka Adelida), perhaps aged between nine and twelve in 1064, adding that as part of the arrangement William would give Harold half of England.[45]

The Norman sources remained relentless in their attempts to establish the premise that an offer of the English throne had been extended to their duke, reinforcing it further by adding that Harold confirmed William's claim to England upon oath on holy relics. The timing of the famous oath is compounded by comparing the *Bayeux Tapestry* with Poitiers' text. On the tapestry, the Brittany campaign is shown before the oath ceremony; the *Gesta Guillelmi* of Poitiers, meanwhile, has it being given ahead of the campaign.[46] The pledge is repeated by Henry of Huntingdon and Symeon of Durham, and it has become central to the question surrounding the legality and validity of the Norman invasion.[47] The Norman sources provide further detail, as expected, but there are areas of disagreement. Wace says that William convened a council at Bayeux, although the significance of Bayeux only grew after the 1060s and Wace may have named it because of its later twelfth-century contemporary importance to him. Meanwhile Poitiers' *Gesta Guillelmi* names the meeting at Bonneville and Orderic's *Ecclesiastical History* locates it at Rouen.[48] Poitiers is likely to be the more accurate, referring to a castle William of Normandy had at Bonneville-sur-Touques, a few miles inland from the coast at Deauville.

The intention to have Harold swear an oath on holy relics seems to have been well planned. According to Poitiers, William gathered 'the most truthful and distinguished men' to witness the pledge, and Harold 'clearly and of his own free will pronounced these words that as long as he lived he would be the vicar of Duke William in the court of his lord King Edward' and 'he would strive to the utmost with his counsel and his wealth to ensure that the English monarchy should be pledged to him (William) after Edward's death'. Poitiers then adds 'that in the meantime the castle of Dover should be fortified by his (Harold's) care and at his expense for William's knights; likewise, that he would furnish with provisions and garrisons other castles to be fortified in various places chosen by the duke'.[49]

Wace's *Roman de Rou* remains our most detailed primary source on this episode. He delves into the ritual surrounding the oath and the relics that William had prepared, and it is worthwhile quoting his full text. He writes that the duke

> ordered all the holy relics to be assembled in one place, having an entire tub filled with them; then he had them covered with a silk cloth so that Harold neither knew about them nor saw them, nor was it pointed out or explained to him. On top of it he placed a reliquary, the finest he could choose and the most precious he could find. Then he (Harold) solemnly swore and affirmed, according to the text someone dictated to him, that he would take Adela (William's daughter) ... and hand England over to the duke ... When Harold had kissed the relics and

was back on his feet, the duke drew him towards the tub. From the tub, he removed the brocade, which has covered everything, and showed Harold the relics inside, over which he had sworn; Harold felt great fear at the relics which he showed him ...[50]

Taken at face value, this long passage infers that Harold was duped and did not voluntarily make a vow in the knowledge it was on holy artefacts.

For good measure, some primary sources add that Harold also committed his youngest sister Ælfgifu in a future marriage to one of William's senior nobles.[51] The *Bayeux Tapestry* has the image of a woman with the name 'Ælfgifu' embroidered in the scene where William brings Harold to Rouen. This may refer to Harold's sister. The scene depicts a cleric shown slapping the woman, and in the border below there is an explicitly naked male figure. This could infer a sexual impropriety involving this 'Ælfgifu'.[52] We are unable to understand the connotation, but it was one presumably understood by contemporaries. The scene may refer to Ælfgifu of Northampton and the claimed illegitimacy of Harold Harefoot; perhaps it was intended to undermine the Anglo-Scandinavian candidates in comparison to Edward and the links Emma of Normandy had to the English throne.[53]

There is still an argument that Harold never set foot in Normandy in 1064. However, in accepting the premise that Harold was at William's court it is an easy step to then conclude he was held there for longer than planned, which logically leads to the deduction he was held against his will and then coerced into swearing an oath before being permitted to leave. His sojourn to Normandy in 1064 has remained a fascinating episode surrounding the debate on the English succession and the Norman Conquest. The general inference from the Norman sources is that Harold could have freely returned home at any time but had happily remained in Normandy and had then willingly offered the oath William required of him regarding the English throne. This concept is as absurd as it sounds. Harold had been a well-treated guest, but a captive guest nonetheless, one only allowed to leave when it suited William. Wace's storyline is revealing, and within it is an aspect William of Poitiers ignores. Why did the Normans hide the relics? Logic would suggest William knew that Harold would not give a vow freely on holy artefacts, and that was why they were hidden from view.

The outcome of the one-sided encounter between Harold and William in the summer of 1064 has been succinctly described as 'the world of subtle compromise practised by the Godwinsons' encountering 'the crude realities of Norman politics' and losing.[54] From Harold's perspective, he was no doubt prepared to agree to anything to free himself from his predicament, although William could not risk asking Harold to knowingly agree to swear on holy relics. The crux of the matter is that unless Harold swore the oath, he would not be free to leave. Academic discussion should not centre on whether a pledge was sworn, but under what circumstances it was conducted and given. An oath sworn under duress was condemned by the Church, and the validity of any such pledge was not binding. If one was forced to give an oath there was no legal or moral obligation to adhere to it.

William was not afraid to exploit a situation. He may have contemplated holding Harold indefinitely, but that could have led to unpredictable outcomes, both in his relationship with the papacy and the chance of replacing Edward peacefully. It was agreed Harold could return to England with Hakon, Swegn's son, but not his brother Wulfnoth, who was to remain a hostage. William of Poitiers noted that 'the second hostage (Hakon), was, out of respect for his person, released', but omits to mention why Wulfnoth was not.[55] The *Bayeux Tapestry* has a scene involving Harold and William where Harold points to a man that is assumed by his beard and long hair to be an Anglo-Saxon. This could depict Wulfnoth, as Normans are depicted with short hair in the tapestry, and perhaps illustrates Harold requesting William to release his brother.[56]

That the Norman duke was already contemplating a move for the English throne by the summer of 1064 is a plausible theory. Whatever our modern interpretations, he may have genuinely believed he had an entitlement. Normandy had by 1064 safely secured control of the county of Maine and reached an agreement with the region of Anjou to the south. Peace had continued with France, and any serious threat from Brittany in the west had disappeared after the campaign of that year. This was also the period, perhaps a few months earlier during the winter of 1063/64, when William of Normandy had, by controlling Maine, secured the custody of Walter of Mantes. Walter was the brother of the deceased Ralph of Mantes, the second son of Godgifu, and was Edward's nephew. Walter, therefore, had a valid entitlement to be considered for the English throne on Edward's death should he wish to make a claim. Is it coincidental, then, that several months before Harold's visit Walter was killed while in William's custody, reputedly by poison?[57]

The *Bayeux Tapestry* portrays Harold's meeting with Edward on his return.[58] The illustration shows the earl, as recorded by Orderic Vitalis, giving 'an account of his crossing and arrival in Normandy and mission there'.[59] Rather than Edward looking satisfied that Harold had delivered his throne pledge to William, in keeping with the Norman version of events, the tapestry appears instead to show Edward admonishing Harold, as if showing his displeasure that Harold had made the journey. The image of the king and his earl is deliberately nuanced, perhaps contrived by the English seamstresses of the tapestry to portray a meaning undetected by the Normans – namely that Edward had not approved of Harold's journey and had not requested Harold to confirm the English succession to William of Normandy.

How should we view Edward's position in 1064? The evidence is strong that he had for a period hoped to be replaced by Edgar, the heir of Edward the Exile. A commitment giving his approval to William of Normandy seems unlikely. In summarising the events of 1064, William of Poitiers was, as observed by historians, writing a panegyric of his duke, and needed to justify William's actions post-1066.[60] Poitiers used three distinct means to support the Norman claim. The first two, the 1051 promise from Edward to William and Harold's oath of 1064, have been addressed. The third was the blood-ties of William to Emma and hence a link to the throne by that means.

On this point, Poitiers writes, 'If anyone asks the reason for this blood claim, it is well-known that he (Duke William) was related to King Edward by close ties of blood, being the son of Duke Robert, whose aunt, Emma, the sister of Richard II and daughter of Richard I, was Edward's mother.'[61] There was a kinship link, but it was not robust enough to gain the approval of the English Witan. The issue of the English succession in this period needs to be given context. Anglo-Saxon England did not follow the rules of primogeniture as would emerge in later centuries, in which the right of inheritance belonged only to the eldest surviving son or blood relative of the previous monarch. That was a Norman and Plantagenet import. Instead, the English constitution relied on the Anglo-Saxon Witan, the secular and ecclesiastic nobles, and they had the right of veto or consent towards any candidate that presented themselves as a successor to the throne.

There are earlier examples of this, relatively recent, such as their acceptance as king of the Dane Sweyn Forkbeard in 1014 when Æthelred II was still alive and in self-exile, and then again when Cnut succeeded in 1016. The Witan was pragmatic; it would approve the man best suited to consolidate the support of the nobility, preserve the peace, maintain the economy and unite the kingdom. Even if Edward had wished personally for Duke William to be his successor, there is no possibility the English system of selection would have approved such a proposal, not in 1051, 1064 or 1066. Duke William's credentials did not meet the necessary criteria.[62] As suggested elsewhere, the Witan's priority was maintaining stability. As a result, in January 1066 they would again choose a replacement with no kinship tie to his predecessor but someone who promised that stability.

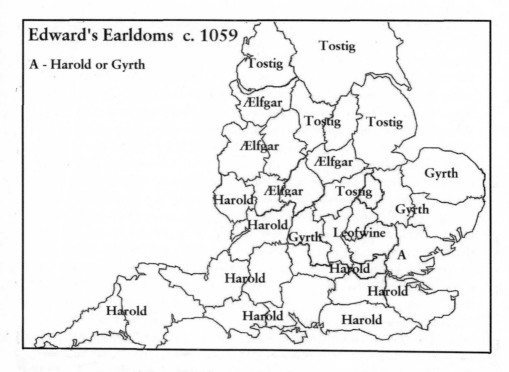

Edward's Earldoms c. 1059

A - Harold or Gyrth

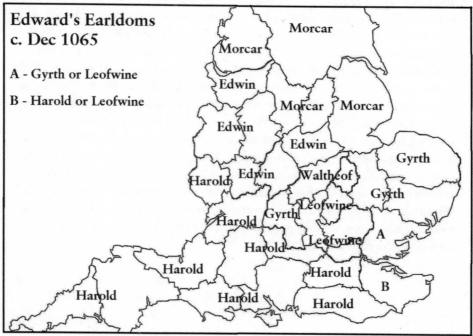

**Edward's Earldoms
c. Dec 1065**

A - Gyrth or Leofwine

B - Harold or Leofwine

13

Harold and Tostig:
A Family Divided

By 1065, Tostig had been Earl of Northumbria for a decade. He is known from later references to have had at least two children, born between 1049 and 1053, but historians are uncertain whether these were from his marriage to Judith or from a previous concubine union.[1] Two boys, Ketil and Skuli, are only referenced after Tostig's death, where they were by then at or near their age of maturity. They have Scandinavian names, but not ones that link them to their grandmother Gytha's background, and had they been Judith's children it is reasonable perhaps to expect them to have been named differently. The *Vita Edwardi* refers to Tostig having at least one more unnamed child described as 'unweaned', born several months before Tostig's death. This child may have died as an infant. Judith is known to have produced three children after 1071 while over the age of thirty-eight from the marriage to her second husband, Welf I of Bavaria.

Tostig's popularity in Northumbria waned after 1061–62. There was likely a gradual mounting discontent, and on Tostig's part perhaps an overconfidence developed from several years of relatively peaceful control. Resentment had likely grown among the mixed Anglo-Scandinavian population against the policies Tostig had pursued on behalf of Edward, the economic and judicial practices that were then in operation further south. Perhaps Tostig's response to Northumbrian disaffection had been to enforce Edward's rules even more strongly, which rather than resolving issues added to the unrest.

He had addressed the separate major concern of lawlessness and had brought in much stricter measures which reduced the incidences of banditry and general disorder. On the face of it, this is to be praised, but even in upholding the law there was a regional problem in Northumbria. Greater enforcement affected the established codes of 'blood-feud' among the various noble factions, a feature of Northumbrian dynastic rivalries since before the ninth century, and a principle more prevalent in the north than in the other regions. Blood-feud was outside of the law and bypassed the existing system of *wergild*, a code of honour and revenge whereby if a kinsman from one faction was killed by another there was a duty to avenge the killing rather than invoke *wergild*.[2]

Nevertheless, several issues – and three in particular – seem to have contributed to a deterioration of Tostig's overall position. The first concerned his protection of Northumbrian-controlled Cumbria and the northern border with Scotland (Alba). In 1058, Malcolm III ('Canmore', i.e. Great Chief) succeeded to the Scottish throne and the following year Edward invited him for talks at Gloucester. He was escorted south by Tostig, along with Archbishop Cynesige of York and Bishop Æthelwine of Durham.[3] At Gloucester, Edward proposed a marriage alliance between Malcolm and Margaret, the thirteen-year-old daughter of the deceased Edward the Exile. Tostig's hand was probably behind this plan, a political arrangement to avert warfare with the Scots. The *Vita Edwardi* scribe noted that Tostig defeated Scottish pressure more by cunning diplomacy than by war.[4] However, the wedding did not proceed and Malcolm later married Ingibiorg Finnsdottir, the widow of Earl Thorfinn Sigurdsson of Orkney and niece of Harald Sigurdsson (Hardrada). Ironically, perhaps, Malcolm would marry Margaret in 1069–70 after Ingibiorg's death.[5]

In 1060–61, while Tostig was undertaking the journey to Rome described in the previous chapter, Malcolm sought to recover territory in Cumbria and north of the River Tweed that had fallen back under Northumbrian control after Earl Siward's campaign of 1054.[6] A Scots army raided into Bernician Northumbria, pillaging the monastery at Lindisfarne and as far as Durham before withdrawing. On his return from Rome Tostig took no reprisal, a sign to the Bernician Northumbrians perhaps that he was not tied to the preservation of the land or the people in the manner of his predecessor Siward. As would be observed, there was a friendship between Tostig and Malcolm, and it was feasibly through Malcolm and Ingibiorg that Tostig would contact the Norwegian king Harald Hardrada during the events of 1066.

The second issue developed in 1063 and concerned further increases in taxation, seemingly a consequence of paying for Edward's Welsh wars, which Tostig had conducted alongside Harold. Tostig may have moved clumsily, although in fairness to him these tax rises were perhaps long overdue. What he was trying to enforce, through one arm of his administration, was a change to bring Northumbrian taxes in line with those imposed elsewhere. The Northumbrian nobility and their vassals had become accustomed to paying low taxes. Both Deira (south of the Tees) and Bernicia (north of the Tees) brought in a much lower rate compared to the other regions, and unlike the south, tax rates had not been assessed on land values per hide or per carucate calculated on soil fertility and production.[7] Tostig was effectively attempting to push the local contribution rate nearer to the 'national' average, but there were vast differences to balance. Even a local increase of 50 per cent would bring the rate to just under a quarter of that paid further south.[8] This attempt to rebalance the economy aggravated those Northumbrian nobles whose support he needed. In simple terms, the Northumbrians did not appreciate paying for the costs of a Welsh war when there was a border with Scotland to defend, especially as Tostig did not seem interested in defending it.

Furthermore, Tostig had failed to distribute fairly the loot pillaged from Wales. Unlike Harold in Wessex, Tostig could not recruit enough levies in his earldom, and to fight in Wales he had recruited Danish or Anglo-Danish warrior mercenaries. These did not come cheap. Two-thirds of revenue went to the royal treasury, but Tostig was entitled to keep a third of the raised tax for his own purposes, and he used it to employ more professional housecarls (huscarls) for his retinue in York rather than use the funds to help defend the northern borders.[9] His behaviour perhaps differed little from that of the earls further south, but the situation in Northumbria had become more volatile and required more tact and delicacy.

The third issue can be identified as a specific incident, which was a direct consequence of the first two. Tostig was not as skilled at diplomacy as Harold. His relationship with his senior nobles had probably already deteriorated, but this incident tipped the balance over the winter of 1063/64 and points towards the problems that lay ahead. Apparently showing a willingness to compromise and discuss the concerns of the discontented nobility, Tostig summoned two leaders of this growing faction, the thegns Gamal, son of Orm, and Ulf, son of Dolfin, to a meeting to discuss their grievances and the newly imposed tax increases.[10] However, he had already decided that rather than listen to their objections he would dispose of them instead and use their fate as a demonstration of his authority. As soon as they arrived at York under his assurance of safe passage and safe-conduct, Tostig had them assassinated.

Gamal and Ulf are Scandinavian names, and their kin were likely associated with the group that had originally arrived with Cnut and later connected to Siward. Some speculation is possible in trying to identify them further. A Scandinavian thegn named Orm Gamalson, the man identified with the inscription at St Gregory's Minster in Kirkdale mentioned previously, had married Æthelthryth, the daughter of Ealdred, the former ruler of Northumbria between the early 1020s and 1038.[11] Gamal is thought to be the child of Orm and Æthelthryth, which made Gamal a kinsman of the previous Northumbrian regime. Tracing the identity of Ulf is more difficult. He was conceivably the descendant of the Dolfin who had been allied to Siward and killed at Dunsinane in 1054. There is an Ulf, perhaps a brother, associated with a Dolfin, the heir of a Gospatric (aka Cospatric).[12] This Gospatric would thereafter become Earl of Northumbria in 1067 under Norman rule. He was the grandson of Uhtred and his wife Ælfgifu, who was a daughter of Æthelred II (the Unready), so if Ulf was related to this Gospatric, he had a blood tie to the former Anglo-Saxon line.

There is another Gospatric: the man who had been in Tostig's party that went to Rome during 1061. Being of a similar age to Tostig, he was unlikely to be Ulf's father, but this Gospatric, son of Uhtred and his second wife Sigen, was to experience the same fate as Gamal and Ulf. During the Christmas festivities of 1064, he was likewise assassinated by Tostig or his agents. However, Edith has also been connected to Gospatric's murder. John of Worcester claims that the assassination was 'a disgraceful death ... whom Queen Edith, on account of her brother Tostig, had ordered to be killed in the king's court on the fourth night of Christmas by treachery'.[13] Edith's involvement in this incident should be taken seriously. She and Tostig are understood to have been close, and that she acted in her favoured brother's best interests with or without her husband's knowledge is credible. The murders of Gamal, Ulf and Gospatric avoided a resurgence of the old Northumbrian regime in Bernicia, but the potential repercussions were ignored. The assassinations had proved to those who wished to challenge his policies that Tostig was not prepared to compromise. Henceforth, the dissatisfied factions would made plans to remove him.

Primary sources tell us little to nothing of the rapport between the Godwinson brothers, not only between Harold and Tostig but likewise their relationships with their other siblings. The family had held together during the emergency of 1051–52, but Harold's reaction to Swegn's exiling and his refusal to return the shires he had gained when Swegn was pardoned tells us two things: first, kinship did not override Harold's ambitions; second, he may have led by example, demonstrating that his brother should not benefit from his wrongdoings.

As already examined, Edith and Tostig seem to have been close, and this is implied in the *Vita Edwardi*. For other personal relationships we are left with supposition. That Leofwine accompanied Harold and not his father when the household were exiled in 1051 suggests Harold may have taken his much younger brother under his wing. Gyrth, with perhaps only a three- or four-year age difference to Tostig, may have been on better terms with him than he was with Harold. The fresh crisis that would hit the Godwinsons in 1065 is often viewed as a conflict between Tostig and Harold, perhaps rightly so, but there is the lack of evidence as to how their brothers reacted to the situation. Ultimately, they would support Harold, but their sympathies may have rested with Tostig.

Assessing the relationship between Harold and Tostig is interesting because of their later decisive dispute. However, unlike their other sibling relationships we have the advantage of detail Edith provided in the *Vita Edwardi*.[14] Being their sister, she is a reliable source and gives an insight not found elsewhere. Edith describes their qualities and differences. Tostig was driven by the need to succeed but was seemingly more temperamental, more secretive than Harold and more inflexible. While both brothers persevered in any course of action, Tostig did so energetically while Harold acted more prudently. She adds that for Tostig success was his overriding aim, while Harold aspired to happiness, which seems at odds with our perception of Harold.[15] Edith further tells us that Tostig always kept his word and compared to Harold was more generous to the Church. He was also faithful to his wife, and clean mouthed. This could be construed as a serious comment on Harold's morals.

Other evidence shows Harold to be equally devout in his religious beliefs, more intelligent than Tostig, less rash and more prone to consider his movements, but more secretive and moodier. Both men could disguise their intentions. The *Vita* adds that they had in common good looks, physical strength, courage, and ability in war. Both were serious and responsible, and never inept or foolhardy. Tostig was more energetic and compulsive than Harold, but Edith rated Harold's abilities and character higher than Tostig's. Physically, Harold was the taller, although exactly how tall is unknown, and he had the greater physical stamina and what has been described as a 'sunnier temperament'.[16] These traits and qualities contain a great deal at variance, but in essence, Harold seems to come across as more easygoing, the more likeable and friendlier of the two. Edith's input on Tostig perhaps hints that his temperament was more akin to her own if we evaluate her relationship with Edward. This may imply Edith and Tostig were more open with each other than with their fellow siblings, and if brother and sister were close Tostig likely had a better insight into her difficulties with her husband. From her perspective, she was probably empathetic to the difficulties Tostig had encountered in Northumbria compared to the easier task Harold likely had in slotting into Godwin's old Wessex earldom.

Edith says little about her other siblings. Her views on Swegn are forthright, and justifiably so, but in contrast we discover nothing about Gyrth or Leofwine or her views on Wulfnoth's imprisonment in Normandy. This oversight about Wulfnoth can perhaps be focused down to the political situation she found herself in after 1066 when completing the *Vita*. However, that she failed to throw some light on the personalities of Gyrth and Leofwine is disappointing. She is not alone in this among the sources. For two men that held such power in the last days of Anglo-Saxon rule, they are almost seen as inconsequential within the primary texts. In reality, the opposite was assuredly the case. From our knowledge of the power of personality displayed by their brothers, and equally that of their parents, it is hard to imagine that Gyrth and Leofwine were not cast from the same mould and matured along similar lines – Swegn excepted – to their siblings.

The assassinations in Northumbria ordered by Tostig, seemingly with Edith's knowledge if not active participation, as discussed earlier, may have opened differences between them and their other siblings, but particularly with Harold. When the facts became known perhaps Harold was aggrieved that Tostig had not thought out the long-term consequences of his actions, although we should be reminded, as Edith had written in the *Vita*, that Tostig was more temperamental, compulsive and secretive.[17] The manner of the assassinations, which took place under assurances of safe conduct, could have broken the accord Harold hitherto had with Tostig. This could have been something that played a factor when Harold was called upon to respond to the Northumbrian rebellion against his brother. From our knowledge of him at moments of crisis, Harold can be assessed as more like Godwin than Tostig, seeking a diplomatic solution first before resorting to alternate courses of action. However, playing devil's advocate, maybe Harold welcomed the opportunity to marginalise his brother in the autumn of 1065 if he saw Tostig as a rival for the throne.[18] Tostig was by all accounts on friendlier terms with Edward, and by that stage Harold may have been vigorously pursuing his own agenda for the succession.

The *Vita* refers to an incident when Harold and Tostig were boys. When playing a game in front of their father, 'so hotly do they play that both are made very angry', and 'one (Harold) the other gives such a blow that it strikes him (Tostig) down there and quite stuns him'.[19] Harold was a few years older, but this episode may be symbolic of their competitiveness. If true, it could support a rivalry that persisted throughout their lives. The writer Aelred (aka Ailred) of Rievaulx recorded a more aggressive disagreement in his *Life of Saint Edward*. When still boys they undertook a wrestling match at the royal court but matters got out of hand. Harold, being the elder and stronger of the two, dragged Tostig to the floor by his hair and began to throttle him before being pulled away, although Aelred adds that Godwin claimed it was only a game.[20] These entries in the *Vita* and *Life of Saint Edward* have so much in common that they may be different versions of the same incident.

Henry of Huntingdon's *Historia Anglorum* refers to a later episode in 1063 which is worth noting. Henry writes that 'in the king's presence in the royal hall at Windsor, as his brother Harold was serving wine to the king, Tosti (Tostig) grabbed him by the hair. For Tosti nourished a burning jealousy and hatred because although he was the first born, his brother was higher in the king's affection. So, driven by a surge of rage, he was unable to check his hand from his brother's head.'[21] We are required to believe here that the brothers, aged either side of forty, were fighting in the king's court, which makes the venue implausible if not the incident. Henry has erred in naming Tostig as the elder of the two. However, his next entry takes the story into fantasy, presumably aimed at exciting his readers, when adding, 'So Tosti, departing in anger from the king and from his brother, went to Hereford, where his brother had prepared an enormous royal banquet. In which place he (Tostig) dismembered all his brother's servants, and put a human leg, head, or arm into each vessel for wine, mead, ale, spiced wine, marat (wine with mulberry juice), and cider.'[22]

If taken at face value, this was effectively a psychotic episode beyond Swegn Godwinson's worst actions and is clearly absurd. Entertaining as this may have been for a certain twelfth-century readership, this extract reminds us that the primary sources do occasionally move beyond realistic narrative. Nevertheless, perhaps the kernel of the story originated from a minor incident between the brothers that grew into something far removed from the original episode. The entry perhaps reflects the national mood at the time Henry was writing. Parts of twelfth-century England may have seen Tostig as the man most responsible for England being under Norman domination, resentful of a regime which by the period Henry was writing had subverted the vast majority of the old Anglo-Saxon population to a reduced sub-status within society.

It would seem Edward, and the Godwinsons in general, based on their known activity, were unaware of the impending storm brewing in Northumbria in the summer of 1065 and ignorant of the weight that Earl Edwin of Mercia was to bring behind the uprising there when it came. In June and July 1065, Harold's attention was put towards building a hunting lodge south of Chepstow, a region recently seized from the Welsh, with the *ASC* noting it was established before Lammas (1 August) at Portskewett.[23] It lay about half a mile from the River Severn, accessed in the eleventh century by a small inlet. Harold's original lodge was west of present-day Sudbrook Road, the area now called 'Harold's Park' near the Church of St Mary, a mile north of the Prince of Wales Bridge where the M4 motorway crosses the Severn. Recent archaeology has identified later structures erected on this site. Harold planned to invite the king there on a hunting trip in September, as Edward had often hunted in the nearby Forest of Dean close to his favoured residence of Gloucester. However, on 24 August, before the lodge was ready, it was looted, and the workforce killed by Caradog ap Gruffydd, the heir of Gruffydd ap Rhydderch, the former king of Gwent and Deheubarth.[24]

Alternative arrangements were prepared for Edward to continue hunting at his estate at Britford in Wiltshire. Harold was likely active in responding to the Welsh assault, so the king invited Tostig to travel south to join him. Britford was 3 miles south-east of Old Sarum and less than 2 miles from present-day Salisbury. There has been no positive archaeology to locate the site of the original Anglo-Saxon manor, although it was possibly on the east side of the village near the River Avon, close to where the Church of St Peter now stands. While Tostig was at Britford news came on 3 October of an uprising in Northumbria. The Northumbrian thegns Gamelbearn, Dunstan, son of Æthelnoth, and Glonieorn, son of Heardwulf, had entered York with a 200-strong warband and slaughtered all Tostig's supporters and any housecarls still in the city.[25] None of these thegns appear in charters prior to this, but Gamelbearn by name association was undoubtedly related to the thegn Gamal whom Tostig had previously assassinated. Furthermore, research into the three ringleaders recognises how they would have been affected by Tostig's recent tax rises, with each of them paying an extra 50 per cent above their previous tax amount.[26]

William of Malmesbury later assumed that Tostig had been in York when the rebellion began but had escaped, writing that the insurgents were 'not liking to kill him out of respect for his earldom'.[27] However, as noted above, Malmesbury was wrong: Tostig was in Wiltshire, not York.[28] The ringleaders had chosen their moment to enter York knowing their earl was in the south. The timing in early October was also relevant. The latest round of tax collecting had been imposed after the recent harvest, which meant that the monies collected by Tostig's reeves were still lying in the treasury at York, with the rebels duly seizing all the gold and silver within it. The thegn Copsig, acting as Tostig's deputy, managed to escape and made his way to Orkney. Only Tostig's supporters were targeted, and the citizens of York welcomed the rebels, with the *ASC* recording that 200 men from Tostig's court were wiped out, English and Danish alike, after making a futile stand on the banks of the River Ouse.[29] The sources highlight that the Danish housecarls Amund and Reavenswart, presumably specifically named because they were close retainers to Tostig, were captured beyond the city walls of York and slain by the rebel thegns,

The Northumbrians declared Tostig an outlaw. However, the rebels had a clear objective and an immediate replacement as earl had been selected ahead of the assault. He was Morcar, the compromise candidate. As Edwin of Mercia's younger sibling, Morcar's appointment gave the Ælfgarsons between them control of the west and central Midlands and the north.

Why a Northumbrian-born candidate was not proffered acknowledges a prior agreement with Edwin, and that a compromise unity candidate had already been decided upon. Native candidates had been available, including Gospatric, the grandson of Uhtred of Bernicia mentioned previously, plus Oswulf (aka Osulf), the heir of the former earl, Eadwulf, and likewise Siward's young son Waltheof.[31] Waltheof was perhaps the most entitled of these three, although still quite young, but the key fact that worked against them was that Morcar was Edwin's brother, and support for the Northumbrian rebellion from Mercia was only assured if Morcar was adopted as earl to replace Tostig. This was the deciding factor. To ensure there were no divisions, Oswulf was later given authority in Bamburgh while Morcar based himself in York. Edwin and Morcar's mother is unknown. However, it has been speculated that she may have been named Ælfgifu, a common name, and had connections going back to Earl Ælfhelm of Northumbria three generations earlier.[30] If true, this would give both Edwin and Morcar a northern connection, and the name of 'Morcar' itself is traceable to Northumbrian roots.

On the news of the insurgency, the king summoned his council to gather at Britford. William of Malmesbury notes that it had 'angered the king, who was much attached to Tostig; but he was handicapped by illness and burdened with old age, and had almost become an object of contempt already, so that he could do nothing for his favourite'.[32] This is not entirely accurate. Edward's health up to this point had been vigorous enough for him to continue hunting, hence why he was at Britford with Tostig. The king had attempted to rule the north through his selected appointee, and it had worked satisfactorily to all intents and purposes under Tostig for nearly a decade, but ultimately the northern earldom had failed to align itself. The wrong move at this point risked the possibility that Northumbria could break away from the English kingdom and its southern administration with immediate effect. Of equal importance was the probability that if Northumbria claimed independence Edwin's Mercia would follow.

The northern rebels meanwhile assembled their forces and headed south, Morcar gathering men from Nottinghamshire, Derbyshire and Lincolnshire. At Northampton, he was met by his brother at the head of a large Mercian fyrd, including additional Welsh levies.[33] Northamptonshire had been assigned to the Northumbrian earldom during Siward's time and had transferred to Tostig when he assumed his earldom. The shire therefore held some political symbolic significance to the rebels, and the Ælfgarsons had chosen it not only as the place to combine their forces but to pillage because it still came under Tostig's jurisdiction.

The meeting at Britford had concluded that Harold should meet Edwin and Morcar for negotiations. Presumably Tostig had wanted to accompany his brother but was persuaded to remain at the king's court to avoid potential confrontation. Edward initially offered to give the rebels legal redress if their case was proven, but reconciliation was to be refused. He may have initially underestimated the situation. Nonetheless, Tostig wanted immediate retribution against the rebels, and the king had the choice of trying to restore Tostig to Northumbria by force or accepting Morcar as the new earl. A plan was formed, but a military response was not the favoured option.

For those nobles within the Witan based across the south and East Anglia, Northumbria was not worth a fight.

Harold was instructed to reach a compromise, but the insurgents refused to negotiate on Edward's terms. William of Malmesbury says that 'the Northumbrians ... were conciliatory, and defended what they had done before him, maintaining that, being born and bred as free men, they could not brook harsh treatment from any superior; "If you wish to keep us in subjection ... set Morcar son of Ælfgar over us, and you will find ... how mildly we have learnt to obey, if we are mildly treated."'[34] Harold, preferring to take lengths to avert civil war, returned to Edward with their message, but there was no immediate consensus on the next move.

Another Witan council was held at Oxford on the eve of the feast of the apostles Simon and Jude, 27 October.[35] This second council seems to have moved decisively against attempts to restore Tostig and to have gone further in appeasing the rebels to evade a larger conflict. Harold may have initially supported his brother but had already readjusted his stance after having met the rebels. Interestingly, none of the sources mention the involvement of Gyrth and Leofwine or their stance in support or otherwise of Tostig in these discussions, although they held large earldoms of their own. Likewise, Edith's opinion is hidden from us, but we can speculate she had tried to influence her husband in support of Tostig to take up arms against Edwin and Morcar when other options to restore him had failed. The *Vita* implies that the king wished at first to crush the insurgents by force and was vexed by having conceded to their demands.[36] Edith likely expected Harold to support Tostig, but the interaction that took place between the Godwinson siblings is hidden from us. Edward's decision, based on the Witan's majority opinion, was to concede to the demands of Edwin and Morcar and agree to the latter replacing Tostig as Earl of Northumbria.

Edward had little choice if he wanted to avoid bloodshed, and his priority was to ensure the kingdom remained united. Reports had already been received that the rebels had done 'great harm around Northampton' and 'did not spare that district, burning, and plundering and killing'.[37] John of Worcester notes, 'While Harold and very many others wished to make peace between Earl Tostig and them, all unanimously spoke against it and they outlawed him and all who had encouraged him to establish his iniquitous rule.'[38] Many believed Tostig had brought matters down on himself. The *ASC* version C tells us that 'Earl Harold ... wanted to work their (Tostig and the Northumbrians) reconciliation if he could, but he could not'.[39] The sources are difficult to interpret, but we can imagine Tostig's was angered they had failed to support his immediate restoration. His foremost vitriol was directed not towards the monarch but reserved for Harold, whom he believed had betrayed him. Tostig had expected them both to support him, but Harold above all else. The *Vita Edwardi* records that there were angry scenes at the council meeting, with some blaming Tostig and Tostig blaming Harold for artfully instigating the revolt.[40] From here matters quickly moved against Tostig, and he was outlawed, perhaps after unproven accusations either against the king or his brother or both.

In fairness to Harold, his ability to overturn the Witan council was restricted. However, if he had recommended the king accept the rebels' terms, which equated to Tostig's removal, Tostig's response is easily explained. There would otherwise be no justification for Tostig's deep bitterness towards Harold and the course of action he later took. Perhaps we can speculate Harold used the situation cynically to increase his importance at his brother's expense. It has been contended that the marginalisation of the Ælfgarsons (first Ælfgar, then Edwin and Morcar) in relative terms to the Godwinsons since 1057–58 could have heightened the personal rivalry between Harold and Tostig.[41] The question of Edward's successor had become more pressing as time passed. Could it be that Harold saw his brother as his most dangerous rival when it came to Edward nominating a successor, particularly as the king appeared more favoured towards Tostig? Furthermore, was Harold playing a longer game, ensuring that by negotiating favourably with the Ælfgarsons he was already envisaging them being useful allies for him in the succession debate when it came?

That there was a potential pact established by Harold with Edwin and Morcar in October 1065 cannot be dismissed. He was soon to marry their sister Ealdgyth, the widow of the Welsh king Gruffydd ap Llywelyn. The merger was not enacted until Harold had taken the English throne, as he would do in January 1066, but the arrangement could have been agreed during the earlier negotiations. Perhaps it had been a stipulation from the Ælfgarsons that was non-negotiable, and Harold had committed to it as part of a pragmatic compromise to reach a peaceful conclusion on behalf of the king. It may have suited Harold to keep such an arrangement to himself, but if he had announced at Edward's council that the betrothal was part of her brothers' peace terms for Tostig's removal it is perhaps not surprising Tostig saw it as betrayal and part of a premeditated plan to remove him.

Morcar was acknowledged and granted the earldom of Northumbria, and Harold gave the king's hand on it back at Northampton and renewed the laws of Cnut.[42] This acknowledgement towards Cnut's laws confirms that Tostig had previously introduced West Saxon law as part of the plan to integrate Northumbria more fully with the rest of the kingdom. This renewal was significant because it reiterated the accord struck at Oxford in 1018–19 whereby Cnut had reconfirmed the laws of King Edgar, wherein both English and Danes were to be treated equally. That arrangement had formed the basis for an Anglo-Danish settlement, so by renewing these laws it was acknowledging that there would be no reprisals against Morcar, and that Northumbria remained as before within the greater kingdom of England.

It is entirely feasible to argue that the combined earldoms of Harold, Gyrth and Leofwine and their vassals could have mustered a substantial army to eventually overcome Edwin and Morcar. However, the outcome for England would have been disastrous, even if the northern earls had been heavily defeated militarily. Once a civil war had been started, the chances of the kingdom uniting again within several years or longer would look remote and the impact on the economy and society considerable. This point has been largely overlooked because of the calamitous events that befell Anglo-Saxon England in 1066, but it should be recognised that the decision to agree to the insurgents' ultimatum at the expense of Tostig was at that stage the rational conclusion agreed by most of the nobility. There were much greater risks that the north would be lost and separated permanently if a compromise had not been realized.

Electing to remove Tostig did not by itself justify his immediate exile. He had not committed obvious or earlier wrongdoings against the king. Perhaps, as noted above, a loss of temper at court with Edward or Harold finally forced the king into pronouncing him an outlaw. Edward could not permit his court to become the setting for an ongoing family feud that would damage his rule. Given time to leave, and reminiscent of the journey made by the Godwinsons fourteen years earlier, Tostig and Judith sailed for Flanders in December 1065, where they were later treated generously, settling at Saint-Omer over the winter of 1065/56.[43] There had been a long-standing alliance between Wessex and Flanders, and blood ties too, because Count Baldwin V was Judith's half-brother. Judith had been Baldwin IVs offspring from his second marriage, to Eleanor of Normandy, and Eleanor was the sister of Duke Robert I of Normandy, the father of the incumbent William of Normandy (soon to be the Conqueror).[44] Baldwin V's daughter Matilda had married Duke William of Normandy during 1051–52. This combination of associations meant that, through his wife, Tostig was linked two ways to Duke William of Normandy, the future Conqueror, firstly through Judith's mother Eleanor and secondly through Judith's niece Matilda.

In terms of the immediate stability of England and its power structures, Tostig's removal was a manageable problem, much more so than the fallout from a civil war. The country was accustomed to dealing with the exiling of important individuals. Nevertheless, the decisions generated in the autumn of 1065 had profound connotations which no one had foreseen. Following Tostig's exiling Edward and Harold, perhaps with the support of Gyrth and Leofwine Godwinson, may have envisaged holding out an olive branch to him. However, none of them, Edith included, expected or anticipated the bitterness recent events engendered in Tostig, least of all Harold, the chief object of Tostig's gnawing resentment. His anger would provide the fuse that would blow the Anglo-Saxon kingdom apart in less than twelve months.

14

Harold Godwinson, King of England

Within ten weeks of Tostig's banishment, in the early days of January 1066, King Edward was dead. His father Æthelred II the Unready had ruled ten years longer, but Edward, aged just over sixty, was in terms of longevity of age the oldest king that England had seen since Offa of Mercia (before the unification of the kingdoms) in the second half of the eighth century. There was a rapid deterioration in the king's health from early November, and it can be speculated that the stress of the previous months had affected him beyond repair. He does not fit the stereotype for a monarch of the period, being more comfortable at court or chapel than out conducting itinerant visits across his realm or leading his armies. From that perspective, he was the opposite of most of the Anglo-Saxon kings who had gone before him. As recently as September, Edward appears to have been in robust health. One of his favourite pastimes was hunting and he was enjoying that activity when word of the Northumbrian rebellion had reached him. Likely brought on by the subsequent political crisis, Edward's condition declined rapidly in mid-December, and it is suggested he may have suffered a series of mild strokes.[1]

By this stage seriously ill, Edward had stayed at Westminster for the 1065 Christmas festivities rather than hold his customary seasonal court at Gloucester. Ostensibly, his decision to remain at Westminster was to oversee and attend the consecration of his long-term project, the rebuilt and extended St Peter's Abbey in stone. Construction work on the church had begun in 1045, laid out with a nave comprising twelve bays and a lantern tower over the crossing.[2] However, by December 1065 the final stages of the building work were still being undertaken. The eastern end, the transepts, the nave, the chapterhouse, and most of the cloisters had been finished; and one later source noted that only the vestibule/porch remained outstanding.[3] Nevertheless, the supposition is that other parts required final embellishment and much of the scaffolding had yet to be removed, and overall the building was still a few weeks away from full completion.

Edward attended the Christmas Day service and banquet, but this seems to have drained him and he spent Boxing Day in his chamber. The decision was made to bring the consecration ceremony for the abbey forward to 28 December (Holy Innocent's Day) because of Edward's declining strength. William of Malmesbury observed that 'the king wore his crown on Christmas Day ... and there too, being struck by the illness of which he knew he would die, he gave orders for the church of Westminster to be consecrated'.[4] The abbey, an image of which appears in the *Bayeux Tapestry*, lay next to the royal palace and would serve as his mausoleum.[5] It was the first such construction in England to follow the Romanesque style, with sections copied from Jumièges Abbey, a style Edward had admired during his years in Normandy, although it was larger than Jumièges. Aside from the cathedral of Speyer in Germany, Westminster Abbey was recognised as the largest religious house to be built north of the Alps since the fourth century.[6] In the intervening centuries there has been considerable reconstruction and elaboration. The only remains of Edward's original house that can be found in the present-day abbey are parts of the main undercroft below where the monks' dormitory once stood.

The Witan council remained at Westminster throughout the last days of Edward's tenure. Witness lists from two charters of 28 December confirm that a host of the major nobility were in attendance.[7] These lists included archbishops Stigand and Ealdred, the Godwinson earls, ten bishops and seven abbots. In addition, Edwin of Mercia signed both charters, and his brother Morcar, the newly installed earl in Northumbria, witnessed one. Discussion about the monarch's imminent death and his successor must have been at the fore, while all the important nobles and churchmen were gathered. Edward drifted on for several days before expiring on 5 January 1066, the eve of the Epiphany (Twelfth Night), and he was buried the following day beside the altar of his new abbey.[8]

The *ASC* added a thirty-four-line prose tribute to Edward and his reign, an unusual departure from the chronicle's normal succinct entries, and it demonstrates the ecclesiastic community's affection for him.[9] Only King Edgar's eulogy in 975 (thirty-eight lines of prose) exceeds the one devoted to Edward the Confessor throughout all versions of the *ASC*. However, his canonisation as 'the Confessor' was a twelfth-century initiative, and only appears after 1161; a confessor was a saint, but not a martyr, who had suffered for their faith and their sanctity in life. The elaborate Saint Edward's shrine seen today in Westminster Abbey was a thirteenth-century addition to incorporate his tomb, which was moved from its original position near the high altar.[10] Surprisingly perhaps, Godwin was also later connected to

Westminster. The abbey's late twelfth-century wax seal shows St Edward trampling on an image of the earl.[11] This seal comes from the period of the Plantagenet kings but shows how deeply sentiment against the Godwinsons had prospered under Norman and Plantagenet monarchs over the century and a half since the demise of Godwin's dynasty.

At the outset, the question of the succession during the last weeks of 1065 was driven by the political situation, particularly given the recent rebellion. The general assumption has been that from 1057 Edward the Exile's son Edgar was being groomed as the successor. Edgar, as Edmund Ironside's grandson, had a direct line to the old West Saxon royal dynasty, and the king and queen had acted as guardians for the ætheling in England since the death of his father. An undated document witnessed at the New Minster in Winchester by Edward, Edith and Edgar, estimated around 1063, suggests that he was still then being positioned to succeed to the throne.[12] Other evidence of intent cannot be found, as Edgar is missing from the charter witness lists and missing from the pre-1066 landholder register in the *Domesday Book*.[13] He was accorded the nomenclature 'Cild' in some texts, which, like Godwin's father Wulfnoth, denoted his high rank.

Nevertheless, it has been argued with some justification that the situation had changed during the final few years of Edward's reign and the young Edgar had been already marginalised by 1064.[14] Much had likely depended on how long Edward lived. If he lived long enough for Edgar to reach his maturity, the Witan may be better inclined to ratify the ætheling's nomination. However, Edgar had only reached fifteen when Edward died. He had no substantive wealth of his own, which meant he could not attract key supporters, and the question remains whether, in the interim, Edward had changed his mind over his preferred successor. By 1064 the growing influence of Harold and the other Godwinsons may well have played a part in Edgar's marginalisation, with Queen Edith perhaps instrumental in convincing her husband to side-line the ætheling in favour of one of her brothers.

The issue that has attracted historians is the manner of Harold Godwinson's succession, and Harold's purported nomination for the throne by the dying king. Detail varies depending on the origin of the source. The *ASC*, for example, says, 'Earl Harold succeeded to the kingdom of England just as the king granted it to him, and also men chose him for it.'[15] Edward's deathbed speech was directed specifically to Harold and Edith if her *Vita Edwardi* is accepted, wherein the king tells Harold, 'I commend this woman (Edith) with all the kingdom to your protection.'[16] Historians have interpreted this in two ways. For those who cast doubt on Edward nominating Harold, the argument is that the king was commending Edith into the earl's care and nothing more. Others have resolved that Edward was commending not only his wife but the whole kingdom into Harold's care.

The twelfth-century Norman writer Wace has the most entertaining version of what took place, even if we accept he may be more imaginative. Wace tells us the English nobles of the Witan pleaded with Edward to hand Harold the throne, 'since they all come to make this request to you, that Harold should be king over your land. We cannot advise you better and we cannot do better.'[17] He then describes the exchange between Edward and Harold: 'He (Edward) said, " … you are very well aware and have heard many times that I have given my kingdom after my lifetime to the Duke of Normandy. What I have given him some of you have sworn to him on oath". Then Harold, who was on his feet, said, "Whatever you have done, my lord, allow me to be king and let your land be mine. I seek nothing more than your acquiescence. You would never do anything for me which you would regret."' Wace then adds that 'the king then turned and said, I do not know whether he did so with a willing heart – "Now let the English create a duke or a king, Harold or another, I grant this." In this way, he made Harold his heir, since he could not have William.'[18] This claimed dialogue makes for inventive writing and Wace has infrequently been dismissed as too imaginative to be reliable, but some truth may lie between the words. Edward may have at one time preferred William to replace him but had subsequently agreed it should be Harold.

The question of Harold's entitlement to the throne occupied many later chroniclers, although William of Poitiers and other immediate contemporaries are silent. The anonymous thirteenth-century work *Lives of Edward the Confessor* chose to support the Norman claim by accusing Harold of having usurped the throne, after having told Edward, 'I dare to swear to you … it had never come into my thoughts to possess your heritage; Duke William of Normandy who to it has right … I have sworn it and he is sure of it I shall keep my covenant … to the kingdom I have no claim or right.'[19]

Elsewhere, the *Bayeux Tapestry* depicts the death of Edward and again Harold's coronation as King Harold II in adjacent scenes.[20] The deathbed scene has Harold, Archbishop Stigand, Queen Edith and Robert FitzWimarc in attendance. We can best turn to the *Vita Edwardi* of Edith, as she was apparently present, and her encomiast writes of the king placing his foreign servants into Harold's care, 'those men who have left their native land … and up till now have served me faithfully. Take from them an oath of fealty, if they should so wish … or send them with your safe-conduct across the Channel.'[21] At initial glance this does not seem important, but as noted by several historians, why give Harold the option of keeping or sending back the Normans at court if the intent had been for the Duke of Normandy to be king?[22] More to the point, if William was Edward's nominated successor with Harold's agreement, as claimed by Norman sources, why had the

Noman duke not been informed that the English king was seriously ill before Christmas? We are told the first he heard of it was on 9 January, while at his estate at Quevilly outside Rouen.[23]

In line with Anglo-Saxon practice, the dying king could not offer Harold the throne per se; it needed ratification from the Witan. Nonetheless, Edward's recommendation was significant. In Anglo-Saxon law a deathbed bequest superseded and revoked any previous donation or instruction, and this is why Edward's exact words on his deathbed became so critical.[24] The contribution from Edith's *Vita* is particularly valid when considering it was written in 1067, as it goes against Norman interests by acknowledging Edward's acceptance of Harold. It has credence because Edith was a first-hand witness. Her priority after Harold's death was not to undermine her brother but to establish her post-Conquest entitlements under a Norman king, so she ensured that the *Vita* included Edward's words which reaffirmed her position and property after his death.[25]

The *ASC* scribes praised Edward's reign and mourned his passing.[26] His contemporaries complimented him on how peaceful and prosperous he had made the kingdom and lauded his capabilities. However, this was not the complete story. Edward was a capable king compared to his father, Æthelred II, but as has been seen he frequently over-relied on the Godwinsons and others throughout much of his regime. After his death, criticism of his tentative leadership, his handling of the succession, and even the nuances within his marriage began to emerge.[27] Edward's legacy was restored somewhat by the later Anglo-Norman kings, so much so it led to his beatification and canonisation as 'the Confessor' on 5 January 1161. More recently, historians remain divided as to his qualities as a monarch.

Some historians see Harold's crowning within hours of Edward's death as an act done with indecent haste.[28] He had by 1066 fabricated a position for himself of unrivalled dominance, and his political skills had attracted men to his cause and given him a guaranteed majority within the Witan. He was the only valid choice open to the English nobility looking to unite the kingdom instantly and smoothly and stabilise the establishment while protecting their interests and safeguarding their wealth. William of Malmesbury tells us that Harold 'exacted an oath of loyalty from the chief nobles [and] seized the crown, though the English say that it was granted to him by the king', and adds that 'this claim, however, rests, I think, more on goodwill than judgement'. Here Malmesbury betrays his view of Harold: ' ... for it makes him (Edward) pass on his inheritance to a man of whose influence he had always been suspicious'.[29] Malmesbury's contemporary John of Worcester remained uncritical, informing us that 'Harold, son of Earl Godwin, whom the king had chosen before his demise as the successor to the kingdom, was elected by the primates of all England to the dignity of kingship, and was consecrated king with due ceremony by Ealdred archbishop of York, on the same day (6 January)'.[30]

Behind Harold's selection rests the crux of the English system as it stood pre-Conquest. Those with blood ties to a deceased monarch were given favoured status but not guaranteed succession. Candidates were assessed on their merits, their aptitude and competence, and the level of support they were likely to receive among the nobility. The primary concern was continuity. Edward had no descendants or direct kin. As considered already, the ætheling Edgar was an option, but his young age, inexperience and general lack of standing meant the Witan needed to look elsewhere. Henry of Huntingdon, like William of Malmesbury, similarly dismissed Harold's validity to replace Edward, and recorded that 'some of the English wanted to advance Edgar ... but Harold, relying on his forces and his birth, usurped the crown of the kingdom'.[31]

From beyond England, two alternative candidates were eyeing the English throne: William of Normandy and Harald Hardrada (Sigurdsson) of Norway. William of Malmesbury returns to the oath of 1064 where in hindsight he advises the Norman duke that 'with regard to the kingdom ... it had been presumptuous to promise on oath a succession that was not his (Harold's), without the general assembly and decision of his council and his folk'.[32] This is revealing, because as argued previously it had not been in Harold's remit to offer such an undertaking to Duke William, forced or otherwise, and neither was it Edward's without the consent of the Witan. William's claims are considered below and elsewhere, and Hardrada's in the following chapter, but in terms of the criteria the English Witan was looking for, blood ties excepted, Harold Godwinson was the outstanding candidate.

Harold had already proved himself able as a military leader over the last decade, and a capable and effective royal advisor and administrator. Bolstered by the nobles of Wessex and the regions that his brothers Gyrth and Leofwine controlled he also importantly had the provisional backing of the heirs of Earl Ælfgar, Edwin in Mercia and Morcar in Northumbria. He was also backed by the three major ecclesiastical figures, archbishops Stigand and Ealdred, and Bishop Wulfstan of Worcester, and further support came from the senior clergies at Rochester and Hereford. The archbishops would appear to have been on as friendly terms with him as they had been with Godwin, and in Wulfstan's case, Harold had helped him secure his bishopric.[33] Stigand was in the group that had surrounded Edward's deathbed and was a witness to substantiate the claim that the old king had nominated Harold.

Harold Godwinson was installed as monarch (Harold II) on the afternoon of 6 January 1066, a few hours after the hasty burial of his predecessor. Some primary sources considered this disrespectful, labelling him a usurper, sworn in quickly before he was prevented from seizing the throne.[34] Normally, a coronation would follow months after a royal accession, but in this instance both were performed together by Ealdred, who had been deliberately chosen in preference to Stigand to avoid the question of the latter's unresolved pallium. For the service, Ealdred adopted a new Third English *ordo* which he had copied from a German text, *Romano-Germanica Pontifical*. However, the *Bayeux Tapestry* later portrayed the non-canonical and excommunicated Stigand performing the ceremony, which was presumably intended to further undermine the validity and legality of Harold's coronation.

Over in Normandy, William of Jumièges says the Norman duke instantly despatched messengers urging Harold 'to renounce this act of folly', while Wace adds that Harold 'would do nothing for him (William); he would neither take his daughter (referring, it is believed to Adeliza) nor hand over the land to him'.[35] Unsurprisingly, William of Poitiers was critical of Harold, noting that 'this mad Englishman could not endure to await the decision of a public election, but on the tragic day when that best of men was buried ... he violated his oath and seized the royal throne with acclamation, with the connivance of a few wicked men'. Poitiers then directs his aim at Stigand, adding that the new king 'received an impious consecration from Stigand, who had been deprived of his priestly office by the just zeal and anathema of the pope'.[36] Poitiers is keen to place Stigand alongside Harold, even though, as mentioned above, Ealdred and not Stigand conducted the service. Orderic Vitalis, writing two generations later in a similar vein, noted, 'Harold son of Earl Godwin had usurped the kingdom of England and ... caused much harm, stained as he was by perjury and cruelty and other vices.'[37] Henry of Huntingdon continues the theme, accepting the Norman source arguments when writing that 'Harold, who had fallen into perjury, had wrongfully usurped the kingdom that by law of kinship ought to have been William's'.[38] The Norman chroniclers were only responding as expected. Exaggeration or distortion was and is an effective tool.

Henry of Huntingdon continues the consensus against the Godwinsons by further reminding us of the events of fifteen years earlier, declaring that William 'was provoked in his mind ... because Godwin and his sons had, by their cunning, exiled from England Bishop Robert (Champart) and Earl Odda and all the Frenchmen'.[39] The texts from the Anglo-Normans William of Malmesbury and Henry of Huntingdon reflect their source materials. Such entries were not designed to ensure historical accuracy. Nonetheless, they are useful in understanding how exposure to several decades of Norman propaganda against the Godwinsons influenced the input of later chroniclers. There are minimal English sources from 1066 to counteract this information. The *ASC* was the only English source contemporary with mid-eleventh-century affairs, and it gives no opinion on Harold's succession other than, 'Here also Harold became consecrated as king.'[40]

After Harold was proclaimed king, there was some initial unrest in the north. As recorded in William of Malmesbury's *Vita Wulfstani* (The Life of Wulfstan), some Northumbrians feared he would restore his exiled brother Tostig to the earldom.[41] Harold's response was to engage Bishop Wulfstan of Worcester and journey to York in late February or March to negotiate with Morcar. Wulfstan had deputised for Ealdred in York occasionally beforehand, and the *Vita Wulfstani* says that Wulfstan appealed to the northern earls on several levels. It is presumed that Edwin of Mercia was involved in the discussions alongside his brother. However, the Ælfgarsons had already made one astute move. Acknowledging that the support from Bamburgh had been crucial to the 1065 rebellion, and perhaps understanding that it required an olive branch to Bernician Northumbria, Morcar, with Edwin's backing, had handed control north of the River Tees to Oswulf, the grandson of Uhtred the Proud, descendent of the noble house of Bamburgh.

Harold had upheld northern grievances in 1065, and in doing so had acted against his own brother's interests, but perhaps Edwin and Morcar sought to extract further assurances in the early months of 1066 knowing that Harold could not contemplate another uprising. Wulfstan apparently reminded the earls of their moral obligations and of the need to avoid destabilizing the north, which would risk an invasion from Scotland or Scandinavia and hence jeopardise their own positions. Negotiations likely included final arrangements for the marriage of their sister Ealdgyth, binding Harold formally to the Ælfgarson family. Ealdgyth was reputedly a famous beauty, but there were good overriding pragmatic reasons for a marriage alliance between the Godwinsons and the Ælfgar family. The formal ceremony may have taken place in York at this time, as the marriage is known to have taken place no later than March or April 1066.

This is therefore a suitable moment to look at Harold's relationship with Edith Swan-neck (the Fair). Their hand-fast marriage had survived over two decades. Their union had required a civil ceremony acceptable to Anglo-Saxon society and approved by the laity, the non-ordained sector of the Church. This was still a common practice in the eleventh century, the same basis as Cnut and Ælfgifu of Northampton's earlier marriage. Any offspring would theoretically have a future entitlement to claim the succession, as Cnut and Ælfgifu's son Harold Harefoot had done. However, the higher Christian clergy did not recognise a hand-fast union and required a church service to validate a marriage. Hence, the Church saw Edith Swan-neck as a concubine not a wife, and this enabled Harold to marry Ealdgyth legally without terminating his relationship with Edith. Anglo-Saxon sources were reticent to record the wedding, although William of Jumièges mentions it, noting that 'Harold married his beautiful widow Edith (Ealdgyth), daughter of the well-known earl Ælfgar'.[42]

With Morcar in Deiran York, and Oswulf holding authority to act for him in Bernician Bamburgh, there was no opening for Siward's remaining son Waltheof in his native earldom. However, an opening could be offered in Huntingdonshire and Northamptonshire. These shires had previously been tied to Northumbria under Siward and had remained so while Tostig was earl. Harold's compromise in the spring negotiations conducted at York likely agreed that Waltheof would be given the authority of these two Midland shires. Harold's new wife accompanied him back south at Easter, 16 April. By late summer she was pregnant, and the child born in 1067 was named Harold Haroldson, after his father.

Having returned to London, the *ASC* recorded that the new king experienced little peace. The scribe refers in the spring of 1066 to a comet, later identified by Edmond Halley in the early eighteenth century as one of the regular seventy-six-year periodic visitations of the same comet named after him.[43] The chronicle noted, 'Then through all England, a sign such as men never saw before was seen in the heavens. Some men declared that it was the star comet which some men called the "haired" star, and it appeared first on the eve of the Greater Litany, that is on 24 April, and shone thus all the week.'[44] The comet, particularly bright on this visitation, appears in a scene in the *Bayeux Tapestry*, above an image of a perturbed Harold II slumped on the throne, which fitted the Norman interpretation of subsequent developments.[45] The ideological beliefs of the period persuaded many that the appearance of the comet was a portent for change. Retrospectively, it was interpreted, following the Norman invasion and the English defeat at Hastings, as an omen that foresaw the end of the Anglo-Saxon control of England. Of course, if Harold had won the battle, it would have been reinterpreted instead as a sign of the coming victory and much prosperity.

Trying to evaluate King Harold II's administration satisfactorily is almost impossible from the limited surviving detail within the primary sources. He was to be king for only forty-two weeks. Most of that period was spent placating the northern earls and cementing his support, organising the defences and militia against a potential Norman invasion, counteracting the movements of Tostig, and, in his last few weeks, dealing simultaneously with two military invasions at the opposite ends of England. Historians accept in the absence of documentary detail that in contrast to his predecessor Harold was far more active in his itinerant movements.[46] He travelled extensively across England and parts of the Continent before 1066, including a visit to Rome, and during his first few months as monarch had visited each region of his kingdom.

Brief though his reign would prove, we would nonetheless normally expect a few charters to have endured. It was common practice for a new king to reward his supporters and to show himself across his new kingdom, and charter productivity can be a useful way to measure these issues. Seeing that Harold had not gained the throne as an ætheling, there would have been even more reason to cement his support in terms of land awards through such charters. Unfortunately, any issued by Harold have been lost. The lack of documentary evidence can be explained not just by the briefness of his kingship but because he was succeeded by William the Conqueror, who systematically destroyed documentary evidence of Harold's kingship as best as he could. In addition, any valid documents prior to the English defeat at Hastings would have soon become worthless as under the new Norman administration land entitlement was redistributed, nearly all of it to the Norman elite.

There is, nonetheless, one surviving writ from Harold's reign.[47] This writ was addressed to Abbot Æthelnoth of Glastonbury, confirming that the judicial and financial rights of Bishop Giso of Wells were to be honoured in keeping with the arrangements made during Edward's reign. This document was basically addressing a dispute over land between two churchmen, but if Harold was communicating on matters of such minor import in relative terms then surely he must have drafted and distributed significantly more charters and writs during his tenure that have not survived.

It was customary for a fresh regime to ring the changes, bringing in men who had shown loyalty while side-lining others because of age or unreliability. Here, again, the lack of surviving charters hides the extent of these changes. We cannot, for example, easily compare a list of Edward's key men with Harold's court of 1066. Some of Edward's supporters who kept their positions during the transformation in January are identified as still being in their positions when the Norman invasion began in October. These included Robert FitzWimarc and William Malet, the chancellor Regenbald, and the stallers (royal officials) Ansgar, Bondi, Eadnoth and Ralph Ælfstan.[48] FitzWimarc and Malet, and possibly Regenbald, were Normans, evidence that Harold had no grievance against foreigners in his court and valued the loyalty they had shown to his predecessor. Presumably, newly promoted thegns were brought in who had served with Harold in the Welsh campaigns or were otherwise trusted advisors from Wessex. In terms of his siblings, we can also imagine that Gyrth and Leofwine were accorded increased prominence alongside their brother, and their principal key supporters similarly gained additional prominence. Harold's relationship with his sister, the widowed queen, during this period is unclear, but Edith had regularly witnessed all her husband's charters during 1065 and the new king likely ensured she remained involved in court affairs.

For details of Harold's real estate ownership as monarch we need to lean heavily on the *Domesday Book*, although it should be remembered that many estates he owned in 1066 were not recorded under his name within the Domesday survey. A summary gleaned from the *Prosopography of Anglo-*

Saxon England *(PASE)* database of the Domesday survey shows that in 1066 Harold owned an impressive 470 estates of varying size across twenty-eight shires.[49] Many of these estates were modest, but they give some surprising data. Harold had over sixty estates in both Herefordshire and Lincolnshire, the latter quantity somewhat surprising. Lincolnshire was a shire under the control of the Ælfgarsons in 1066, so perhaps significant estates had been turned over to Harold as part of the agreement reached with Edwin and Morcar, or maybe these were formerly owned by Tostig in his role as Earl of Northumbria.

Harold also held many estates in Essex and Norfolk, within his former earldom of East Anglia, substantial holdings in Sussex, Wiltshire, Yorkshire, Somerset and Cornwall, and significant numbers in Surrey, Devon and Berkshire.[50] Some of these were formerly owned by Tostig, although the survey also lists many estates under Tostig in 1066 that presumably had already been transferred after his exiling. Nonetheless, ahead of the events of 1065, Tostig can be seen to have held many estates throughout all the English shires. His major holdings were in Yorkshire, but he held many also in Nottinghamshire, and somewhat unexpectedly large acreages across shires such as Buckinghamshire and Hampshire. As seen in the Domesday survey, Harold would have been lord to many more estates that had been assigned to various thegns and supporters under vassalage to him. Furthermore, as king, he would have assumed ownership of those formerly owned by Edward even though the Domesday survey describes them as transferring directly from Edward to William I and bypassing Harold's reign completely.

Comments on Harold's kingship are few. Orderic Vitalis condemned it by noting that, 'In a short time the kingdom which he had nefariously seized was polluted with crimes too horrible to relate.'[51] Once again the Norman agenda is clear. However, some positive comment did eventually surface. John of Worcester is the best advocate in favour of Harold's rule. In opposition to Orderic's *Ecclesiastical History* John's *Chronicle* tells us that Harold 'destroyed iniquitous laws, and set about establishing new ones ... becoming a patron of churches and monasteries, cultivating and venerating at the same time bishops, abbots, monks and clerks; showing himself pious, humble and affable to all good men; detesting malefactors, for he ordered the earl, ealdormen, sheriffs, and his officers generally to seize thieves, robbers, and disturbers of the realm, and exert themselves by land and sea for the defence of their country'.[52]

Even accepting that some chroniclers and writers were frequently prone to exaggeration, this panegyric of Harold is full of praise from a writer whose words are usually in more clipped tones. Perhaps John's text gives us a measure of Harold's reign that is both genuine and illuminating. It would be agreeable to those seeing Harold as a hero not a villain in the last years of Anglo-Saxon England if some reliability could be placed on this concise summary of his kingship. Symeon of Durham added that Harold's was a 'firm and just government', and William of Malmesbury added perhaps disgruntled praise when noting that 'he (Harold) might well have ruled the kingdom, to judge by the figure he cut in public, with prudence and fortitude, had it come to him lawfully'.[53] From this little evidence from inside England, albeit Anglo-Norman writers, we have a picture of a king that may well have proved to be an exceptional ruler had he lived longer.

Harold looks to have brought to his rule the energy he had displayed in his role as senior earl, renewed and released from the confines of his predecessor's semi-retired mindset. His ten-month sovereignty, some suggest, can be expressed in three themes: political unity, centralised economic power, and military preparation.[54] We are unfortunate to not have better evidence of his government and administrative directives, but we know something of Edward's administration and Harold would have operated along similar lines. Reeves appointed to each of the shires acted as the king's sheriff and tax collector, administering the law and collecting royal revenues. Harold's full law codes have not survived in written form, but his predecessor had not issued any codes and Harold most likely reiterated the statutes of Cnut, which had reinforced the laws of King Edgar going back to the tenth century. Harold's earlier dealings with the Welsh and the Welsh border seem to have remained an important issue with him. It is interesting that he promulgated a law that any Welshman found with a weapon on the English side of Offa's Dyke should have his right hand cut off.[55] This was an obvious demonstration that he would not allow the Welsh to cause the same problems to his administration as they had done during Edward's tenure.

The collection of revenue remained extremely efficient, with the weight of the coinage changed to aid control of inflation and deflation. During the 1040s a penny weighed 18 grains, in 1051 it shot up to 27 grains, it was back at 21.5 by 1059, then 17 in 1062 and back to 21.5 by 1065.[56] At each of these dates the population was required to exchange the coinage to control the number of coins in circulation. The general deflation that took place after 1050 suggests greater prosperity. During Harold's reign new dies were cut, and a penny had stabilised at 21.5 grains. The levels of production infer his keenness to replace the coins in circulation from Edward's reign quickly as representative of a fresh regime. A surprising number of the coins minted during his reign have survived and been identified as coming from forty-two of the seventy or more mints active across England in the mid-1060s.[57] The new coinage had Harold's image on the obverse turned to face left, not right. The quantity of his coins that have endured suggests that the nation was prosperous, and that coin production was being undertaken in high volume. Minting of coins increased royal revenues because the charges for bullion and new coin dyes gave increased income into the treasury.

In more general terms Harold followed the Christian practices of his forebears, displaying his religious conviction through patronage. Perhaps more so than their father, Harold, Tostig and Edith had been keen to contribute to local foundations and support the honouring of saints and their relics. This was not with cynical intent. They saw their contributions as increasing their chances of avoiding purgatory in the afterlife. The *Bayeux Tapestry* shows Harold entering the family church at Bosham ahead of his Normandy trip in 1064, and before that in 1056–57 he had taken a pilgrimage to Rome, as had Swegn before him and Tostig and Gyrth afterwards. Belief in Christian ideology was genuine and devout, but it is difficult today to comprehend the contradictions in their daily lives that encompassed religious worship on one hand and violent warfare on the other.

Harold's patronage and enlargement of a collegiate church at Waltham with Lotharingian influences is particularly notable.[58] Aside from donating 70 hides of land to support the canons, he endowed it with costly furnishings and nearly sixty separate religious relics from across England and Europe, including from Rome.[59] This visit to Rome, his second, was not recorded by primary sources, but was probably undertaken during a period of relative stability, sometime during 1058 or early in 1059. Waltham Abbey was not on the scale of Edward's Westminster project but was a more personal investment. Whether Harold planned to expand the site further given a longer tenure cannot be established. As already seen, his wealth had rivalled that of the king before 1066, and when assuming the throne he no doubt continued to donate large sums to several churches as he had done as earl. Besides Waltham, he is recognised to have committed his support for several notable religious houses, including Malmesbury, Abingdon, Durham and Peterborough. Aside from his influence in the careers of archbishops Ealdred and Stigand and Bishop Wulfstan, Harold also appointed two new abbots: one at Abingdon, also named Ealdred, and Thurstan at Ely.[60]

In periods of peace monarchs would lavish land and funds upon their favoured clerics or institutions, but in times of war the king required funds from the Church. Edward was favourably looked on by ecclesiastics as he had been fortunate to reign during a period of relative peace and prosperity within England. Much of this relative peace had been down to the Godwinson family for more than two generations. However, Harold would need considerable funds from the late spring of 1066 to support an extended period of military alertness to deal with the threats from overseas. Although they were often excused from contributions to the royal treasury, we can assume religious houses were called upon during the emerging period of crisis to contribute financially to the defence of England. Based on the necessities of that arrangement, praise for his relationship with the Church among clerical scripts is hard to find.

15

Tostig and the Road to Stamford Bridge

Harold would spend much of the summer and early autumn of 1066 watching the Channel coast after receiving information that Duke William was preparing an invasion armada. However, his first concern was with Tostig. We cannot know if Harold expected his brother to respond as it would transpire, but we can imagine he knew him well enough to appreciate he would attempt something. What he did not foresee perhaps, or even understand, was the depth of Tostig's anger. He underestimated the lengths to which his younger sibling would go to enable him to recover his position. Tostig's need for revenge would override anything else, including the long-term security of England. Those familiar with the events of 1066 will know of the prelude to Hastings, and Tostig's alliance with Harald Hardrada (Sigurdsson) of Norway, but what is less adequately established is what alliances Tostig attempted before that, and how those activities affected later developments. The role he played in the downfall of Anglo-Saxon England cannot be underestimated.

No serious moves were made over the winter of 1065/66. Perhaps, as some argue, Tostig had hoped after Edward's death that Harold would summon him back to England and return him to a position of authority.[1] He was to be disappointed, and Harold's refusal to hold out an olive branch at this stage probably decided his next steps.

There is sufficient primary source detail for us to piece together Tostig's movements. Flanders and his brother-in-law Count Baldwin V proved unable or unwilling to finance an assault on England. Baldwin's long-standing alliance with the Godwinsons and his need to keep on terms with the new English king would have formed his response to Tostig. Tostig then looked for another kinship affiliation, his cousin Swein II (Estrithsson) in Denmark. The Norwegian Snorri Sturluson, the writer of the *Heimskringla*, tells us that Tostig urged Swein to invade England but was rebuffed, with

Snorri mischievously adding that the Danish king had replied, 'I know my limitations.'[2] Swein was perhaps still recovering from the protracted war against Harald (Hardrada) of Norway that had ended only two years earlier, and to provide Tostig with military aid would have left him exposed to a potential fresh assault from Hardrada. In similar fashion to Baldwin V, Swein would not wish to make an enemy of his cousin Harold or interfere in English matters. It has been suggested that Swein instead directed Tostig towards Norway, and it was probably in the spring of 1066 that Tostig first met Hardrada.[3] This would make perfect sense from Swein's perspective because if he had suspected a new build-up of Norwegian forces early in 1066 and was concerned Hardrada was planning to renew the war against Denmark a good strategy would be to divert Hardrada's military efforts elsewhere.

The timing of Tostig's meeting or meetings with Hardrada cannot be verified. It may have come immediately after he had visited Swein Estrithsson but probably came later in the year. What is often ignored, however, is Tostig's attempt to recruit Duke William of Normandy to his cause ahead of his final alliance with Hardrada. William, of course, was already considering his options. Tostig's chances of gaining support in Normandy would seem slim but the link between Tostig and William has been understated by many historians, and Tostig was prepared to explore any possibility. Not one but two kinships linked Tostig and William, and this is often ignored or undervalued. The first was through Baldwin V of Flanders, as noted previously. Baldwin's daughter Matilda had married the Norman duke, and Matilda was the niece of Tostig's wife Judith. Secondly and furthermore, there was a blood tie through Judith's mother Eleanor of Normandy, who was William of Normandy's aunt.

Orderic Vitalis recorded, 'For some time they had been close friends and by marrying two sisters had strengthened the bonds between them.'[4] Actually, as mentioned above, Judith and Matilda were aunt and niece. Describing Tostig and William as 'friends' is perhaps an exaggeration, but the kinship link between them has not been sufficiently appreciated as it explains why Tostig approached William and sought his support. The Norman duke might have been initially surprised but then used the opportunity to his advantage. It is entirely plausible that Tostig had been made aware beforehand that William was considering, or indeed planning, an invasion of England.

We learn that the duke would begin constructing an invasion fleet in the spring of 1066. Did this coincide with a visit from Tostig, or was it Tostig's visit that led to William's decision to plan an invasion?

Sources concentrate on the later Tostig–Hardrada alliance, but a possible meeting between Tostig and William conceivably proved critical to how things played out in the months ahead. Reference to their meeting comes primarily within two Norman sources, William of Jumièges' *Gesta*

Normannorum Ducum and Orderic Vitalis' *Ecclesiastical History*.[5] However, interestingly, Jumièges excludes reference to Tostig and William's kinship connection, perhaps because it was not ideal for William's invasion to be linked to information given by, or plans arranged with, the English king's brother. Orderic writes that Tostig 'himself hurried to Normandy ... and swore that he would faithfully secure the crown for him (Duke William) if he would cross to England with a Norman army', and tells us plainly that 'the duke sent Earl Tostig to England'.[6] In acceptance that the two met, we can only speculate what William promised Tostig. Tostig's immediate use to William was in potentially gaining inside knowledge of the machinations of the English court and advance intelligence of the level of loyalty for Harold.

As seen when he later allied himself with Harald Hardrada, Tostig had likely claimed he could attract many men to his banner to overturn his brother. This exaggerated the depth of his former powerbase in England, although Orderic acknowledges that Tostig had already 'resolved to oppose him (Harold), and openly declared war on him'.[7] William knew that Tostig was unlikely to provide much in the way of ships and soldiers and did not offer any military assistance directly from Normandy, but the intelligence he gained from Tostig concerning Harold's support and the military situation in England was likely significant and played a part in his later invasion plans. The Norman duke was independently preparing what would prove to be a large invasion fleet, but he would have been encouraged by the affirmation that the two senior Godwinson brothers were now enemies.

It is easy to conclude that William and Tostig could have remained in contact, and through Tostig the Norman duke was made aware of Hardrada's planned invasion. Although many historians dismiss the premise, the two offensives against England a few months afterwards, Norse and Norman, were linked. It presumes too much to say that William and Hardrada worked together to overthrow Harold, but if they did know of each other's intent, perhaps directly through Tostig or other intermediaries, they would understand their invasions had more chance of success if they were launched in parallel.[8] This hypothesis lacks hard evidence, beyond the fact that their invasions, when they came, were fortuitously synchronised. The Norwegian fleet would enter the River Humber in mid-September, and the Norman fleet would first set sail from Dives in mid-September. It was only poor weather in the Channel that diverted the Norman fleet to Saint-Valéry and delayed its landing in England another few weeks. Had the weather in the Channel not intervened, Hardrada and William's invasion fleets would have arrived on English shores almost simultaneously.

By May 1066, Tostig had mustered from one source or another a mercenary fleet of several dozen vessels. The principal sources are clear that he first set sail from either Flanders or Normandy. This was probably no later than mid-

May because the *ASC* records that it came soon after the appearance of the 'haired star' (Halley's Comet), which had shone throughout the last week of April.[9] William of Malmesbury notes that 'Tostig sailed with a fleet of sixty ships from Flanders to the Humber', and Henry of Huntingdon similarly agrees that Tostig first made for the Humber.[10] However, this detail is questionable. Other main sources, which have preference among historians, refer to his earlier movement along the English Channel before he headed further north. Orderic claims Tostig embarked from the Cotentin in western Normandy (possibly Cherbourg or Carentan), while John of Worcester names Flanders.[11] John and the *ASC* version C name Tostig's landing point as the Isle of Wight, suggesting his point of departure was more likely to have been western Normandy.[12] After provisioning his ships on the island, Tostig sailed back east to Sandwich, 'and did harm everywhere along the sea-coast where he could get to'.[13]

He was joined at Sandwich, presumably as arranged beforehand, by his thegn Copsig, his loyal deputy who had fled from York at the time of the rebellion and had since successfully recruited mercenaries in Orkney and possibly also Northumbria. The Norman writer Gaimar records that Copsig brought with him seventeen additional shiploads of fighting men.[14] Questions need to be asked as to the whereabouts of the main English fleet at this time, because evidently it was not at anchor at Wight or Sandwich. Harold had possibly assembled it at London or in the River Medway ahead of pushing into the Channel, for when he heard news of his brother reaching Sandwich he had already 'gathered a greater ship-army and a land-army than any king in the land had ever gathered before ... because he was told for certain that Earl William from Normandy ... wanted to come here and win this land'.[15] This confirms Harold was preparing for a Norman invasion, and Tostig's timing was unlucky or unwise. Harold set off for Sandwich by land and water, but his brother withdrew northward. At this juncture, he looks to have needed to pressgang further crews, as John of Worcester records, he took some seamen with him 'whether they wished to go or not'.[16]

Tostig then landed in East Anglia at the mouth of the River Burnham.[17] It had probably not been his original intention. East Anglia was controlled by his brother Gyrth, but whether Tostig was hoping for assistance from him is unclear. Perhaps of all his brothers he was closest to Gyrth; they had travelled together to Rome a few years earlier. Nonetheless, it is conceivable Tostig planned to pillage East Anglia if he had concluded that Gyrth had betrayed him and supported Harold the previous autumn. In any case, Tostig's squadron soon sailed further north and entered the River Humber sometime around the end of June. Landing either on the south bank of the Humber or moving into the River Trent, his mercenaries, perhaps numbering well over a thousand, devastated Lindsey, the region now identified as

Lincolnshire. Lindsey was part of Mercia and under the authority of Earl Edwin, so Tostig's reason for targeting this area is obvious.

However, Tostig was possibly surprised by the speed of Edwin's reaction. The *ASC* and John of Worcester confirm that while Tostig's forces were pillaging the region, 'Earl Edwin and Earl Morcar ... came there and drove him out of the land'.[18] Many of Tostig's mercenaries were killed, and there would have been significant desertions, as confirmed by the *ASC* when the scribe notes that 'the boatmen deserted him; and he went to Scotland with twelve cutters'.[19] He had lost around 80 per cent of his vessels and their crews since entering the Humber. The remnants of Tostig's fleet then continued north, where he sought exile with Malcolm III (aka Canmore), King of the Scots, at Forteviot, 5 miles south-west of modern Perth, accessed by the River Tay, or at Dunfermline, accessed via the Firth of Forth. It seems their earlier personal relationship had remained strong, and Tostig stayed at Malcolm's court for several weeks. Nevertheless, the Scottish king refused to give any military aid.[20] In 1070, at Dunfermline, Malcolm would link himself to the old Anglo-Saxon royal line by marrying Margaret, the daughter of Edward the Elder and sister of Edgar ætheling.

The question of when Tostig first met Harald Hardrada will probably never be settled. As mentioned previously, it could have been in the spring of 1066 but was likely a few months later. We know for certain it could not have been during May or June, the period when Tostig had moved along the English Channel into the North Sea and the Humber and then finally to King Malcolm's Scottish court. Maybe they met at Orkney in August, which was Hardrada's first stop after leaving Norway. The Norwegian writer Snorri Sturluson in his text the *Heimskringla* tells us that Tostig and Hardrada had initially agreed to assault England in concert, with Tostig attacking Wessex and Hardrada Northumbria.[21] If this is accurate, Tostig's failure to gain any traction in the south forces a change of plan. Missing from the primary source chronology is whether Tostig had been influential in persuading the Norwegian, if he needed it, to undertake an invasion of England.

The chronicler Orderic Vitalis acknowledges again Tostig's Norman connection by noting that when he first met Harald Hardrada he 'was well received by the king and saw that he could not possibly fulfil the promises he had made to Duke William'.[22] We can only surmise what that promise had been, but his earlier failure left Tostig with little bargaining collateral. It would be fair to assume he had exaggerated his influence in England during his discussions with the Norwegian monarch. Orderic Vitalis gives us the most fascinating record of Tostig's plea to Hardrada, which acknowledges an earlier meeting in the spring of 1066; although Orderic wrongly suggests in his *Ecclesiastical History* that Tostig believed himself to be older than Harold and thus the rightful claimant to the English throne.

Orderic provides Tostig with a dramatic narrative which is worth relaying in full, and which he is depicted as delivering to Hardrada:

> Great king, I approach your throne as a suppliant, offering myself and my service in good faith ... in the hope of being restored by your aid to the honour which is mine by right of inheritance. For Harold, my brother, who ought rightly to obey me as the firstborn, has treacherously risen against me and presumptuously on false pretences made himself king of England. Destroy my brother's upstart strength in war, keep half England for yourself, and let me have the other half to hold as your faithful vassal as long as I live.[23]

Hardrada would have known of the 1065 rebellion and Tostig's unpopularity within Northumbria. How much he knew is uncertain, but it was enough to encourage him to prepare his invasion fleet. His campaign is evidence that he saw the north of England as unstable under a new earl in 1066 and ripe for invasion, and York was always going to be the key to Northumbria.

To what extent Tostig ultimately benefitted Hardrada's campaign is another question. He could contribute little militarily after his forces had been blunted in Lindsey, and his presence in the invasion force would likely prove more negative than positive once the Northumbrians knew of his direct involvement. From Hardrada's perspective, he perhaps saw Tostig as only marginally useful, valuable mostly for his insights into the Northumbrian leadership and his direct knowledge of the landscape around York and the defensive lines and movements Morcar and Edwin might employ. Whether Hardrada intended to give Tostig half of England when and if successful, as suggested, never needed to be answered. However, the Anglo-Scandinavian population across Northumbria, particularly around Deiran York, would not have easily accepted Tostig's return, and it is difficult to see another region that would have accepted him peacefully as ruler if the Norse invasion had succeeded.

Harald Hardrada's justification, his legal argument, for claiming the English throne was based on him being the uncle and successor of Magnus (the Good) Olafsson of Norway, who had succeeded to the throne of Denmark on the death of Harthacnut in 1042 based on their earlier arrangement made between 1036–39. In replacing Magnus, Hardrada had therefore inherited, so he claimed, that arrangement between Magnus and Harthacnut whereby each was to be the heir of the other.[24] Whichever of the two survived longest would inherit the thrones of both Denmark and Norway. When Harthacnut died, Magnus reinterpreted and extended this provision to incorporate England, the third country in Cnut's North Sea empire. The Anglo-Saxon Witan would not have recognized or conceded to that arrangement, so it is extremely unlikely any pact between Harthacnut and Magnus encompassed a promise of the English throne; in any case, it would be invalid.

As seen previously, Magnus had during the 1040s threatened to invade England in pursuit of his interpretation of the arrangement, writing to Edward that he (Magnus) should have inherited Harthacnut's throne and would invade and 'then govern it who wins the victory'.[25] His invasion never materialised and no written agreement survives, but historians generally accept the settlement covered only Norway and Denmark. There are similarities here in the Norwegian case with the Norman claims concerning Harold Godwinson's offer of the English throne to Duke William. In terms of the English succession, it had not been for Harthacnut to promise the throne of England to Magnus any more than for Edward or Harold to promise it to William. Hardrada therefore had no real justifiable claim to the English throne based on a claimed agreement by his predecessor thirty years earlier. Regardless of this, it is astounding that his professed legal entitlement to England has gained such credibility within some secondary sources.

Despite Hardrada having won an important sea battle in 1062 against Swein II Estrithsson at Nisa on the west coast of Danish-controlled southern Sweden, the Norwegian king had by 1064 conceded any future rights to the Danish throne. This needs emphasising, because in conceding his rights to Denmark Hardrada was also conceding that the original treaty between Magnus and Harthacnut had lapsed, disqualifying him from any claimed entitlement to England. Any argument over the original pact was thereafter irrelevant. His invasion accordingly would have no legal basis. Rather, its origins come from the fact that after peace had been made with Denmark Hardrada needed to pursue another military avenue to retain his popularity within Norway, and an invasion of England was the chosen outlet. We can perhaps summarise the Norse invasion as opportunism, nothing better than an illegal military power grab in the true tradition of earlier Viking armies that had invaded England countless times in previous generations. The recent political uncertainty and manoeuvrings within England gave the Norwegian king the perfect opportunity to strike in 1066.

Harald Hardrada had prepared 300 ships, and in mid-August the armada left Norway.[26] The sources tell us Tostig met the Norwegian fleet with his remaining twelve ships in Scotland, seemingly around early September, before they moved down the North Sea to the River Tyne.[27] They had probably joined forces at the estuary of the River Tay, as acknowledged by the writer Geffrei Gaimar in his *L'Estoire des Engleis* (History of the English People).[28] Historians have formed various assessments as to the size of Hardrada and Tostig's forces. The vessels were filled primarily with warriors, and with it being just after harvest time they did not need to carry additional provisions but planned to pillage. Assuming an average warship carried a conservative estimate of thirty warriors, fighting numbers were at least 9,000 and some historians have estimated they numbered over 10,000.[29]

Re-embarking at Tynemouth, the allied fleet continued down the North Sea coast, sacking and burning Scarborough in mid-September before entering the Humber Estuary. The landing at Scarborough may be pertinent. It is plausible some warriors had disembarked to march on York, which was only 35 miles distant. Hardrada, with Tostig's advice, may have envisaged investigating Morcar's preparations or surprising some of his forces. Nonetheless, the contingent had re-joined the fleet by the time the ships entered the River Humber. Within a week they would fight a decisive battle against the northern English earls south of York.

While the Norse had been planning their expedition, Harold Godwinson had been preparing throughout the summer to counteract the impending invasion from Normandy. He had been organising his defences even before Tostig's incursions into Wessex. News had been circulating since the spring that William of Normandy was assembling a large invasion fleet at the port of Dives-sur-Mer, which is now a suburb of present-day Cabourg between Quistreham and Deauville. We know Harold used agents to gain intelligence of Duke William's activities because William of Poitiers refers to the duke having captured one of Harold's spies in Normandy.[30] Unlikely as a successful assault across the Channel in sufficient numbers might have seemed at this stage, it was looking plausible that the Normans could launch one before the autumn.

Harold had taken the threat seriously, and the regional fyrd had been summoned. Based on the standard recruiting criteria of one warrior or soldier for every five hides of productive land in England, amounting to approximately 70,000 hides, there was a conservative estimate of 14,000 men available based on rotational enlistment.[31] This equated to one man from every eleven or twelve families, and could be expanded if required. Guarding the southern coastline was exclusively Harold's remit, both as king and as Earl of Wessex. The earldoms of Gyrth and Leofwine, with the latter perhaps having authority over Kent by this juncture, would have also had men available on standby. The combined forces of the Godwinson earldoms alone probably amounted to between 8,000 and 9,000 men. Perhaps half this number were conscripted to guard the south coast, with the others on standby to move as necessary. They were in their positions no later than mid-June.

Back in the north, Edwin and Morcar would have cause to send out their summons to assemble the northern fyrds, perhaps bringing together an initial strength of between 4,000 and 6,000 men. This demonstrates England could muster two armies simultaneously, one in the south and another in the north, without undue difficulty. In the crisis that followed Harold had need to extend these basic numbers by necessity, able to summon two armies into the field within the space of a few weeks. The combined numbers that were to fight on the English side at the three battles of Fulford, Stamford Bridge and Hastings totalled somewhere between 16,000 and 20,000. In consideration of those housecarls and thegns who were to fight at two battles (Stamford Bridge and Hastings), an estimated minimum of 15,000 individuals were engaged.

Harold had moved the English navy to the Isle of Wight by early June. The *ASC* tells us that the ships lay at Wight 'all the summer and the autumn'.[32] The number of vessels is not recorded but being on high alert there were likely several dozen ships based at Wight, perhaps more, with others at significant ports from Dorset to Kent. Two men had been given command of the Wight flotilla: Eadric the Steersman, and Abbot Ælfwold of St Benet's in East Anglia. The latter's East Anglian origin suggests Harold had known the abbot since his own period as earl in that region.

Perhaps the original fyrd conscription, which required only three months' service, was upwards of 5,000. A new intake would replace them at the end of that period if needed. It was necessary to monitor the coastline from Dorset to the Isle of Thanet, stretching over 180 coastal miles, and men were placed, as noted by John of Worcester, 'at strategic places around the coast'.[33] The greatest numbers were garrisoned in Hampshire and Sussex on the intelligence that William was preparing his armada in western Normandy at Dives-sur-Mer. As a general observation, Harold's ability to organise such a comprehensive and effective defensive screen says much about his aptitude in coordinating the machinery of government. It also acknowledges that his personal coffers, the royal treasury and the country in general were in rude financial health, because to maintain land and sea forces on this scale for three months of service in a state of inactivity was a major commitment. The choice he was to make regarding a new conscription when the moment came in September would be key, and a combination of factors would soon unite to work against his best-laid plans.

ESTATES HELD BY GODWINSONS AS PER DOMESDAY SURVEY

No. of Shire Estates Holder (H) or Lord (L)	Harold		Edith (Q)		Gyrth		Leofwine		Gytha		Edith Sw		Tostig		Godwin	
	H	L	H	L	H	L	H	L	H	L	H	L	H	L	H	L
Bedfordshire		5	3	7	1	1							5	10		
Berkshire	16	5	6	3	2	1				1			2			
Buckinghamshire	5	27	8	18			8	21			1	4	4	6		
Cambridgeshire	4	13			4	6					25	76		2		
Cheshire	4															
Cornwall	24	22							2							
Devon	19		8				7		14							
Dorset	14	1	11				1		2					1		
Essex	44	28	5		1		4				6	1				
Gloucestershire	7	9	1						1				1	1		
Hampshire	8	6	9	5	1				4				12	4	2	15
Herefordshire	65	18	34	1									1			
Hertfordshire		39		7		4	2				5	10				
Huntingdonshire	4	1											2			
Kent	1	4		1			9	3							15	15
Leicestershire	15		6	3												
Lincolnshire	63	7	56	40												
Middlesex	1	6		1			1	7								
Norfolk	38	144			20	82								1		
Northamptonshire			15										3			
Nottinghamshire													12			
Oxfordshire	6		3										1			
Rutland	1		3													
Shropshire	1		1													
Somerset	25	4	18	5			1		5				1			
Staffordshire	1															
Suffolk	3	61	7	12	14	46					3	25				
Surrey	15	12	6				2	3	1				2			
Sussex	26	8	5		3	1	2	1	7	1			1		34	53
Wiltshire	27		8						7				3			
Worcestershire	1		2	3												
Yorkshire	32	28											34	9		

Note 1) H = Estates held directly; L = Estates held through vassals
Note 2) Edith (Q) = Queen Edith; Edith Sw = Edith Swan-neck (aka the Fair)
Note 3) All estates are as listed in the Domesday Book as formerly owned prior to conquest of 1066
Note 4) Harold's listings do not include all royal estates transferred from Edward the Confessor
Note 5) Tostig is identified in the DB as holding these estates in 1066, although he would have lost ownership in 1065
Note 6) Godwin's estates would have been transferred on his death in 1053, and they were already incorporated into his wife and children's holdings. The DB lists his estates with no known successor
Note 7) Data compiled from the Domesday Book (Penguin, London, rev edn.2003) and from the Prosopography of Anglo-Saxon England database (www.pase.ac.uk)

16

The Norse Invasion

The story of how events in the south unfolded will be returned to in the following chapter, but we first need to look at developments in the north that would culminate with the Battle of Stamford Bridge. Having sailed up the River Humber, the Norse fleet of Harald Hardrada, with Tostig, entered the Humber's major tributary of the River Ouse and moved towards York. Reconnaissance of the route ahead would have told them that the English flotilla further up the Ouse, a combination of vessels from Mercia and Northumbria, had retreated in front of them. The English ships had probably already withdrawn as far as Ulleskelf on the River Wharfe.[1] The English earls Morcar and Edwin would have monitored their enemy's movements and had chosen not to attack but to make a defensive stand closer to York. Hardrada, as recorded by John of Worcester, beached his longboats, and disembarked at Riccall (on the river's east bank), a few miles downstream from where the Wharfe fed into the Ouse from the west.[2] Surprisingly, John is the only major primary authority to name the location as Riccall, presumably a detail garnered from an earlier lost source.

Riccall was not a random choice but an ideal site. The timing and speed of the tidal flow of the Ouse would have played a part in how such a huge fleet manoeuvred upriver towards York, but it is plausible that Riccall was already the pre-planned landing site dependent on the movements of the English. Tostig's prior knowledge of the area would have been invaluable. Riccall lies on the north side of a broad bend of the River Ouse, 8 miles south of central York on foot but 14 miles by water. Just west of it the Ouse twists to the west and south, almost 180 degrees. In the eleventh century, this meant that the fast-flowing tide on the bend at Riccall cut into the eastern banks as it passed, eventually forming what has been described as an extensive swampy hinterland akin to an oxbow lake.[3] When taken during a high springtide, this allowed Hardrada's large fleet to row into the slack water and beach safely. Hardrada was probably at this stage still not fully appreciative of the dispositions of the English fyrd, but the additional benefit of Riccall, which Tostig knew, was that it lay less than a mile from one of the major north–south roads to York.

By this stage, Edwin and his Mercian forces had joined up with Morcar. It is likely many Mercians had arrived earlier on the ships that were now lying at Ulleskelf. The brothers knew that the king would only have heard of the enemy's arrival days earlier, which was not enough time for Harold to come to their aid – assuming he would anyway – before the Norse attacked York. Perhaps the brothers should have withdrawn and allowed the city to be taken, to unite themselves with Harold's army on his arrival in the north. However, there is no obvious reason to believe the earls had expected Harold's arrival at all, and with that in mind, there was no reason to sacrifice York uncontested. Furthermore, there was a political element to be considered. Avoiding an encounter was not an option. Morcar had been in place as earl only a matter of months, and to leave the city undefended was unthinkable; to do so would spell the end of his authority in Northumbria, whatever the military outcome.

In response to their enemy's movements, Morcar and Edwin had chosen a defensive position at Fulford, blocking the north–south road to York. Fulford lay adjacent to the east bank of the Ouse, straddling the road (modern A19) about 2 miles south of the city close to where a tributary of the Ouse known as the Germany Beck joined the main river. Their fyrds formed up on the north bank of this beck, and it would be there that the earls would make a stand, on the eve of St Matthew the Apostle's Day, 20 September.[4] Bearing in mind Edwin had needed to leave behind men to protect Mercia, we can estimate that he may have brought between 1,500 and 2,000 under his command to add to Morcar's 3,000 or more Northumbrians. These figures are mere speculation, but the English were evidently outnumbered. Tostig's contingent alongside those recruited from Orkney may have numbered several hundred or more, and with Hardrada's Norwegians, the allied army at Fulford could have numbered around 6,000–6,500.[5] Furthermore, a substantial number of warriors had been left to guard the Norse longboats. In total the allied army that had sailed up the Ouse probably numbered between 7,500 and 8,500 men, as noted earlier, although some historians have argued for much larger numbers in excess of 10,000.[6]

Details of the battle at Fulford are omitted from several of the leading primary sources and it simply receives a brief mention in the *ASC*.[7] John of Worcester gives us a little more detail, but the best source for what took place comes from the Scandinavian Snorri Sturluson in his *Heimskringla* saga.[8] Some text within Snorri's work has elaborations, but most of the basic details about the battle are accepted, and recent detailed research by local historians has matched the original topography of the battlefield to the present-day landscape.[9] Looking at the formation from the English perspective on the north bank of Germany Beck, Morcar had placed the bulk of his army on his left (eastern) flank butting up against the adjacent marshland. The watercourse was shallow, and probably no more than 20 metres wide. Edwin's Mercians secured the right (western) flank by the road ford crossing near where the beck joined the River Ouse.

The natural terrain restricted the width of the battlefield – one reason why the outnumbered English had chosen the position – and their shield wall, lying between the Ouse and the marshland, ran to a maximum of 400–450 metres. However, the ground on the south bank was higher, giving Hardrada a better view of the battlefield than Morcar. Some of the best Norse warriors under Hardrada were kept in reserve, hidden from view behind the rising ground. The Orcadians under their leader Siward were given the centre ground and Tostig controlled the right (eastern) flank opposite Morcar. More experienced fighters were placed towards the left, facing Edwin's Mercians between the ford crossing and the Ouse, and Hardrada would take charge of that wing as the battle progressed.

In the initial stages of the fighting there was stalemate. Then Tostig's wing began to be pushed back and many of the Northumbrians broke their formation and crossed the beck to pursue them. This was potentially a tactical move by the allies rather than a forced withdrawal. Most of the Norse army had not yet been fully committed, but from his vantage point Hardrada had identified a weakness in the English line. He immediately led a major assault on the left flank across the beck to confront Edwin's Mercians.[10] Caught by surprise at the scale of this sudden attack, many of Edwin's soldiers' broke ranks, and as more Norse gained the solid ground north of the watercourse, the Mercians were either forced westward into the Ouse or began fleeing back north towards York. The inherent weakness of the English position was exposed, for in losing this flank the entire line was made vulnerable.[11] Morcar was not initially aware that his brother's right wing had folded, and with Edwin neutralised Hardrada's warriors had already moved behind the Northumbrians on the north bank and began to roll up the centre of Morcar's forces.[12] Simultaneously, and likely as part of the battle plan, Tostig had reformed his men and crossed the beck, trapping many of Morcar's Northumbrians between the marsh to their rear and the Norse attacking them from their flank. Forced back eastward into the swampy ground, those Englishmen not killed at this stage of the fighting drowned in the marsh.

The primary sources tell us that the Norse 'made great slaughter; and there many of the English people were killed and drowned and driven in flight', with 'more of them drowned in the river than had fallen in battle'.[13] Total casualties were heavy, with some estimates giving a mortality rate of nearly 30 per cent (perhaps 3,000 of the combatants), most of them English.[14] The *Heimskringla* of Snorri Sturluson, being a Scandinavian saga, gives Harald Hardrada centre stage while Tostig Godwinson gets the briefest of mentions.[15] Despite the defeat, both English earls survived. Edwin had fled the field northward with his remaining Mercians, but more surprisingly perhaps considering the fatalities, Morcar had extricated himself and escaped with a section of his forces before Hardrada had pushed the remaining Northumbrians into the marsh.

The centre of the original battlefield, the Norwegian side, can be found today south of what remains of Germany Beck between Selby Road (A19) and Fordlands Road on Fulford Playing Fields. There is a modest ground plaque, hard to locate, dedicated to the battle, lying on the western edge of the field about 50 metres south of the Beck. During the 1990s, remains of a medieval burial site were discovered during redevelopment work at Fishergate in York. Many of these skeletons were identified as suffering violent deaths and carbon-dating of bone was identified to the mid-eleventh century. One suggested possibility is that they are the bones of Anglo-Saxons killed at Fulford, although it should be pointed out that there were several separate acts of warfare in the general area around York which are traceable to this era.[16]

Hardrada and Tostig entered York unopposed on 22–23 September on the understanding no looting or further slaughter would be undertaken. Morcar had made himself absent, probably to avoid Tostig, but Edwin may have negotiated peace terms on behalf of Northumbria and Mercia.[17] A select party of Norse jarls and warriors entered York while the bulk of the army remained in camp to the south. Some returned to Riccall to re-join those guarding the ships. Tostig would have been prominent in the negotiations, appreciating better than most the existing seniority among the remaining Northumbrian nobility. He would have taken pleasure in extracting oaths from those within the city that had gone against him in 1065 and drawing up the list of required hostages.

The *ASC* tells us that Hardrada and Tostig 'were given hostages from the town, and given provisions, and so went from there to ship, and spoke of complete peace provided that they would all go south with them and win this land'.[18] This last point makes sense. Hardrada was trying to appeal to the dominant Anglo-Scandinavian background of the Northumbrian populace, and therefore negotiating in terms of becoming their ally, not a conqueror. John of Worcester added that the English and Norse agreed to exchange 150 hostages, although this seems generous from Hardrada and Tostig's perspective, and reinforces the suggestion Hardrada was seeking immediate cooperation.[19] Contrarily, it was said Tostig had insisted on more hostages, perhaps up to 500, from across Deira and Bernicia.[20] Undoubtedly, there were a few individuals he specifically wanted, and the Northumbrians were given several days to assemble them. In hindsight, this delay proved crucial.

As part of the agreed terms the Norse army withdrew to Stamford Bridge, a crossing place over the River Derwent 7 miles north-east of York. Stamford Bridge was significant in that not only did several roads converge there at the crossing point, but it also lay adjacent to Catton, one of Harold's estates, which ensured additional easy provisions in the interim.[21] The transfer to there may have taken place on the morning of 24 September, which was less than a day before Harold was to arrive in the north. The *Heimskringla* tells us that one in every three from the Norse army returned to Riccall, including Hardrada's young son Olaf Haraldsson and the earls of Orkney Paul and Erlend under the leadership of jarl Eystein Orri, the intended future husband of Hardrada's daughter Maria.[22]

Harold Godwinson's response on hearing of the Norse invasion was remarkably swift. He had already disbanded the fyrd and navy guarding the south coast, and Orderic's *Ecclesiastical History* links the date of the disbandment in the south, to be looked at later, to explain why Harold was able to lead a powerful army northward.[23] However, this is not a reasonable interpretation, because the southern levies that disbanded in early September were not the same infantry that would fight at Stamford Bridge but the ones that formed the bulk of the force that would fight at Hastings. The claim that the whole English fyrd force-marched 200 miles from London to York in several days, albeit a gripping story, is therefore an exaggeration of the facts.

The speed with which Harold arrived in Yorkshire was extraordinary, but those who departed from London alongside him were not foot soldiers but mounted contingents, comprising his retinue, housecarls (huscarls) and thegns, perhaps a thousand men in total. More mounted men would join as he rode north, and perhaps Gyrth had joined him with a mounted contingent from East Anglia. In contrast, the foot soldiers who were to fight at Stamford Bridge were not from London but from further north and they had received advance instructions to join from various points in the shires along Harold's route and liaise with the mounted troops at Tadcaster. It has been calculated, based on the rule of one fyrdman per five hides, that Harold could probably raise an additional 5,000 men, mounted and infantry, en route northward.[24]

Harold's fastest route north from London was via the Roman Ermine Street and the Great North Road, which crossed the River Trent near Newark and the River Don at Doncaster. As has been acknowledged, the quality of the roads at this period would normally limit mounted travel to 25 miles a day, while the rate of infantry movement was about 15 miles a day.[25] The *ASC* tells us he 'went northward, by day and night, as quickly as he could gather his army'.[26] Accepting the urgency of the situation, and because we know that Harold reached Tadcaster on 23 or 24 September, we can safely increase the rate of mounted travel to 35 miles a day and calculate he left London no later than 17 September, in other words before Fulford had been fought. The suggestion has been put that Harold's haste was fed by concern that his new brothers-in-law might agree peace terms with Hardrada and Tostig to avoid battle.[27] The counter-argument is that it was highly unlikely Morcar and Edwin would have compromised on any agreement involving Tostig. Morcar's position would have looked untenable thereafter if he had done so.

When he arrived at the River Wharfe at Tadcaster, only 9 miles from York, Harold would soon have been informed of the English defeat at Fulford. He would also have learned that a large remnant of the enemy had remained or returned to their ships at Riccall, and that his brother and the Norwegian king were at that moment in the process of moving the majority of their army several miles east of York to await hostages. Armed with this knowledge, Harold delayed for twenty-four hours (24 September) so that late arrivals could add to his strength. There is an interesting adjunct to this, as the scribe for *ASC* version C noted that Harold's army came to Tadcaster 'and there (he) marshalled his fleet'.[28] No other primary source mentions a fleet, so these must have been Edwin's vessels that had been at Ulleskelf. They could not have been ships from the south because to reach the Wharfe they would have had to pass Riccall, which would have alerted the Norse.

Maintaining secrecy at this juncture was paramount, and it was to play a crucial role in the forthcoming encounter. Nevertheless, it is astounding that the Norse remained unaware Harold's fyrd was in the vicinity and extraordinary that a token force was not left behind in York, men who could have warned Hardrada at Stamford Bridge or those at Riccall who were still oblivious to the English forces assembling at Tadcaster. Hardrada's complacency was grounded in the view that it would be impossible for an English army to reach York from the south so soon after the encounter at Fulford. Perhaps equally surprising is that Tostig had seriously underestimated his brother.

Perhaps only upon reaching Tadcaster and learning of his enemy's movements did Harold adopt his final strategy when it became clear they knew nothing of his approach. His forces advanced the final 9 miles to York in the early hours of 25 September, still with the element of surprise, but to find the city devoid of Norse was a further unexpected bonus. After perhaps an hour or two's rest, the English army left York at mid-morning and marched the final 7 miles to Stamford Bridge. The element of surprise was maintained to the end, with Snorri Sturluson's *Heimskringla* noting that the first the Norse knew was when 'they saw the cloud of dust raised by horses, and under it, fine shields and shining coats of mail'.[29] The Norse, having previously removed their armour, were found relaxing in the sunshine on either side of the narrow bridge crossing the Derwent. When Hardrada became aware that the approaching force was hostile he immediately sent horsemen to ride to Riccall to summon the men guarding the fleet.

The *Heimskringla* supplies us with the most detail of the day's events, although the primary aim of Snorri's work was a saga of Harald Hardrada, so writing in a storytelling style was his priority. Henry of Huntingdon's *Historia Anglorum* says that 'they engaged at dawn' and 'continued steadfastly until midday', although Henry is not supported by other reports.[30] Other sources suggest the fighting began nearer to midday, while Snorri adds that 'the day was excellent, with hot sunshine', which supports the premise that the English had set out from York mid-morning.[31] Those Norse caught unawares on the north bank of the Derwent suffered casualties as they rapidly withdrew across the bridge, and while a contingent tried to hold the crossing the majority of the command moved up onto the high ground half a mile to the south of the river to form a shield wall. This area would become the centre of the fighting, subsequently known as Battle Flats.

One of the most frequently recounted details from the battle concerns the bridge over the Derwent at Stamford, although it should be mentioned that the eleventh-century bridge was sited 100 metres to the east of the modern road bridge (A166), nearer to the present-day centre of the village.[32] It was doubtless wide enough to carry carts, but version C of the *ASC* leads us to imagine it was thinner when the scribe writes of one Norwegian warrior delaying the English from crossing. Interestingly the tale of this champion is not included in Snorri's *Heimskringla*. Nevertheless, the myth of the sole Viking guarding the crossing was well entrenched by the time William of Malmesbury and Henry of Huntingdon were writing in the early twelfth century.[33] Malmesbury wrote that the hero held up the English 'for many an hour', and it was 'a thing posterity may hardly believe' before he was finally killed.[34] The warrior was eventually slain by a single Englishman taking a small coracle under the bridge and spearing the Viking from below as the boat passed under him.[35] The episode epitomises the bravery of the professional warrior of the day, but the incident is likely allegory not fact as surely Harold would have used some of his archers to dispatch this individual.

Harold delayed his main assault to allow all his command to form up on the south bank. This had equally given Hardrada and Tostig time to form their lines on Battle Flats 500 metres south of the river at the crest of the ridge. Snorri's *Heimskringla* describes a brief exchange, of sorts, between Harold and Tostig ahead of the action. The English king and some housecarls rode up to the Norse shield wall, where Harold purportedly offered his brother a third of England if he would agree not to fight. Tostig is claimed to have replied, 'That is an offer different from the one of last winter, when I was shown contempt and hostility … If I should accept this, what will he offer King Harald Sigurdsson for his pains?' Snorri adds that the English king's reply was succinct: 'Seven feet of English soil.' With that, Tostig declined the overture and the English horsemen retired down the slope. Hardrada is then said to have asked Tostig, 'Who was that man who spoke so well?' When Tostig told him it had been Harold, the Norse king replied, 'Too late were we told of that … they had approached our army so close this Harold would not have lived to tell of our men's death.' Tostig responded that he would not be the cause of his brother's death and added, 'But I would rather that he slayed me than I him'.[36]

This text adds to the scene, but the supposed conversation was primarily designed to entertain Snorri's contemporary audience. It would be fitting to imagine that the Godwinson brothers had one last chance to talk before the conflict began, but Harold is unlikely to have risked a close approach to the Norwegian lines ahead of the main battle, and at best riders would have been sent to offer Tostig a pardon. Furthermore, the fictional element in Snorri's version is clear because Harold would never have offered away a third of his kingdom. Conversely, we need to place ourselves in Tostig's position. If we suppose that he was truly made this offer, how could he possibly extricate himself safely from the Norwegian lines without risking the wrath of Hardrada? The Norwegian would not have accepted such an arrangement; he was, after all, trying to conquer England himself.

The main English attack began in the early afternoon. The principal sources do not reveal the numbers involved, but Harold may have had a force of 6,000. Hardrada's army was likely smaller, because although the original allied force had numbered perhaps over 8,000 fighting men two factors had reduced this significantly. First, the allied casualties at Fulford likely exceeded a thousand; and second, 25–30 per cent of the Norse fighting strength that remained was still at Riccall. After the initial earlier losses at the riverbank the allies probably had no more than 5,000 men, maybe less, forming the shield wall on the ridge. Historians disagree on the English tactics and on the extent that the English used cavalry at Stamford Bridge.[37]

We know Harold had with him a large contingent of mounted thegns, and Hardrada formed his shield wall into a circle to prevent a cavalry attack from the rear, as 'the English horsemen rode down upon the Norwegians'.[38] It was not customary practice during this period for the English to use cavalry on the battlefield, but the terrain at Battle Flats probably aided cavalry tactics and enabled Harold to effectively encircle the Norse position. However, the main hand-to-hand fighting began when the English infantry had reached the crest of Battle Flats to confront the enemy shield wall. In this the Norse were further disadvantaged because, as recognised, many of them were not wearing their full armour.

The battle was long and bloody, but perhaps late in the afternoon came the breakthrough when Harald Hardrada fell. Snorri's *Heimskringla* tells us he was shot in the throat by an arrow as he led a charge out from behind the remains of his shield wall, although this is not mentioned by other primary sources.[39] The use of English archers, as with cavalry, remains an ongoing debate among historians, particularly when trying to compare Stamford Bridge to Hastings. Some archers would have been present at Stamford Bridge, although we cannot be certain of their impact. It is plausible Hardrada was slain by an arrow, but equally possible he was hacked down in hand-to-hand fighting.

Snorri tells us there was a brief lull in the action near the end after the death of Hardrada, during which Harold is said to have offered an amnesty to his brother and the remaining Norse warriors.[40] This was refused, although the *Heimskringla* does not inform us of Tostig's response, and soon afterwards Tostig was killed.[41] Paradoxically, it was then that the Norse warriors from Riccall began to arrive at Stamford to renew the fighting under the leadership of Eystein Orri. These Norse were fully armoured, but they had run 13 miles over difficult terrain and were exhausted. It had taken them around three hours via Wheldrake and Kexby, where they had crossed the River Derwent, before approaching Stamford Bridge through High Catton or Low Catton.[42] Had these 1,500 or so men reached Stamford an hour earlier the outcome might have been different, but they were arriving in divided units not a single united force, and they were soon running back the way they had come. Eystein Orri and many of the newly arrived warriors were slaughtered and it turned into a rout as Harold used his cavalry to best effect by harassing the retreating Norse and cutting them down as they fled.

The English mounted thegns hounded the survivors most of the way to Riccall. The *ASC* version D scribe wrote, 'The English fiercely attacked them from behind until some of them came to ship, some drowned, and some also burnt, and thus variously perished, so that there were few survivors.'[43] This burning of the ships may add an extra factor to the eventual fate of many of the remaining Norse. Perhaps the Mercian ships that had earlier retreated to Ulleskelf had sailed back into the Ouse on news that the Riccall Vikings had been summoned to Stamford Bridge and had been able to set the unguarded Viking ships aflame virtually unhindered.[44]

The leading sources record that Harold gave the survivors quarter and obtained oaths and hostages from Hardrada's son Olaf and Paul, Earl of Orkney, before allowing them to board their ships and leave freely. This group included Tostig's sons Skuli and Ketil. Depending on which source is accepted, the Norse survivors sailed away in only twenty or twenty-four ships compared to the 300-plus they had first arrived with.[45] Assuming perhaps forty or fifty men in each ship, little more than 800 to 1,000 men had survived.

What became of Hardrada's corpse is unclear, and only William of Malmesbury provides any detail on what happened to Tostig. According to Malmesbury, Tostig's body was 'recognised by the evidence of a wart between the shoulder-blades'.[46] This is like the later story surrounding the identification of Harold's corpse after Hastings, and Malmesbury may have conflated the two events. However, it is likely that his armour, presumably of high quality befitting a man of his status, had already been stripped from him. This was common practice. Armour and weaponry were expensive, and the victors would always take the spoils from the battlefield. A similar outcome would await the English dead at Hastings, as evidenced in the *Bayeux Tapestry*.[47] That Tostig was recognisable only from a wart on his back implies his face had been disfigured beyond recognition, so presumably Harold, or perhaps Gyrth or Leofwine if they were there, had identified the body.

 Harold had his brother's corpse taken back to York, and it was recorded that Tostig thereafter 'received the honour of a burial at York'.[48] How long his tomb remained undisturbed cannot be answered, but the original eleventh-century minster was replaced many centuries ago. Visitors to the village of Stamford Bridge will today find two memorials associated with the battle. The first site is found in a small memorial courtyard on the north side of Main Street (A166) about 100 metres east of the village square. It comprises a 4-foot headless stone cross on a plinth with two plaques at its base, one in English and the other in Norwegian, combined with a separate inscribed polished granite slab inserted into the wall behind the cross, which was erected in 1956. The second is at Battle Flats overlooking the site of the heavy fighting at the top of the ridge and close to the likely spot where Hardrada and Tostig died. From the village centre, it can be found by following Church Road into Moor Road and to the end of Whiterose Drive. It comprises a 3-foot memorial stone and plaque erected in 2016.

17

The Norman Invasion

Harold's famous victory at Stamford Bridge has taken us ahead of ourselves regarding developments in the south of England. In hindsight, he could have allowed the Norse attack to take its course, perhaps sending Gyrth and Leofwine to assist the northern earls while staying in the south himself. The English king, as has been seen, was well prepared to counteract a potential Norman invasion. His spies had informed him of Duke William's activities around Dives-sur-Mer. A scene in the *Bayeux Tapestry* depicts an English spy being captured in Normandy and permitted to return to England to report back William's intentions.[1] It has often been assumed Harold disbanded his forces along the south coast when news came of the Norse invasion in the north. However, the timeline was somewhat different. Harold had ordered the disbandment of the southern fyrd and the navy more than a week before Hardrada and Tostig's armada entered the River Humber, fully twelve days before Edwin and Morcar were to fight at Fulford. In simple terms, Harold had hedged his bets that Duke William had left it too late in the season to cross the Channel in assured safety, and the Norman invasion, if or when it came, would now arrive no earlier than the spring of 1067.

The fyrd levies were demobilised, as recorded by the *ASC*: 'When it was the Nativity of St Mary (8 September) the men's provisions were gone, and no one could hold them there any longer. The men were released to go home.'[2] Harold had not thought it necessary to replace them with fresh levies, and part of the reasoning given is that they were called upon to gather the harvest. However, gathering the harvest may have not been an issue. 8 September in the Julian Calendar, which was in force during the eleventh century, equates to a revised date of 19 September in the Gregorian Calendar (see introductory chapter).[3] Dates within the primary sources are based on the Julian Calendar and in real terms it was eleven days later in the yearly seasonal cycle. By that date, the harvest for 1066 would have been gathered.

The weather in the Channel from September onwards was thought to be poor for naval manoeuvres, particularly on the scale the Normans were planning. Harold had calculated that the threat had passed for the moment, and he could reassemble his forces in the coming spring. Even with his forces dispersed, Harold could probably assemble a new fyrd rapidly. The English military system by this period was efficient and adaptive, and in the context of the Norman invasion the disbandment was not the insurmountable problem that it might appear to have been. Nevertheless, the absence of men guarding the south coast was relevant, as it gave the Normans time to establish a strong beachhead before needing to fight the English. If William had met immediate strong resistance on first arrival, his chances of success would have been slim and probably extinguished quickly and permanently.

The deciding consideration was the twin invasions at opposite ends of the country within a week of each other, and Harold could only be in one place at a time. The English king and his housecarls were more than 200 miles from Sussex when the Norman fleet landed. Looking at it from William's perspective, his decision to launch his invasion in the autumn of 1066 rather than risk waiting until 1067 seems a logical one. Based on the news that Harold had disbanded the fyrd, alongside the plausible chance William was aware of Hardrada's parallel plans, meant there would not be a better opportunity for the Normans. In addition, an issue sometimes overlooked was that William could not afford to keep his forces on duty for five or six further months. The expense would have been punitive, and those nobles who had provided him with soldiers and ships would have withdrawn their support.

Months earlier, Duke William had called together his senior nobles to persuade them to back his venture on the promise of great returns on their capital. Over the late spring and summer of 1066, William had assembled what would become a considerable fleet in the estuary of the River Dives at Cabourg, 7 miles east of modern-day Oustreham. A contemporary list of those identified as the largest contributors of ships and men included Count Robert of Mortain, Bishop Odo (William's brother-in-law), Count Richard of Evreux, William FitzOsbern, Count Robert of Eu, Hugh of Avranches, Robert of Montgomery and Roger of Beaumont.[4] Nobles flocked to join, either to garner favour with William or to seek fame and fortune, 'attracted partly by the well-known liberality of the duke, but all fully confident of the justice of his cause'.[5]

Some Norman sources portray the expedition in terms of a crusade, with Duke William having papal support and an obligation to seek justice for being deprived of the English throne by a usurper. William of Poitiers emphasises the moral argument best, confirming that 'seeking the approval of this pope (Alexander II), whom he had informed of the business in hand, the duke received a banner with his blessing, to signify the approval of St Peter, by following which he might attack the enemy with greater confidence and safety'.[6] Alexander purportedly gave his blessing along with a papal ring and a Saint George Cross standard.[7] It was important that those attracted to the cause believed they were acting with a papal mandate.

However, the papal response was more likely negative than positive, and it is argued this is linked to the building of Battle Abbey. William's post-1066 project to establish an abbey on the site of the victorious battle was accredited to his earlier pledge if he successfully defeated Harold. Nevertheless, there is serious doubt over this claim. He was instead probably compelled to build the abbey as absolution for the bloodshed he had caused, because Pope Alexander had not approved of the invasion of another Christian country or the killing of a Christian monarch. Penances that were imposed on the Norman soldiery by the papal legate Ermenfrid after the Conquest acknowledge that his papal predecessor had not sanctioned the violation. Additional Norman propaganda claimed William had 'recently made a friendly pact with Henry, emperor of the Romans ... by the terms of which Germany would if requested, come to his aid against any enemy', and 'Swein, king of the Danes, also pledged his faith to him through ambassadors'.[8] These claims can also be seen to be false, particularly the notion that Swein II (Estrithsson) would have acted against his cousin Harold.

Vessels were constructed or customised to transport the more than 2,500 warhorses that were a key part of William's invasion army. Some wildly excessive figures have been given for the size of the Norman fleet. William of Jumièges records there were up to 3,000 vessels, but aside from the logistics of coordinating such an armada it would have been impossible to find adjacent safe landing spots for that number of ships.[9] Wace recalled that his father had told him as a young lad that there had been 'seven hundred ships less four ... carrying weapons or equipment'.[10] This latter figure seems nearer the numbers for men, horses and material combined based on the other information available. Using this maximum capacity of 700 warships and transports some historians have claimed such a fleet could have carried up to 12,000 men plus 2,500 horses.[11] The *Bayeux Tapestry* illustrates that some vessels had men and horses, while others had just men.[12] This perhaps interprets the tapestry detail too strictly, giving us a mean average of seventeen men and about four horses per vessel. Besides, it excludes any prerequisite of the deck space needed for provisions, materiel, weapons, food (for horses and men) and the pre-constructed timber sections the Normans brought for their preliminary fortifications (forts), which would have taken up significant space in the fleet.

The consensus among historians for the Norman forces averages out at 7,500–8,000 soldiers, consisting of 4,000 foot-soldiers, 1,000 archers, and up to 3,000 cavalry.[13] An additional 4,000 non-fighting men likewise seems excessive (to arrive at the 12,000 noted above), and a figure of 2,000 for the artisans, engineers and labourers may be nearer the mark. We can venture to modify the ship configurations and hypothesise that horses and fighting men occupied 550 of the vessels with fifteen men and five horses per vessel, but with no provisions, while the remaining 150 ships each held about thirteen non-fighting men and all the equipment and provisions.

The logistical planning behind the invasion was impressive. One estimate is that it would have taken 8,400 men three months to construct 700 vessels requiring 624 hectares of forest, the equivalent of about seventy-four trees per ship.[14] However, only about half of this number were new constructions, as many vessels had been requisitioned from ports all along the coast from as far away as Flanders. To maintain the large body of men that had accumulated around Dives-sur-Mer necessitated a massive task requiring about 9,000 cartloads of food and supplies per month, plus 13 tons a day of both grain and hay to feed 3,000 horses.[15] The land required to produce this amount of food could have been as much as 550 square kilometres.[16]

Ahead of the invasion, William would have been aware of the local geography of Sussex through his contacts with Fécamp Abbey. Fécamp had been granted the minster at Steyning and its estates in Sussex by Edward, including a thriving port, and in 1047 ecclesiastical jurisdiction for it had passed directly to the papacy.[17] Earl Godwin had seized Steyning's lands from the abbey, and they had later passed to Harold. Harold was effectively overruling papal control of those estates, and William used this argument to further bolster his claim with the pope. Among the Fécamp estates was a specific estate named Rameslie, and it held extensive holdings including Rye, Old Winchelsea, Brede, and territory east of Hastings.[18] The advance intelligence obtained from the monks at Fécamp has been underplayed, as they were able to advise the best landing sites in the area that could accommodate the large Norman fleet. This was perhaps a factor in why William first transferred from Dives to the Somme Estuary.[19] Evidence of links to Fécamp Abbey ahead of the conquest is found in a cleric named Remigius, who was to provide a ship and twenty knights for the Norman expedition, and was later made Bishop of Dorchester-on-Thames, and then later of Lincoln, by William in gratitude.[20]

The chosen landing site or sites needed to accommodate 700 ships with an average beam of 4 metres with drafts varying between 20–50 centimetres, assuming the boats beached 3 metres apart, required a minimum of 3 miles of landing space.[21] If they were 5 metres apart, it would be 4 miles. In the region of the planned landing only Pevensey Bay, Combe Haven and the Brede Estuary had suitable tidal flows and sufficient landing points to sustain such a fleet. William's delay, whether by accident or design, has been the subject of much discussion. The English squadron was plausibly still at anchor at the Isle of Wight and if William had invaded before the English ships or the fyrd disbanded, it would have ended in disaster. However, the weather in the Channel was likely to deteriorate, so his window of opportunity was limited.

As noted by William of Poitiers and Orderic Vitalis, the expedition had planned to sail in mid-August but 'unfavourable winds delayed him for a month at the mouth of the Dives'.[22] News had subsequently reached William that the English forces had dispersed on 8 September and had not been replaced by a new conscript, and it was this that must have given him the green light to risk the weather. If this was not calculated, it was a fortuitous coincidence, because had the Normans sailed to their original timetable they would have encountered the English navy and Harold's fyrd, making William's chances of establishing a bridgehead virtually impossible. However, Dives would prove to be a false start. Poitiers adds that 'the whole fleet ... was blown from the mouth of the Dives ... where they had long waited for a south wind ... and was driven by the breath of the west wind to moorings at Saint-Valéry'.[23] There is a strong argument that William deliberately delayed until he was assured the English king had disbanded his fyrd.[24]

Working in reverse, the Norman fleet had left the Dives Estuary one week after the English fyrd had demobilised. Some primary sources record incorrectly that the Norman fleet first sailed from Saint-Valéry-sur-Somme. It was to eventually cross from there on 28 September. The sailing distance from Dives to West Sussex was approaching 110 miles, but it was only 60 miles from the Somme to East Sussex. What happened between the two sailings (Dives and Saint-Valéry) has been omitted from many primary sources, but the transfer to Saint-Valéry may hide the fact that the Normans had encountered bad weather in the Channel after leaving Dives. Alternative suggestions are that part of the Norman armada clashed with a few of the English ships that were still withdrawing up the Channel to Sandwich.[25] However, if an encounter took place, we need to question the response from Harold and the English command. We talk in detail of Harold's fyrd, but we overlook what was happening with his navy. If the English knew that the Normans had sailed in numbers, why would they fail to return down the Channel when the weather window improved? For this reason alone, we can probably dismiss the idea that there had been a clash of navies.

Nevertheless, it is clear the Norman fleet suffered some difficulty. William of Poitiers' *Gesta Guillelmi* notes the duke, 'whom neither the delay nor the contrary wind nor the terrible shipwrecks ... could shake ... concealed as far as he could the loss of those who had been drowned, by burying them in secret'.[26] This tells us the Normans had lost men and ships and had found port again in Normandy, reassembling 100 miles north-east of Dives in the Somme Estuary at Saint-Valéry. A scheduled transfer up the Norman coast to be nearer the English coast is credible, but it is also plausible the main offensive had been attempted first from Dives-sur-Mer and had been thwarted by factors outside William's control. Conditions in the Channel had caused casualties among the English too, because while some of Harold's disbanded ships were returning to London 'many perished before they came there'.[27]

The Norman fleet sailed from the Somme Estuary on the evening of 27 or 28 September. It was so large that many ships lost contact and were instructed to rest overnight at anchor in the open sea 'until they see a lamp lit at his (Duke William's) masthead and hear the sound of a trumpet as a signal to sail on'.[28] There is some disagreement whether the invasion began on the morning of 28 or 29 September. The *ASC* tells us it was the earlier date (the eve of the Feast of St Michael), whilst the *Carmen* of Guy of Amiens, and also Orderic Vitalis, prefers the following day.[29] The two contemporary Norman authorities, Poitiers and Jumièges, give no date, saying only that it was five days after Harold's victory at Stamford Bridge.

Where exactly the Norman fleet landed on English shores is worthy of discussion. Pevensey Bay was, and remains, the location favoured by most academics, but in recent years the topic has been more widely debated and more in-depth consideration is appropriate. Part of the problem in consolidating the primary source detail is their different definitions of Hastings and Pevensey (i.e. 'Hastinga' or 'Heastinga', and 'Pevensae', 'Pevenisel' or 'Penevesellum'). Sources use different interpretations of 'Pevensey' to describe not just the area around Pevensey Castle but also the Hastings peninsula as far as the estuary of the River Brede. Similarly, 'Hastings' has been used to define the peninsula and alternatively everything between the port of Hastings and Pevensey, including Combe Haven and Bulverhythe. It is these alternative interpretations within the main sources that have widened the debate.

The central consensus is that William arrived at Pevensey, occupied and fortified the old Roman fort there, and then proceeded to Hastings, where he established a fortification of earthworks and two forts using the materials the fleet had transported.[30] This is summarised in Orderic's *Ecclesiastical History* and the *ASC*: 'They took possession of Pevensey and Hastings and gave them into the charge of chosen soldiers as a base for the army and shelter for the fleet ... [and] made a castle at Hastings.'[31] Wace's *Roman de Rou* adds that the Normans 'threw down from the ships and dragged on land the wood which the Count of Eu had brought there, all pierced and trimmed' and 'built a small castle with it and made a ditch round it, creating a great fortress there', as per the scenes in the *Bayeux Tapestry*.[32]

Understanding the local topography around Pevensey and Hastings as it looked in the mid-eleventh century is fundamental to any discussion on this subject. What today is occupied partly by 'Pevensey Levels National Nature Reserve' and crossed by the modern A259 road from Pevensey to Bexhill and the minor road through Normans Bay was at that time an extensive tidal bay. Godwin had previously utilised it at least twice to shelter his ships. In present-day terms the shallow bay reached inland north to Herstmonceux, to the edge of Polegate in the west, and the outskirts of Bexhill in the east.[33] Being tidal, much of its northern reaches was perhaps only underwater for two hours a day.[34] Pevensey Castle lay on a promontory into the bay on its western edge, reached from the higher ground via Westham. The old fort was ideal for defence, but it was unsuitable for launching a wider advance. Had the Normans concentrated at Pevensey and remained there, they would have been hemmed in without room for manoeuvre. Today, the castle is a mile from the sea and the bay is dry land interspersed with a few minor watercourses including Hurst Haven and Waller's Haven. Due to a combination of silting, tidal flows and land reclamation, the landscape has been transformed. Geologists have estimated that in 1066 the sea level at high tide at Pevensey, when counter-adjusted to remove subsequent soil deposition, was between 2 to 3 metres higher than it is today.[35]

On consideration of the landing site, Wace noted that the Normans 'arrived near Hastings and first found land there; they gathered their ships all together, putting one ship up against another', and 'the first day they arrived there they stayed close to the shore and the next day they came to the castle called Pevensey'.[36] These entries are not as contradictory as they first appear if we theorise that the Normans initially landed at two or three sites, sent out scouting parties between Pevensey and Hastings, and then consolidated their ships in one place the following day. There is logic in the assumption 700 ships would not initially have all beached at one site. Duke William knew thanks to advance local intelligence from Fécamp Abbey that Pevensey Bay could accommodate many ships, but there was another extensive shallow harbour to the east at Combe Haven with its associated port of Bulverhythe on the western margin of the Hastings peninsula.

The premise that the Normans later chose the inlet at Bulverhythe as their primary base is highly likely. The name itself has two interpretations in Old English, translating as 'the harbour of the people of the burh' or 'the landing place of the people'.[37] Today, Bulverhythe is dry land between Bexhill and St Leonards, but in the eleventh century it served as one of the ports for the burh on the Hastings headland. The port lay about a mile inland from the present seafront, near to Redgeland Wood, just south of Crowhurst Road and the newly constructed A2690.[38] Beyond eleventh-century Bulverhythe lay the extended inlet of Combe Haven, where boats could sail almost to Crowhurst and Henley's Down with a water depth of a few metres. The inlet was sealed from shipping after a major storm in 1252 deposited large volumes of silt, permanently blocking the entrance to the harbour and the haven.

Bulverhythe and Combe Haven are now separated from the sea by the raised sandbar from Bexhill. The Haven lies in the reclaimed area known as 'Combe Valley Countryside Park', beyond where the A2690 road now bisects the northern end of the original tidal zone. During the 1930s a longship, possibly Norman, complete with dragon prow, was evidently discovered within a drainage ditch while major work was being carried out to level the area for Pebsham Aerodrome, although the ship was immediately reburied to avoid a delay to the completion of the airfield. The small airfield closed in 1959, and the site has not been excavated further. It is understood this story of the discovery was widespread among residents for many years, and if accepted, the remains of this longship will still be there, somewhere below or next to the fields now identified as Bulverhythe Recreation Ground.

The Normans probably initially landed at both Pevensey and Bulverhythe. It is a pointless argument debating between them; utilising both meets the primary source detail and explains the later construction of the temporary fort at Hastings. The traditional association of Bulverhythe with the Norman landing is embodied in the 3-by-2-metre flat sandstone slab that can be found on the seafront at St Leonards between Marina Drive (A259) and the promenade, opposite the Royal Victoria Hotel. The stone was originally sited a short distance away in Maze Hill Gardens and has since been transferred twice before being placed at its present position. It is known locally as 'William the Conqueror's Stone', and rests on a concrete plinth with a bronze plaque denoting the stone's reputed connection with the Norman landing. Folklore says it was employed as the table where Duke William, his brother-in-law Bishop Odo of Bayeux and the other leading Norman lords ate their first meal on English soil. The table scene is depicted in the *Bayeux Tapestry*.[39] It shows only one diner eating fish, which is presumed to denote Bishop Odo because the clergy could not eat meat on a Friday. This therefore places the meal scene as taking place on Friday 28 September 1066.

William of Jumièges and William of Poitiers record the Normans built a fortification at Pevensey, but this cannot have been the case.[40] The pre-constructed sections the Normans had shipped over were instead used to build their two forts at Hastings, one near to Bulverhythe and the other on the headland. Defending Pevensey was not William's key strategy. The fort at Pevensey had originally been built as a defence against sea attacks and did not afford sufficient protection from the landward direction. The land journey from Pevensey to Hastings in the eleventh century required a circuitous route via what is now Polegate, Hailsham, Herstmonceux, Catsfield and Crowhurst, an estimated minimum of 22 miles. By comparing estate values before and after 1066 taken from the *Domesday Book*, the evidence of the pillaging caused by the Normans immediately following their arrival supports the case that the estates around Pevensey were relatively unspoilt compared to those nearer to Combe Haven and Crowhurst.[41] In some cases, the differences are stark.

Some historians point to the omission of Hastings itself within the Domesday survey of 1086, although its exclusion may be because it had simply ceased to exist by that date because of the Norman destruction twenty years earlier.[42] The evidence that the Norman pillaging was responsible for most of the devaluations that took place is interesting. There are indeed several estates around Pevensey that devalued by up 50 per cent, but the worst affected area was on the Hastings Peninsula and around Combe Haven and Crowhurst, where twice the number were impacted with losses of two-thirds of their pre-1066 values. In several cases, estates such as Hastings remained 'wasted' and did not recover ahead of *Domesday Book*.[43]

This data supports the premise the Normans centred all their ships and men to the area around Bulverhythe and then erected the initial Norman fort on the eastern edge of the Bulverhythe–Combe Haven inlet as their main base camp, to the west of and below the headland at Hastings.[44] There was an old Anglo-Saxon burh fort on the promontory, and it was here that, shortly afterwards, William, uncertain of Harold's whereabouts, erected the second of his forts.[45] Some of the mound (motte) for this survives as part of the late eleventh-century Norman castle. However, it is estimated that the cliff headland may have eroded by somewhere between 300 and 800 metres since 1066, taking with it the earlier Anglo-Saxon burh.[46] The peninsula had defensive advantages, protected by Combe Haven to the west and the Brede Estuary to the east, with only one significant road out of it. The River Brede was formerly considerably wider, flowing past Winchelsea and continuing almost due west to Sedlescombe just 2 miles from where the road from the peninsula came up to the ridge at Senlac (that is, Battle).

More recently local historians have suggested that the main Norman landing was via the Brede Estuary.[47] The strength of this claim rests primarily on a new interpretation of the location of what eleventh-century contemporaries understood to be 'Hastinge Portus' (the Port of Hastings) and 'Penevessel' (the Port in the Wash).[48] Instead of the limited definition of Pevensey as we accept it today, some academics have suggested 'Penevessel' was formerly applied to define a much wider region abutting the Hastings peninsula. As mentioned, Fécamp Abbey held the manor of Rameslie on the northern fringe of the Hastings peninsula near the mouth of the Brede Estuary, which served the peninsula as another port. Rameslie no longer exists, but it was situated somewhere near the estate of Guestling, which today lies south of the River Brede a mile or more from the original mouth of the river.[49]

In 1066, the Brede combined with the River Rother and other smaller streams to form a large body of water with a catchment area much larger than Pevensey or Combe Haven.[50] There was tidal access at either end of a long and wide shingle bar extending between Fairlight and Old Romney. Further deposition would eventually seal this, but prior to the fourteenth century ships could have accessed the Brede at full tide. In accepting the Norman fleet could theoretically have beached along the Brede at Rameslie, we acknowledge the proposition put by local historians that Sedlescombe may be the location of the later battle. This will be looked at in more depth in chapter eighteen.[51] Nonetheless, unlike the decline of the estate valuations discussed above there is little evidence to support serious pillaging having taken place around Rameslie, although that may be explained by it being under the ownership of the Norman monks at Fécamp. South of the Brede Estuary, further down the peninsula, the evidence of declining estate values is upheld.

Once established, William began pillaging for food and supplies, and an image of the Norman destruction appears in the *Bayeux Tapestry*.[52] The suggestion has been put that these actions were intended provoke Harold into rushing headlong for Hastings without waiting to assemble his full army. As recorded by William of Malmesbury, 'fate surely was hurrying him to his doom, unwilling as he was to get together any reinforcements'.[53] It is questionable whether Harold took William's plundering into account. The only heavily pillaged estate the English king held in the neighbourhood was Crowhurst. From Harold's perspective, his speed in reaching the south coast was based on catching William unprepared in the same way he had surprised Hardrada and Tostig.

For William, luring Harold to move hastily was desirable, but he needed to be careful his defensive position on the Hastings peninsula did not trap his forces indefinitely and disadvantageously. He had not broken out into the wider countryside, despite plentiful opportunities to do so, and his decision for remaining at his base camp must be questioned.[54] Could he have used the greater mobility of his cavalry to raid much further afield before Harold's arrival? Probably, but he nevertheless remained cautious, because unlike the English William would not be receiving reinforcements, and so he needed to entice Harold into a single decisive battle rather than slowly lose men he could not replace. More importantly, moving away from the Hastings peninsula too soon risked his ships being destroyed to his rear, leaving him without the critical option of escaping by ship if the coming battle went badly. Even this option may have already been closed to him if we assume that the English navy had returned to the Channel.

Harold may have been aware as early as 29 September that the Normans had landed, if we accept the premise that a system of beacon fires was in operation.[55] Leaving York in the hands of Marleswein the Staller, he headed south, repeating in reverse the hard ride he had undertaken only eight or nine days before. As discussed earlier, it is a marvellous story to imagine the troops marching headlong down the Great North Road in just a few days to confront their second army of invasion in a fortnight, but this was not the reality. For speed, Harold travelled south with a large contingent of mounted men and not foot soldiers. The fyrdmen who would later march into Sussex with Harold, unlike the mounted thegns, were not the same men that had been engaged at Stamford Bridge. Harold's mounted force, comprising housecarls and thegns, would have been back in London by perhaps 6 or 7 October, and word would have gone ahead, as he travelled, for levies to converge at London in readiness. Gyrth and Leofwine would have been active in raising men from their earldoms to join their brother. The list of some English fatalities at the Battle of Hastings confirms that senior nobles and their men had answered this second summons from across the Midlands, East Anglia and the south-east.

A dozen miles north of London, Harold stopped off at his foundation church at Waltham to pray for divine support. The *Waltham Chronicle* later told of a dire omen seen by the monks, but not by Harold, while he prayed; and two monks, Osgod Cnoppe and Æthelric Childemaister, were assigned to go with him, with instructions to take charge of the king's body if things went badly.[56] In London Harold waited several more days for the troops to gather, but when he left there sometime around 9–10 October many of the fyrd conscripts had still not arrived. More later joined en route to Hastings, but John of Worcester notes that Harold reached Hastings 'before a third of his army had been drawn up'.[57]

It is difficult to determine whether Harold hoped to catch out William as he had done Hardrada, or if he already had news that William was not budging from the Hastings peninsula. Three different primary sources – the *Ecclesiastical History* of Orderic Vitalis, Wace's *Roman de Rou*, and the *Gesta Regum Anglorum* of William of Malmesbury – tell us of earlier discussions between Harold and Gyrth in London. The essence of these texts is that Gyrth tried to persuade his brother to remain in London, because unlike Harold he had not given an oath to the Norman duke and could therefore not break any pledge, whereas Harold would perjure himself. This reference reminds us that the oath reputedly given to William remained a constant source of propaganda against Harold's character.

The sources say Gyrth argued that he should lead the English fyrd, so if the battle was lost Harold could still fight another day. Wace warmed to the task of attributing their conversation, with Gyrth saying, 'Stay here (in London) but let me have your troops. I will take the risk and do battle with William. But if I am conquered or captured, you, who would still be alive, could, if it pleases God, gather your troops together to do battle.'[58] Malmesbury included Leofwine in the family discussion, and adds, 'If you enter the lists yourself, you may be put to flight or killed, whereas, if we alone fight ... you will be able to restore the situation if we flee, and avenge us if we fail.'[59] However, Harold ignored the advice, because 'he refused to lend a patient ear to good advice' and because 'they would consider him a coward ... and many would rebuke the man who sent his good supporters to a place to which he did not dare go himself'.[60]

These entries were aimed at their contemporary readership, and conversation narratives such as those quoted here were often added to provide additional interest. However, there may be a hint of truth within these conversation pieces. Rationally, Gyrth was right. Harold did not need to accept the risk, and part of the alleged response from him to Gyrth accords with how we perceive his character. Harold had shown he was prepared to take the initiative, and it is only in hindsight that we can see wrong choices were made. Nevertheless, there was pressure to act decisively.

It has been suggested Harold acted in haste because he believed the Normans would be receiving reinforcements.[61] However, this argument is hard to justify. As noted above, it is far from certain William would have had the full freedom of the Channel after the initial landing, even putting weather conditions aside. The whereabouts of the English fleet in the weeks following the Norman landing is a mystery. It was only in the weeks after his victory at Hastings that William had the luxury of bringing over reinforcements without fear of being challenged at sea.

The direct route between London and the Hastings area, although not the quickest, was through the great forest of Andredsweald, the ancient, sparsely populated forest that in the Middle Ages stretched west to east from the Hampshire–Sussex border to Ashford and the Kent Downs, and north to south from Sevenoaks to just north of Lewes and Rye.[62] The Andredsweald was best avoided, and consequently historians have concluded that the English army likely followed one of two alternate routes. Both were a similar distance, about 60 miles. The first was along the old Roman road to Lewes via Titsey and Edenbridge as far as Maresfield, before turning east past Buxted and Netherfield towards Hastings. The second was along Watling Street via Dartford to Rochester, then along the Roman road through Maidstone and Sissinghurst to Cripps Corner near Sedlescombe.[63] This latter route was faster, but it meant crossing the River Rother near Bodiam. At Sedlescombe, the track turned west before fording the River Brede along a shallower section nearer to Caldbec. In 1876, over 1,000 coins minted during the reign of Edward the Confessor were discovered at Sedlescombe. These could be linked to the events of 1066, possibly coins from Harold's lost army pay chest connected to the alternate battle site near Sedlescombe discussed in the next chapter.[64]

The Anglo-Saxon military system relied on a combination of thegns and militia levies, but the elite core of the army were the housecarls. Many housecarls had been casualties at Stamford Bridge, and the need to engage in another major battle so soon afterwards limited their available numbers. The call to arms to counteract the Normans, as the *ASC* describes, was to assemble the army north of the Hastings peninsula at 'the grey apple-tree'.[65] This rather oblique reference has become famous as part of the storyline behind the coming battle. This tree was evidently a location marker known throughout the district, possibly designating a significant boundary between two administrative hundreds. Many historians suggest this tree was probably on Caldbec Hill, half a mile north of Senlac Hill and the later Battle Abbey. At Caldbec Hill the English were somewhere between 3 and 5 miles from the Norman camp.

In contrast, Orderic Vitalis implies that the English united to the south of Caldbec, noting that they 'flocked together from all sides to the place whose early name was Senlac', taken from the Old English word *sandluca*, meaning 'sand stream' or 'sand lake', thereafter adopted for the name of the hill overlooking the traditional battleground.[66] The term has alternately been used for the Brede Estuary, known as 'Sandy Loch'.[67] Documents show that Battle Abbey had in later centuries a tithing of land known as Santlache.[68] Men continued to filter into the English camp, but Harold is said to have fought the following day (14 October), 'before all his raiding-army had come'.[69]

Norman sources describe envoys being sent between Harold and William on the eve of battle, one of them being the Breton Robert FitzWimarc, who was sent to dissuade William from fighting Harold. FitzWimarc, it should be remembered, was one of those individuals depicted at Edward's deathbed scene in the *Bayeux Tapestry*, so was part of Harold's trusted elite. Failing to dissuade William, FitzWimarc nevertheless remained in the Norman camp, although whether this was voluntarily or otherwise is unclear. Guy of Amiens' *Carmen* and Wace's *Roman de Rou* are the most detailed on this phase of communications pre-battle.[70] These help in understanding the ongoing propaganda. William of Poitiers, for example, maintains the rhetoric he knew appealed to his Norman audience in his *Gesta Guillelmi*. He returns to his favourite topic, the alleged offer of the English throne made to William in 1051, when writing as his duke's voice, 'I have crossed the sea to enter this land, of which my lord and kinsman King Edward says made me his heir ... certainly he did not do this without the consent of his magnates, but in truth with the advice of Archbishop Stigand, Earl Godwin,

Earl Leofric, and Earl Siward, who also confirmed with a handfast oath, that after the death of Edward they would receive me as their lord.'[71]

Nevertheless, in his desire to re-emphasise William's legitimate entitlement, Poitiers made two errors regarding the 1051 claim. Firstly, as noted previously, Earl Godwin could not have given his backing or any pledge supporting the Norman duke's claim because when William purportedly visited Edward that year Godwin was at that moment in exile in Flanders. Secondly, the Archbishop of Canterbury in 1051 had been the Norman Robert of Jumièges (Champart). Stigand could not have confirmed any oath as archbishop because his promotion only came after the return of the Godwinsons from exile towards the end of 1052. Poitiers presumably made these mistakes because he had little or no knowledge of the major issues that had taken place in England fifteen years earlier. He was attempting to revise history to suit his argument irrespective of the facts.

18

Hastings: The Battle and Its Location

Hastings is the most written-about battle in English history. At a conservative estimate, there are over twenty books in print today in which the battle forms the principal subject directly or more roundly in general terms of the Norman Conquest. Similarly, the battle is given some attention later in this chapter alongside a consideration of the structure of the two armies. However, much of the following focuses the discussion on where the encounter took place, an issue less frequently addressed in standard academic works but which has gained increased interest in recent years.

We first need to glance at the unique structures of the two armies. Hastings was a clash of two different military systems. Each army had a large contingent of elite semi-professional fighting men: housecarls (huscarls) for the English, and cavalry (mounted knights) on trained warhorses (destriers) for the Normans. Housecarls are consistently portrayed as being skilled in the use of the two-handed battle-axe. The *Bayeux Tapestry* provides the strongest evidence for the weaponry and armour that was employed by both sides, and this appears typical of the period. Professional warriors wore chainmail coats, conical helmets with or without nasal guards, and padded leggings, and carried either a round or kite-shaped shield. The English fyrd militias had rudimentary protection, perhaps padded jerkins, and the mercenary archers used by the Normans possibly even less protection. The weapon of choice was the double-edged sword, but an array of other weapons, including spears and javelins, were shared by both armies. The English used axes and clubs and projectiles, and the Norman cavalry lances, but whereas the archers formed a valuable part of William's army there were far fewer archers available to Harold.

The topic of archery and cavalry has been touched on previously. The English did on occasion use warhorses in battle, as seen at Stamford Bridge, and the war-gear demanded by the king on the death of a thegn includes reference to their horse and confirms that horses were part of the inventory of the military nobility.[1] However, unlike Stamford Bridge, Harold did not deploy cavalry at Hastings, a decision likely based on a combination of the available terrain and his overall strategic approach. Why there were so few English bowmen cannot be answered. The *Bayeux Tapestry* depicts a single English bowman among its scenes, and they did not impact the fighting.[2] The Normans, as depicted in the tapestry, employed a large contingent of archers and crossbowmen from Normandy and beyond, although the terrain of the battlefield did not allow William to use them to their best effect until near the end of the fighting.

Where the two armies assembled their troops and in what formation has been continuously debated, although a consensus has been reached on how they initially formed ranks. The English established a multi-ranked infantry shield wall, and the Normans had combinations of infantry on the wings and horsemen in the centre, with archers being sent forward at stages. Harold was not unaware of the potency of the Norman mounted knight; he would have seen first-hand their effectiveness during the Norman campaign in Brittany in 1064. Traditionally, the housecarls and the fyrd fought on foot behind the shield wall. This was not a hard and fast rule, but the traditional battle site, alongside each of the other sites discussed later, favoured the English king adopting a defensive infantry formation. In contrast, the Norman infantry would prove ineffective on the chosen battlefield, but Duke William utilised a combination of archery and cavalry to good effect as the day progressed.

The location where the Battle of Hastings took place has become a topic more openly discussed than it once was. Until relatively recently historians have almost unanimously agreed, based on interpretation of the various primary source evidence, that it took place where the ruins of Battle Abbey stand today, the hill known as Senlac Hill. This is unequivocally supported by English Heritage, the owners of the abbey and the adjacent land. This location has been argued for vociferously, but there is no hard archaeological evidence other than the tradition that the Norman abbey was constructed on the spot where the English shield wall had stood and where Harold Godwinson was killed. However, some academics and local historians have recently put their heads above the parapet to suggest alternative locations for the battlefield, and these are worthy of examination alongside the traditional site.

Conclusive archaeological evidence is non-existent, not just for the traditional site but for all the alternative proposed sites, and the long-held acceptance of the Battle Abbey site will not be critically challenged unless substantial archaeology emerges elsewhere. However, we should nonetheless approach this with an open mind, looking at all the evidence applicable, and this means assessing the primary source texts in parallel with evaluating the data gathered from new advances in landscape sciences. We may never know with total clarity where Harold fought William, but an assessment of all the plausible options may, if nothing else, give pause for thought. The aim should not be to support or refute the traditional site come what may, but rather to give alternative scenarios some space for consideration.

Apart from the English Heritage traditional site, there are four other locations of varying suitability worthy of assessment, with the case for these alternate sites resting heavily on geographical analysis using quantitative data combined with the data derived from the primary sources.[3] The first is very close to the conventional site, only 200 metres east of the abbey, its centre at or near to the present-day roundabout where Upper Lake, Lower Lake and Marley Lane meet in the village of Battle, on what can be termed the eastern edge of Senlac Hill. The second alternate location is at Caldbec Hill, half a mile to the north of the abbey, and a third is between Telham Hill and Crowhurst, about a mile and a half south of Battle.[4] All these, including the traditional spot, are based on the evidence that the initial Norman landing site was at Pevensey or Combe Haven (Bulverhythe) or a combination of both, and that the Norman camp was at or just to the west of the modern centre of Hastings. But there is a fourth option, radically different, suggested near Sedlescombe between the rivers Rother and Brede.[5] The premise here is, as considered in the previous chapter, that the Norman fleet entered the body of water east of the Hastings peninsula at high tide, near Winchelsea, and sailed up the River Brede. From there, they made camp and in due course ventured out to fight the English army near Sedlescombe.

Before assessing these alternate options, we should first work on the basis that the fighting took place at the traditionally recognised site when looking at how the battle unfolded, although most of the known or speculated events of the day can be easily slotted into the other battle site scenarios too. William had been keen to draw Harold towards him but had nearly been caught out by the speed of Harold's march into Sussex. Traditionally, Harold and his bodyguard were at the highest point of Senlac Hill (Battle Hill), but crucially Harold was on foot, which was to prove a serious disadvantage as the day progressed. Gyrth and Leofwine and their retinues of housecarls may have been alongside their brother, as stated by William of Malmesbury, but it is possible they were deployed to control and oversee the flanks of the English defensive line.[6] The *ASC* tells us that 'William came upon him (Harold) by surprise before his people were marshalled'.[7] The Normans had left their base camp and reached the top of Telham Hill before 8.00 a.m. and had moved to the foot of Senlac Hill within the hour.

The *Carmen de Hastingae Proelio* of Guy of Amiens says Harold 'planted his standard on the summit, and ordered all other banners to be joined to his'.[8] The primary tactic was to defend the restricted fighting front and prevent the Norman cavalry outflanking the shield wall, with the housecarls and thegns being perhaps over 50–60 per cent of the total standing in the front few ranks with the fyrd militia behind them. Some primary sources wildly exaggerate the numbers, but historians accept that the English army probably numbered between 7,000 and 9,000.[9] Accepting the conventional alignment at Senlac, the English faced south and Harold would have had to defend a minimum front of 450 metres to cover his flanks. However, in the alternative scenario at the 'Battle roundabout', which will be considered later, the shield wall was aligned to face more to the south-east at the optimum angle of the ridge based on the eleventh-century topography, requiring a reduced shield wall length closer to 350 metres. Given that a man in the first rank would have taken up a 3-foot space to fight effectively, there would have been about 490 men in a 450-metre shield wall or 380 men along a 350-metre shield wall. Assuming an army of 8,000 men, that would give us a depth of sixteen ranks in the initial instance or twenty-one ranks in the second instance.

The Normans had similar numbers to the English. The truly destructive wing was the mounted knights, numbering more than 2,500. There were also several hundred archers and crossbowmen and about 4,000 infantry. The *Carmen* confirms William placed his French allies on his left wing and his Breton allies on his right, with the Normans, incorporating all the cavalry, occupying the centre.[10] According to William of Poitiers, the archers were initially in the front rank and the infantry immediately behind them. The mounted knights, from which William directed operations on horseback, were initially kept in the rear.[11] The armoured knight and his mount combined to form a highly efficient fighting weapon which the English had not encountered beforehand, but as already suggested Harold would have known of their effectiveness. This was to be primarily nullified by the landscape for most of the fighting, in that being forced to charge uphill they could not use their extra mobility to any great profit, and Harold had selected perhaps the strongest defensive site available aimed at nullifying the Normans' most potent weapon.

William of Poitiers' only mention of the battlefield topography is that the ground was rough and the Normans had to 'climb slowly up the steep slope', and that the English 'had the advantage of the higher ground'.[12] The *Carmen* refers to a 'steep hill', but nothing else.[13] Wace's *Roman de Rou* refers to the terrain ahead of and during the early stages as a 'ditch behind the Normans, who had passed round the side of it'.[14] Meanwhile, John of Worcester writes of 'the English being drawn up in a narrow place' while William of Malmesbury and the *ASC* give no indications of the immediate landscape or conditions.[15] Much if not all the textual evidence for Senlac Hill comes from the *Chronicle of Battle Abbey* and the immediate physical evidence of the abbey ruins, in which the altar of the church was said to have been located on the spot where Harold fell.[16] However, several recent excavations around the conventional site have produced nothing of note. This is not entirely surprising; most non-perishable items would have been gathered or retrieved immediately after the battle, and during the subsequent construction of the abbey at the epicentre of the encounter the ridge previously defended by the English underwent major landscaping that removed or destroyed other evidence. Furthermore, the soil around Hastings and Battle is acidic and likely destroyed bone and even metal objects over the intervening millennium.

Those who question the traditional site have argued that the ridge at Senlac was not a sufficient obstacle to prevent Norman cavalry outflanking the English shield wall. The slope has been calculated to have had a gradient of 8 per cent facing due south, but only 4.5 per cent (i.e. 1 in 22) on Harold's east flank and just 3 per cent (i.e. 1 in 33) on his west flank.[17] For William to attack the English directly from the south he would have had to pull his men off the Hastings road at the foot at the south-easterly approach to Senlac Hill and swing them to the west to form up facing the slope towards Senlac. Doing so would have necessitated forming his army partly upon marshland. A glance at the enclosed illustration section showing the estimated groundwater levels in the eleventh century infers unsuitable ground, particularly for his mounted troops, which were initially in the rear.

The best detailed contemporary information for the battle is provided by the Norman sources of William of Poitiers' *Gesta Normannorum Ducum* and Guy of Amiens' *Carmen de Hastingae Proelio*, both of which were produced only a few years after 1066. The *Bayeux Tapestry* is another invaluable source completed during the 1070s, providing an illustrative depiction of the encounter. Further primary detail is provided within the *ASC* and from later writers of various Anglo-Norman or Norman origin, including William of Jumièges, Geffrei Gaimar, Wace, Orderic Vitalis, William of Malmesbury, John of Worcester and Henry of Huntingdon. Orderic confirms that the fighting started 'from the third hour', in other words three hours after sunrise, which in mid-October was 9.00 am. The Norman bowmen and infantry failed to make an early impression on the English shield wall, so William sent in his mounted knights to attack the shield wall. Both sides then traded blows without either gaining any significant advantage, although William of Poitiers refers to the foot soldiers and the Breton knights giving way.[18]

The *Carmen* of Guy of Amiens tells of how, at the height of the fighting, 'the French (i.e. Normans) ... cunningly pretend to flee as though they had been defeated'.[19] They were pursued by many of the English, and Poitiers writes, 'they wheeled around and deliberately feigned flight', then 'suddenly wheeled round their horses, checked and encircled them, and slaughtered them to the last man'.[20] Many historians have accepted this as a deliberate stratagem. It is perfectly plausible that it was preconceived, but it was a risky tactic at a crucial stage. A medieval battlefield was noisy and disorderly, with individual men reduced to concentrating on the opponent directly facing them. To enact such a manoeuvre would have required high discipline and perfect coordination. The stratagem would not have been relayed across the whole of the Norman front line, particularly the infantry, who would have thought it a real retreat, which risked demoralising them.

Some academics refer to a similar ploy used by the Normans in their Italian campaigns. However, the circumstances and conditions in which that tactic was employed are unknown, so is not a satisfactory argument to conclude a similar scenario at Hastings. It is unlikely there was any deliberate feint, but that this describes a real flight.[21] We will never know the reality. The sources relate that the English who had pursued their enemy were soon cut off from their lines, surrounded by the Norman cavalry and wiped out. The *Bayeux Tapestry* illustrates that it was at this juncture, in this isolated group, that Gyrth and Leofwine were killed.[22] Nevertheless, it is hard to imagine the king's brothers had led this charge unless we adopt the premise it was a major counterattack ordered by Harold. Other authorities place Gyrth and Leofwine's demise towards the end of the fighting, perhaps on the summit alongside their brother. The fighting raged on for several more hours. William of Poitiers tells us that William had three horses slain under him, with the Normans on one occasion believing their duke had fallen.[23] The duke is said to have cried out, 'Look at me, I am alive, and with God's help I will conquer. What way is open to escape? Not one of you will escape death by flight.'[24] The *Bayeux Tapestry* shows William, late in the day, raising his helmet so his soldiers could see he still lived.[25] In describing this, Poitiers inadvertently confirms that during the clamour a section of the Norman army was in real retreat.

By late afternoon many of the seasoned English warriors, the housecarls and the thegns, had been killed or injured. The Norman infantry and a good percentage of their cavalry had suffered equally heavily, but they had taken fewer fatalities among their elite fighters in comparison. As the sun fell the English shield wall still held, but the rear ranks of militia were increasingly needed to fill the gaps. However, they were less equipped and capable of holding cavalry at bay. Duke William then made his last big effort to break through the English, brought on by the knowledge that if he did not win before it was dark his invasion would fail.[26] If the English still occupied the ridge overnight Harold could expect to receive new reinforcements the following day to swell their numbers, while there was no hope of additional men to replace Norman losses in the days that would follow. In these final stages, with the English ranks thinning, William deployed his bowmen to better effect, using them nearer to the English lines and ordering them to fire at a higher trajectory. These archers were using short bows with a lethal range of only about 50 metres, but they were now firing from closer range. Combinations of cavalry charges and arrow volleys took their toll as the English tired. The *Bayeux Tapestry* depicts Norman horsemen attacking English warriors from both left and right, which indicates they had gained a foothold on the ridge and were now behind at least one of the English flanks.[27]

Everyone knows the famous story of how Harold Godwinson was slain by an arrow in the eye. It appears in a scene in the *Bayeux Tapestry* and was recorded by, among others, William of Malmesbury, Henry of Huntingdon and the Norman writer Wace.[28] Versions differ as to whether Harold died immediately from this, but there are other concerns over the story's validity. A new assessment of the *Bayeux Tapestry* scene showing an Englishman being struck in the eye under the text 'Here King Harold is killed' (*Hic Harold rex interfectus est*) has found that the original tapestry needlework has been altered since it was first completed. Not is all as it seems, because the text extends over the next illustration of a Norman knight hacking at a falling English warrior, and many academics have concluded this image also represents Harold.[29]

During the eighteenth or nineteenth century the 'arrow in the eye' scene was altered, changed from a warrior holding up a spear shaft into a missile, and lowering its angle so that the projectile meets the line of the warrior's (and so Harold's) head. The alteration appears to have been designed to fit later medieval literary traditions that support the 'arrow in the eye', whereas their earlier primary source counterparts fail to mention it. Wace tells us Harold was 'suffering great pain from his eye, as it had been put out'.[30] In theory, he could have survived this injury if the missile did not enter his brain, but this is difficult to accept. Wace concurs with Guy of Amiens, William of Malmesbury and Henry of Huntingdon that Harold was slain when a group of knights broke through the last remnants of the shield wall, rode him down, and slaughtered him.[31] John of Worcester says Harold fell at dusk, along with 'Earls Gyrth and Leofwine', but does not record how he perished.[32] The tapestry text more likely refers to the slumping figure, not the preceding figure, although it is entirely plausible both images are of Harold. The eye disfigurement may have been added because it has symbolic meaning, as some historians argue that the piercing of the right eye was a symbol of the punishment for perjury.[33]

According to the *Carmen*, the fighting was nearing its conclusion when Duke William gathered Eustace of Boulogne, Hugh of Ponthieu and another knight named Gilfard (Walter Giffard), and charged towards the English king. The *Carmen*, in dramatic style, then tells us the first knight pierced Harold's shield and chest with his lance, the second 'cut off his head below the protection of his helm', the third then 'liquefied his entrails with his spear', and 'the fourth cut off his thigh and carried it some distance away'.[34] Wace omits most of this but does mention Harold being struck in the thigh. However, it is William of Malmesbury that highlights why these events were later reworked. He writes that the knight that hacked at Harold's thigh 'was branded with disgrace by William for a dastardly and shameful act and degraded from his knighthood'.[35] Evidently Harold's body was attacked after his death and his corpse mistreated. This was unacceptable in eleventh-century codes of honour. William later distanced himself from this and Walter Giffard, the knight accused of committing the most serious mutilations, was stripped of his title and sent back to Normandy in disgrace. The mutilation of Harold's body may explain why his death by arrow became a more acceptable version for the Normans to promote.

As discussed above, investigation of the reverse of the *Bayeux Tapestry* has identified potential stitch-holes which suggest that the falling warrior was originally depicted with a projectile in the head that was subsequently removed at a later period.[36] This is intriguing, and perhaps we can speculate that the first figure was not meant to portray Harold but the second one was. To complete the deception, and to further hide the memory of the manner of his eventual demise, a missile was added to the standing figure so that later generations would assume that figure was representing Harold's last moments.

Harold's death fractured the remaining morale of those men still fighting around him. Surviving fyrdmen were already fleeing from Senlac Hill northwards. If Gyrth and Leofwine had not been slain in the earlier incident, then they had fallen alongside their brother in the last stages. The final rout in the dusk would have seen heavy casualties as the English ran with their backs to the Norman cavalry. Less than a mile or so from the battlefront the English formed a stand at what was later called the Malfosse ('evil ditch'), a natural feature which some have argued can be identified as Oakwood Gill to the north of Caldbec Hill. William of Poitiers described it as a 'broken rampart and labyrinth of ditches', and Orderic Vitalis added that the English, 'reformed their ranks there and unexpectedly made a stand, inflicting heavy slaughter on the Normans'.[37] In the final summary, the English defeat may be put down to the length of the engagement and the reduced numbers of elite warriors available after the losses at Stamford Bridge. It has been succinctly put that Harold 'lost the battle because his men were unequal to the stress of a purely defensive engagement too long protracted'.[38] The English suffered perhaps 4,000 or more wounded or killed compared to Norman casualties of half that number.[39]

We can now return to consider the potential alternative locations for the battlefield. Some historians have suggested Harold not only gathered his army at Caldbec Hill but that the main fighting took place there, it being a better position on which to fight defensively.[40] A recent appraisal of the local topography using GIS (Geographic Information Systems) and LIDAR (Light Detection And Ranging) has placed Caldbec as a strategically strong option.[41] The rise is steeper than Senlac, with a substantial slope on its north face, but a less daunting approach from the south.[42] The advantage of Caldbec is that the summit is narrow and less open on the flanks, although its narrowness would have created its own difficulties in forming a defensive position, and the shield wall would have had to assemble slightly down the hill. On that basis, Harold could theoretically create a continuous unbroken shield wall circle. To fully encircle the summit at the optimum level, Harold's shield wall would need to be 1,250 metres long, much longer than needed for Senlac Hill, but with less depth in its ranks.

Full defensive advantage would depend on the direction of approach of the Normans. The north-facing slope of Caldbec is considerably more substantial but is not a relevant factor if the Normans were attacking in an arc somewhere from the south-west across to the south-east, the angle of their likely advance. The slope facing south-east rises by one in eight (50 metres in 400 metres) and the approach from the south or the east was a rise of only 25–30 metres to where the English shield wall would have formed 400–500 metres distant. The topography here better suited the Norman cavalry, and they faced a climb of merely 1 in 16 to attack the English shield wall, although it should be borne in mind that factors such as the level of tree cover and vegetation remain unclear.

Caldbec is perhaps best placed when trying to identify the whereabouts of the Malfosse. Many historians now acknowledge that it could well be where Oakwood Gill lies at the foot of the northern slope of Caldbec Hill.[43] Today there is a mix of mature trees lying in a gully through which a small stream passes, but it would have constituted a significant problem for Norman cavalry in 1066. Its closeness to the summit of Caldbec Hill supports the case for Caldbec being the battle site, but the two are not exclusive. Oakwood Gill is only 990–1050 metres from Senlac Hill. Those escaping Senlac did not need to climb Caldbec but could have reached Oakwood Gill skirting around the hill's western slope. The distance from Senlac compared to Caldbec may have given the English survivors time to regroup, thus confirming the primary source detail. In contrast, arguably Oakwood Gill is too close to Caldbec to enable a rearguard to form.

Moving on from Caldbec there are three other suggested battle sites which have received varying degrees of attention in recent years. The first lies between Crowhurst and Telham Hill, adjacent to the road that takes us from the A2100 at Telham into Crowhurst. It is argued that Harold built two or three lines of defence north to south, on a battlefield which stretched across Forewood Lane close to and to the north of the present position of St George's church at Crowhurst.[44] Telham Hill (not to be confused with Telham) gives us a good view of Battle Abbey to the north and was the route the Normans are understood to have taken in October 1066. The road out of the Hastings peninsula did not follow the modern A2100 but passed instead over Telham Hill. There is a track down towards Battle which gives us an indication of the original line. On approaching Battle this trail joins the A2100 just south of the railway track, but in 1066 it would have curved east to avoid the waterlogged ground below Senlac Hill to access the higher ground leading up to the ridge at the foot of Battle Hill.

The argument for Crowhurst rests on the Normans having constructed their temporary fort at Upper Wilting at the northern point of Combe Haven, and to have moved their army directly northward from there. This scenario relies on accepting that Harold had advanced south beyond Telham Hill and had constructed a defence on the incline leading down into Crowhurst ahead of the Normans reaching that spot.[45] The likelihood of the English advancing undetected that close to the Norman camp and having time to construct a three-tier defence seems difficult to comprehend. It is less than 1½ miles from Wilting to Crowhurst. The local landscape and proposed Crowhurst battleground, including specifically either side of Forewood Lane north of the present-day church, would seem to be a risky choice for Harold, even if he had time to build a defence. For the Normans, the route from their camp at Wilting towards Crowhurst required crossing or bypassing marshland and watercourses at the top section of Combe Haven, so William was unlikely to have diverted via Crowhurst if exiting the Hastings peninsula across Telham Hill. Furthermore, we should not assume the Norman options leaving their Wilting base camp were limited. They were not prevented from sweeping to the east of Crowhurst and hitting the English from the rear on terrain that would have negated any English advantage in the landscape.

Some primary sources note that the Normans advanced on the English before they were prepared. The suggested Crowhurst site would have caused difficulty when attacking from the south, but unless the landscape was heavily wooded it did not give the English shield wall enough protection on their flanks. The major question mark over Crowhurst is not necessarily the battleground itself but its closeness to the Norman camp. Surely William had been warned of Harold's advance, and knew the best or worse terrain on which to challenge the English. Why therefore allow himself to be blocked in so close to his base? The wider question for Crowhurst would be that William had the opportunity of taking the less arduous route to Telham Hill, thereby skirting around the prepared defences of the English.

The next alternate proposed battle site at Sedlescombe relies on an acceptance of the idea that the Norman fleet did not land at Pevensey or

Bulverhythe but had instead entered the Brede Estuary and built their fort on the south bank of the River Brede.⁴⁶ According to the proponents for this preference, Harold had chosen the eastern approach route to Hastings via Rochester and Bodiam and had diverged to cross the River Rother and moved south to Cripps Corner. It was there or just south of it he supposedly rested his army the night before the battle.⁴⁷ The theorists for Sedlescombe have proposed that Harold only realized his proximity to his enemy after reconnoitring north of the Brede and seeing the Norman camp on the opposite bank, following which he was forced to make a defensive stand at short notice. A rudimentary embankment and ditch (fosse) were hastily constructed, and Wace says that this ditch was 'to one side which ran through the fields'.⁴⁸ This supports the idea that the English were defending a short battlefront.

Researchers looking at the region between Cripps Corner and the Brede have identified a battlefield location at a hill named Great Sanders Ridge, which they claim was also the location of the English camp the previous evening.⁴⁹ This can be found about 1,000 metres to the north-east of Sedlescombe village along Hurst Lane. The ridge runs north to south, rising at its south-facing edge by about 30 metres over 300 metres. This 1-in-10 incline would have been difficult to attack, but the topography suggests that the contours on the flanks were even more tortuous, meaning the Norman cavalry could not outflank the English defensive line. Harold's advantage was the narrowness of his frontline facing the enemy, basically the smallest sector of an elongated rectangle. In effect, he needed to defend less than 100 metres to his immediate front but required a shield wall with fewer ranks perhaps 300–350 metres either side to secure his flanks. The premise is that the Normans were for a long period confined to charging the front-facing section of the shield wall because of the waterlogged terrain either side that restricted cavalry movement. The area around Great Sanders Ridge was still covered with watercourses and ditches centuries later from evidence of a map dated from 1780, so was likely even more challenging in 1066.⁵⁰

The Sedlescombe battlefield seems more credible than Crowhurst because it appears to have given Harold better possibilities of forming a defensive position that restricted the Norman cavalry from attacking his flanks. However, other aspects of Sedlescombe pose problems, in particular a lack of any connection to Battle Abbey. It also means accepting beyond question that the whole Norman fleet had entered the Brede Estuary. The alternative venue for 'Pevenisel' being near to the Fécamp estate at Rameslie is not entirely convincing, and to link the Brede under the umbrella of the Hastings estate is stretching the evidence.⁵¹ It is also hard to imagine Harold would have committed his army to cross the River Rother, which was wider than the Brede and required his troops to be ferried across. That he was surprised soon afterwards by the closeness of William's force implies that he did not know William's whereabouts at that stage, and hence was unlikely to risk being caught undergoing a major river crossing in ignorance of his enemy's exact position.

In general terms the debate over the landing site or sites of the Norman fleet hinges on interpreting the Sussex coastline and the sea levels in 1066 as considered in the previous chapter. However, what is perhaps not fully appreciated is the groundwater level inland from Hastings. As determined in the enclosed illustrations section, the higher water levels limited the route available out of the peninsula to a single neck of solid ground just to the south-east of the Senlac Ridge. The track over Telham Hill and the trail from the eastern end of the peninsula met south of a 250–300-metre-wide pinch point, roughly where the present-day Battle railway track and Powdermill Lane meet the A2100 between Senlac Hill to its north and Battle Hill to its south. In 1066 the low-lying ground adjacent to the later route of the railway was not necessarily underwater all year round but was potentially marshland for much of it. A scene in the *Bayeux Tapestry* illustrates that some fighting took place in or near to water, and the English deployment may have extended into the lower ground near to a watercourse.[52]

Discussion of the topography and groundwater levels in 1066 brings us back full circle to Battle and Senlac Hill to review the last alternate recently suggested battle site. This is so near to the conventional site some argue it is not a valid alternative. However, the key is in assessing the local eleventh-century topography and how Harold's army consequently aligned their shield wall. Several years ago, research into the landscape around Battle brought forward some new and interesting detail by amalgamating data from assessments of water levels during the eleventh century with data captured from aerial surveys using LIDAR.[53] These aerial surveys used remote sensing to generate precise three-dimensional details which illustrate the shape and characteristics of the natural ground surface. The compiled data leads us to question the accepted alignment of the traditional battlefield, and from this data it is possible to form an argument that the centre of Harold's shield wall was 200 metres to the east of where Battle Abbey now stands and not on the spot that tradition upholds. Many historians are sensitive to this alternate argument, and some vociferously dispute it, but the aerial evidence provides detail worthy of consideration. The proposition is that Harold set his shield wall facing south-east at roughly a 90-degree angle to the road out of the peninsula where it rises from the foot of Battle Hill to meet the eastern edge of the Senlac Ridge. The front rank would be where the present-day Upper and Lower Lake roads and Marley Lane converge, only 200 metres east of the conventional location.

Traditionalists have argued that this newly proposed battlefield is still located partially in the grounds of Battle Abbey and is therefore not worthy of separate consideration. However, it is perhaps more useful to consider its merits without trying to prove or disprove the validity or otherwise of the English Heritage location. The key should surely be the direction of the Norman approach and the orientation of the two armies in relation to the topography facing them and the contours of Senlac Hill. The enclosed illustrations, the maps showing the land elevation and the LIDAR image, provide clear evidence of the topography which confronted both Harold and William.[54] The LIDAR image is particularly interesting. It shows us the approximate north–south alignment of the conventional battlefield to the topography and the height above sea level, and, as hinted at earlier, it is fair to assume that in 1066 the lowest levels were either permanent marshland or frequently waterlogged. To form up on this terrain, William would need to take his men off the drier ground on which the road lay. On the conventional battlefield William had only 80–100 metres of guaranteed solid ground to assemble his troops and cavalry between the front of the English shield wall and the waterlogged ground to his rear, which surely restricted his ability to deploy 7,000 men or give his mounted knights the mobility necessary.

In contrast, the alternate battlefield option at the eastern edge of Senlac Ridge meant Harold had to form his shield wall on a north-east to south-west axis to take best advantage of the topography and to directly face the Norman advance approaching from the foot of Battle Hill. This alignment may have allowed the English to extend part of their right flank down the slope to the south towards the watercourse, further depriving the Norman cavalry access to the dry ground below the hill referred to earlier and forcing them to ride across the marshy ground if trying to outflank the English shield wall. When comparing this alignment to the traditional site it more readily explains why the Norman cavalry were unable to outflank the English and remained relatively ineffective for much of the fighting.

As seen in the enclosed LIDAR image, the valley between Senlac Hill and Battle Hill, combined with the higher water table, would have enabled Harold to organise his defence along the eastern fringe of the Senlac Ridge, and the geography limited William's ability to manoeuvre his cavalry around the flanks.[55] On this basis, an argument supporting a reorientation of the English defensive position can be justified. Harold did not have to hold the highest part of the ridge, only secure the thinner neck of land at its eastern edge. The fundamental key was not the gradient of the slope the Norman cavalry faced – it was about 1 in 12, much like the central slope of the traditional site – but rather the narrow width of solid ground which William had available to best deploy his knights, his primary weapon.

The debate will continue. English Heritage has invested heavily in the traditional location. There is a permanent exhibition centre inside the Battle Abbey grounds detailing the various aspects of the encounter and a circular walk can be taken around the rear of the claimed Norman position and back up to the abbey ruins. Some sections of the Norman abbey complex have survived, but only the bare foundations of the original location of the main church at the summit remain above ground level. There is a memorial stone dedicated as the spot where Harold was killed, and where the abbey altar was located when the building was first completed.

All these alternate battlefield sites have their adherents to a varying degree. Ultimately, the debate will continue unless conclusive evidence comes to light. In terms of the two sites in Battle village, the so-called 'roundabout' spot at the eastern end of Senlac Ridge suggested by the LIDAR evidence is not radically different from the conventional site and has viability. Much of the fighting would have taken place on the same piece of land that thereafter became the eastern section of the grounds of Battle Abbey. This reorientation of Harold's shield wall and moving the English battleline 200 metres east does not contradict the primary source entries connecting the abbey with the battle. We know the Normans later flattened the top of the ridge when constructing their church. The image of Harold centring himself on what would be a roundabout a millennium later has amused some historians. Nevertheless, it is unlikely to have been the place where Harold finally fell. The traditional spot, later marked by the siting of the high altar of the abbey, could equally apply to the scenario of our alternate battle site, if we agree that the English were slowly forced back up the slope, allowing their flanks to be exposed before Harold died towards the end of the fighting.

19

End of a Dynasty

The battle on 14 October 1066 had been bitterly fought for most of the day, with the outcome uncertain for much of it. Only when the English had suffered too many casualties and could no longer prevent the Norman cavalry gaining the ridge was it decided. Harold's death was inevitable once the shield wall had been outflanked and broken. Perhaps there had been a fleeting opportunity for Harold, and perhaps Gyrth and Leofwine also, to escape to the rear and ride away from the battlefield while some of their remaining housecarls held a rearguard action. The suspicion is that in his role as a king and leader Harold declined to run and preferred to die with honour next to his men. The Norman cavalry, with Eustace of Boulogne prominent among them, had pursued the English escaping northward, but had lost horsemen unnecessarily in the last hour of fighting at the Malfosse. On the battlefield lay the bodies of three Godwinson brothers. Although the *ASC* records the deaths of Gyrth and Leofwine, only John of Worcester notes that they fell at dusk alongside the king, while William of Poitiers tells us that 'his brothers ... had perished'.[1] What became of Gyrth and Leofwine's bodies afterwards remains unclear. As depicted in the *Bayeux Tapestry*, the mail coats and other armour were stripped from the dead soldiers and weapons gathered.[2] The Normans are reported to have buried their dead but to have left the English to see to theirs.[3]

Later writers were keen to tell their audience what happened to Harold's body immediately after the fighting had ceased. There are two key notions, plus a third that even suggested he had survived the battle. The first of the traditional stories is that Edith Swan-neck, who had remained at Waltham, was summoned to Sussex by Osgod and Æthelric, the Waltham monks who had accompanied Harold, so she could help them identify his body. Edith must have been in the vicinity already, perhaps searching the battleground in the early hours of the following day after the Normans had returned to their basecamp. She could only recognise Harold 'by certain marks, not by his face, for he had been despoiled of all signs of status'.[4] This implies he had been badly mutilated, supporting the version of events that four Norman knights had cut him to pieces.

The narrative then goes that the monks took Harold's body back to Waltham Abbey, although we are left to imagine how this was brought about if he had been cut to pieces. Tradition has it his remains were embedded by the high altar of the abbey church at Waltham. The abbey was subsequently reconstructed in the early twelfth century, albeit reusing the Saxon foundations and some of Harold's earlier stonework. An eighteenth-century account noted that his remains had been moved from the site of the former altar at Waltham to the choir during this reconstruction. The author of the *Waltham Chronicle* claims to have seen the translation of Harold's remains in 1120.[5] The translation was an attempt by the Anglo-Norman establishment, if we accept this rendition of events, to minimise the cult of pilgrimage that had grown around Harold's memory. However, this seems a little late for that purpose. In 1086, when the *Domesday Book* was being compiled, William wanted no reference to Harold's kingship in its pages, so it is hard to believe he, or indeed his successors William Rufus (William II) and Henry (Henry I), would have permitted Harold's tomb at Waltham to be a place of open pilgrimage for half a century after the Conquest.

The church choir at Waltham was destroyed during the dissolution, and if we accept the proviso that he had first been taken there, Harold's remains were likely moved more than once. There is a story that in the eighteenth century a coffin bearing the inscription 'Haroldus Rex' was discovered during excavations to extend the cellar in the manor house next to the abbey. The coffin was apparently displayed in the cellar but was lost and destroyed after a major fire and the house was later demolished in 1770.[6] There is no way of verifying this story, but it adds to the legend. A memorial stone for Harold's resting place was installed in 1964 on what was believed to be the location of his original tomb. Today, there is a marker stone and plinth in the grounds of the church close to the east end of the present-day building, where the altar may have been located before the dissolution. The inscription reads, 'This stone marks the position of the altar behind which King Harold is said to have been buried in 1066.' However, recent research has suggested that these marker stones may not lie within the perimeter walls of Harold's earlier and smaller eleventh-century church building, although the ongoing story persists in some quarters that Harold lies there. There is a variation on the Waltham story in which he survived the battle and was buried at this spot when an old man thirty years later. In recent years, a geophysical survey has been undertaken over and around the marked site in the church grounds, but no suitable evidence supporting any findings was produced.

A parallel tradition to Edith Swan-neck having identified Harold's torso was added by the chronicler Orderic Vitalis, but he places Harold's mother Gytha and not Edith at centre stage as the identifier. Perhaps they had both searched the battleground. We are told that Gytha offered to pay Duke William 'Harold's weight in gold for his body; but the high-minded conqueror refused to make such a bargain, for he thought it wrong that the man whose ambition had caused thousands to lie unburied should be buried wherever his mother chose'.[7] A similar tale has William otherwise accepting Gytha's offer, and allowing her to retrieve his body, which with the help of the monks she takes and then buries at Harold's foundation church at Waltham.[8] Both these stories rely on the idea that Gytha and Edith Swan-neck were only hours from the battle site during the fighting. If Gytha negotiated with William, it poses a question: with the influence she could still bring to any Anglo-Saxon resistance, why did William not detain Gytha? It should be remembered that even though the duke had killed the English king, his ultimate victory was far from certain in October 1066. No mention is made of Gytha trying to reclaim the bodies of her other sons, Gyrth and Leofwine, which she surely would have done in parallel with trying to retrieve Harold.

The second major theme surrounding Harold's fate involves Duke William's actions soon after the fighting. It is claimed by Norman writers that Harold's body was taken back to William's camp, presumably still identifiable and so in conflict with the dismemberment account described earlier. The duke 'entrusted his burial to William surnamed Malet, not to his mother (Gytha), though she offered his weight in gold for the body of her beloved son. It was said in jest that he should be placed as guardian of the shores and sea.'[9] William Malet had been one of the Normans brought over by Edward who stayed at Harold's court initially, but had, along with Robert FitzWimarc, seemingly transferred his allegiance to William just before the battle. This report of Harold's burial is confirmed by Orderic, tying in with his entry that William had refused to hand over Harold's remains to Gytha, adding that 'the conqueror commanded William Malet to bury the body near to the sea-shore'.[10] The location of this burial spot remains a mystery. Maybe it overlooked Pevensey Bay or Hastings. Perhaps Harold was deliberately laid in unhallowed ground, the suspicion being that William did not want the grave to be identified if Harold's burial place risked becoming a shrine and a place of pilgrimage for Anglo-Saxons. The same argument would certainly cast some doubt on the Normans accepting Harold's formal burial at Waltham.

The third theme, that Harold instead lived to old age, first appeared in the thirteenth-century work *Vita Haroldi*.[11] The text is a deliberate 'romance' to engender a myth around the last Anglo-Saxon monarch. One version is that

Harold lived as a hermit and died forty years later. This appears fanciful, although one or two historians have argued that he may have survived the arrow in the eye and was taken from the battlefield to safety just before the final Norman assault. However, the report of Harold's survival originated at Waltham Abbey years after Hastings, so it seems odd that the monks contemporary to 1066 would have promoted the tale of him being entombed in their building only to subsequently admit they had deceived the pilgrims and he was still alive and living somewhere else in the country.

The *Vita Haroldi* adds that Harold had been wounded at Hastings but then recovered from his wounds in Winchester and travelled to Germany and Scandinavia, trying and failing to get military support to retake the throne. It would be an understatement to call this far-fetched, but its primary purpose was to maintain the myth that Anglo-Saxons would one day recover their throne. Returning to England, Harold then lived out his life as a hermit before dying at Chester.[12] We can safely label all of this as fiction. Harold died at Hastings. However, the tale of his survival reveals the continued importance of retaining symbols of Anglo-Saxon nationalism two centuries after his death while England was being ruled by an elite that spoke French, not English.

Finally, the discovery of a stone coffin in 1954 in the floor below the chancel arch of Holy Trinity Church at the former Godwinson estate at Bosham has led to speculation that it may have been the last resting place of Harold.[13] The coffin had been seriously vandalised sometime centuries earlier because only a fractured left leg thigh (femur) bone and pelvic bone fragments were still inside. Forensic investigation of these remains suggested a man aged between forty and sixty, with the femur having been fractured at the time of death.[14] This detail has led to speculation that the femur damage was consistent with Guy of Amiens' *Carmen* entry on Harold, where he noted that the Norman knights had 'cut off his head' and 'cut off his thigh and carried it some distance away'.[15] If we accept the speculation, then only part of his body was recovered and later buried at Bosham.

Maybe also we have the possibility that part of Harold ended up at Bosham, and part of him at Waltham. This would follow the practice whereby the remnants of Christian saints were often distributed as relics to various religious houses. Putting aside speculation, the coffin at Bosham, made of Horsham stone, implies the occupant was an important figure. Nevertheless, the bone analysis suggests the occupant was too old to presuppose it to have been either Gyrth or Leofwine. Unless further research on the bones is undertaken using modern scientific techniques, we remain no wiser. The latest request in 2004 to exhume the remains for further analysis was denied by the Holy Trinity Church authorities.

When the news reached London of the English defeat at Hastings, the surviving leadership was divided as to how to react. Archbishop Ealdred, and possibly Archbishop Stigand, wished to raise the ætheling Edgar to the throne, but the support of the recently arrived earls Edwin and Morcar would be required. The primary sources are a little confused. Some proposed the young Edgar as king, but the Witan could not agree. The *ASC* scribe blames the two northern earls, noting that despite them having promised to fight for Edgar, 'when it should have been furthered ... day to day the later the worse it got'.[16] William had supposed after his victory and Harold's demise that the English secular leadership would come to him and surrender the throne. Still waiting several days later, he advanced his army to Dover, perhaps while more ships returned to Normandy for reinforcements. The citizens and garrison at Dover did not surrender immediately, and part of the township was burnt down. Matters were made worse when dysentery spread among the Norman troops and many died.[17]

After this unavoidable delay, William then moved on to receive the surrender of Canterbury. However, after next advancing to Southwark before mid-November, the Normans failed in their attempt to storm London and were prevented from crossing the Thames by the London garrison. Burning everything he could find on the south bank, William pillaged a route south-west across Surrey and northern Hampshire to Winchester to seize the exchequer there. Meanwhile, John of Worcester recorded that the Normans laid waste to Sussex, Kent, Middlesex and Hampshire.[18] Researching estate values and their deflation pre-and post-1066, a method not agreed by all historians, has given us a reasonable idea which route the Norman army followed from Southwark. Following this defined line of destruction, they had moved via Godstone, Leatherhead, Guildford and Micheldever towards Winchester.[19]

The dowager queen Edith had remained at Winchester, and much of the royal treasury was likely still held there. News of the Norman army's destructive march had travelled ahead of them. After his victory, William may have expected the Godwinson women to recognise the fait accompli without further discord. In this, he had mixed success. Edith remained in Winchester to await William's arrival for reasons not entirely obvious, but Gytha and Gunhild, and probably Harold's sons Godwin, Edmund and Magnus, if they had been with their grandmother, had already left for the West Country. It can be imagined that Gytha had tried to persuade her eldest daughter to join her in forming a resistance to the Norman invasion, but Edith had distanced herself from continuing the fight.

Edith was to formally hand over control of Winchester and what remained of the exchequer to William, but we should without hesitation assume that her mother and sister had emptied a large part of the treasury before the Normans arrived. It seems Edith chose to negotiate, but why she did not arrange for the remainder of the royal treasury to be moved to safety far away from Norman hands in the weeks after hearing of her brother's defeat is perplexing. There had been ample time to do it, and it would have provided critical additional funding for her mother's later plans to rally the thegns in the West Country. In contrast to her mother, Edith, either willingly or by coercion, appears to have cooperated with the conquering Normans.

The writer Guy of Amiens adds that the city elders of Winchester had advised Edith to accept and submit to William's demands.[20] This perhaps only tells us part of the story. The elders may have feared William looting and burning the city, and from Edith's perspective she was probably granted assurance that her estates would not be confiscated in return for giving her public support to the new Norman regime. While we cannot know, Edith may have been held in close custody for several weeks, perhaps until William's coronation on Christmas Day. Acknowledgement from the dowager queen of his rightful entitlement was symbolically important for William, particularly if it came while many of the English hierarchy beyond the south-east were still assessing their options. Her compliance ensured she would not become the focus of support for the Godwinsons but would importantly persuade many waverers to abandon their support for the ætheling Edgar. The accommodation Edith came to with William ensured that she would still hold her wealth and position.

We have an image of a woman that may still have carried some resentment for her own family after Tostig's exiling, prepared to place her future comfort above anything akin to dynastic loyalty. Before the Conquest, Edith held lands valued between £1,570 and £2,000 per annum, but from the detail in the *Domesday Book* she still held land worth over £520 afterwards.[21] Edith's peaceful submission may have encouraged William to extend similar terms to her mother. It has been proposed that Gytha too was initially permitted to keep her estates.[22] Prior to Hastings she had held, as designated by the Domesday survey, a significant number of estates throughout Wessex, most of them in Devon, Somerset and Wiltshire, and she had been the fifth richest landowner in England.[23] However, Gytha's influence was not initially seen as a threat by William. She was now in her sixties and politically isolated from the centre of government.

William's priority after seizing Winchester was to gain the submission of what remained of the English secular leadership that had rallied around the ætheling Edgar in London after the death of Harold. More Norman reinforcements may have arrived through Portsmouth and the Solent to join William at Winchester, and from there the Norman army again divided. Through assessment of the post-1066 decline in estate valuations caused by pillaging, the left flank of the Norman army is believed to have moved north through Andover, Lambourne and Wantage while the right flank marched through Highclere and East Isley before both sections combined to cross the River Thames at Wallingford.

It was at Wallingford that Archbishop Stigand, who had left London and looks to have deliberately sought out William, submitted to him. William's plan after being repulsed at Southwark was to isolate London by destroying a broad belt of land around it.[24] He had initially employed this south of the river and was to continue it through the Home Counties to the west and north of the city. From Wallingford, the army moved on via the Icknield Way to pillage across a wide arc through Oxfordshire, Hertfordshire and Buckinghamshire, including Risborough, Wendover, Aylesbury, Buckingham, Bedford and Luton.[25] The significance of this deliberate destruction is clear. The English leaders who remained loyal to young Edgar were being given the option of accepting vassalage to William or acknowledging that further destruction would ensue. The Norman duke was giving a simple message that he would destroy London too if necessary.

It was now probably the second week of December. At Berkhamsted, 25 miles north-west of London and Westminster, William halted, and a delegation from London rode out to meet him. This included the ætheling Edgar, Archbishop Ealdred of York, Bishop Wulfstan of Worcester, Bishop Walter of Hereford, and, according to the main primary sources, the brothers Edwin and Morcar.[26] The *ASC* scribe noted that they 'submitted from necessity when the most harm was done, and it was a great folly that it was not done this earlier'.[27] Terms were agreed whereby the English leadership formally surrendered London, gave vassalage to William, and that upon their oaths he would be crowned king. On returning from Berkhamsted, Edwin and Morcar immediately arranged for their pregnant sister Ealdgyth, Harold's widow, to be taken to Chester for safety. Carrying Harold's unborn baby meant that Ealdgyth was a potential future threat to the new regime and was in danger of being eliminated. Orderic Vitalis later recorded that Edwin and Morcar and all the leading thegns of Mercia then formally submitted to the Normans at Barking in January 1067.[28] They would lead a failed rebellion against the Normans in 1068 but play no further part in the story of the Godwinsons. Edgar was killed in 1071 and Morcar was later imprisoned long-term by William, and again by the Conqueror's successor William II Rufus, before dying sometime around 1090.

While we know Ealdgyth was removed to Chester, the whereabouts of Harold's long-term hand-fast wife Edith Swan-neck remain unclear. She may have followed Gytha and the other Godwinsons into Devon. Gytha had been active in raising support for a potential rebellion centred at Exeter. She had used her wealth to buy new allies and rallied others who had previously given notable vassalage to her family. These included West Country supporters Abbot Sihtric of Tavistock, Abbot Saewold of Bath, and Abbot Ealdred of Abingdon.[29] Exeter was to act as the new centre of operations for the remaining Godwinsons, one that had sea access but was far removed from immediate Norman interference. Gytha and Godwin had long owned property in Exeter, and the Church of St Olave's in present-day Fore Street was founded as a house chapel by Gytha in 1053 after her husband's death so that prayers could be offered for him.

The situation in the south-east was quite different. William and his army entered London peacefully in December. The ætheling Edgar was left unhindered but was kept close to William's court. He would later be taken to Normandy when William returned there in 1067 as assurance he would not become a rallying figure for ongoing English resistance in William's absence. The *ASC* tells us that the Norman duke was crowned as William I, King of England, at Westminster Abbey on Midwinter's Day (21 December) 1066, although John of Worcester records the coronation was symbolically on Christmas Day.[30] Because there was still some dispute over Stigand having received his pallium canonically the service was conducted by Archbishop Ealdred.

William of Poitiers tells us that the coronation service was interrupted when 'the men who, armed and mounted, had been placed as a guard around the minster, on hearing the loud clamour in an unknown tongue, thought that some treachery was afoot and rashly set fire to houses near to the city'.[31] Reading between the lines, there is no confusion here. The London citizens appear to have shown displeasure for their new king and had revolted, which was put down forcefully by the Norman soldiery. The coronation did not end the question of a successful English candidate returning to the throne. There is often a misconception that all of England surrendered to the Normans in 1066, but this was far from reality. It would take several years to conquer all the country and quell the rebellions in the north. However, although the chances of a Godwinson returning to the throne in the shape of Harold's sons remained theoretically alive for another year or two, the Norman grip on the south would soon extinguish that hope. Elsewhere, there was no similar appetite for supporting the Godwinson cause in Mercia or Northumbria.

To commemorate his achievement, William is said to have ordered the building of the abbey at the site of his victory over Harold, and the later Norman writers support the premise it was built as a monument to his success. The *Chronicle of Battle Abbey*, a work completed in 1176 and written to describe the history of the abbey's foundation, further supported this idea.[32] However, not all sources support this premise and some suggest instead that Battle Abbey was commissioned as part of William's penance for the invasion. In 1067, Pope Alexander II was to instruct his legate Ermenfrid of Sion to enact a penitential ordinance that had been composed by the bishops in Normandy calling for atonement to be undertaken by those who had taken part in the violation of the English kingdom.[33]

This act acknowledges that the papacy considered the Norman invasion to have been unfounded. More than that, it was enacted by Alexander II, the same pope that Norman propagandists had earlier claimed had approved and blessed William's actions with a papal banner ahead of his invasion. This exposes the earlier distortion. Rather than a papal blessing for the Norman invasion of England, the complete opposite was true: the papacy had strongly disapproved. The construction of Battle Abbey, William's penance, was therefore a direct consequence of that ordinance. Work started in 1070 at levelling the ridge at Senlac and it would be another twenty-four years, beyond William's lifetime, before the complex was finished.

Finally, we have a window into the domination of the Godwinsons in terms of land ownership across England ahead of the Conquest. The *Domesday Book* gives us a picture of the estates that the Godwinson family members owned or that were assigned to their vassals at the end of the Anglo-Saxon reign.[34] As mentioned previously, both Godwin and Tostig still appear as the last named landholders pre-Conquest in many of these estates. Godwin is named in fifty-five and Tostig in eighty-one, plus another 116 which were owned by their various vassals. Clearly this would not have been the reality by 1066, as all the estates of Godwin and Tostig would have already been transferred to other members of the household or other vassals after their deaths. By 1065 Tostig likely held several hundred across the country that were reallocated soon after his exiling. Likewise, the estates entered as belonging to Edward (the Confessor) would have already transferred into Harold Godwinson's hands in his role as the new monarch.

The Domesday survey is not entirely precise on the property that the surviving family members had held just ahead of the Battle of Hastings. Based on the Domesday entries, but excluding the royal estates under Harold that had formerly been Edward's, the family members were identified as holding control over most of the land across Wessex, East Anglia and Mercia, and additional considerable territory north of the Humber. Most of these estates were less than 10 hides in area (about 300 modern acres), although some were larger than 50. According to the Domesday survey, Harold held, minus his royal residences, 470 estates as holder and a further 448 as lord to a vassal. Combining the 'holder' and 'lord' estates, but excluding the royal properties, most of these 918 were in Norfolk (182), Herefordshire (83), Essex (72), Lincolnshire (70) and Suffolk (64).[35]

The other dynastic distribution had been:

Gytha – Estates across nine shires – 43 as the holder, mostly in Devon, Wiltshire, Sussex, and Somerset, the largest being Rushall and Aldbourne (Wilts), Harting (Sussex) and Otterton (Devon).

Edith – Estates across twenty-four shires – 215 as the holder, and 106 as lord, principally in Lincolnshire, Herefordshire, and Buckinghamshire, the largest being Iford (Sussex), Westbury (Wilts), Reigate (Surrey) and Martock and Keynsham (Somerset).

Gyrth – Estates across nine shires – 46 as the holder, and 141 as lord, mostly in Norfolk and Suffolk, the largest being Aylesham (Norfolk) and Washington (Sussex).

Leofwine – Estates across ten shires – 37 as the holder, and 35 as lord, chiefly in Buckinghamshire, the largest being Leckhampstead (Bucks) and Cuddington (Surrey).[36]

These numbers seem a little disjointed, and presumably Edith's figures include estates she had gained while still queen. Similarly, both Gyrth and Leofwine's holdings are much fewer than would have been expected. There must have been considerably more acreage under their ownership pre-Conquest, but the Domesday survey failed to register their previous interest ahead of the transfers to Norman nobles after 1066. Edith the Fair, whom we have previously assumed was the woman we know as Edith 'Swan-neck', Harold's hand-fast wife, also owned forty estates and another 116 as 'lord' under vassalage. More than a hundred of these were in Cambridgeshire, with another large grouping in Suffolk. Even assuming Harold had awarded her some of these, it acknowledges Edith's family wealth had originated in Cambridgeshire and she was already a wealthy woman when she had first met him. Finally, the *Domesday Book* also includes details of two small estates in Somerset which were owned by Harold's young son Godwin in 1066.[37]

Anglo-Saxon, Danish, and Norman lines of Succession - Genealogy Chart

20

The Last of the Godwinsons

The Normans would take several years to establish control over the whole of England. However, our concern here is with the fate of the surviving members of the Godwinson family and tracing them through from 1067 to their last days. Harold's second wife, Ealdgyth, had been pregnant when Harold had fallen at Hastings, and in the early months of 1067 she gave birth to a son, named Harold after his father. Some historians suggest that Ealdgyth had twins, another boy named Ulf alongside Harold, although as mentioned in a previous chapter this Ulf is usually credited to be the fourth and last of Harold's sons to his hand-fast wife Edith Swan-neck, and to have been born much earlier during the 1050s.[1] Ealdgyth had been safely removed to Chester by her brother Edwin before the Normans had gained the submission of London.[2] The child, Harold Haroldson, had reached the age of two before the Normans had conquered all the south and had advanced northward in numbers. Had the Normans detained his mother it is unlikely the child, theoretically the legitimate heir to the English throne, would have been permitted to live.

Ealdgyth and her child likely remained in Chester until the Normans had established control across the Midland shires and it was no longer safe. This may have been in the early months of 1070, because the forces of Ealdgyth's brothers Edwin and Morcar suffered a major defeat near Stafford in 1070. After that the movement of Ealdgyth and her child becomes blurred. From Chester, she may have left via the River Dee for Ireland. Alternately, some additional research possibly links her subsequently to the Auvergne in southern France, well removed from Norman influences but perhaps having moved there via Ireland. The monks of La-Chaise-Dieu Abbey recorded that years later an English 'Queen Edith (Ealdgyth)' was cured of leprosy there, perhaps while travelling on pilgrimage to Rome. This Edith became a generous benefactor of the abbey, and lived out her last days in the Auvergne, being buried at the abbey during the 1080s.[3]

If this was not Harold's widow, we have no other trail to follow. The fate of the boy Harold Haroldson is equally difficult to define, but he appears to have aligned himself later in life with Scandinavians in Ireland or the Western Isles. After a long gap, when Harold would have reached the age of thirty-one, an entry by William of Malmesbury for the year 1098 refers to 'Harold, son of Harold the late English king' travelling with King Magnus III Olafsson, the grandson of Hardrada, on raids to Orkney and Anglesey.[4] Perhaps he perished during those raids because after this he disappears from the historical record. The Norwegian connection is well justified. Magnus had likely welcomed Harold Haroldson into his service in remembrance over thirty years earlier of Harold Godwinson having allowed the then young Magnus, who had been at Riccall with the Norse fleet in 1066, to return freely to Norway after Stamford Bridge. As recorded by Malmesbury, 'it was in memory of this kindness that he treated Harold's son Harold so kindly'.[5]

By the autumn of 1067, full Norman control had still been limited to the south-east, in an arc from Hampshire around to East Anglia. That had allowed Gytha and her allies to continue to gather strength in western Wessex, centred at Exeter, in a region where there remained vigorous support for her house. However, over the winter of 1067/68, the Normans made their first move to confront her and her supporters. Harold's young sons Godwin, Edmund and Magnus were alongside their grandmother and William clearly saw them as a serious threat to his position. Marching an army into Devon, he placed Exeter under siege, but it would take eighteen days and many Norman casualties before the city was taken.[6] Orderic Vitalis describes events in detail. A combination of disunity and unpreparedness among the leaders inside Exeter, led by the treachery of a few thegns, allowed William finally to gain entry into the city.[7] William of Malmesbury adds that Exeter was easily subdued 'when part of the walls collapsed of its own accord and gave him admittance'.[8] Gytha, her daughter Gunhild, and her grandsons fled the city.

While Godwin, Edmund and Magnus headed for Ireland hoping to raise mercenary support, Gytha's party, including her daughter Gunhild, made their way to the north Somerset coast. From there they took ship to Flat Holm Isle, out in the Bristol Channel, 6 miles north-west of present-day Weston-super-Mare and 3 miles from the Welsh coast at Lavernock. The isle was less than one-tenth of a square mile and was not the most hospitable of refuges, but it was on the sea lane from Ireland to Bristol and the River Severn. It allowed Gytha and her supporters access to news from her grandsons in Ireland and contact with other areas not yet under Norman control. They remained undisturbed on Flat Holm for some while but decided to leave in the autumn of 1068 or spring of 1069 when it became clear that her grandsons would not be successful in gaining a foothold back in England. The sources tell us that after gathering 'a great store of treasure ... Gytha and the wives of many good men ... went across the sea to St Omer (Flanders)'.[9]

Gunhild Godwinsdottir accompanied her mother into exile in Flanders. There is evidence, as noted below, that despite setbacks Gytha was still looking to restore her family's fortunes and she may have immediately travelled back to her native Denmark, perhaps intending to try and gain Danish support from her nephew King Swein II (Estrithsson). The Danish scribe Saxo Grammaticus, in his *Gesta Danorum* (Deeds of the Danes), records members of the Godwinson family travelling to Denmark after their exile. This included not just mother and daughter Gytha and Gunhild, but also the two eldest of Harold's sons, Godwin and Edmund, and Harold's daughter, the younger Gytha.[10] That Grammaticus makes no mention of Magnus being with his brothers implies this was after Magnus had already died, which places the Danish trip after 1068. Gytha looks to have been successful in persuading her nephew to attempt an invasion of northern England. In 1069 it is known Swein Estrithsson sent across a fleet and joined forces with the ætheling Edgar, who had already fled William's court, and for a while their forces controlled York. However, Swein was to accept payments from William to withdraw from England and Edgar was forced to seek exile in Scotland. Gytha disappears from the historical record around this time, aged in her late sixties. She likely lived in Denmark until her death, which may have been during the early 1070s.

We know that Gytha's daughter Gunhild spent her final moments in Bruges in Flanders, so maybe she returned there after her mother's death. Gunhild had formerly held two estates in Somerset before the Conquest but had never married. It is suggested by some sources she had probably become a nun when young, despite her activities outside of any nunnery. This is not as unusual as it appears. It is acknowledged that women living under religious vows in this period were not necessarily confined to nunneries, and before 1066 Gunhild would have maintained herself from the income from her estates.[11] Back at Bruges, she donated holy relics and a psalter to the local church, and the psalter was said to have survived until the sixteenth century. In her last years, she renewed her vows and entered the nunnery at St Omer. There is some confusion over her date of death, which was either on 24 August or 9 September 1087.[12] She was the last surviving daughter of Godwin and Gytha, and outlived all but one of her siblings, her youngest brother Wulfnoth. An inscription on a plaque in St Saviour's Cathedral museum in Bruges, believed to have originally been inside Gunhild's tomb, records her death on 9 September. There is an ironic coincidence in this: it was on that exact date in 1087 at Rouen that William the Conqueror expired in pain from a combination of illness and injury.

Harold's hand-fast wife Edith Swan-neck may have reached Exeter with the remaining Godwinsons, including her own sons, after Hastings. Through a combination of her East Anglian kinship inheritance and her connection with Harold, she was by 1066 a rich woman. She had held perhaps over 400 hides of land across Suffolk, Essex, Cambridgeshire, Buckinghamshire and Hertfordshire, with an estimated value of £500.[13] It can reasonably be concluded William was keen to punish her for her long association with Harold. In immediately moving her legal ownership of estates into Norman hands she was treated no differently than most of the English nobility at this period. However, there is a contrast here between Edith Swan-neck and Queen Edith and how they responded to the Norman occupation. Maybe she had declined the same terms her namesake had accepted.

What finally became of her is unknown. It is plausible Edith may thereafter have travelled with Gytha and Gunhild to Flanders. It is likewise plausible that the later link to the 'Edith' in Aquitaine noted above, although usually interpreted as referring to Ealdgyth, could have been Edith Swan-neck.[14] Alternately, an unidentified stone tomb in the vaults of St Michael's Church at Bishop Stortford, a building originally founded in the eighth century but significantly rebuilt by the Normans, may contain her remains. The *Domesday Book* acknowledges that the estate at Stortford was owned by Edith, and she may have been lain to rest there.

Harold's brothers Gyrth and Leofwine had both died alongside him at Hastings. Disappointingly, nothing was recorded previously within contemporary texts about their personal lives. We do not know the names of their wives, nor any details of potential children. This is not as unusual as it may appear, and as has been seen, beyond the witnessing of charters neither brother features in any great significance within most of the primary sources. Our assumption is that men in their position would have been given marriages that were politically desirable and beneficial, perhaps betrothals arranged by their father when they were still young men, or alliances made soon after Godwin's death to cement regional support within their respective newly awarded earldoms. It is possible that one or both never married. Nevertheless, it is unfortunate that nothing is known of their descendants.

Tostig's widow Judith remained in Flanders after 1066. In late 1070, when aged about thirty-eight, a new marriage was negotiated for Judith with Duke Welf I of Bavaria. The evidence suggests that she exaggerated her former position to secure a wedding, claiming that she was a former queen in waiting of England on the grounds that her erstwhile spouse had intended to supplant his brother the king. That this was believed at the time is hard to support. Nonetheless, she did marry and move to Bavaria, and although advancing in years Judith had three children by Welf from this marriage. The evidence for it appears in Judith's obituary, kept in Weingarten monastery in Bavaria, which acknowledges that she died there on 5 March 1094.[15.]

Tostig Godwinson's sons Skuli and Ketil had accompanied their father on his 1066 campaign. Perhaps because of their youthful age, the eldest being no older than sixteen, they had remained behind with the Norse ships at Riccall and were not involved in the fighting at Fulford or Stamford Bridge. They were among the survivors pardoned by their uncle alongside Earl Paul of Orkney and Hardrada's young sons Olaf Haraldsson (aka Olaf Kyrre) and Magnus and were on the small flotilla of ships that returned to Norway after the Norse defeat. When Olaf became King of Norway (Olaf III) in 1067, the *Heimskringla* of Snorri Sturluson tells us Skuli and Ketil both gained favour with him and Skuli became one of his senior advisors, marrying one of the king's cousins, a niece of Harald Hardrada.[16]

As seen, Harold and Edith Swan-neck had four sons: Godwin, Edmund, Magnus and Ulf. Even though they had a claim to the English throne, there was no significant show of immediate support for them in England. Godwin, the eldest, was probably aged nineteen at most. After the fall of Exeter, the eldest three had left their grandmother and travelled to Ireland to raise ships and mercenary troops using some of the accumulated family wealth. As seen already, there had been previous ties of friendship between the Godwinsons and the High King of Dublin-Leinster, Diarmait mac Máel na mBó. Diarmait had expired in 1064 but his son Donnchad had succeeded him, and he aided the brothers in gathering mercenaries and providing ships. In the summer of 1068, the *ASC* tells us that the Godwinsons (or Haroldsons) 'came by surprise from Ireland into the mouth of the Avon with a raiding ship-army, and straightway raided across all the region'.[17]

They tried unsuccessfully to seize Bristol before moving south into Somerset, but they were confronted by their father's old follower Eadnoth the Staller at the head of the local levies. The two forces clashed at Bleadon, 3 miles inland from Weston-super-Mare. The sources recorded that 'Eadnoth ... was killed there, together with many good men on either side', along with one of the Godwinson brothers.[18] Most historians have accepted it was Magnus Haroldson that perished in this battle. However, a monument on the wall of the church of St John sub-Castro over in Lewes in Sussex commemorating a hermit named Magnus has been claimed to be a reference to Magnus Haroldson. The monument includes the inscription 'of the royal Danish line, who had served the Church', and suggests that he died much later than 1068.[19] Perhaps Magnus was seriously wounded at Bleadon and was finally laid to rest in Lewes because it was near to one of his former estates pre-1066. The battle at Bleadon may have been a Godwinson victory, as noted by the chronicler Symeon of Durham.[20] If so, it was a pyrrhic victory, because Godwin and Edmund were forced to return to Ireland with their remaining ships.

This was not their last attempt. Godwin and Edmund were to return with a new band of mercenaries. Version D of the *ASC* adds that in midsummer the same year (1068) the sons of Harold came with sixty-four ships into the River Taw at Barnstaple.[21] However, as most other primary sources suggest, this second campaign was more likely launched in 1069.[22] This time they were confronted by Earl Brian, William's Breton vassal, newly placed in control of Devon following the Godwinsons withdrawal from Exeter. At an unspecified place, the two forces clashed. The Norman writer William of Jumièges describes two battles on the same day, with the Godwinsons (Haroldsons) losing 1,700 men.[23] Orderic Vitalis adds that only two small boatloads of survivors made it back this time to Ireland.[24] Godwin and Edmund had probably exhausted their available family finances and could not raise further ships and men for a third campaign.

Their efforts had been limited to the south-west, and at no stage did Harold's sons directly impact the outcomes of the larger uprisings that were taking place against the Normans in the north and east Midlands between 1067 and 1071. The relative insignificance of these attempts to regain their father's kingdom in comparison to the ongoing uprisings against Norman rule further north is perhaps surprising, and lingers only as a footnote to the Conquest. Their involvement in English affairs ended in 1069 at Barnstaple, although the brothers likely moved on to Denmark with their grandmother to try and gain support from their kinsman Swein Estrithsson. Swein declined to help them directly, although, as noted previously, he was to join forces with the ætheling Edgar in 1069 in a failed attempt to seize Northumbria. Perhaps it is reasonable to surmise that Godwin and Edmund joined that campaign and thereafter settled permanently in Denmark, although one suggestion is that they moved on from Denmark to join their sister Gytha in Smolensk (see below) before disappearing from the primary record.

For reasons unclear, their youngest brother Ulf Haroldson seems to have fallen into Norman hands soon after 1066 and became a hostage of the Conqueror.[25] He may have been taken while staying with his aunt Edith in Winchester. Rather than execute him William took him to Normandy in 1067 and he joined his uncle Wulfnoth in custody. Like Wulfnoth, Ulf was held until the Conqueror's death in 1087, when he would have been aged perhaps around thirty, but unlike his uncle, he was fortunate to fall into the hands of William's eldest son, Robert Curthose, and not the second son and future king William Rufus. Rather than be held in confinement, Ulf was given a position close to the Norman court by Robert. He possibly survived well into the twelfth century, but as he would have subsequently adopted a Norman name he consequently disappears from the primary record. Of the descendants with blood ties going back to his grandfather Earl Godwin, Ulf was perhaps the longest-lived member of the dynasty and we can speculate that he may even have lived into the 1120s.

Harold's sister Edith, widow of Edward and now a dowager queen, retained many of her estates after the Conquest. It was not in her interests to be associated with any of her family's uprisings against Norman rule, including the gathering at Exeter supported by her mother. Edith may well have formally acknowledged and endorsed William as her husband's rightful successor. William, now William I (the Conqueror), could therefore hardly dispossess the property of the widow of the man through which he directly claimed his right to be heir to the throne. In the months that followed Edith distanced herself further from her family's legacy and instead aligned herself in the role as Edward's dutiful widow. This is most evident in the *Vita Edwardi*, written by her anonymous Flemish encomiast, which was resumed during 1067. As accepted by historians, she had commissioned the *Vita* ahead of the Conquest. The work had originally been intended as a panegyric on her dynastic family, the House of Godwin. However, post-1066 the scope and subject were revised under Edith's later instructions, as the title of work acknowledges, to highlight instead her deceased husband's life and reign.[26] Nevertheless, the work still provides a valuable insight into the Godwinsons, containing detail of the family not included in any other text. The change of focus further reflected the new political reality. Comment on the rights or wrongs of the Norman claims to the English throne were avoided, as is any direct mention of the Battle of Hastings.[27]

Edith spent most of her later years between Winchester and the nunnery at Wilton, her former convent school. She had sponsored the rebuilding of Wilton Abbey in stone and had seen it consecrated in 1065. It remained largely an English community under an English abbess, and more and more of her time was spent there. In the last few years of her life, she had to fend off renewed long-standing suspicions from the Church that she had committed adultery when married to Edward. This debate was related to the possible claimed celibacy, perhaps virginity, of Edward, and his celibacy was something that the Church had been keen to promote after his death. William of Malmesbury writes that Edith voluntarily confirmed on oath on her deathbed her perpetual virginity to reinforce Edward's celibacy during their marriage.[28] Aged somewhere around fifty, Edith died at Winchester on 18 December 1075.[29] William I seems to have taken considerable care to give Edith a respectful burial at Westminster Abbey, close to the tomb of her husband, and it was 'lavishly decorated with gold and silver'.[30] Later medieval lists recorded she was reburied on the left side of Edward's new shrine, perhaps in the late twelfth century, and that a lamp burned by the high altar in her memory.[31] The abbey was extensively altered in the late thirteenth century, and there is nothing today to mark the whereabouts of Edith's tomb in the present-day abbey.

Moving on to Harold's two daughters, the fortunes of Gytha and Gunhild followed different paths. Gytha Haroldsdottir was likely the elder of the two and was named after her grandmother. Gunhild was probably named after their aunt, who had perhaps been Harold's favoured sister. The young Gytha had accompanied her grandmother and aunt to Exeter, to Flat Holm, and then to Flanders. As recorded by the Danish writer Saxo Grammaticus in his *Gesta Danorum*, Gytha then accompanied her family to the Danish court.[32] This was probably in 1069 after her brothers' unsuccessful campaigns in the south-west. She was perhaps offered as part of a potential marriage alliance when aged about sixteen, but several years later in 1075 Swein Estrithsson is believed to have arranged a marriage alliance for her with Prince Vladimir II Monomach of Smolensk in Russia.[33] This was the first of three marriages for Vladimir. Debate still surrounds her identity, although her date of death is recorded as being 7 May 1107, and in the absence of new evidence we can adopt the premise that this unnamed wife was likely to be our Gytha.[34] One child born to this marriage, named Mstislav, was given the baptismal name of 'Harold', which strongly supports the premise.

Gunhild Haroldsdottir did not follow the movements of her sister and grandmother in the weeks and months after Hastings. She was already living at Wilton Abbey, having been placed there when aged about eleven a few years before 1066. Her aunt Edith probably encouraged her to remain at Wilton after the Conquest. Gunhild remained a long-term resident there, apparently without having taken religious vows, and she was still there well beyond her aunt's death and into the 1090s. Towards the end of Gunhild's stay another royal resident arrived, the young Edith (aka Matilda) of Scotland. This Edith was the daughter of the Scottish king Malcolm III (aka Canmore) and his wife Margaret, and through her mother's bloodline the young Edith/Matilda was the granddaughter of Edward the Exile and therefore great-granddaughter of Edmund Ironside.

Bishop Wulfstan of Worcester is said by William of Malmesbury to have visited Gunhild and Edith at Wilton while en route to councils at Winchester, but the middle-aged Gunhild and the young Anglo-Scot Edith were to leave Wilton dramatically in 1093.[35] Edith of Scotland was removed by her father after King William II (Rufus) had refused to sanction her wedding to the Breton Count Alan the Red. Count Alan escorted Edith from Wilton to her father, but he also took with him from the abbey Gunhild Haroldsdottir. She was now almost forty, but still by all accounts as beautiful as her mother Edith Swan-neck. This was not initially or purely a romantic arrangement. Alan the Red held many of the estates formerly owned by Gunhild's mother, and associating himself with Gunhild further legitimised his usurpation of her mother's estates and reinforced his standing among his tenants, many of whom had pre-1066 associations.[36] Matters took a further twist when Alan died within the year. Despite pressure placed on her by Archbishop Anselm, Gunhild refused to return to Wilton and instead became the wife or concubine of Alan the Red's brother Alan the Black when the latter inherited the former's position and estates in Richmond in Northumbria. Alan the Black died in 1098 and the eventual fate of Gunhild thereafter is unknown. Meanwhile, there is one further point of interest about Edith (aka Matilda) of Scotland. She was to marry William the Conqueror's third son, Henry, within weeks of him succeeding to the throne as King Henry I in 1100. This marriage thereby linked the Anglo-Norman succession of Henry to the original Anglo-Saxon royal house of Edmund Ironside.[37]

Swegn Godwinson, the black sheep, as noted in a previous chapter, has been credited with having two sons. The elder was Hakon, held hostage by Duke William for thirteen years. The younger, a less convincing connection, was named Tostig Reinald (Ranig). Some historians have argued that one, or both, were the sons of the abducted abbess Eadgifu of Leominster, as described in chapter seven, but it is more likely they were the children of concubines. Unlike his fellow hostage Wulfnoth, Hakon had been freed from Norman custody in 1064. There are suggestions he fought and died, on the English side, at either Stamford Bridge or Hastings, and he disappears completely from the primary source record thereafter. Evidence for Tostig Reinald being Swegn's offspring is much thinner, and his only mention is a brief entry in the works of the Norman writer Gaimar.[38]

Finally, we reach Wulfnoth Godwinson, the youngest child of Godwin and Gytha. In the years before 1066, William had kept Wulfnoth in custody in Normandy, presumably to use as a bargaining chip if the opportunity arose. That moment had come in 1064 when Harold was the 'guest' of the Norman duke, but William had declined to release Wulfnoth when freeing Hakon. After 1066, the chances of him being released worsened. It would have been unwise for William to allow Godwin's last surviving son to be free to raise potential support for the Anglo-Saxon cause. Wulfnoth was therefore detained in Normandy. He reappears as one of several important English hostages whom William ordered to be released just before his death at Rouen in September 1087. William's second eldest child, William Rufus, had hurried across the Channel to England to claim the now vacant throne ahead of his brothers, and when doing so he ensured Wulfnoth Godwinson was brought along in close custody. As soon as Rufus reached Winchester and secured the throne, he went against his father's recent instructions and had Wulfnoth imprisoned once again.[39]

Unlike the image of his imprisonment suggested by William of Malmesbury, in which Wulfnoth 'grew old in chains', his remaining days were likely spent in relative comfort as befitted his status.⁴⁰ Wulfnoth adapted to the reality of the Norman Conquest. It is feasible that both before and after 1087 he occasionally travelled with the Anglo-Norman court and remained under direct supervision. Although the evidence is disputed, documents reveal that he appeared in several witness lists during the 1080s and early 1090s.⁴¹ Nonetheless, more than a generation after the Norman Conquest, Rufus was still concerned that the last son of Godwin might grow to be a figure that the Anglo-Saxon majority could rally around. Most primary sources did not record his death, and the *ASC* scribes failed to mention him once. However, both William of Malmesbury and Orderic Vitalis note that Wulfnoth died at Salisbury, and a surviving undated obituary poem for him has been assessed to suggest he died in 1094.⁴³

21

The Verdict of History

The lifespan of the House of Godwin, from Godwin's birth to the deaths of most of his known descendants, was relatively brief. The dynasty flourished in a period of history that reflects in many ways our archetypal image of Anglo-Saxon England, but it was a period which saw England conquered by two foreign powers in the space of fifty years. Nevertheless, the Godwinson dynasty has etched itself a permanent and prominent place in English history. Much of this is reliant, perhaps unfairly, on the events of 1066. The Norman Conquest by design consigned the achievements of the family, expediently and prematurely, into a metaphorical historical vacuum, but ironically it was Harold's defeat at Hastings that kept their legacy alive.

At a contemporary level, by the early years of the twelfth century, only Godwin's granddaughters Gytha and Gunhild can be confirmed as still alive. Other kinfolk, the grandchildren that had been forced by circumstances to transfer themselves to Denmark, Norway, Russia, Ireland or Flanders, or other places unknown, fade from the historical record before the end of the eleventh century. It is entirely likely that two or three had married and had had children, and they in turn had children, and so forth. However, tracing Godwin's family tree through the intervening centuries is open to a mixture of error, guesswork and wild speculation, although more than a few individuals in modern times have claimed blood heritage. While these claims are impossible to verify beyond reasonable doubt, it is nevertheless reasonable to argue that somewhere across Europe there are possible descendants of the Godwinsons alive today, unaware of their connection with Godwin and their Anglo-Saxon ancestry. For Godwin, his burial in the Old Minster in Winchester emphasises how his Anglo-Saxon contemporaries viewed his contribution to the nation, his personal legacy. To be buried inside the Old Minster was an honour previously limited to royalty or senior ecclesiastics. This alone illustrated his importance and standing as Earl of Wessex within the establishment and the level of respect he received from the people. We are told that he was carried to his resting place 'amidst scenes of great grief', and was mourned by all people as a father and a protector of the kingdom.[1]

In 1093, the Old Minster was replaced by the new Norman cathedral and Godwin's remains, along with those of many others, were exhumed and transferred inside the new building. Whether they were reinterred and then later moved during the Reformation is unclear, but by the sixteenth century his bones and those of other individuals had been transferred into eight mortuary chests inscribed with the names of eight kings, two bishops and a queen (Emma). In the seventeenth-century English Civil War, parliamentary troops broke into the chests and scattered the bones, and as the authorities could not differentiate the remains they were thereafter restored haphazardly into six surviving chests. In 2015, the cathedral authorities permitted the contents to be examined and around 1,300 separate bones from twenty-three individuals were identified. Radiocarbon dating revealed that the remains were all pre-1200. Some of Godwin's bones are likely to be within them. Examination by anthropologists continues, but as there are several individuals among the group that died at a similar age to Godwin precise identification is impossible.

Of the other direct family members, only knowledge of Queen Edith's burial place seems to have survived beyond a couple of generations. As already seen, she was entombed alongside her husband in Westminster Abbey in her own lavish burial.[2] However, her tomb was moved in the thirteenth century and the fate of her remains is unknown. Her mother Gytha, brothers Swegn, Tostig, Gyrth, Leofwine and Wulfnoth, and sister Ælfgifu, disappeared from the historical record even more swiftly. Gytha was buried in Denmark or Flanders, Tostig had been buried in York, Swegn somewhere in Turkey, and Wulfnoth probably at Salisbury, but no precise records survive for them. Edith's other sister Gunhild was entombed in St Donation's Church at Bruges. The building was destroyed in 1799 and what happened to Gunhild is unclear. However, the lead plaque mentioned previously, believed to have originally rested under her head inside the tomb now residing in the museum of St Saviour's at Bruges, gives a brief biography of her earlier life in England and praises her devotion to God and her piety.[3] Not much more can be said for the remaining family members. We can summarise that Harold's two wives, Edith Swan-neck (the Fair) and Ealdgyth of Mercia, are thought to have died in Flanders or East Anglia and Francia respectively, his sons Godwin and Edmund in Denmark or Russia, and their brother Ulf in Normandy. His son by Ealdgyth, Harold Haroldson, was last understood to be in Orkney. Harold's daughter Gytha died in Russia and his other daughter Gunhild in Richmond (Yorkshire). Tostig's sons Skuli and Ketil ended their days in Norway, and Swegn's son Hakon had likely died alongside his uncle at Hastings.

What happened to Harold's remains has been addressed in some detail beforehand. If he was laid to rest at Waltham Abbey, the gravestone and plaque laid in 1964 that marks the original spot do not seem to mark his tomb now. Results from ground radar surveys in 2014 across the ground where the earlier church would have extended singled out an area near the east wall worthy of investigation, but Church authorities and English Heritage have refused so far to give archaeologists approval to excavate further. The other potential site associated with Harold, below the floor of Holy Trinity Church at Bosham, has also been refused new permissions to examine the remains again, although in 1999 a ground radar survey was permitted in the nave and chancel and the results strongly indicated signs of a third grave on the north side of the aisle, which has yet to be examined further. Other than the memorial stone (the Harold Stone) at Waltham Abbey for Harold, and the plaque at St Saviour's in Bruges for his sister Gunhild, there are no other memorials or links to any other Godwinson directly related or associated to their place of burial. Harold has the stone memorial at Battle Abbey which was placed there to mark the spot where he was purportedly killed on 14 October 1066. That being accepted, the memorial also marks the site where his brothers Gyrth and Leofwine fell if they died fighting alongside their brother the king.

Beyond these, it is difficult today to find further hard evidence of the Godwinsons. There are no monuments for Godwin, which is perhaps to be expected, but there is a statue of Harold, in a niche on the exterior south wall of Waltham Abbey Church, erected in 1964 at the same time as the memorial stone in the churchyard grounds. There is also an 1875 marble sculpture on a concrete and brick stand in Grosvenor Gardens at St Leonards between Sea Road and Grosvenor Crescent, which romantically but unrealistically depicts Harold being held by Edith Swan-neck after she had reputedly found him on the battlefield. The piece is in a poor state of repair, and in 2019 a plate with the wording 'Edith finding the body of Harold on the battlefield at Hastings' was fixed to the plinth. Elsewhere there is the image of Harold's mother Gytha in a stained-glass window feature at St Nectan's Church in Hartland, Devon, built on the original site of the collegiate church she founded there.[4] This is about the sum of all the monuments that can be identified with the dynastic house.

At a personal level, Godwin was clearly a man to be reckoned with. To gain a position of power effectively second only to the king, and to maintain it for thirty-five years during this period under four separate monarchs – five if we include Edmund Ironside – shows him to have been a man of extraordinary ability, able to master the diplomacy and politics of his age in a way that exceeded any of his peers.[5] Godwin adapted to the Danish conquest and expanded his power during it and beyond it, and he adapted again to the return of Anglo-Saxon control, under Edward (the Confessor), and his family prospered yet further. Let us be under no illusion: Godwin was of critical importance in stabilising the reigns of both Cnut and Edward. He has been described as not always being scrupulous, but his virtues outweighed his vices.[6] Godwin was an effective political chameleon, a vital characteristic during a period of volatile changes within England. However, he was not merely a political figure in the mould of an Eadric Streona. Godwin won the respect of those above and below him as someone that ultimately could be trusted. Others were just as rapacious, but the prudent and shrewd Godwin just did it better than the rest.[7]

At a wider level, as has been seen throughout the book, many of the later primary sources paint a negative picture of the Godwinsons in the era building up to the Norman Conquest.[8] This is not particularly surprising; history, as they say, is written by the victors, and there is no doubt that the Norman version of events dominates this later period. This is often repeated by some historians without recourse but is not necessarily always the most accurate or reliable version of what probably or possibly happened. It is worthwhile repeating here some examples. William of Poitiers in his *Gesta Guillelmi* writes, 'We address you Godwin, whose name even after your death is infamous and hateful.'[9] Poitiers, Duke William's former chaplain, did not know of Godwin when making these comments, but he saved his strongest barbs for Harold. There are many to choose from, among them that 'he was a man soiled with lasciviousness, a cruel murderer, resplendent with plundered riches, and an enemy of the good and just', and 'the execrable tyrant which was forcing you (William of Normandy) into servitude'.[10] These quotes tell us all we need to know about Poitiers' agenda. The Norman Wace added that 'Godwin was cruel and treacherous and did a great harm in the country'.[11] Eadmer, a monk at Christ Church, Canterbury, tells us that Godwin was 'a bitter enemy of the Church of Canterbury', a not unfamiliar response seen within Church communities to the secular nobility.[12] Other later writers took their inspiration from the earlier Norman sources. Henry of Huntingdon considered Godwin to be 'a mighty earl and a ruthless traitor'.[13] Things had not improved by the late twelfth century, with the *Vita Haroldi*, written by a monk in the rebuilt Waltham Abbey, describing Godwin as having 'incredible cunning and audacity'.[14] By the early thirteenth century, Godwin's reputation could reach no lower. Walter Map's *De Nugis Curialum* (The Trifles of Courtiers) describes him as 'ignoble, grasping and unprincipled', and the *Flores Historiarum* (Flowers of History) of Roger of Wendover calls Godwin 'a dog and a traitor; unworthy of Christian burial'.[15]

Not all was negative, however. William of Malmesbury writes of Godwin being 'a man of assumed charm and natural eloquence in his mother tongue, with remarkable skill in speaking and in persuading the public to accept his decisions', and that 'Godwin and his sons, they say, were men of noble spirit and great energy, founders, and pillars of Edward's reign as king'.[16] Godwin's qualities which impressed Cnut were his intelligence, steadfastness and courage, and his supporters reputedly praised his loyalty, justice, bravery, caution and eloquence.[17] Beneath the bias of his daughter Edith's recollections in the *Vita Edwardi*, there appears an able administrator with good negotiating skills and an ability to persuade men to his point of view and create a consensus around him. The ordinary people, perhaps epitomised in the incident at Dover that led to the Godwinson's exile, saw him as a champion of their rights.[18]

It is fair to suggest that Godwin's wife Gytha was a formidable and powerful woman in her time. We can imagine that she not only gave stable support to her husband at moments of crisis but was highly influential in many of the key decisions. Her strength of character and belief in her Anglo-Danish dynasty is displayed by her two-year struggle at the forefront of resistance to the Norman Conquest, and from this we can perhaps assume she had been equally forthright and outspoken in previous decades. Unfortunately, we have perhaps less primary source detail on her than any of the other members of her family. Individually, both Godwin and Gytha were powerful independent characters. A lot of their positive qualities were passed down to Harold, Tostig and Edith, who often displayed the energy and intelligence they had inherited from their parents. Presumably their other offspring possessed similar qualities, some of which is recognised in Gyrth and Gunhild, but we are reduced to speculation. Nothing further can be added about Swegn; he remains something of an enigma. He had been given the same opportunities to shine through his father's contacts, even more so perhaps than his siblings, but clearly squandered his opportunities. Maybe the pressure to follow in his father's footsteps proved too much.

Tostig and Harold, as recorded by Edith, had many similarities. However, Tostig was unable to avoid the pitfalls that came with responsibility, and this is perhaps what separates the two of them. While Harold acted evenly and rationally to almost every situation thrown at him, Tostig was more impulsive and prone to rash decisions. Edith was ruthless if her interests or those of her brothers, particularly Tostig, were threatened, while at diverse times she showed compassion and understanding that can be seen in her devotion to her much older husband and her patronage of the Church. Edith is the intelligent but unfulfilled wife who became more like a mother to her partner in later years, and it may be fair to argue that her childless, unfulfilled marriage gradually made her more resentful as time passed. Historians have compared her to Emma of Normandy. Both had difficult marriages and lived through difficult times. Nevertheless, Emma's legacy seems to have survived in a more positive light in later sources, a contrast created between the munificent Emma and the more predatory Edith.[19] The root of this likely stems from Edith's response to the Norman Conquest. Unlike her mother, or indeed Emma of Normandy in her desire to see her sons retain power, Edith's 'capitulation' to the Norman hierarchy did not go down well among the English and her legacy has suffered. She is the only member of the Godwinson family who after 1069 was not dead, confined or exiled.

Gyrth and Leofwine are in all respects the least remembered of Godwin's sons. Even Wulfnoth is more noticeably remembered than them because of his life spent as a hostage. Nevertheless, from the little we know of Gyrth and Leofwine they fit their father's mould. Despite the lack of primary detail, they look to have been steadfastly loyal to their family. We can only speculate. Perhaps we can place them both somewhere between their parents and Harold on one side, and Tostig, Edith and Swegn on the other, acting as political and diplomatic mediators at both household and national level within the king's court.

Much like his father, Harold was an extraordinary man in his own right. He combined his father's ambition and diplomacy with perhaps a more astute approach to politics. This may be unfair to Godwin because Harold was fortunate in being handed his position through Godwin's lifetime of diplomatic adroitness. Godwin had started with little in comparison. Nevertheless, Harold was to emerge as the cornerstone of Edward (the Confessor's) government and military arm for more than a decade, taking on the mantle of ensuring that the king's withdrawal from decision-making processes did not negatively impact the country's wealth and defences. The Anglo-Norman chronicler Orderic Vitalis added from an unexpected corner that 'he was a valiant man, strong and handsome, pleasant in speech, and a good friend to his own followers'.[20] Harold is said to have shown kindness and patience towards men of goodwill but was 'lion-like' in his hostility towards lawbreakers, thieves and robbers.[21]

As has been seen, Harold was in 1065 to sacrifice Tostig's career to avoid civil war for the greater benefit of his house and the kingdom. This was arguably in contrast to his father, who when faced with something similar had supported his son Swegn against the king, which had risked the permanent ruin of the household in 1051.[22] For Harold, his ultimate downfall came when he was confronted with the unprecedented task of facing two foreign invasions within a week of each other. He nevertheless faced this extraordinary situation undaunted, coming within inches of success. It has been argued that had Harold beaten the Normans after defeating the Norse it is likely we would remember him as one of England's most successful kings.[23]

How, then, has the House of Godwin fared within the historiography? Surveying the available evidence we have from immediate contemporary sources, the dynasty was looked upon with respect and deference. Because of its success and influence it also naturally attracted envy from some of its peers. The Godwinsons were to be remembered in their lifetimes and over several generations as epic heroes, or indeed anti-heroes.[24] Stories of the survival of Harold way beyond 1066 show how traumatic the end of the Godwinson dynasty was, and, as alluded to above, the myth of Harold's survival after Hastings was perpetuated as a hopeful reminder to some English of how things had been, and as an echo of the former indestructibility of the Godwinsons.

Nevertheless, following the Norman Conquest the need to repress any memory of the Godwinsons was deliberately orchestrated, certainly within the top tiers of society. By the twelfth century the writings of scribes such as William of Malmesbury and Orderic Vitalis illustrate that much of the positive sentiment that had remained for the family had been largely squashed as part of the overall Norman-centric dominance of the historical record. There then followed several centuries where the dynasty was effectively forgotten, although it is fair to argue that this was little different than the fate suffered by most of their contemporaries from the Anglo-Saxon period. Matters changed during the late Victorian era, when a new vitality and curiosity towards early English history gathered pace within academia. The deeds of such figures as Alfred the Great, Cnut and Edward the Confessor were revisited and the primary sources reassessed and researched in greater depth. The role of Harold Godwinson within the events surrounding 1066 came to the fore. By the mid-twentieth century a comprehensive library of secondary works on 1066 and the Norman Conquest had surfaced, and it was followed in subsequent decades by new interest in Harold's relationship with Tostig, and Edith's marriage to Edward. From there, further in-depth research among academics and scholars has resurrected debate about the Godwinsons and their place in history and enabled us to understand more about the lives of Godwin and Gytha and the rest of the dynastic family tree.

The outcome has been a more positive resurrection of the Godwinson legacy, enabling us to better assess their lives, both good and bad, within the historical record. As seen from the content of this book, the family must be recognised from so much more than the narrow viewpoint of Harold's defeat in 1066. In particular, the personal significance of Godwin can be more roundly appreciated alongside a greater awareness of the important standing several of the Godwinsons held in eleventh-century England. The demise of the House of Godwin can be put down to a combination of unfortunate circumstances and a self-inflicted calamity that grew from a tragic quarrel between Harold and Tostig. Without this disagreement between the brothers, it is reasonable to conclude that the Norman Conquest would not have succeeded. Unfortunately, the family name has often been evoked not for its achievements but for a family dispute which proved fatal to the dynasty.

Ironically perhaps, but understandably, the House of Godwin is best remembered for Harold's defeat at Hastings. A re-enactment of the battle takes place in the grounds of Battle Abbey every October attended by large crowds. Most of them cheer for the re-enactors representing the Anglo-Saxon English, even though the outcome is predetermined. This show of patriotism is an interesting one. England pre-1066, as argued, was no paragon of proto-parliamentary sovereignty and freedom; but the views on the battle re-enactment continue to be shaped by present notions of nationhood and how these are transposed on the past.[25] Despite an inevitable diluting of our Anglo-Saxon DNA in the intervening centuries, we still see ourselves connected to those who fought and died for Harold at Hastings rather than their Norman counterparts. Invasion by a foreign power is a strong concept, and we have been fortunate; the English Channel has protected England, and the British Isles, from the wars across Europe that devastated many nations on many occasions, none more so than the wars of the twentieth century. Having experienced no similar trauma of such magnitude for nearly a millennium because of that geographical quirk of fate, the events of 1066 have remained raw in the English psyche. There is not necessarily any logic behind this, but we have held the memory of that strongly ever since, and it connects us to the Godwinsons.

Chronology

May–Aug 1016	English victories at battles of Penselwood, Sherston, Brentwood and Otford, between Edmund Ironside and the Danes
18 Oct 1016	Danish victory at Battle of Ashingdon (Assandun) by Cnut over Edmund Ironside; betrayal of English by Eadric Streona
Oct–Nov 1016	Meeting at Deerhurst between Edmund Ironside and Cnut; agreement to divide kingdom: Edmund to hold Wessex, Cnut to hold Mercia, Northumbria, and London
30 Nov 1016	Death of Edmund (possibly murdered)
Dec 1016	Cnut elected King of England by Witan
Jan–Feb 1017	Cnut sends Edmund Ironside's infant sons Edmund and Edward to Sweden, possibly to be killed; Swedish king allows them to be taken to safety in Russia and they afterward settle in Hungary during 1040s;
1017	Cnut appoints Thorkell the Tall, Eric of Hlathir and Eadric Streona as earls; Cnut has Ætheling Eadwig, the last of the sons of Æthelred II and Ælfgifu, killed
Jul 1017	Marriage of Cnut to Emma of Normandy
Nov 1017	Eadric Streona executed by Cnut
1018	Birth of son Harthacnut to Cnut and Emma
1018	Godwin first signs a charter of Cnut
1019–22	Godwin appointed as earl of central Wessex
1019	Death of Cnut's brother Harold (King of Denmark)
1019–20	Cnut claims Danish throne, campaigns in Denmark accompanied by Godwin
1020	Æthelnoth (possible brother of Godwin) becomes Archbishop of Canterbury
1020–21	Marriage of Godwin and Gytha Thorkelsdottir
1021	Birth of Swegn, eldest son of Godwin and Gytha
1021	Earl Thorkell the Tall outlawed by Cnut
1023	Cnut's second visit to Denmark, possibly accompanied by Godwin
1023	Death of Thorkell the Tall
1023–24	Birth of Harold, second son of Godwin and Gytha
1025–26	Cnut's expedition against Ulf and Eilaf; Godwin acts as regent in England
1025–26	Birth of Edith (Eadgyth), eldest daughter of Godwin and Gytha
1025–27	Godwin appointed as earl over all of Wessex (including Kent)
1026	Cnut loses battle of the Holy River to Norwegian/Swedish coalition

1027	Cnut visits Rome
1027–28	Birth of Tostig, third son of Godwin and Gytha
1027–29	Birth of Edith Swan-neck (Eadgyth the Fair), future wife of Harold Godwinson
1027–31	Leofric, son of Ealdorman Leofwine, appointed Earl of Mercia
1028	Cnut successfully invades Norway, Olaf Haraldsson driven into exile; Godwin again acts as regent of England
1028	Cnut leaves his son Harthacnut to act as governor in Denmark
1030	Cnut's governor in Norway, Hakon Ericsson, dies in shipwreck
1030	Danes defeat Norwegians at battle of Stiklestad; Olaf Haraldsson killed
1030	Cnut sends his wife Ælfgifu of Northampton and eldest son Svein Cnutsson to Norway to replace Hakon as regents
1031–35	Birth of Judith of Flanders, future wife of Tostig Godwinson
1031	Cnut's possible second visit to Rome
1031–33	Birth of Gyrth, fourth son of Godwin and Gytha
1032–33	Siward appointed earl of southern Northumbria (Deira)
1033	Possible attempt by Robert I of Normandy to bankroll failed plans to invade England (in support of ætheling Edward)
1033–35	Birth of Gunhild, second daughter of Godwin and Gytha
1034	Svein Cnutsson and his mother Ælfgifu of Northampton are expelled from Norway; Magnus I (the Good), illegitimate son of Olaf Haraldsson, succeeds as King of Norway
1035	Death of Svein Cnutsson, eldest son of Cnut
12 Nov 1035	Death of Cnut; English succession not confirmed; Harthacnut succeeds in Denmark
Dec 1035	Witan council held at Oxford; Harold Harefoot (Ælfgifu of Northampton's son) elected regent in England in absence of Emma's son Harthacnut; Godwin supports Emma and succession of Harthacnut
Jan–Feb 1036	Harefoot seizes treasury held by Emma in Winchester; Godwin remains neutral
Feb 1036	Ælfgifu of Northampton returns to England
Jun–Jul 1036	Emma sends letter to her sons, the æthelings Edward and Alfred in Normandy, to intervene in England
Aug 1036	Edward attempts invasion and lands in The Solent; forced to retire back to Normandy

Sep–Oct 1036	Alfred attempts invasion and lands in Kent; met by Godwin in Surrey on premise of escorting him to Emma in Winchester
Oct 1036	Alfred's men are captured and executed at Guildford by Godwin or supporters of Harefoot; Godwin also implicated in subsequent death of Alfred although Harefoot probable perpetrator
Oct–Nov 1036	Godwin acknowledges Harefoot's entitlement to English throne (possibly earlier)
1036–7	Birth of Leofwine, fifth son of Godwin and Gytha
1037–40	Birth of Ælfgifu, third daughter of Godwin and Gytha
Mar 1037	Harold Harefoot formally elected king (Harold I) by Witan
Mar–Apr 1037	Emma banished and seeks refuge in Flanders
1038	Emma summons her son Edward to Bruges, but he refuses to launch new claim for English throne
1039	Peace treaty agreed between Harthacnut and Magnus I of Norway
Oct–Dec 1039	Harthacnut joins his mother Emma in Flanders
1039–40	Birth of Wulfnoth, sixth and youngest son of Godwin and Gytha
17 Mar 1040	Death of Harold Harefoot
Mar–Apr 1040	Ælfgifu of Northampton seeks refuge in Francia
Mar–Apr 1040	Invitation sent by Witan for Harthacnut to return to England as king
17 Jun 1040	Harthacnut and Emma arrive at Sandwich; Harthacnut proclaimed king
Jun–Jul 1040	Godwin accused by Harthacnut of being complicit in his stepbrother Alfred's death, but gains approval and remains as Earl of Wessex
Jun–Jul 1040	Godwin and others forced to help exhume corpse of Harefoot by Harthacnut, which is then thrown into the River Thames
1041	Earl Siward gains control of all northern Northumbria (Bernicia); Ætheling Edward arrives back in England on Harthacnut's invitation; Emma commissions the *Encomium Emmae Reginae*; in Harthacnut's reprisal for murder of tax collectors Godwin and other senior earls forced to pillage Worcester
8 Jun 1042	Death of Harthacnut at feast; Edward nominated as successor by Witan
Jun 10142	Magnus I of Norway succeeds to Danish throne
1042–43	Possible date for birth of Ælfgifu, third daughter of Godwin and Gytha

23 Apr 1043	Edward (the Confessor) consecrated king; Godwin appointed as senior advisor
16 Nov 1043	Edward confiscates his mother Emma's property in Winchester; Godwin and other earls instructed to assist and seize treasury; Swegn Godwinson appointed Earl of Herefordshire, Gloucestershire, Oxfordshire, Somerset and Berkshire
23 Jan 1045	Marriage of Edward and Godwin's daughter Edith (Eadgyth) to Edward the Confessor; Edith begins to witness charters
1045	Harold Godwinson appointed earl of East Anglia; possible year for the hand-fast marriage of Harold and Edith Swan-neck (the Fair); Beorn (brother of Swein Estrithsson of Denmark) appointed Earl of East Midlands
1046–51	Births of Godwin, Edmund and Magnus, first children of Harold and Edith Swan-neck
1046	Bishop Ealdred succeeds Bishop Lyfing at Worcester
Mar–Jun 1046	Swegn Godwinson and Gruffydd ap Llywelyn raid in South Wales
Oct–Dec 1046	Swegn Godwinson abducts Abbess of Leominster and is exiled and spends winter in Flanders before travelling to Denmark
Dec 1046	Osgod Clapa outlawed
1047	Harald Hardrada (Sigurdsson) becomes joint King of Norway with Magnus I; Bishop Stigand appointed to Winchester; Swein Estrithsson of Denmark, Godwin's nephew, appeals for aid against Magnus of Norway; Edward declines despite urging from Godwin
May–Jul 1047	Swegn Godwinson and Osgod Clapa sail to Denmark to assist Swein Estrithsson
25 Oct 1047	Death of Magnus I, King of Norway and Denmark
Nov 1047	Swein Estrithsson succeeds as King of Denmark; Harald Hardrada succeeds as King of Norway
1048	Swein of Denmark again appeals for aid from England against Norway without success; peace agreed between Swein of Denmark and Harald Hardrada of Norway
Jun–Aug 1049	Swegn Godwinson seeks unsuccessful reconciliation with Edward
Sep 1049	Swegn murders his cousin Beorn Estrithsson and seeks asylum in Flanders
Jun–Aug 1050	After urging from Godwin, Swegn pardoned again by Edward the Confessor

1051	Robert of Jumièges appointed Archbishop of Canterbury by Edward and receives pallium in Rome; Spearhavoc appointed Bishop of London
29 Jun 1051	Robert of Jumièges returns from Rome and refuses to consecrate Spearhavoc
Aug 1051	Marriage of Tostig Godwinson and Judith of Flanders
end Aug 1051	Arrival of Eustace of Boulogne (Edward's former brother-in-law) in Kent; incident with townsfolk of Dover
1–7 Sep 1051	Godwin refuses to comply with Edward's instructions to punish people of Dover
8 Sep 1051	Edward summons council at Gloucester
mid Sep 1051	Stand-off near Gloucester between the Godwinsons and Edward (with earls Leofric and Siward)
24 Sep 1051	Edward summons the Godwinsons to attend Witan meeting at London, but they are not given assurances and withdraw ahead of meeting
25 Sep 1051	Godwin and all his family are declared outlaws by Edward; Godwin, Gytha, Tostig, Gunhild and Gyrth seek asylum in Flanders; Harold and Leofwine travel to Ireland
end Sep 1051	Ælfgar of Mercia replaces Harold as Earl of East Anglia; Edward sends his wife Edith, Godwin's daughter, to nunnery at Wherwell
Oct–Nov 1051	Alleged visit of William (Duke of Normandy) to his kinsman Edward (note: William's grandfather Duke Richard II of Normandy was the brother of Emma of Normandy)
1052–60	Births of Ulf, Gunhild and Gytha, son and daughters of Harold Godwinson and Edith Swan-neck
1052–54	Possible birth of Tostig's sons Skuli and Ketil
6 Mar 1052	Death of Emma of Normandy at Winchester
1052	Swegn Godwinson sets out from Flanders on pilgrimage to Jerusalem; Edith is relocated to Wilton Abbey
Apr–Jun 1052	Godwin finalises plans in Flanders to return to England to restore his position and title
23 Jun 1052	Godwin's first landing in England to assess support; evades royal fleet under Ralph and Odda
Jul 1052	Harold and Leofwine set sail from Ireland and land at Porlock, and are challenged by local fyrd; they then sail around into the English Channel; Godwin launches second attempt and establishes base at Isle of Wight
Jul–Aug 1052	The fleets of Godwin and Harold join forces at Portland and move east

15 Sep 1052	Meeting of Witan held; confrontation avoided and Edward pardons the Godwinsons, restoring them to their lands and earldoms
Sep 1052	Godwinsons gather additional ships and men along the south coast and arrive unchallenged at Southwark; Archbishop Robert flees for Normandy, possibly taking with him as hostages Wulfnoth Godwinson and Hakon (son of Swegn Godwinson); Edith restored as queen
end Sep 1052	Godwin suffers serious illness, but recovers
29 Sep 1052	Death of Swegn Godwinson in Lycia, Turkey, while returning from pilgrimage to Jerusalem
Oct 1052	Stigand appointed Archbishop of Canterbury
Jan 1053	News of Swegn's death reaches Godwin
12 Apr 1053	Godwin suffers stroke while dining with Edward at Winchester or Odiham
15 Apr 1053	Death of Godwin after remaining unconscious for three days; Harold succeeds as Earl of Wessex and Ælfgar replaces Harold as Earl of East Anglia
Apr 1053	Godwin buried at Old Minster, Winchester
1054	Edmund, brother of Edward the Exile and eldest son of Edmund Ironside, dies in Hungary
1054–55	Bishop Ealdred of Worcester sent to Germany by Edward to locate Ætheling Edward (the Exile), son of Edmund Ironside; returns a year later unsuccessfully
Feb–Mar 1055	Death of Earl Siward of Northumbria
Mar 1055	Tostig Godwinson appointed Earl of Northumbria
Mar–Jun 1055	Ælfgar exiled and joins forces with Gruffydd ap Llywelyn of Gwynedd; Gyrth Godwinson appointed Earl of East Anglia
24 Oct	Ælfgar and Gruffydd ap Llywelyn defeat Earl Ralph near Hereford
1055–56	Harold launches successful campaign against Gruffydd
1056	Second attempt by Edward to locate Edward the Exile with assistance of Harold; the Exile persuaded to return, with promise of future English succession; Ælfgar reinstated to East Anglia; Gyrth perhaps retains Northamptonshire
31 Aug 1056	Death of Earl Odda
Feb–Mar 1057	Edward the Exile arrives back in England
19 Apr 1057	Sudden death of Edward the Exile through unknown causes
Aug–Oct 1057	Death of Earl Leofric of Mercia; his son Ælfgar succeeds him; Gyrth Godwinson reappointed Earl of East Anglia
21 Dec 1057	Death of Earl Ralph of Mantes

1057–58	Leofwine Godwinson replaces Ralph as earl in Middlesex, Bedfordshire, Hertfordshire, and Buckinghamshire
1058	Harold Godwinson given additional responsibility as Earl of Herefordshire after death of Ralph
1058	Ælfgar exiled for second time, joins forces again with Gruffydd
1058–59	Ælfgar soon reinstated again by Edward
1059	Tostig escorts Malcolm III of Scotland to meeting with Edward in Gloucester
1060	Ealdred appointed as Archbishop of York
3 May 1060	Harold's foundation at Waltham Cross consecrated
1061	Tostig visits Rome; Malcolm of Scotland raids northern Northumbria in his absence
1061–62	Death of Earl Ælfgar of Mercia; his son Edwin succeeds him
Nov–Dec 1062	Harold Godwinson conducts raid on Gruffydd ap Llywelyn's base in Rhuddlan
May–Jul 1063	Harold and Tostig Godwinson conduct successful campaigns on land and sea against Gruffydd ap Llywelyn
5 Aug 1063	Gruffydd ap Llywelyn killed by his own men
1063–64	Tostig arranges for murder of Northumbrian thegns Gamal and Ulf
Jun–Sep 1064	Harold journeys across English Channel, possibly to negotiate release of his brother Wulfnoth and nephew Hakon (held since 1052); purportedly gives oaths to William of Normandy regarding the English succession before allowed to return to England; Hakon released but Wulfnoth retained in confinement; Harold's daughter Gytha joins nunnery at Wilton
29 Dec 1064	Tostig arranges for murder of Northumbrian thegn Gospatric, possibly aided by Edith
1064–5	Possible year of death of Godwin's youngest daughter Ælfgifu
Aug 1065	Harold's new lodge at Portskewet (near Chepstow) pillaged by Caradog ap Gruffydd
3 Oct 1065	Northumbrian rebels attack and seize control of York while Tostig is in the south with Edward
mid Oct 1065	Rebel army led by earl Edwin (son of Ælfgar) and his brother Morcar march south; Harold Godwinson meets them in Northamptonshire to discuss terms
27 Oct 1065	Witan meeting held at Oxford; Edward sends Harold back with agreement to accept rebels' terms; this may have included Harold agreeing to marry Edwin and Morcar's sister Ealdgyth

end Oct 1065	Morcar succeeds as Earl of Northumbria
end Oct 1065	Tostig rejects outcome and accuses Harold of betrayal; Tostig outlawed by Edward
Nov 1065	Tostig seeks exile in Flanders with his brother-in-law Baldwin V; Edward's health declines
25 Dec 1065	Edward brings forward consecration day of his new foundation of Westminster Abbey due to ill health
5 Jan 1066	Death of Edward; purportedly offers succession to Harold on deathbed
6 Jan 1066	Harold Godwinson consecrated king (Harold II) by Witan
Feb 1066	William of Normandy disputes Harold's entitlement and prepares initial plans to build invasion fleet and army
Feb–Mar 1066	Harold travels to York to agree terms with Edwin and Morcar, including finalising marriage to their sister Ealdgyth (widow of Gruffydd ap Llywelyn)
24–30 Apr 1066	Halley's Comet appears brightly for one week, is seen by contemporaries as an omen
Apr–May 1066	Tostig travels to Normandy, Denmark and Norway in attempts to raise military support for invasion of England
May–Jul 1066	Tostig raids southern and eastern coasts of England; defeated on the Humber by forces of Edwin and Morcar and sails to Scotland
Jun 1066	Harold summons fleet and fyrd to south coast in preparation for Norman invasion
Jul 1066	Tostig has final meeting with Harald Hardrada and helps persuade him to attempt Norwegian invasion of England despite Hardrada's lack of valid entitlement
Aug 1066	William of Normandy completes final preparations to invade England at Dives-sur-Mer
Sep 1066	Norse fleet under Harald Hardrada invades England via Humber and sails towards York accompanied by Tostig as ally
8 Sep 1066	Harold disbands fleet and fyrd guarding southern England believing Norman invasion will not be until following year
mid Sep 1066	Norman fleet first sails from Dives-sur-Mer but is forced back to Normandy (Saint-Valéry-sur-Somme) with losses due to bad weather
20 Sep 1066	Norse victory at Battle of Fulford near York by Harald Hardrada against army of earls Edwin and Morcar; Edwin and Morcar survive
22 Sep 1066	Hardrada awaits hostages and takes his army to Stamford Bridge; Harold Godwinson advances English army north to confront him

25 Sep 1066	Harold defeats Norse army led by Harald Hardrada and Tostig at Battle of Stamford Bridge near York; both Hardrada and Tostig killed; Tostig purportedly buried in York
end Sep 1066	Harold allows remnants of Norse fleet to sail back to Norway
28–29 Sep 1066	Norman invasion fleet sails from Saint-Valéry-sur-Somme and lands unopposed on Sussex coast
2–4 Oct 1066	Harold first hears news of Norman invasion while still at York
4–12 Oct 1066	Harold gathers new fyrd before continuing into Sussex to oppose Normans
14 Oct 1066	Harold defeated by William of Normandy at Battle of Hastings; Harold, Gyrth and Leofwine all killed during battle, possibly also their nephew Hakon
Oct 1066	Harold Godwinson's body purportedly recognised and removed from battlefield; Harold's final resting place uncertain, possibly at Waltham Abbey, Bosham, or near to Hastings
end Oct 1066	Witan nominate Edgar the Ætheling (son of Edward the Exile) as king
Oct-Nov 1066	Surviving members of Godwinson family, except Edith, move west into Devon
Oct-Nov 1066	Norman army marches through southern shires and seizes Edith at Winchester
Nov 1066	Ealdgyth of Mercia, second wife of Harold, is sent to Chester for safety by her brothers Edwin and Morcar
early Dec 1066	English surrender to William at Berkhamsted and Normans enter London
25 Dec 1066	Duke William of Normandy is crowned William I of England
1066–67	Birth of Harold Haroldson, son of Harold and Ealdgyth of Mercia
Jan 1067	Edith accepts Norman rule
Feb–Mar 1067	Gytha, wife of Godwin, and other family members, leave Exeter during siege and arrive at Flat Holm in Bristol Channel
1067–72	English Resistance against Norman Conquest continues to varying degree in the north and west and other areas but ultimately unsuccessful
1067–68	Edith commissions the *Vita Edwardi Regis*
Jun–Aug 1068	Harold's sons Godwin, Edmund, and Magnus leave base in Ireland with mercenary fleet to seek landing at Bristol; defeated at battle in Somerset

Jun-Aug 1069	Gytha and Gunhilda travel to exile in Flanders; Harold's sons conduct further raids and attempted landings in North Devon and Somerset; Magnus killed
11 Sep 1069	Death of Ealdred, Bishop of Worcester and Archbishop of York
Mar–Apr 1070	Gytha, her daughter Gunhild, and Harold's children Godwin, Edmund and Gytha travel to Denmark
May–Aug 1070	Ealdgyth, second wife of Harold Godwinson, leaves Chester for Wales; Gytha and Gunhild move from Denmark to St Omer in Flanders; Stigand deposed as Archbishop of Canterbury
1071	Tostig's widow Judith of Flanders marries Welf I of Bavaria
1072–4	Death of Godwin's wife Gytha
1075	Marriage of Harold's daughter Gytha to Vladimir Monomach of Russia
18 Dec 1075	Death of Edith, eldest daughter of Godwin and Gytha, buried at Westminster Abbey
1080s	Death of Ealdgyth of Mercia, widow of Harold
24 Aug 1087	Death of Gunhild, daughter of Godwin and Gytha; release from confinement in Normandy of Wulfnoth Godwinson, youngest son of Godwin, and Ulf, youngest son of Harold Godwinson
Sep 1087	Wulfnoth re-imprisoned by William II Rufus and held in Winchester until his death
1093	Harold eldest daughter Gunhild leaves Wilton Abbey and elopes with Count Alan the Red (Rufus) the Breton; Alan soon dies and Gunhild marries his brother Alan the Black
1094–5	Death of Wulfnoth
1098	Harold Haroldson (son of Harold Godwinson) joins campaign of Magnus Olafsson (Barefoot) of Norway to Orkney, Isle of Man, and Anglesey
1100	Edith (aka Matilda), daughter of Malcolm III of Scotland and Margaret (daughter of Edward the Exile), marries Henry I (son of William I) of England
7 May 1107	Death of Gytha, daughter of Harold
1110s	Decade which probably saw the deaths of Ulf and Harold Haroldson and Gunhild, the last surviving children of Harold Godwinson

Notes

The following abbreviations have been used in the more frequently referenced works in the endnotes

ASC	The Anglo-Saxon Chronicles
BT	Bayeux Tapestry
DB	Domesday Book
CHP	Carmen de Hastingae Proelio of Guy Bishop of Amiens
CJW	Chronicle of John of Worcester (vol 1)
EE	Estoire des Engleis of Geffrei Gaimar
EER	Encomium Emmae Reginae
EHD	English Historical Documents (vol 1 & 2)
EHOV	Ecclesiastical History of Orderic Vitalis (vol 2)
GG	Gesta Guillelmi of William of Poitiers
GND	Gesta Normannorum Ducum of William of Jumièges (vols 1 & 2)
GPA	Gesta Pontificum Anglorum of William of Malmesbury
GRA	Gesta Regum Anglorum of William of Malmesbury (vols 1 & 2)
HA	Historia Anglorum of Henry of Huntingdon
HSS	Heimskringla of Snorri Sturluson
LEC	Lives of Edward the Confessor
RR	Roman de Rou of Wace
SMO	Symeonis Monachi Opera Omnia of Symeon of Durham
VER	Vita Edwardi Regis

Note: Charter numbers have the prefix 'S' taken from the cataloguing system first adopted by Professor Peter Sawyer in 1968 which is in common usage.

A Note on Primary Sources

1. A. Hern, *The Mythical Battle: Hastings 1066* (Marlborough, 2017) p.17
2. F. Barlow, *Edward the Confessor* (New Haven; London, rev edn. 1997) pp.127–8

3. E. M. C. van Houts, 'Historical Writing' in *A Companion to the Anglo-Norman World*, (Woodbridge, 2007) pp.107
4. Hern, p.30
5. *The Anglo-Saxon Chronicles*, rev. edn, ed. and trans. by M. Swanton (London, 2000)
6. S. Baxter, 'Edward the Confessor and the Succession Question', in *Edward the Confessor: The Man and the Legend*, ed R. Mortimer (Woodbridge, 2009) pp.109–10
7. E. M. C. van Houts, 'Historical Writing' p.113
8. T. Licence, 'A New Source for the Vita Ædwardi Regis' in *Journal of Medieval Latin*, No.29 (2019)
9. E. M. C. van Houts, 'Historical Writing' p.108
10. VER, pp. xxix-xxxiii
11. I. W. Walker, *Harold: The Last Anglo-Saxon King* (Stroud, repr. 2010) p. xxi
12. Barlow, p.225
13. H. J. Grills, *The Life and Times of Godwine Earl of Wessex* (Swaffham, 2009) p.203
14. A. Bridgeford, 'Was Count Eustace II of Boulogne the patron of the Bayeux Tapestry?' in *Journal of Medieval History*, No.25 issue 3 (Sept 1999)

1 Wulfnoth Cild and the Danish Conquest

1. F. Barlow, *The Godwins: The Rise and Fall of a Noble Dynasty* (Edinburgh, 2002) p.21
2. A. Wareham, 'Transformation of Kinship and the Family in late Anglo-Saxon England', in *Early Medieval Europe, Vol 10*, (2001) p.385–99
3. CJW, P.461
4. N. R. Ker, 'Hemming's Cartulary: A Description of Two Worcester Cartularies in Cotton Tiberius A. xiii', in R. W. Hunt, et al (eds.), *Studies in Medieval History Presented to Frederick Maurice Powicke* (Reprint of 1948 Oxford University Press ed.). Westport, CT: Greenwood Press (1979) pp.49–75
5. ASC, p.138
6. Barlow, *The Godwins*, pp.23–4; P. Rex, *The Last English King: The Life of Harold II* (Stroud, 2008) p.22
7. VER, pp.8–9
8. H. J. Grills, *The Life and Times of Godwine Earl of Wessex* (Swaffham, 2009) p.19
9. E. Mason, *The House of Godwine: The History of a Dynasty* (Hambledon & London, 2004) p.25; Charters S862, S885, S895, S911
10. ASC, p.138
11. Prosopography of Anglo-Saxon England (www.pase.ac.uk)
12. Grills, p.32
13. A. Williams, 'Land and Power in the Eleventh Century: The Estates of Harold Godwineson', in *Anglo-Norman Studies III: Proceedings of the Battle Conference 1980* (Woodbridge, 1081), p.183
14. Walter Map, *De Nugis Curialium*, (Oxford, 1914) pp.206–7
15. *Knytlinga Saga*, attr. to Olaf Thordarson, trans. by H. Palsson and P. Edwards (Odens: 1986) pp.32–4; F. Barlow, *The Feudal Kingdom of England 1042–1216*, (Abingdon; Routledge, 2014) p.45
16. ASC, p.138
17. GRA, p.275
18. ASC, p.138
19. CJW, p.461

20. CJW, p.461
21. ASC, p.138
22. ASC, p.138
23. HA, p.347
24. ASC, pp.138–9; CJW, p.463
25. E. John, 'The Return of the Vikings', in *The Anglo-Saxons*, ed A. Campbell (London, 1991) p.209
26. S. D. Keynes, *The Diplomas of King Æthelred 'the Unready', 978–1016* (Cambridge, 1980)
27. EHD, vol 1, pp.548–9
28. S. D. Keynes, 'Edward the Ætheling', in *Edward the Confessor: The Man and the Legend*, ed. by R. Mortimer (Woodbridge, 2009) p.54
29. ASC, p.144
30. ASC, p.145
31. ASC, p.145
32. D. Whitelock, ed and trans. *Anglo-Saxon Wills* (Cambridge; 1930), p.60
33. F. Barlow, *Edward the Confessor* (New Haven; London, rev edn. 1997) pp.29, 34–51; A. Williams, *Æthelred the Unready: The Ill-Counselled King* (London: 2003)
34. ASC, pp.145–6
35. CJW, p.481
36. ASC, p.146
37. ASC, p.146
38. ASC, p.146
39. ASC, p.147
40. ASC, p.148
41. EER, p.31
42. ASC, p.148
43. EE, lines 4198–9
44. ASC, p.149
45. CJW, p.487
46. CJW, p.487
47. EER, p.21; EE, line 4229
48. ASC, p.151
49. *Knytlinga Saga*, pp.32–4
50. Walter Map, *De Nugis Curialium*, pp.206–7
51. ASC, p.151; F. M. Stenton, *Anglo-Saxon England* (Oxford, 1971) p.391
52. CJW, p.491
53. A. Williams, *Æthelred the Unready: The Ill-Counselled King* (London, 2003) p145
54. ASC, p.152; CJW, p.491; EER, pp.24–5
55. CJW, p.491
56. ASC, pp.152–3; HA, pp.359–61
57. ASC, p.153
58. ASC, p.153
59. CJW, p.493; HA, p.361
60. GRA, p.319
61. HA, p.361
62. EE, lines 4420–5
63. S. D. Keynes, 'The Æthelings in Normandy', in *Anglo-Norman Studies XIII: Proceedings of the Battle Conference 1990* (Woodbridge, 1991) pp.173–205

2 Godwin's Rise to Power

1. M. Biddle, 'Capital at Winchester', in *The Vikings in England and their Danish Homeland*, ed E. Roesdahl et al (1981) pp. 165–70
2. E. Mason, pp.83–4
3. ASC, p.154
4. A. Williams, *Kingship and Government in Pre-Conquest England, C.500–1066*, British History in Perspective (New York, 1999) pp.131–2
5. ASC, p.154
6. CJW, p.495
7. N. J. Higham, *The Death of Anglo-Saxon England* (Stroud, Sutton Publishing, 1997) p.85
8. GRA, p.319
9. ASC, p.155
10. GRA, p.323
11. *The Chronicon of Thietmar of Merseburg*, ed D. A. Warner (Manchester, 2001) c.40; Ian Howard, *Harthacnut: The last Danish King of England* (Stroud, 2008) p.15
12. H. O'Brien, *Queen Emma and the Vikings: The Woman Who Shaped the Events of 1066* (London, 2006) p.103
13. Charter S997a
14. CJW, p.503
15. GRA, p.319 n. WOM mistakenly named Edmund as Eadwig, confusing him with Ironside's brother of that name)
16. GRA, p.319
17. G. Ronay, *The Lost King of England: The Eastern European adventures of Edward the Exile* (Woodbridge, 1989) p.81
18. GRA, p.321
19. GRA, p.321; EE, lines 4470–5
20. EER, p.33
21. M. K. Lawson, *Cnut: England's Viking King 1016–35* (Stroud, 2nd edn. 2011) p.90
22. Barlow, *The Godwins*, p.37
23. C. Jones, *The Forgotten Battle of 1066: Fulford* (Stroud, 2007) p.87
24. HA, pp.367–9
25. EE, lines 4700–29
26. *Bede's Ecclesiastical History of the English People*, eds, J. McClure and R. Collins (Oxford: New York, rev edn. 2008) p.193
27. G. W. Marwood, *The Story of the Holy Trinity Church* (Chichester, 1995) pp.3–15
28. ASC, p.154
29. R. Fletcher, *Bloodfeud: Murder and Revenge in Anglo-Saxon England* (London, 2002) p.101
30. D. Hill, 'An urban policy for Cnut?', in A. R. Rumble, ed. *The Reign of Cnut: King of England, Denmark and Norway* (London, 1994) p.103
31. ASC, pp.154–5
32. P. Stafford, 'The Laws of Cnut and the history of Anglo-Saxon royal promises', in *Anglo-Saxon England, Vol. 10*, (1981) pp. 173–90
33. P. Hill, *The Road to Hastings: The Politics of Power in Anglo-Saxon England* (Stroud, 2005) p.62
34. HA, p.365
35. HA, p.365
36. Charters S955, S956
37. W. B. Bartlett, *King Cnut and the Viking conquest of England 1016* (Stroud, 2017) p.169

38. Charter S956
39. A. Anscombe, 'The Pedigree of Earl Godwine', in *Translations of the Royal Historical Society, 3rd series, Vol. VII*, pp. 129–50
40. I. W. Walker, *Harold: The Last Anglo-Saxon King* (Stroud, repr. 2010) pp.65–6
41. S. D. Keynes, 'Cnut's Earls in the reign of Cnut', in *The Reign of Cnut: King of England, Denmark and Norway*, ed A. Rumble (London, 1994) p.73
42. E. Mason, p.31; R. Frank, 'Scaldic Poetry', in *Old Norse Icelandic Literature: A Critical Guide*, eds C. Clover & J. Lindow (New York; Ithica, 1985) p.179
43. M. Lapidge et al, eds. *The Blackwell Encyclopaedia of Anglo-Saxon England*, repr. (Oxford, 2007) p.99
44. M. K. Lawson, *Cnut: England's Viking King 1016–35*, pp.66–7
45. M. Lapidge et al, eds. *The Blackwell Encyclopaedia of Anglo-Saxon England*, p.100
46. GRA, p.331
47. Prosopography of Anglo-Saxon England (www.pastscape.org.uk)
48. ASC, p.155; CJW, p.507
49. Grills, p.84
50. A. Williams, *Kingship and Government in Pre-Conquest England, C.500–1066*, p133
51. GRA, p.363
52. J. Tshan, trans. *Adam of Bremen: Gesta Hammaburgensis Ecclesiae Pontificum History of the Archbishops of Hamburg, Vol. II* (New York; 1999) pp.124–5
53. Saxo Grammaticus, *Danorum Regum Heroumque Historia*, trans and ed by E. Christiensen (Oxford; 1980) p.35
54. VER, p.6
55. S. D. Keynes, 'Cnut's Earls in the reign of Cnut', p.60–4
56. F. M. Stenton, *Anglo-Saxon England* (Oxford, 1971) p.417; M. K. Lawson, *Cnut: The Danes in England in the early 11th Century* (New York, 1993) p.188
57. J. Brondsted, *The Vikings* (London, 1960) p.94
58. VER, p.5–6
59. S. D. Keynes, 'Cnut's Earls in the reign of Cnut', pp.73, 84–6
60. K. DeVries, *The Norwegian Invasion of England in 1066* (Woodbridge, 1999) pp.108–14

3 Establishing a Dynasty

1. J. Tshan, trans. *Adam of Bremen: Gesta Hammaburgensis Ecclesiae Pontificum History of the Archbishops of Hamburg, Vol. II* (New York; 1999) p.92
2. N. R. Ker, 'Hemming's Cartulary', pp.275–6
3. Mason, p.35
4. BT, Scene 18
5. M. B. Missuno, 'Contact and Continuity: England and the Scandinavian Elites in The Early Middle Ages', in *Nordic Elites in Transformation c.1050–1250, vol II*, eds. K. Esmark et al (New York, 2020) p.122
6. Prosopography of Anglo-Saxon England (www.pase.ac.uk)
7. HSS, p.262
8. VER, p.24
9. Charter S950
10. Charters S950, S955, S956, S958, S980, S984
11. P. H. Sawyer, ed. *The Charters of Burton Abbey* (New York: Oxford, 1979) p.xliii
12. EER, p.31
13. Barlow, *The Godwins*, p.21
14. ASC, pp.154–7

15. ASC, p.156
16. P. H. Sawyer, *Kings and Vikings: Scandinavia and Europe AD700–1100* (London, 1996) p.8
17. HSS, pp.441–4
18. HSS, p.445
19. VER, pp.10–11
20. GRA, pp.323–5
21. Geffrei Gaimar, *Estoire des Engleis (History of the English)*, ed. and trans. by I. Short (Oxford; New York: Oxford University Press, 2009)
22. GRA, p.325
23. A. A. M. Duncan, *The Kingship of the Scots 842–1292: Succession and Independence* (Edinburgh, 2002) pp.31–2
24. B. T. Hudson, 'Cnut and the Scottish Kings', in *English Historical Review, Vol. 107*, (1992) pp.357–8
25. N. J. Higham, *The Death of Anglo-Saxon England* (Stroud, 1997) p.104
26. Stenton, *Anglo-Saxon England*, p.404
27. ASC, pp.156–8
28. HA, p.367; GRA, p.325; CJW, p.513
29. H. Wolfram, *Conrad II, 990–1039: Emperor of Three Kingdoms*, with trans by D. A. Kaiser (Pennsylvania, 2006) p.102
30. ASC, p.157; HSS, pp.510–17
31. GRA, pp.325–9; CJW, pp.513–9
32. CJW, p.517
33. EHD, vol 1, pp.477–8
34. Prosopography of Anglo-Saxon England (www.pase.ac.uk)
35. Pentland Firth – the stretch of water between John o'Groats and the Orkneys
36. HSS, pp.541–2
37. Charter S968
38. Mason, p.34–5
39. ASC, pp.158–9; E. B. Fryde et all, eds. *Handbook of British Chronology, 3rd rev ed* (Cambridge, 1996) p.222
40. GRA, p.333
41. *Rodulfus Glaber Opera*, ed. J. France et al (Oxford, 1989)
42. Howard, *Harthacnut: The last Danish King of England*, p.46
43. H. Fuhrmann, *Germany in the High Middle Ages c.1050–1200*, with trans by T. Reuter (Cambridge, 1995) p.40
44. ASC, p.158
45. Lawson, *Cnut: England's Viking King 1016–35*, p.113; Charter S975

4 Godwin and the Anglo-Danish Succession, 1035–1036

1. DB; Prosopography of Anglo-Saxon England (www.pase.ac.uk)
2. DB; Prosopography of Anglo-Saxon England (www.pase.ac.uk)
3. Mason, p.36
4. *Liber Eliensis: A History of the Isle of Ely from the Seventh Century to the Twelfth,* trans J. Fairweather (Woodbridge, 2005)
5. Stenton, *Anglo-Saxon England*, p.420
6. ASC, pp.159–61
7. ASC, p.159; CJW, p.521
8. ASC, p.161; P. Hill, *The Road to Hastings: The Politics of Power in Anglo-Saxon England* (Stroud, 2005) p.69
9. HA, p.369

10. SMO, p.158
11. Barlow, *Edward the Confessor*, p.44
12. Tshan, J., trans. *Adam of Bremen: Gesta Hammaburgensis Ecclesiae Pontificum History of the Archbishops of Hamburg, Vol. II* (New York; 1999) p.134
13. GND, vol 2, pp.78–9
14. P. Stafford, *Queen Emma and Queen Edith: Queenship and Women's Power in Eleventh Century England* (Oxford, 2001) pp.238, 244
15. CJW, p.521
16. Grills, p.90
17. HA, p.369
18. ASC, pp.159–61
19. EER, pp.39–41
20. CJW, p.521
21. EER, pp.39–41; Grills, p.93
22. EER, pp.41–3
23. GND, vol 2, pp.77–9
24. Mason, p.37
25. CJW, pp.522–3
26. ASC, pp.158–9; CJW, p.523
27. GND, vol 2, p.105; GG, p.3
28. GND, vol 2, p.107
29. GND, vol 2, p.107
30. RR, p.143
31. ASC, pp.158–9
32. LEC, p.191; GND, vol 2, p.107
33. CJW, p.523
34. ASC, p.159
35. HA, p.373; CJW, p.523
36. GG, p.5
37. ASC, p.158
38. CJW, p.523
39. GG, p.5
40. EER, p.45; RR, p.143; EE, lines 4826–30
41. ASC, p.158
42. EE, line 4815
43. A. W. G. Lowther, 'The Saxon Cemetery at Guildown, Guildford', in *Surrey Archaeological Collections*, Vol. 39 (1931) pp.1–50, and Vol 41 (1933) pp. 119–22
44. S. Harrington & S. Welch, *The early Anglo-Saxon kingdoms of southern Britain AD450–650: Beneath the Tribal Hidage* (Oxford: Philadelphia, 2014); D. Bird, 'Guildown Reconsidered', in *Surrey Archaeological Society, Bulletin 464, Oct 2017*
45. Grills, p.103
46. RR, p.143
47. GRA, p.337 (Gillingham in Kent)
48. Mason, p.39
49. D. G. J. Raraty, 'Earl Godwine of Wessex: The Origins of his Power and his Political Loyalties', *History*, 74, (1989) pp.14
50. EER, p.43
51. EER, p.43
52. EER, pp.45–7
53. *Liber Eliensis*, p.160
54. EER, p.43
55. Howard, *Harthacnut: The last Danish King of England*, p.98

56. Mason, pp.37–8
57. O'Brien, p.173
58. EER, pp.41–3
59. T. Licence, *Edward the Confessor*, p.68

5 Godwin and the Anglo-Danish Succession, 1037–1042

1. ASC, pp.158–9
2. P. Stafford, *Unification and Conquest: A Political and Social History of England in the Tenth and Eleventh Centuries* (London, 1989) p.79
3. ASC, p.160
4. Stenton, *Anglo-Saxon England*, p.421
5. Stafford, *Queen Emma and Queen Edith*, p.237
6. EER, p.41
7. D. G. J. Raraty, 'Earl Godwine of Wessex: The Origins of his Power and his Political Loyalties', *History*, 74, 1989, p.14
8. I. Howard, 'Harold II: A Throne-Worthy King', in *King Harold II and the Bayeux Tapestry*, ed G. R. Owen-Crocker (Woodbridge; Boydell Press, 2005) pp.40–44
9. ASC, p.160
10. EER, p.47
11. GRA, p.337
12. Charter S1392
13. Lawson, *Cnut: England's Viking King 1016–35*, pp.116–7
14. Stenton, *Anglo-Saxon England*, p.421
15. GRA, p.335
16. EER, p.41
17. J. Stevenson, ed 'The History of Ingulf', in *Church Historians of England, Vol ii* (London, 1854)
18. F. Barlow, *The English Church 1000–1066: A History of the Later Anglo-Saxon Church*, 2nd edn (New York, 1979) p.41
19. ASC, p.160
20. EER, p.49
21. Stenton, *Anglo-Saxon England*, pp.421–2
22. ASC, p.161
23. ASC, p.161
24. Charter S994
25. M. Evans, *Death of Kings: Royal deaths in Medieval England* (London, 2006) p.22
26. Oxford Dictionary of National Biography, M. K. Lawson, 'Harold I' (www.oxforddnb.com)
27. W. H. Stevenson, 'An alleged son of King Harold Harefoot', in *English Historical Review, No.109* (1913) pp.112–17
28. ASC, p.161
29. GRA, p.337
30. Stenton, *Anglo-Saxon England*, pp.422–3; Stafford, *Unification and Conquest*, p.80
31. CJW, p.531
32. ASC, p.162; SMO, p.160
33. Mason, pp.39–40
34. CJW, p.531–3
35. GRA, p.339; CJW, p.531
36. Howard, *Harthacnut: The last Danish King of England*, pp.114–5
37. ASC, p.162
38. SMO, p.91

39. CJW, pp.529–31
40. CJW, p.531
41. ASC, pp.161–3; HA, p.371
42. Lawson, *Cnut: England's Viking King 1016–35*, p.163
43. CJW, p.533
44. CJW, p.533
45. Charters S983, S1394, S1395, S1396
46. Charters S982, S993, S994
47. EER, p.53
48. Licence, *Edward the Confessor*, p.76
49. Grills, p.116
50. Barlow, *Edward the Confessor*, p.52
51. ASC, pp.162–3; CJW, p.533
52. Howard, *Harthacnut: The last Danish King of England*, pp.61–2
53. GG, p.7
54. CJW, p.535

6 Politics, Queen Edith, and the Rise of the Godwinsons

1. ASC, p.162
2. CJW, p.535
3. Fletcher, pp.113–4
4. Tshan, J., trans. *Adam of Bremen: Gesta Hammaburgensis Ecclesiae Pontificum History of the Archbishops of Hamburg, Vol. II* (New York; 1999) p.108
5. Tshan, J., trans. *Adam of Bremen*, pp.108, 136
6. Saxo Grammaticus, *Danorum Regum Heroumque Historia*, trans and ed by E. Christiensen (Oxford; 1980) p.210
7. GRA, p.349
8. GRA, p.353
9. Mason, p.43
10. GRA, pp.351–3
11. A. Hern, *The Mythical Battle: Hastings 1066* (Marlborough, 2017) p.28
12. VER, pp.14–15
13. GRA, p.353
14. EE, lines 4900–14
15. VER, pp.13–14
16. Charter S1000
17. Charter S998
18. Barlow, *Edward the Confessor*, p.75
19. GRA, p.349
20. R. Fleming, Kings and Lords in Conquest England (Cambridge, 1991) p.102
21. Charters S1000 to S1006
22. Raraty, Earl Godwine of Wessex, p.14
23. GRA, p.351
24. Stafford, *Queen Emma and Queen Edith*, pp.249, 251
25. ASC, p.163
26. CJW, p.535
27. HA, p.407
28. Stafford, *Queen Emma and Queen Edith*, pp.248–50
29. Charters S998 to S1002, S1006, S1011, S1062
30. CJW, p.541

31. SMO, p.163
32. Grills, p.138
33. R. Higham, 'The Godwins, Towns and St Olaf Churches: Comital investment in the mid-11th Century', in *The Land of the English Kin*, eds A. J. Langlands and R. Lavelle (Leiden, 2020)
34. Oxford Dictionary of National Biography, F. Barlow, 'Lyfing' (www.oxforddnb.com)
35. *Eadmer's History of recent events in England (Historia Novorum in Anglia)*, trans. by G. Bosanquet (London, 1964) p.6–8; N. Brooks, *The Early History of the Church of Canterbury* (Leicester, 1984) p.301
36. ASC, p.164
37. VER, p.24; Barlow, *Edward the Confessor*, p.65
38. J. L. Nelson, 'Early Medieval rites of Queen-making and the shaping of early medieval Queenship', in *Queens and Queenship in Medieval Europe*, ed A. J. Duggan (Woodbridge, 1997)
39. VER, pp.22–3
40. VER, p.23
41. RR, p.144
42. HA, 373
43. GRA, p.353
44. GRA, pp.353–5
45. Pope Alexander III approved Edward the Confessor's canonisation in 1161
46. P. Rex, *The Last English King: The Life of Harold II* (Stroud, 2008) p.29
47. Walker, p.68
48. Prosopography of Anglo-Saxon England (www.pase.ac.uk)
49. Walker, p.222; Barlow, *The Godwins*, p.170
50. Charters S1002, S1003, S1019, S1044, S1055, S1057, S1058
51. Grills, p.78
52. Charter S1000
53. Prosopography of Anglo-Saxon England (www.pase.ac.uk)
54. Charters S1010c, S1020, S1022
55. Charter S1011
56. L. Palle, *A History of the Kingdom of Denmark*, with trans by D. Hohnen (Copenhagen, 1960) pp.57–9
57. Swein was known by his mother's name, hence Estrithsson not Ulfsson
58. Stafford, *Queen Emma and Queen Edith*, p.251
59. ASC, p.166
60. ASC, p.164; CJW, p.543
61. P. Rex, *King and Saint: The Life of Edward the Confessor* (Stroud, 2008) p.113
62. ASC, p.164
63. Barlow, *Edward the Confessor*, p.88
64. CJW, p.545
65. ASC, pp.165–7
66. G. Jones, A History of the Vikings (London, 1973) p.406
67. Rex, *King and Saint*, p.115
68. S. Baxter, 'Edward the Confessor and the Succession Question', in *Edward the Confessor: The Man and the Legend*, ed R. Mortimer (Woodbridge, 2009) p.83

7 Swegn, the Black Sheep

1. N. R. Ker, *Hemming's Cartulary*, pp.275–6
2. Mason, p.57

3. Ker, *Hemming's Cartulary*, pp.275–6
4. Barlow, *Edward the Confessor*, p.74
5. Charter S1000
6. ASC, p.164
7. ASC, p.164
8. Ker, *Hemming's Cartulary*, pp.275–6
9. Barlow, *The English Church 1000–1066*, p.58
10. CJW, p.549
11. CJW, p.549
12. Mason, p.54
13. ASC, p.164
14. CJW, p.549
15. ASC, p.166
16. Walker, p.27
17. G. Jones, *A History of the Vikings*, p.406
18. Charters S1008, S1009, S1010, S1012, S1015, S1019, S1057
19. CJW, p.549
20. ASC, p.169
21. ASC, p.168
22. CJW, p.551
23. ASC, p.168
24. ASC, pp.168–9
25. Walker, p.29
26. ASC, p.168
27. CJW, p.551
28. Grills, p.157
29. ASC, pp.168–9
30. ASC, p.168
31. ASC, pp.169–71; CJW, pp.549–51
32. ASC, p.171
33. ASC, p.171; HA, p.375
34. L. M. Larson, 'The King's Household in England before the Norman Conquest', in *Anglo-Norman Warfare: Studies in Late Anglo-Saxon and Anglo-Norman Military Organisation and Warfare*, ed M. Strickland (Woodbridge, 1992) p.3
35. R. Huscroft, *The Norman Conquest: A New Introduction* (Harlow, 2009) p.90
36. Mason, pp.57–8
37. HA, p.375
38. Charter S1021
39. Anglo-Saxon Writs nos. 78 & 79
40. H. R. Loyn, & A. L. Brown, eds., *The Governance of England. Vol 1: The Governance of Anglo-Saxon England, 500 – 1087*, repr. (London, 1991) p.121
41. Walker, p.31
42. ASC, p.170
43. VER, pp.30–1
44. N. Brooks, *The Early History of the Church of Canterbury*, p.303
45. CJW, p.557
46. GRA, pp.353–5
47. ASC, p.171
48. GPA, p.24
49. The pallium was a woollen vestment conferred by the Pope to archbishops as a symbol of their position
50. J. Hudson, ed and trans, *The History of the Church of Abingdon* (Oxford, 2002) pp.103–5

51. ASC, pp.171–2
52. C. R. Dodwell, *Anglo-Saxon Art: A New Perspective* (Manchester, 1982) pp.363–5
53. GPA, p.121
54. Barlow, *Edward the Confessor*, p.89
55. Pastscape, (www.pastscape.org.uk)
56. P. Hill, *The Road to Hastings*, p.104
57. Hill, *The Road to Hastings*, p.105

8 Crisis and exile

1. Mason, p.59
2. H. J. Tanner, *Family, Friends and Allies: Boulogne and Politics in Northern France and England c.879–1160* (Brill, 2004) p.113, 263
3. ASC, p.181; GRA, p.357
4. ASC, pp.172–3; GRA, p.357; CJW, p.559
5. ASC, p.172; GRA, p.357
6. CJW, p.559
7. ASC, p.172
8. Mason, p.60
9. ASC, p.172
10. ASC, p.172
11. CJW, p.559
12. ASC, p.175; GRA, p.357; CJW, p.559
13. Hill, *The Road to Hastings*, p.104; Mason, p.67
14. EHOV, pp.205–7
15. ASC, p.172
16. GRA, p.357
17. ASC, p.172
18. GRA, p.357
19. GRA, pp.357–9
20. Grills, p.205
21. CJW, p.559
22. GRA, p.359
23. ASC, pp.173, 175
24. The 'hundred' was the administrative sub-division of the shire (about 12,000–13,000 acres)
25. ASC, p.175
26. CJW, p.559
27. ASC, p.173
28. CJW, p.561
29. Hill, *The Road to Hastings*, p.105
30. CJW, p.561
31. GRA, p.359
32. ASC, p.174
33. Stenton, *Anglo-Saxon England*, p.564
34. ASC, p.174
35. ASC, p.174
36. Walker, p.34
37. Grills, p.178; Licence, p.139
38. ASC, p.175
39. GRA, p.359

40. VER, p.36
41. CJW, p.561
42. GPA, p.24
43. ASC, pp.174–5; GRA, pp.359–61
44. GRA, p.361
45. VER, p.17
46. Wherwell Abbey was an important house during this period but the building that Edith knew was to be burnt down in the twelfth century. During the 1980s and 1990s, archaeologists and geophysicists identified the foundations of the original church in the grounds of present-day Wherwell Priory house. K. Clark & E. Roberts, 'Wherwell Abbey: New Evidence', in *Proceedings of Hampshire Field Club Archaeological Society, No.55* (2000) pp.21–5
47. Stafford, *Unification and Conquest*, p.92
48. T. Licence, *Edward the Confessor*, p.142
49. GRA, p.353
50. Pastscape, (www.pastscape.org.uk)
51. Barlow, *Edward the Confessor*, p.96–7
52. J. L. Grassi, 'The Vita Ædwardi Regis: The Hagiographer as Insider' in *Anglo-Norman Studies XXVI: Proceedings of the Battle Conference 2003* (Woodbridge, 2004) p.93
53. The ASC and John of Worcester name it as 'Thorney' (a small isle to the west of Bosham).
54. CJW, p.563
55. VER, pp.36–7
56. VER, p.38
57. ASC, p.176
58. VER, pp.38–41; Licence, p.151
59. VER, pp.38–41
60. ASC, pp.176–7; HA, p.377
61. Grills, p.186
62. ASC, p.176
63. SMO, p.168; CJW, p.563; GG, p.121; RR, p.151
64. Baxter, 'Edward the Confessor and the Succession Question', p.92
65. D. C. Douglas, 'Edward the Confessor, Duke of Normandy, and the English succession', in *English Historical Review, No.68* (1953) p.545
66. Licence, p.144
67. GG, p.121
68. RR, p.153
69. S. D. Keynes, 'The Æthelings in Normandy', in *Anglo-Norman Studies XIII: Proceedings of the Battle Conference 1990* (Woodbridge, 1991) pp.196–8, 204–5
70. Grills, p.166
71. F. McLynn, *1066: The Year of the Three Battles* (London, 1999) p.158
72. GG, p.121
73. GRA, p.363; GG, p.21
74. RR, p.151

9 Return of the Godwinsons

1. VER, pp.40–1
2. VER, pp.40–1
3. ASC, p.172, 176
4. ASC, p.179; GRA, p.361

5. Grills, p.191
6. ASC, p.177
7. GRA, p.361
8. CJW, p.569
9. ASC, p.177
10. ASC, p.178
11. ASC, p.178
12. Prosopography of Anglo-Saxon England (www.pase.ac.uk)
13. ASC, p.179; CJW, p.567
14. The ASC, p.179. The ASC D scribe names Land's End as 'Penwith Tail
15. ASC, pp.178–9
16. Grills, p.180
17. ASC, p.178
18. HA, p.377
19. Barlow, *Edward the Confessor*, p.172
20. CJW, p.569
21. ASC, p.179
22. HA, p.377
23. ASC, pp.179–80
24. R. Mortimer, *Edward the Confessor: The Man and the Legend* (Woodbridge, 2009) p.11
25. ASC, p.181; CJW, p.569
26. Walker, p.53
27. CJW, p.569
28. CJW, p.569
29. ASC, p.181; CJW, p.571
30. ASC, p.181
31. ASC, p.181; CJW, p.571
32. CJW, p.571
33. ASC, pp.180–1
34. ASC, p.181
35. *Eadmer's History of recent events in England (Historia Novorum in Anglia)*, trans. by G. Bosanquet (London: Cresset Press, 1964) pp.5–6
36. Grills, p.181
37. ASC, p.181
38. GRA, p.361
39. ASC, pp.181–2
40. CJW, p.571
41. ASC, p.181
42. CJW, p.573
43. T. Licence, *Edward the Confessor*, p.156
44. Walker, p.104
45. GPA, p.24

10 The Death of Godwin and the Emergence of Tostig

1. Barlow, *Edward the Confessor*, p.191
2. Charters S1023, S1025
3. GRA, p.361
4. ASC, pp.182, 185
5. English Heritage, (www.english-heritage.org.uk)
6. ASC, p.182

7. GRA, pp.363–5; CJW, p.571
8. Grassi, pp.93–4
9. ASC, pp.182–3; Barlow, *Edward the Confessor*, p.126
10. ASC, p.182
11. ASC, p.183
12. HA, p.379
13. RR, p.152; Richard of Devizes, *Annals of Winchester* (Cambridge; Corpus Christi College, MS339)
14. Pastscape, (www.pastscape.org.uk)
15. DB, p.90; 'British History Online', (www.british-history.ac.uk)
16. P. H. Hase, 'The Church in the Wessex Heartlands', in *The Medieval Landscape of Wessex*, eds. M. Aston and C. Lewis (Oxford, 1994)
17. ASC, p.182
18. CJW, p.573
19. GRA, p.355
20. LEC, pp.271–3
21. LEC, pp.271–3
22. ASC, p.182; CJW, p.573
23. Williams, 'Land and Power in the Eleventh Century: The Estates of Harold Godwineson', in *Anglo-Norman Studies III: Proceedings of the Battle Conference 1980*, (Woodbridge, 1081), pp. 183
24. Grills, *Godwine: Earl of Wessex*, pp.220–3
25. Grills, pp.224–5; DB
26. CJW, p.573
27. T. Talvio, 'The design of Edward the Confessor's coins', in *Studies in Late Anglo-Saxon Coinage in memory of Bror Emil Hildebrand*, ed K. Jonsson (Stockholm, 1990) pp.492, 495
28. Barlow, *Edward the Confessor*, p.189
29. VER, pp.22, 64
30. F. Lot, ed. *Chronique de l'abbaye de Saint Riquier* (Paris, 1894) pp.237–8
31. Barlow, *Edward the Confessor*, p.200
32. ASC, pp.184–5
33. R. L. Graeme Ritchie, *The Normans in Scotland* (Edinburgh, 1954) p.3
34. *The Annals of Ulster (to A.D.1131)*, eds. S. Mac Airt and G. Mac Niocaill (Dublin, 1983)
35. ASC, p.185; GRA, p.349; CJW, p.573
36. HA, pp.379–81
37. ASC, p.184
38. HA, p.381
39. GRA, p.365
40. Barlow, *Edward the Confessor*, p.196
41. C. Hurt, 'William Malet and His Family', in *Anglo-Norman Studies XIX: Proceedings of the Battle Conference 1996* (Woodbridge, 1997); H. Licence, *Edward the Confessor*, p.184
42. ASC, pp.185–6
43. ASC, p.185; CJW, p.577
44. H. Licence, p.183
45. ASC, pp.184–7; CJW, p.577
46. ASC, pp.185–6
47. VER, p.50
48. Stenton, *Anglo-Saxon England*, p.466
49. Walker, p.119

50. Mason, p.124
51. Symeon of Durham, *Libellus de Exordio atque Procursu istius, hoc est Dunhelmensis Ecclesie*, ed D. W. Rollason (Oxford, 2000) p.175
52. Symeon of Durham, *Libellus de Exordio*, p.177
53. Walker, p.104
54. Kirkdale Churches (www.kirkdalechurches.org.uk)
55. A. Williams, 'Thegnly piety and ecclesiastical patronage in the late old English kingdom', in *Anglo-Norman Studies XXIV: Proceedings of the Battle Conference 2001* (Woodbridge, 2002) pp.10–11
56. CJW, p.577
57. ASC, p.184
58. ASC, p.184; CJW, p.577
59. ASC, p.186
60. CJW, p.579
61. Pastscape, (www.pastscape.org.uk)
62. ASC, p.186 n.
63. V. King, 'Ealdred, Archbishop of York: The Worcester Years', in *Anglo-Norman Studies XVIII: Proceedings of the Battle Conference 1995* (Woodbridge, 1996) pp.128–9
64. ASC, p.186; Barlow, *Edward the Confessor*, pp.207–8
65. ASC, pp.186–7
66. ASC, pp.186–7

11 The Earldoms and the Search for the Exile

1. Baxter, 'Edward the Confessor and the Succession Question', p.82
2. G. Ronay, *The Lost King of England: The Eastern European adventures of Edward the Exile* (Woodbridge, 1989) pp.43–8
3. Tshan, J., trans. *Adam of Bremen: Gesta Hammaburgensis Ecclesiae Pontificum History of the Archbishops of Hamburg, Vol. II* (New York; 1999); Geffrei Gaimar, *Estoire des Engleis (History of the English)*, ed. and trans. by I. Short (Oxford; New York, 2009); H. Summerson, 'Tudor Antiquaries and the *Vita Edwardi*', p.157–84
4. Ronay, p.53
5. GRA, p.417
6. ASC, p.185; CJW, pp.575–7
7. Ronay, pp.110, 134
8. Ronay, p.135
9. P. Grierson, 'A visit of Earl Harold to Flanders in 1056', in *English Historical Review, Vol 51* (1936) pp.90–97
10. Mason, p.91
11. Baxter, 'Edward the Confessor and the Succession Question', p.80
12. ASC, p.187; Ronay, p.137
13. Mason, p.93
14. CJW, pp.503–5
15. ASC, pp.187–8; HA, p.381; CJW, p.583
16. ASC, p.188
17. GRA, p.417
18. Ronay, pp.137–8
19. Saxo Grammaticus: *The History of the Danes*, ed. H. E. Davidson, trans by P. Fisher (Woodbridge, 1979)
20. Ronay, pp.138–9
21. Hern, p.73

22. E. John, 'Edward the Confessor and the Norman Succession', in *English Historical Review, No.94* (1979) pp.242, 248

23. Mason, p.92

24. Ronay, p.141

25. *The Liber Vitae of the New Minster and Hyde Abbey,* Early English manuscripts, ed. S. D. Keynes (Copenhagen, 1996); D. N. Dumville, 'The Aetheling: A Study in Anglo-Saxon Constitutional History', in *Anglo-Saxon England,* 8 (1979), pp.7–10

26. ASC, p.187

27. ASC, p.188; CJW, p.583

28. Roger of Wendover, *Flowers of History, Comprising the History of England from the descent of the Saxons to AD1235,* trans by J. A. Giles, 2 vols (London, 1849) p.314

29. CJW, p.583

30. DB

31. ASC, p.188

32. Walker, pp.233–4, 238; Mortimer, Maps (p.116–7)

33. S. Baxter, 'The death of Burgheard, son of Ælfgar, and its context', in *Frankland: The Franks and the world of the early Middle Ages,* eds. P. Fouracre and D. Ganz (Manchester, 2008) pp.266–84

34. A 'Staller' was a military position, the title given to a royal constable

35. ASC, p.188

36. ASC, pp.188–9

37. CJW, p.585; *Annales Cambriae,* ed. J. Williams ab Ethel (London; Rolls Series XX, 1866)

38. EHOV, p.217

39. VER, pp.60–3

40. H. Licence, *Edward the Confessor,* p.209

41. Charter S1026

42. Prosopography of Anglo-Saxon England (www.pase.ac.uk)

43. Stenton, *Anglo-Saxon England,* p.657

44. Walker, p.62; DB

45. DB; P. A. Clarke, *The English Nobility under Edward the Confessor* (Oxford, 1994)

46. Walker, pp.62–3; DB

47. P. A. Clarke, *The English Nobility under Edward the Confessor* (Oxford, 1994)

48. R. H. Davies, 'The lands and rights of Harold, son of Godwine, and their distribution by William I', unpublished dissertation (Cardiff, 1967)

49. P. Rex, *The Last English King: The Life of Harold II* (Stroud, 2008) p.75

50. DB

51. Walker, p.77

52. *The Waltham Chronicle,* ed and trans by L. Watkiss and M. Chibnall, Oxford Medieval Texts (Oxford; New York, 1994) pp.31–3

53. R. Fleming, 'The New Wealth, the New Rich, and the New Political Style in Late Anglo-Saxon England', in *Anglo-Norman Studies XXIII: Proceedings of the Battle Conference 2000* (Woodbridge, 2001) p.14

54. Stenton, *Anglo-Saxon England,* pp.465–6

55. Barlow, *The English Church 1000–1066,* p.306

56. E. C. Fernie, 'The Romanesque Church of Waltham Abbey', in *Journal of the British Archaeological Association, Vol. 138* (1985)

57. ASC, p.189

58. *Vita Haroldi: The Romance of the Life of Harold, King of England: From the Unique Manuscript in the British Museum,* ed and trans. W. de Gray Birch (London, 1885)

59. *The Waltham Chronicle*

60. Charter for year 1055 is S1026

12 The Norman Connection

1. VER, pp.52–5
2. Mason, p.96
3. GPA, p.167
4. GPA, p.168
5. VER, pp.54–5
6. VER, pp.54–5
7. GPA, p.168
8. Charter S1037a
9. K. L. Maund, 'The Welsh Alliances of Earl Ælfgar and his family in the mid-eleventh-century', in *Anglo-Norman Studies XI: Proceedings of the Battle Conference 1988* (Woodbridge, 1989) p.188
10. Barlow, *Edward the Confessor*, p.210
11. Baxter, 'The death of Burgheard, son of Ælfgar, and its context', pp.266–84; Mason, p.96
12. ASC, p.191; CJW, p.593
13. Gatehouse Gazetteer (www.gatehouse-gazetteer.info)
14. ASC, p.191; CJW, p.593
15. CJW, p.593
16. VER, p.87
17. ASC, p.191
18. CJW, p.593
19. L. Thorpe, ed and trans. *Gerald of Wales: Journey through Wales* (Harmondsworth, 1978) p.266
20. ASC, p.191
21. *Annals of Ulster*, p.501
22. Hill, *The Road to Hastings*, p.132
23. *Vita Haroldi*, pp.17–21, 117–121
24. Baxter, 'Edward the Confessor and the Succession Question', p.105
25. G. Garnett, 'Conquered England 1066–1215', in *Oxford Illustrated History of Medieval England*, ed N. Saul (Oxford, 1997) p.67
26. A. Bridgeford, *1066: The Hidden History of the Bayeux Tapestry* (London, 2004) p.89
27. GRA, p.417
28. BT, Scenes 4–6
29. EHOV, p.135; GND, p.161; GG, p.69
30. DB, p.40
31. Baxter, 'Edward the Confessor and the Succession Question', p.106
32. RR, p.153
33. RR, p.153
34. GRA, p.417
35. GRA, p.417
36. RR, p.154
37. RR, p.154
38. GG, p.71
39. GRA, p.419
40. RR, p.154
41. GG, p.71
42. BT, scene 20
43. GRA, p.419
44. GRA, p.419

45. GND, p.161
46. BT, scenes 20 & 26; GG, p.71
47. HA, p.381; SMO, p.184
48. EHOV, p.134; GG, p.71
49. GG, p.71
50. RR, pp.154–5
51. Symeon of Durham, *A history of the kings of England*, trans by J. Stevenson (London, 1855) p.135
52. BT, scene 18
53. Higham, *The Death of Anglo-Saxon England*, p.157
54. C. Jones, *The Forgotten Battle of 1066: Fulford* (Stroud, 2007) p.100
55. GG, p.77
56. BT, scene 17;
57. Bridgeford, p.79
58. BT, scene 28
59. EHOV, p.137
60. Barlow, *Edward the Confessor*, p.225
61. GG, p.151
62. Stafford, *Unification and Conquest*, p.92

13 Harold and Tostig: A Family Divided

1. Mason, p.104
2. *Wergild* was the compensation payment owing to a victim or their family by the perpetrators of a crime
3. SMO, p.174
4. VER, p.66
5. A. A. M. Duncan, *The Kingship of the Scots 842–1292: Succession and Independence* (Edinburgh, 2002) p.43
6. R. Oram, *David I: The King who made Scotland* (Stroud, 2004) p.21
7. A 'hide' was approx 120 acres, a 'carucate' was the equivalent in the former Danelaw regions, but both could vary in size dependent on production values
8. Walker, p.123
9. E. W. Kapelle, *The Norman Conquest of the North: The Region and its Transformation 1000–1135* (Carolina, 1979) p.95
10. CJW, p.599
11. Prosopography of Anglo-Saxon England (www.pase.ac.uk)
12. Prosopography of Anglo-Saxon England (www.pase.ac.uk)
13. CJW, p.599
14. VER, pp.38–51
15. VER, pp.50–1; Mason, p.104
16. VER, pp.50–1; Barlow, *Edward the Confessor*, p.195
17. VER, pp.50–1
18. N. J. Higham, *The Death of Anglo-Saxon England* (Stroud, 1997) p.166
19. LEC, p.267
20. Aelred of Rievaulx, *The life of Saint Edward: King and Confessor*, trans by J. Bertram, (Guildford, 1990) pp.87–8
21. HA, p.383
22. HA, p.383
23. ASC, p.190
24. ASC, p.191; CJW, p.597
25. CJW, p.597

26. Walker, p.108
27. GRA, p.365
28. ASC, p.190
29. ASC, pp.190–1, CJW, p.599
30. Walker, p.118
31. Hill, *The Road to Hastings*, p.138
32. GRA, p.467
33. ASC, pp.191–3
34. GRA, p.365
35. ASC, p.192
36. VER, pp.80–1
37. ASC, pp.192–3; HA, p.385
38. CJW, p.599
39. ASC, p.192
40. VER, pp.78–82
41. Hern, p.76
42. ASC, pp.192–3; EHOV, p.139
43. ASC, pp.192–3; EHD, vol 1, pp.454–67
44. P. Grierson, 'The Relations between England and Flanders before the Norman Conquest', in *Transactions of the Royal Historical Society, Vol. 23* (1941) pp.109–110

14 Harold Godwinson, King of England

1. Barlow, *Edward the Confessor*, p.247
2. ASC, p.193; E. C. Fernie, 'Edward the Confessor's Westminster Abbey', in *Edward the Confessor: The Man and the Legend*, ed. R. Mortimer (Woodbridge, 2009) pp.150
3. W. Rodwell, 'New glimpses of Edward the Confessor's Abbey at Westminster', in *Edward the Confessor: The Man and the Legend*, ed. R. Mortimer (Woodbridge, 2009) pp. 150, 166
4. GRA, p.419
5. BT, scenes 29–32
6. G. Hindley, *A Brief History of the Anglo-Saxons* (London, 2006) p.325
7. Charters S1041, S1043
8. ASC, p.193; CJW, pp.599–601
9. ASC, pp.192–5
10. Westminster Abbey, (www.westminster-abbey.org/abbey-commemorations)
11. Westminster Abbey, (www.westminster-abbey.org/abbey-commemorations)
12. Baxter, 'Edward the Confessor and the Succession Question', p.100
13. Baxter, 'Edward the Confessor and the Succession Question', pp.101–2
14. G. Garnett, 'Conquered England 1066–1215', in *Oxford Illustrated History of Medieval England*, ed N. Saul (Oxford, 1997) p.67
15. ASC, p.197
16. VER, p.122
17. RR, p.155
18. RR, p.156
19. LEC, p.281
20. BT, scenes 30–31
21. VER, p.124
22. Barlow, *Edward the Confessor*, pp.249–51; Hill, *The Road to Hastings*, pp.142–4
23. B. R. Patterson, *Harold and William: The Battle for England 1064–1066* (Stroud, 2004) p.57

24. Baxter, 'Edward the Confessor and the Succession Question', pp.115
25. VER, pp.122–3
26. ASC, pp.192–5
27. Barlow, *Edward the Confessor*, pp.132
28. Douglas, *William the Conqueror*, pp.182
29. GRA, pp.419–421
30. CJW, p.601
31. HA, p.385
32. GRA, p.447
33. Fleming, *Kings and Lords in Conquest England*, p.79
34. Baxter, 'Edward the Confessor and the Succession Question', pp.114
35. GND, p.161; RR, p.157
36. GG, p.101
37. EHOV, p.135
38. HA, p.387
39. HA, pp.385–7
40. ASC, pp.194–5
41. William of Malmesbury, *Vita Wulfstani: Lives of Saints Wulfstan, Dunstan, Patrick, Benignus and Indract*, eds. R. M. Thomson and M. Winterbottom, Oxford Medieval Texts (Oxford, 2002)
42. GND, pp.161–3
43. Comet was named after Edmond Halley, Astronomer Royal between 1718–42, for accurately calculating the comet's repeat orbit around the sun as being every 76 years
44. ASC, p.194; CJW, p.601
45. BT, scene 33.
46. Barlow, *Edward the Confessor*, pp.169
47. Writ S1163
48. Rex, *The Last English King: The Life of Harold II*, p.215
49. Prosopography of Anglo-Saxon England (www.pase.ac.uk)
50. Prosopography of Anglo-Saxon England (www.pase.ac.uk)
51. EHOV, p.139
52. CJW, p.601
53. GRA, p.421; SMO, p.179
54. DeVries, p.163
55. C. C. J. Webb, ed. *John of Salisbury, Johannis Saresbiriensis episcopi Carnotensis Policraticus* (London; Methuen, 1909) p.19–20
56. Barlow, *Edward the Confessor*, pp.183
57. M. Dolley, *Anglo-Saxon Pennies* (Trustees of the British Museum, 1964) pp.29–30
58. Mason, p.51
59. Walker, pp.142–3
60. D. Knowles, et al, eds. *The Heads of Religious Houses: England & Wales, I, 940–1216,* 2nd edn (Cambridge, 2009) pp.24, 45

15 Tostig and the Road to Stamford Bridge

1. DeVries, p.230
2. HSS, pp.643–4
3. Jones, *The Forgotten Battle of 1066*, pp.67–8
4. EHOV, p.141
5. GND, p.163
6. EHOV, p.141; GND, p.163
7. EHOV, p.139

8. DeVries, p.234
9. ASC, pp.194–5
10. ASC, p.197; GRA, p.421; HA, p.387
11. EHOV, pp.139–43; CJW, p.601
12. ASC, p.194
13. ASC, p.194
14. EE, lines 5158–66
15. ASC, p.194
16. CJW, p.601
17. Stenton, *Anglo-Saxon England*, p.587
18. ASC, p.196; CJW, p.601
19. ASC, p.197
20. CJW, pp.601–3
21. HSS, pp.644–5
22. EHOV, p.143
23. EHOV, pp.143–5
24. Howard, *Harthacnut: The last Danish King of England*, pp.58–61; K. Larson, *History of Norway* (Princeton, 1948) p.113
25. Larsen, p.114
26. EHOV, p.169
27. ASC, pp.196–7; GRA, p.421; HA, p.387
28. EE, lines 5191–96
29. DeVries, pp.264–5
30. GG, p.107
31. Barlow, *Edward the Confessor*, pp.171
32. ASC, p.194
33. CJW, p.603

16 The Norse Invasion

1. Jones, *The Forgotten Battle of 1066*, pp.171
2. CJW, p.603
3. Jones, *The Forgotten Battle of 1066*, pp.169
4. ASC, p.196; CJW, p.603
5. Jones, C., *Finding Fulford: The search for the first battle of 1066* (London, 2011) pp.202–3
6. DeVries, pp.264–5
7. ASC, pp.196–7
8. CJW, p.603; HSS, pp.649–50
9. Jones, *The Forgotten Battle of 1066*, pp.173–96
10. HSS, p.649
11. DeVries, p.255
12. Jones, *The Forgotten Battle of 1066*, pp.190–1
13. ASC, p.196; CJW, p.603
14. Jones, *The Forgotten Battle of 1066*, pp.195–6
15. HSS, pp.649–50
16. P. Warren, *Battleground Britain: 1066 The Battles of York, Stamford Bridge and Hastings* (Barnsley, 2004) p.72
17. Jones, *The Forgotten Battle of 1066*, p.199
18. ASC, p.197
19. CJW, p.603
20. Patterson, p.124

21. Walker, p.182
22. HSS, p.651
23. EHOV, p.169
24. Brown, R. Allen., 'The Battle of Hastings', in *Anglo-Norman Studies III: Proceedings of the Battle Conference* 1980 (Woodbridge, 1981) p.6–7
25. Walker, p.181
26. ASC, p.196
27. Hern, p.84
28. ASC, pp.197–8
29. HSS, p.651
30. HA, p.387
31. HSS, p.651
32. Warren, p.161
33. ASC, p.198; HA, pp.387–9
34. GRA, p.421
35. ASC, p.198
36. HSS, pp.653–4
37. Walker, p.184; Warren, p.161–2
38. HSS, p.655
39. HSS, p.655
40. HSS, p.656
41. ASC, pp.198–9
42. McLynn, p.204
43. ASC, p.199
44. Jones, *The Forgotten Battle of 1066*, p.205
45. ASC, p.199; CJW, p.605
46. GRA, p.469
47. BT, scenes 71–3
48. GRA, p.469

17 The Norman Invasion

1. BT, scene 31; A. Bridgeford, *1066: The Hidden History of the Bayeux Tapestry* (London, 2004), p.116
2. ASC, p.194
3. The Julian Calendar was not superseded by the Gregorian Calendar in Great Britain until AD1752
4. E. M. C. van Houts, 'The ship list of William the Conqueror', in *Anglo-Norman Studies X: Proceedings of the Battle Conference 1987* (Woodbridge, 1988) pp.169–71
5. E. M. C. van Houts, *The Normans in Europe* (Manchester, Manchester, 2000) p.105
6. GG, p.103
7. GG, p.105
8. GG, p.105
9. GND, p.165
10. RR, p.163
11. C. Oman, *A History of the Art of War in the Middle Ages*, 2nd edn. (London, 1924)
12. BT, scenes 40–3
13. R. Glover, 'English Warfare in 1066' (p.173–188), in *The Battle of Hastings, Sources and Interpretations*, ed S. Morello (Woodbridge, 1996) pp.181–2
14. C.M. Gillmor, 'Naval logistics of the Cross-Channel Operation 1066', in *The Battle of Hastings: Sources and Interpretations*, ed. S. Morillo (Woodbridge, 1996) pp.122–3

15. B. S. Bachrach, 'Some observations on the military administration of the Norman Conquest', in Anglo-Norman Studies VIII: Proceedings of the Battle Conference 1985 (Woodbridge, 1986) pp.11–15
16. Gillmor, pp.124–5
17. Steyning Museum (www.steyningmuseum.org.uk/fecamp)
18. K. Foord, and N. Clephane-Cameron, *1066 and the Battle of Hastings: Preludes, Events and Postscripts*, 2nd repr (Battle and District Historical Society, 2018), p.46
19. Mason, p.146
20. GPA, pp.45, 211
21. J. Starkey, and M. Starkey, *The Battle of Hastings at Sedlescombe* (Sussex, 2018) pp.22–3
22. GG, p.103; EHOV, p.169
23. GRA, p.449; GG, p.109
24. F. Neveux, *A Brief History of the Normans: The Conquests that changed the face of Europe*, with trans by H. Curtis (London, 2006) p.134
25. Mason, p.147; Walker, p.171
26. GG, p.109
27. ASC, p.196
28. GG, p.111
29. ASC, p.199, EHOV, p.171; *The Carmen de Hastingae Proelio of Guy Bishop of Amiens,* ed and trans by F. Barlow (Oxford; New York, 1999) p.7
30. ASC, p.199; GND, p.167; GG, pp.113–5
31. ASC, p.199; EHOV, p.171
32. BT, scene 50; RR, p.164
33. Topographic-Map' (www.en-gb.topographic-map.com/maps/du6e/East-Sussex)
34. A. Pearson, *The Roman Shore Forts: Coastal Defences of Southern Britain* (Stroud, 2002)
35. Topographic-Map' (www.en-gb.topographic-map.com/maps/du6e/East-Sussex)
36. RR, pp.163–5
37. Foord & Clephane-Cameron, p.32; N. Austin, N., *Secrets of the Norman Invasion* (Crowhurst, 2012) p.175
38. Austin, p.110
39. BT, scene 48
40. GND, p.167; GG, p.115
41. Austin, p.9
42. Austin, pp.101–2
43. DB; Austin, pp, 9, 46–9
44. Hill, *The Road to Hastings*, p.168
45. BT, scenes 47 & 50
46. Foord & Clephane-Cameron, p.48
47. Starkey & Starkey, pp.40–42; Tyson, K., trans & transcript. *Carmen Widonis: The First History of the Norman Conquest* (2018)
48. Tyson, *Carmen Widonis: The First History of the Norman Conquest*
49. Starkey & Starkey, pp.39–40
50. Starkey & Starkey, p.50
51. Tyson, *Carmen Widonis: The First History of the Norman Conquest*
52. BT, scene 51
53. GRA, p.451
54. Walker, p.189
55. P. Poyntz-Wright, *Hastings* (Gloucester, 1996) p.43
56. *Waltham Chronicle*, pp.146–7
57. CJW, p.605

58. RR, p.168
59. GRA, p.451
60. GRA, p.453; RR, p.169
61. McLynn, p.213
62. P. Brandon, *The Kent & Sussex Weald* (2003)
63. I. Margary, *Roman roads in Britain*, 3rd edn (London, 1973)
64. W. A. Raper, 'On the silver pennies of Edward the Confessor found at Sedlescombe', in *Sussex Archaeological Collections, Vol.33* (1883) p.1–19
65. ASC, p.199
66. EHOV, p.173
67. Tyson, *Carmen Widonis: The First History of the Norman Conquest*
68. *The Chronicle of Battle Abbey*, ed and trans by E. Searle (Oxford; New York, 1980) pp.62–5
69. ASC, p.198
70. *The Carmen de Hastingae Proelio*, pp.19–21; RR, pp.167–71
71. GG, pp.121

18 Hastings: The Battle and Its Location

1. C. W. Hollister, *Anglo-Norman Military Institutions* (Oxford, 1962) p.140
2. BT, scene 62
3. C. M. Hewitt, 'Was the Battle of Hastings Really Fought on Battle Hill? A GIS Assessment', in *Historical Geography, Vol. 44* (2016) p.145
4. N. Austin, N., *Secrets of the Norman Invasion*; J. Grehan, and M. Mace., *The Battle of Hastings 1066 – The Uncomfortable Truth: Revealing the true location of England's most famous battle* (Barnsley, 2012); Hewitt, 'Was the Battle of Hastings Really Fought on Battle Hill? A GIS Assessment'.
5. Starkey & Starkey, *The Battle of Hastings at Sedlescombe*; Tyson, K, *Carmen Widonis: The First History of the Norman Conquest*
6. GRA, pp.453–5
7. ASC, p.199
8. *The Carmen de Hastingae Proelio of Guy Bishop of Amiens*, p.23
9. R. Glover, 'English Warfare in 1066' (p.173–188), in *The Battle of Hastings, Sources and Interpretations*, ed S. Morello (Woodbridge, 1996) pp.181–2
10. *Carmen*, p.25
11. GG, p.127
12. GG, p.129
13. *Carmen*, p.23; EHOV, pp.173–5; GND, p.169
14. RR, p.182
15. CJW, p.605
16. *The Chronicle of Battle Abbey*, ed and trans by E. Searle, Oxford Medieval Texts (Oxford; New York, 1980)
17. Poyntz-Wright, p.80
18. GG, p.129
19. *Carmen*, p.27
20. GG, p.133
21. Poyntz-Wright, p.93
22. BT, scene 64
23. GG, pp.129, 135
24. GG, p.131
25. BT, scene 68

26. Walker, p.202
27. BT, scenes 61–5
28. BT, scene 72; GRA, p.455; HA, pp.393–5; RR, p.190
29. Bridgeford, pp.144–52; Foys, M. K., *The Bayeux Tapestry: New Interpretations* (Woodbridge, 2009)
30. RR, p.190
31. *Carmen*, p.33; GRA, pp.455–7; HA, p.395; RR, p.190
32. CJW, p.605
33. D. J. Bernstein, *The Mystery of the Bayeux Tapestry* (London, 1986)
34. *Carmen*, p.33
35. GRA, pp.455–7
36. D. J. Bernstein, 'The blinding of Harold and the meaning of the Bayeux Tapestry', in *Anglo-Norman Studies V: Proceedings of the Battle Conference 1982* (Woodbridge, 1983) p.64
37. GG, p.139; EHOV, p.177
38. Stenton, *Anglo-Saxon England*, p.595
39. P. Warren, Battleground Britain, p.149
40. Grehan & Mace, p.125
41. Hewitt, p.127
42. Hewitt, p.143
43. Grehan & Mace, p.153
44. Austin, pp.250–4, 269–74
45. Austin, pp.269–74
46. Tyson, K, *Carmen Widonis: The First History of the Norman Conquest*
47. Starkey & Starkey, pp.97–100
48. RR, p.179
49. Starkey & Starkey, pp.105–8
50. Starkey & Starkey, p.108
51. Tyson, K, *Carmen Widonis: The First History of the Norman Conquest*
52. BT, scene 66; M. K. Lawson, *The Battle of Hastings: 1066* (Stroud, 2016) p.204
53. Archeurope Educational Resources, (http://anglosaxon.archeurope.info/index)
54. Archeurope Educational Resources, (http://anglosaxon.archeurope.info/index)
55. Archeurope Educational Resources, (http://anglosaxon.archeurope.info/index)

19 End of a Dynasty

1. ASC, p.199; CJW, p.605; GG, p.137
2. BT, scenes 71–3
3. J. Bradbury, *The Battle of Hastings* (Stroud, 1998) p.213
4. GG, p.141
5. *Waltham Chronicle*, pp.50–7
6. Barlow, *The Godwins*, p.158; D. Dean, *Evidence of the Burial of King Harold II Godwinsson at Waltham Abbey*
7. EHOV, pp.179–81
8. GRA, p.461
9. GG, p.141
10. EHOV, p.179
11. *Vita Haroldi: The Romance of the Life of Harold, King of England: From the Unique Manuscript in the British Museum,* ed and trans. W. de Gray Birch (London, 1885)
12. A. T. Thacker, 'The Cult of King Harold at Chester', in The Middle Ages in the North-West, eds. T. Scott and P. Starkey (Oxford, 1995) pp.155–76

13. Pollock, J., *Harold Rex: Is King Harold buried in Bosham Church* (Bosham, 4th ed 1996 suppl. 2002)
14. Pollock, *Harold Rex*
15. *The Carmen de Hastingae Proelio of Guy Bishop of Amiens*, p.33
16. ASC, pp.199–200
17. GG, pp.143–5
18. CJW, p.607
19. J. Beeler, *Warfare in England 1066–1189* (New York, 1966) pp.26–9; Bradbury, p.220
20. *The Carmen de Hastingae Proelio of Guy Bishop of Amiens*, pp.36–9
21. DB; P. Stafford, *Queen Emma and Queen Edith: Queenship and Women's Power in Eleventh Century England*
22. A. Williams, *The English and the Norman Conquest* (Woodbridge, 1997) p.10
23. Mason, p.180
24. Stenton, *Anglo-Saxon England*, p.597
25. 25. Beeler, pp.26–9
26. ASC, p.200; CJW, p.607
27. ASC, p.200
28. EHOV, pp.194–5
29. Walker, pp.210–11
30. ASC, p.200; CJW, p.607
31. GG, p.151
32. *The Chronicle of Battle Abbey*, ed and trans by E. Searle, Oxford Medieval Texts (Oxford; New York, 1980)
33. P. Rex, *1066: A new history of the Norman Conquest* (Stroud, 2009) p.117
34. DB; Prosopography of Anglo-Saxon England (www.pase.ac.uk)
35. DB; Prosopography of Anglo-Saxon England (www.pase.ac.uk)
36. DB; Prosopography of Anglo-Saxon England (www.pase.ac.uk)
37. DB; Prosopography of Anglo-Saxon England (www.pase.ac.uk)

20 The Last of the Godwinsons

1. Barlow, *The Godwins*, p.168
2. CJW, p.605
3. G. Beech, 'England and Aquitaine in the Century before the Norman Conquest', in *Anglo-Saxon England, No.19* (1990) pp.94–5
4. GRA, p.571
5. GRA, p.481
6. ASC, p.201
7. EHOV, pp.210–15
8. GRA, p.463
9. ASC, p.202; EHOV, p.225
10. Saxo Grammaticus, *Danorum Regum Heroumque Historia*, trans and ed by E. Christiensen (Oxford; 1980) p.58
11. Mason, p.183
12. Barlow, *The Godwins*, p.167
13. DB
14. Grills, pp.210–11
15. E. M. C. van Houts, The Norman Conquest through European eyes', in *English Historical Review, No.110* (1995) pp.838–9; 'Judith of Flanders', Oxford Dictionary of National Biography, (www.oxforddnb.com)
16. HSS, p.660; Mason, p.197
17. ASC, p.203

18. ASC, p.203; John of Worcester, *The Chronicle of John of Worcester, Vol 3*, ed and trans by P. McGurk (New York, 1998) p.7
19. Barlow, *The Godwins*, p.169
20. SMO, p.186
21. ASC, p.203
22. GND, pp.181–3; John of Worcester, *The Chronicle of John of Worcester, Vol 3*, p.9
23. GND, pp.181–3
24. EHOV, p.225
25. Mason, p.196
26. Mason, p.186
27. VER, pp.84–91
28. GRA, p.353
29. ASC, p.212
30. GRA, p.503
31. Westminster Abbey, (www.westminster-abbey.org/abbey-commemorations)
32. Saxo Grammaticus: *The History of the Danes*, ed. H. E. Davidson, trans by P. Fisher (Woodbridge, 1979)
33. Mason, pp.200–1
34. Grills, p.215
35. William of Malmesbury, *Vita Wulfstani: Lives of Saints Wulfstan, Dunstan, Patrick, Benignus and Indract*, eds. R. M. Thomson and M. Winterbottom (Oxford, 2002) p.83
36. R. Fleming, *Kings and Lords in Conquest England*, p.125
37. C. W. Hollister and A. C. Frost., *Henry I* (New Haven, 2003) p.130
38. EE, line 5408
39. John of Worcester, *The Chronicle of John of Worcester, Vol 3*, p.47
40. GRA, p.363
41. Barlow, *The Godwins*, p.164
42. EHOV, p.179; T. Wright, ed. *The Anglo-Norman Satirical Poets and Epigrammatists of the Twelfth Century, vol II* (London, 1872) p.148

21 The Verdict of History

1. VER, pp.46–7; Grills, p.200
2. GRA, p.503
3. J. C. Crick, and E. M. C. van Houts, eds., *A Social History of England, 900–1200* (Cambridge; New York, 2011) p.228
4. Grills, p.204
5. Hill, *The Road to Hastings: The Politics of Power in Anglo-Saxon England*, p.203
6. Barlow, *Edward the Confessor*, p.89
7. Barlow, *The Godwins*, p.37
8. Grills, p.14
9. GG, p.5
10. GG, pp.115, 157
11. RR, p.151
12. *Eadmer's History of recent events in England (Historia Novorum in Anglia)*, trans. by G. Bosanquet (London, 1964) p.6–7
13. HA, p.373
14. *Vita Haroldi*, pp.113–4
15. Walter Map, *De Nugis Curialium*, (Oxford, 1914), pp.416–7; Roger of Wendover, *Flowers of History, Comprising the History of England from the descent of the Saxons to AD1235*, trans by J. A. Giles, 2 vols (London, 1849) p.312

16. GRA, pp.353–5
17. Barlow, *Edward the Confessor*, p.89; Barlow, *The Godwins*, p.38
18. Grills, p.200
19. Stafford, *Queen Emma and Queen Edith*, p.148
20. EHOV, p.171
21. VER, pp.48–9
22. Walker, p.225
23. Walker, pp.226–7
24. Mason, p.201
25. Hern, pp.11, 197

Bibliography

Primary Sources

Aelred of Rievaulx, *The life of Saint Edward: King and Confessor*, trans by J. Bertram, (Guildford, 1990)

Annales Cambriae, ed. J. Williams ab Ethel (London; Rolls Series XX, 1866)

Barlow, F., ed and trans. *Vita Ædwardi – The Life of King Edward who rests at Westminster* (Oxford; New York: Oxford University Press, 2nd edn. 1992)

Bede's Ecclesiastical History of the English People, eds, J. McClure and R. Collins (Oxford: New York; Oxford University Press, rev edn. 2008)

Campbell, A., ed, *Encomium Emmae Reginae,* Royal Historical Society (Cambridge: Cambridge University Press, 1998)

Domesday Book: A Complete Translation (London: New York; Penguin, 2003)

Douglas, D. C., and G. W. Greenaway, eds. *English Historical Documents, 1042–1189*, 2nd edn (London: Eyre Methuen, 1981)

Eadmer's History of recent events in England (Historia Novorum in Anglia), trans. by G. Bosanquet (London: Cresset Press, 1964)

Geffrei Gaimar, *Estoire des Engleis (History of the English)*, ed. and trans. by I. Short (Oxford; New York: Oxford University Press, 2009)

Henry of Huntingdon, *Historia Anglorum: The History of the English People*, ed., and trans. by D. E. Greenway, Oxford Medieval Texts (Oxford: Clarendon Press, 1996)

John of Worcester, *The Chronicle of John of Worcester*, Vol. 2, ed. by R. R. Darlington and P. McGurk, trans. by J. Bray and P. McGurk, Oxford Medieval Texts (Oxford; New York: Clarendon Press, 1995)

John of Worcester, *The Chronicle of John of Worcester, Vol 3*, ed and trans by P. McGurk, Oxford Medieval Texts (New York; Oxford University Press, 1998)

Ker, N. R. (1979). 'Hemming's Cartulary: A Description of Two Worcester Cartularies in Cotton Tiberius A. xiii', in R. W. Hunt; W. A. Pantin; R. W. Southern (eds.), *Studies in Medieval History Presented to Frederick Maurice Powicke (Reprint of 1948 Oxford University Press ed.). Westport, CT: Greenwood Press. pp. 49–75*

Knytlinga Saga, The History of the Kings of Denmark, attr. to Olaf Thordarson, trans. by H. Palsson and P. Edwards (Odens: 1986)

The House of Godwin

Liber Eliensis: A History of the Isle of Ely from the Seventh Century to the Twelfth, trans J. Fairweather (Woodbridge; Boydell Press, 2005)

Lives of Edward the Confessor, ed by H. R. Luard (New York: Cambridge University Press, rep. 2012)

Richard of Devizes, *Annals of Winchester* (Cambridge; Corpus Christi College, MS339)

Rodulfus Glaber Opera, ed by J. France, N. Bulst and P. Reynolds (Oxford: Oxford University Press, 1989)

Roger of Wendover, *Flowers of History, Comprising the History of England from the descent of the Saxons to AD1235*, trans by J. A. Giles, 2 vols (London; Bohn, 1849)

Saxo Grammaticus, *Danorum Regum Heroumque Historia*, trans and ed by E. Christiensen (Oxford; 1980)

Saxo Grammaticus: *The History of the Danes*, ed. H. E. Davidson, trans by P. Fisher (Woodbridge; Boydell & Brewer, 1979)

Snorri Sturluson, *Heimskringla: History of the Kings of Norway*, trans. by L. M. Hollander (Austin, TX: University of Texas Press, 2007)

Symeon of Durham, *A history of the kings of England*, trans by J. Stevenson (London, 1855)

Symeon of Durham, *Libellus de Exordio atque Procursu istius, hoc est Dunhelmensis, Ecclesie*, ed D. W. Rollason (Oxford; Clarendon Press, 2000)

Symeon of Durham, *Symeonis Monachi Opera Omnia: Vol. 1, Historia Ecclesiae Dunelmensis.*, ed. by T. Arnold, rev edn 2012 (New York: Cambridge University Press, 2012)

The Anglo-Saxon Chronicles, rev. edn, ed. and trans. by M. Swanton (London: Phoenix Press, 2000)

The Annals of Ulster (to A.D.1131), eds. S. Mac Airt and G. Mac Niocaill (Dublin; Dublin Institute of Advanced Studies, 1983)

The Bayeux Tapestry, intro by D. M. Wilson (London, Thames and Hudson, rev edn 2004)

The Carmen de Hastingae Proelio of Guy Bishop of Amiens, ed and trans by F. Barlow, Oxford Medieval Texts (Oxford; New York: Oxford University Press, 1999)

The Chronicle of Battle Abbey, ed and trans by E. Searle, Oxford Medieval Texts, (Oxford; New York: Oxford University Press, 1980)

The Ecclesiastical History of Orderic Vitalis, Vol II, ed and trans by M. Chibnall, Oxford Medieval Texts (Oxford; New York: Oxford University Press, 1990)

The Liber Vitae of the New Minster and Hyde Abbey, Early English manuscripts, ed. S. D. Keynes (Copenhagen, 1996)

The Waltham Chronicle, ed and trans by L. Watkiss and M. Chibnall, Oxford Medieval Texts (Oxford; New York: Oxford University Press, 1994)

The Chronicon of Thietmar of Merseburg, ed D. A. Warner (Manchester; Manchester University Press, 2001)

Thorpe, L., ed and trans. *Gerald of Wales: Journey through Wales* (Harmondsworth, 1978)

Tshan, J., trans. *Adam of Bremen: Gesta Hammaburgensis Ecclesiae Pontificum History of the Archbishops of Hamburg, Vol. II* (New York; 1999)

Vita Edwardi Regis: The Life of King Edward who rests at Westminster, ed and trans F. Barlow (Oxford; Oxford University Press, 1992)

Vita Haroldi: The Romance of the Life of Harold, King of England: From the Unique Manuscript in the British Museum, ed and trans. W. de Gray Birch (London; Elliott Stock, 1885)

Wace, *Roman de Rou, The History of the Norman Peoples*, ed and trans by G. S. Burgess (Woodbridge, Boydell Press, 2004)

Walter Map, *De Nugis Curialium*, (Oxford: Oxford University Press, 1914)

Webb, C. C. J., ed. *John of Salisbury, Johannis Saresbiriensis episcopi Carnotensis Policraticus* (London; Methuen, 1909)

Whitelock, D., ed. *English Historical Documents, 500–1042*, 2nd edn (London: Eyre Methuen, 1996)

William of Jumièges, Orderic Vitalis and Robert of Torigni, *Gesta Normannorum Ducum, Vol. 1*, ed. & trans by E. M. C. Van Houts, Oxford Medieval Texts (Oxford; New York: Oxford University Press, 1992)

William of Jumièges, Orderic Vitalis and Robert of Torigni, *Gesta Normannorum Ducum, Vol. 2*, ed. & trans by E. M. C. Van Houts, Oxford Medieval Texts (Oxford: Oxford University Press, 1995)

William of Malmesbury, *Gesta Regum Anglorum: The History of the English Kings, Vol. 1*, ed. & trans. by R. A. B. Mynors, R. M. Thomson and M. Winterbottom, Oxford Medieval Texts (Oxford; New York: Clarendon Press, 1998)

William of Malmesbury, *Gesta Regvm Anglorvm: The History of the English Kings. Vol. 2: General Introduction and Commentary*, ed. by R. M. Thomson, Oxford Medieval Texts, reprinted (Oxford; New York, Clarendon Press, 2003)

William of Malmesbury, *Gesta Pontificum Anglorum, The History of the English Bishops*, trans. by M. Winterbottom and R. M. Thomson (London; New York: Oxford University Press, 2007)

William of Malmesbury, *Gesta Pontificum Anglorum, The Deeds of the Bishops of England*, trans. by D. Preest (Woodbridge: Boydell Press, 2002)

William of Malmesbury, *Vita Wulfstani: Lives of Saints Wulfstan, Dunstan, Patrick, Benignus and Indract*, eds. R. M. Thomson and M. Winterbottom, Oxford Medieval Texts (Oxford; Oxford University Press, 2002)

William of Poitiers, *Gesta Guillielmi, The Deeds of William*, ed and trans by R. H. C. Davis and M. Chibnall, Oxford Medieval Texts (Oxford: Oxford University Press, 1998)

Secondary Sources

Anscombe, A., 'The Pedigree of Earl Godwine', in *Translations of the Royal Historical Society, 3rd series, Vol. VII*, pp. 129–50

'Archeurope Educational Resources' <http://anglosaxon.archeurope.info/index> [accessed 15 January 2020 to 12 March 2020]

Aston, M, and C. Lewis., *The Medieval Landscape of Wessex* (Oxford; Oxbow, 1994)

Atherton, M., *The Making of England: A New History of the Anglo-Saxon World* (London New York: I.B. Tauris, 2017)

Austin, N., *Secrets of the Norman Invasion* (Crowhurst: Ogmium Press, rev edn. 2012)

B S Bachrach 'Some observations on the military administration of the Norman Conquest', in Anglo-Norman Studies VIII: Proceedings of the Battle Conference 1985 (Woodbridge: Boydell Press, 1986) pp.1–25

Barlow, F., *Edward the Confessor* (New Haven; London: Yale University Press, rev edn. 1997)

Barlow, F., *The English Church 1000–1066: A History of the Later Anglo-Saxon Church*, 2nd edn (New York; Longman, 1979)

Barlow, F., The Feudal Kingdom of England 1042–1216, 5th ed, (Abingdon; Routledge, 2014)

Barlow, F., *The Godwins: The Rise and Fall of a Noble Dynasty* (Edinburgh: Pearson, 2002)

Barlow, L. W., 'The Antecedents of Earl Godwine of Wessex'. *New England Historical and Genealogical Register (1957), pp. 30–38*

Bartlett, W. B., *King Cnut and the Viking conquest of England 1016* (Stroud: Amberley, 2017)

Bates, D., *Normandy before 1066* (London; New York: Longman, 1982)

Bates, D., '1066 in 2016', in *The Historian, No.131* (2016), pp.6–11

Baxter, S., 'Edward the Confessor and the Succession Question', in *Edward the Confessor: The Man and the Legend*, ed R. Mortimer (Woodbridge: Boydell Press, 2009) pp.77–118

Baxter, S., 'The death of Burgheard, son of Ælfgar, and its context', in *Frankland: The Franks and the world of the early Middle Ages*, eds. P. Fouracre and D. Ganz (Manchester; Manchester University Press, 2008) pp.266–84

Baxter, S., *The Earls of Mercia: Lordship and Power in late Anglo-Saxon England* (Oxford: Oxford University Press, 2007)

Beech, G., 'England and Aquitaine in the Century before the Norman Conquest', in *Anglo-Saxon England, No.19* (1990) pp.81–101

Beeler, J., *Warfare in England 1066–1189* (New York: Cornell University Press, 1966)

Bennett, M., *Campaigns of the Norman Conquest* (Oxford: Osprey Publishing, 2001)

Bernstein, D. J., 'The blinding of Harold and the meaning of the Bayeux Tapestry', in *Anglo-Norman Studies V: Proceedings of the Battle Conference 1982* (Woodbridge; Boydell Press, 1983) pp.40–64

Bernstein, D. J., *The Mystery of the Bayeux Tapestry* (London; Weidenfeld and Nicolson, 1986)

Bibbs, H., *The Rise of Godwin Earl of Wessex* (Canada: Northwest & Pacific Publishing, 3rd edn, 1999)

Biddle, M., 'Capital at Winchester', in *The Vikings in England and their Danish Homeland*, ed E. Roesdahl et al, 1981, pp. 165–70

Bird, D., 'Guildown Reconsidered', in *Surrey Archaeological Society, Bulletin 464, Oct 2017*

Bjork, R. E., ed, *The Oxford Dictionary of the Middle Ages, vols. 1–4* (New York: Oxford University Press, 2010)

Bolton, T., *The Empire of Cnut the Great: Conquest and Consolidation of power in Northern Europe in the early Eleventh Century* (Leiden: Koninklijke Brill, 2009)

Bønløkke Missuno, M., 'Contact and Continuity: England and the Scandinavian Elites in the Early Middle Ages' in *Nordic Elites in Transformation, c. 1050–1250, Volume II*: ed by K. Esmark, L. Hermanson, H-J. Orning (New York; Routledge, 2020)

Bradbury, J., *The Battle of Hastings* (Stroud: Sutton Publishing, 1998)

Bramley, P., *A Companion and Guide to the Norman Conquest* (Stroud: History Press, 2012)

Brandon, P., *The Kent & Sussex Weald* (Phillimore, 2003)

Bridgeford, A., 'Was Count Eustace II of Boulogne the patron of the Bayeux Tapestry?' in Journal of Medieval History, No.25 issue 3 (Sept 1999) pp.155–85

Bridgeford, A., *1066: The Hidden History of the Bayeux Tapestry* (London: Harper Collins, 2004)

'British History Online', <http://www.british-history.ac.uk> [accessed 21 August 2019]

Brondsted, J., *The Vikings* (London; Penguin, 1960)

Brooke, C., *The Saxon and Norman Kings* (Oxford: Blackwell Publishers, 3rd edn. 2001)

Brooks, N., *The Early History of the Church of Canterbury* (Leicester; Leicester University Press, 1984)

Brooks, R., *Cassell's Battlefields of Britain and Ireland* (London: Weidenfeld & Nicolson, 2005)

Brown, R. Allen., ed. *Anglo-Norman Studies I: Procedures of the Battle Conference on Anglo-Norman Studies 1978* (Woodbridge; Boydell Press, 1979)

Brown, R. Allen., 'The Battle of Hastings', in *Anglo-Norman Studies III: Proceedings of the Battle Conference 1980* (Woodbridge; Boydell Press, 1981) pp.1–21

Brown, R. Allen., ed. *Anglo-Norman Studies V: Proceedings of the Battle Conference 1982* (Woodbridge; Boydell Press, 1983)

Brown, R. Allen., ed. *Anglo-Norman Studies VIII: Proceedings of the Battle Conference 1985* (Woodbridge: Boydell Press, 1986)

Brown, R. Allen., ed. *Anglo-Norman Studies XI: Proceedings of the Battle Conference 1978* (Woodbridge: Boydell Press, 1979)

Bucknill, R., *The Foundations of Wherwell Abbey* (Salisbury, 2010)

Campbell, A., ed. *The Anglo-Saxons* (London: Penguin, repr. 1991)

Campbell, M. W., 'Earl Godwin of Wessex and Edward the Confessor's promise of the throne to William of Normandy', in *Traditio, Vol. 28*, 1972

Cavendish, R., 'The Rebellion of Earl Godwin', in *History Today, Vol. 51*, 2001

Chibnall, M., ed. *Anglo-Norman Studies XIII: Proceedings of the Battle Conference 1990* (Woodbridge, Boydell Press, 1991)

Chibnall, M., *The Debate on the Norman Conquest* (Manchester & New York: Manchester University Press, 1999)

Clark, K, and E. Roberts., 'Wherwell Abbey: New Evidence', in *Proceedings of Hampshire Field Club Archaeological Society, No.55* (2000)

Clarke, H. B, 'Economy', in *A Companion to the Early Middle Ages: Britain and Ireland, c.500–c.1100*, Ed P. Stafford (Wiley-Blackwell; Oxford, 2009) pp.57–75

Clarke, P. A., *The English Nobility under Edward the Confessor* (Oxford: Oxford University Press, 1994)

Clephane-Cameron, N., J. Lawrence and D. Sawyer., *The 1066 Malfosse Walk* (Battle: Battle and District Historical Society, 2000)

Crick, J. C., and E. M. C. van Houts, eds., *A Social History of England, 900–1200* (Cambridge; New York: Cambridge University Press, 2011)

Crouch, D., *The Normans: The History of a Dynasty* (London: Hambleton, 2002)

Davies, R. H., 'The lands and rights of Harold, son of Godwine, and their distribution by William I', unpublished dissertation (Cardiff; University College, 1967)

Davies, W., ed, *From the Vikings to the Normans* (Oxford: Oxford University Press, 2003)

Dean, D., *Evidence of the Burial of King Harold II Godwinsson at Waltham Abbey* (2001)

DeVries, K., *The Norwegian Invasion of England in 1066* (Woodbridge: Boydell Press, 1999)

Dodwell, C. R., *Anglo-Saxon Art: A New Perspective* (Manchester; Manchester University Press, 1982)

Dolley, M., *Anglo-Saxon Pennies* (Trustees of the British Museum, 1964)

Douglas, D. C., 'Edward the Confessor, Duke of Normandy, and the English succession', in *English Historical Review, No.68* (1953) pp.526–45

Douglas, D. C., *William the Conqueror* (New Haven; London: Yale University Press, rev edn. 1999)

Dumville, D. N., 'The Aetheling: A Study in Anglo-Saxon Constitutional History', in *Anglo-Saxon England*, 8 (1979), 1–33

Duncan, A. A. M., *The Kingship of the Scots 842–1292: Succession and Independence* (Edinburgh; Edinburgh University Press, 2002)

'English Heritage', <https://www.english-heritage.org.uk> [accessed 7 June 2019 to 5 March 2020]

Evans, M., *Death of Kings: Royal deaths in Medieval England* (London, Continuum, 2006)

Fernie, E. C., 'Edward the Confessor's Westminster Abbey', in *Edward the Confessor: The Man and the Legend*, ed. R. Mortimer (Woodbridge: Boydell Press, 2009) pp.139–50

Fernie, E. C., 'The Romanesque Church of Waltham Abbey', in *Journal of the British Archaeological Association, Vol. 138* (1985) pp.48–87

Fleming, R., *Britain after Rome: The Fall and Rise 400 to 1070* (London, Penguin, 2011)

Fleming, R., *Kings and Lords in Conquest England* (Cambridge; Cambridge University Press, 1991)

Fleming, R., 'The New Wealth, the New Rich, and the New Political Style in Late Anglo-Saxon England', in *Anglo-Norman Studies XXIII: Proceedings of the Battle Conference 2000* (Woodbridge: Boydell Press, 2001) pp.1–22

Fletcher, R., *Bloodfeud: Murder and Revenge in Anglo-Saxon England* (London: Allen Lane/Penguin Press, 2002)

Foord, K, and N. Clephane-Cameron, *1066 and the Battle of Hastings: Preludes, Events and Postscripts*, 2nd repr (Battle and District Historical Society, 2018)

Forte, A. D. M., R. D. Oram and F. Pedersen, *Viking Empires* (Cambridge; New York: Cambridge University Press, 2005)

Foys, M. K., *The Bayeux Tapestry: New Interpretations* (Woodbridge; Boydell Press, 2009)

Frank, R., 'Scaldic Poetry', in *Old Norse Icelandic Literature: A Critical Guide*, eds C. Clover & J. Lindow (New York; Ithica, 1985) pp.157–96

Fryde, E. B., et al, *Handbook of British Chronology (Third revised ed.).* (Cambridge, UK: Cambridge University Press, 1996)

Fuhrmann, H., *Germany in the High Middle Ages c.1050–1200*, with trans by T. Reuter (Cambridge; Cambridge University Press, 1995)

Garnett, G., 'Conquered England 1066–1215', in *Oxford Illustrated History of Medieval England*, ed N. Saul (Oxford, 1997)

'Gatehouse Gazetteer', <http://www.gatehouse-gazetteer.info> [accessed 7 June 2019 to 11 November 2019]

Gillingham, J., ed. *Anglo-Norman Studies XXIII: Proceedings of the Battle Conference 2000* (Woodbridge: Boydell Press, 2001)

Gillingham, J., ed. *Anglo-Norman Studies XXIV: Proceedings of the Battle Conference 2001* (Woodbridge, Boydell Press, 2002)

Gillingham, J., ed. *Anglo-Norman Studies XXVI: Proceedings of the Battle Conference 2003* (Woodbridge: Boydell Press, 2004)

Gillmor, C. M., 'Naval logistics of the Cross-Channel Operation 1066', in *The Battle of Hastings: Sources and Interpretations*, ed. S. Morillo (Woodbridge: Boydell Press, 1996) pp.113–28

Glover, R., 'English Warfare in 1066' (p.173–188), in *The Battle of Hastings, Sources and Interpretations*, ed S. Morello (Woodbridge; Boydell Press, 1996) pp.173–88

Graeme Richie, R. L., *The Normans in Scotland* (Edinburgh; Edinburgh University Press, 1954)

Grassi, J. L., 'The Vita Ædwardi Regis: The Hagiographer as Insider' in *Anglo-Norman Studies XXVI: Proceedings of the Battle Conference 2003* (Woodbridge; Boydell Press, 2004) pp.87–102

Grehan, J., ed, *The Battle of Hastings and the Norman Conquest*, (Stamford; Key Publishing, 2016)

Grehan, J., and M. Mace., *The Battle of Hastings 1066 – The Uncomfortable Truth: Revealing the true location of England's most famous battle* (Barnsley: Pen & Sword, 2012)

Grierson, P., 'A visit of Earl Harold to Flanders in 1056', in *English Historical Review, Vol 51* (1936)

Grierson, P., 'The Relations between England and Flanders before the Norman Conquest', in *Transactions of the Royal Historical Society, Vol. 23* (1941) pp.71–112

Grills, H. J., *The Life and Times of Godwine Earl of Wessex* (Swaffham: Anglo-Saxon Books, 2009)

Hadley, D. M., 'Viking Raids and Conquest', in *A Companion to the Early Middle Ages: Britain and Ireland, c. 500–c. 1100*, ed. by Pauline Stafford (Wiley-Blackwell, 2009), pp. 193–211

Harper-Bill, C, and E. M. C. van Houts, eds, *A Companion to the Anglo-Norman World*, (Woodbridge; Boydell Press, 2007)

Harper-Bill, C., ed. *Anglo-Norman Studies XVIII: Proceedings of the Battle Conference 1995* (Woodbridge; Boydell Press, 1996)

Harper-Bill, C., ed. *Anglo-Norman Studies XIX: Proceedings of the Battle Conference 1996* (Woodbridge; Boydell Press, 1997)

Harrington, S., and M. Welch, *The early Anglo-Saxon kingdoms of southern Britain AD450–650: Beneath the Tribal Hidage* (Oxford: Philadelphia; Oxbow Books; 2014)

Harvey-Wood, H., *The Battle of Hastings* (London: Atlantic Books, 2008)

Hase, P. H., 'The Church in the Wessex Heartlands', in *The Medieval Landscape of Wessex*, eds. M. Aston and C. Lewis (Oxford; Oxbow, 1994) pp.47–81

Hawkes, S.C., *Weapons and Warfare in Anglo-Saxon England*, ed by S.C. Hawkes (Oxford: Oxford University Committee for Archaeology, 1989)

Hern, A., *The Mythical Battle: Hastings 1066* (Marlborough: Robert Hale, 2017)

Hewitt, C. M., 'Was the Battle of Hastings Really Fought on Battle Hill? A GIS Assessment', in *Historical Geography, Vol. 44* (2016) pp.127–48

Higham, N. J., *The Death of Anglo-Saxon England* (Stroud, Sutton Publishing, 1997)

Higham, N. J., and M. J. Ryan, *The Anglo-Saxon World* (New Haven: Yale University Press, 2013)

Higham, N. J., 'The Godwins, Towns and St Olaf Churches: Comital investment in the mid-11th Century', in *The Land of the English Kin*, eds A. J. Langlands and R. Lavelle (Leiden, Brill, 2020)

Hill, D., *An Atlas of Anglo-Saxon England*, Reprinted (Oxford: Blackwell, 1989)

Hill, D., 'An urban policy for Cnut?', in Rumble, A., ed, *The Reign of Cnut: King of England, Denmark and Norway*, A. R. Rumble, ed. (London: Leicester University Press, 1994) pp.101–105

Hill, P., *The Anglo-Saxons at War, 800–1066* (Barnsley, South Yorkshire: Pen & Sword Military, 2012)

Hill, P., *The Road to Hastings: The Politics of Power in Anglo-Saxon England* (Stroud: Tempus, 2005)

Hilton, L., *Queens Consort: England's Medieval Queens* (London: Weidenfeld & Nicolson, 2008)

Hindley, G., *A Brief History of the Anglo-Saxons* (London: Robinson, 2006)

Hollister, C. W., *Anglo-Norman Military Institutions* (Oxford, Clarendon Press, 1962)

Hollister, C. W, and A. C. Frost., *Henry I* (New Haven; Yale University Press, 2003)

Houts, E. M. C. van., 'Historical Writing' in *A Companion to the Anglo-Norman World*, (Woodbridge; Boydell Press, 2007) pp.103–21

Houts, E. M. C. van., The Norman Conquest through European eyes', in *English Historical Review, No.110* (1995) pp.832–53

Houts, E. M. C, van., *The Normans in Europe* (Manchester, Manchester University Press, 2000)

Houts, E. M. C, van., 'The ship list of William the Conqueror', in *Anglo-Norman Studies X: Proceedings of the Battle Conference 1987* (Woodbridge; Boydell Press, 1988) pp.159–84

Howard, I., 'Harold II: A Throne-Worthy King', in *King Harold II and the Bayeux Tapestry*, ed G. R. Owen-Crocker (Woodbridge; Boydell Press, 2005) pp.35–52

Howard, I., *Harthacnut: The last Danish King of England* (Stroud: History Press, 2008)

Howard, I., *Swein Forkbeard's Invasions and the Danish Conquest of England, 991–1017* (Woodbridge, UK: Rochester, NY: Boydell Press, 2003)

Hudson, B. T., 'Cnut and the Scottish Kings', in *English Historical Review, Vol. 107*, (1992) pp.350–60

Hudson, J., ed and trans, *The History of the Church of Abingdon* (Oxford; Oxford University Press, 2002)

Hurt, C. R., 'William Malet and his Family', in *Anglo-Norman Studies XIX Proceedings of the Battle Conference 1996* (Woodbridge, Boydell Press, 1997) pp.123–66

Huscroft, R., *Making England 796–1042* (London; New York: Routledge, 2018)

Huscroft, R., *Ruling England 1042–1217* (London; New York: Routledge, 2004)

Huscroft, R., *The Norman Conquest: A New Introduction* (Harlow; Pearson/ Longman, 2009)

John, E., 'Edward the Confessor and the Norman Succession', in *English Historical Review, No.94* (1979) pp.241–67

John, E., 'The Return of the Vikings', in *The Anglo-Saxons*, ed A. Campbell (London: Penguin, repr. 1991) pp.192–213

Jones, C., *Finding Fulford: The search for the first battle of 1066* (London; Writers Print Shop, 2011)

Jones, C., *The Forgotten Battle of 1066: Fulford* (Stroud: History Press, 2007)

Jones, G., A History of the Vikings (London, Oxford University Press, 1973)

Kapelle, W. E., *The Norman Conquest of the North: The Region and its Transformation 1000–1135* (University of North Carolina Press, 1979)

Kempen, A, Van, 'The Mercian Connection, Harold Godwineson's Ambitions, Diplomacy and Channel-Crossing 1056–1066', in *History, Vol. 94*, pp. 2–19

Keynes, S. D., 'Cnut's Earls in the reign of Cnut', in *The Reign of Cnut: King of England, Denmark and Norway*, ed A. Rumble (London: Leicester University Press, 1994) pp.43–88

Keynes, S. D., 'England, c.900–1016', in *The New Cambridge Medieval History*, ed. by T. Reuter (Cambridge: Cambridge University Press, 1999), iii, pp. 456–84

Keynes, S. D., 'Edward the Ætheling', in *Edward the Confessor: The Man and the Legend*, ed. by R. Mortimer (Woodbridge: Boydell Press, 2009) pp.41–62

Keynes, S. D., *The Diplomas of King Æthelred 'the Unready', 978–1016* (Cambridge; 1980)

Bibliography

Keynes, S. D., 'The Æthelings in Normandy', in *Anglo-Norman Studies XIII: Proceedings of the Battle Conference 1990* (Woodbridge, Boydell Press, 1991) pp.173–205

King, V., 'Ealdred, Archbishop of York: The Worcester Years', in *Anglo-Norman Studies XVIII: Proceedings of the Battle Conference 1995* (Woodbridge; Boydell Press, 1996) pp.123–38

'Kirkdale Churches' <http://www.kirkdalechurches.org.uk> [accessed 19 January 2020)

Knowles, D, and C. N. L. Brooke and V. C. M. London, eds. *The Heads of Religious Houses: England & Wales, I, 940–1216,* 2nd edn (Cambridge, Cambridge University Press, 2009)

Lapidge, M., J. Blair, S. D. Keynes & D. Scragg, eds. *The Blackwell Encyclopaedia of Anglo-Saxon England*, repr. (Oxford: Blackwell, 2007)

Larsen, K., *History of Norway* (Princeton; Princeton University Press, 1948)

Larson, L. M., 'The King's Household in England before the Norman Conquest', in *Anglo-Norman Warfare: Studies in Late Anglo-Saxon and Anglo-Norman Military Organisation and Warfare*, ed M. Strickland (Woodbridge; Boydell Press, 1992) pp.153–71

Lawson, M. K., *Cnut: England's Viking King 1016–35* (Stroud, History Press, 2nd edn. 2011)

Lawson, M. K., *Cnut: The Danes in England in the early 11th Century* (New York: Longman, 1993)

Lawson, M. K., *The Battle of Hastings: 1066* (Stroud: History Press, repr. 2016)

Licence, T., *Edward the Confessor: Last of the Royal Blood* (New Haven & London; Yale University Press, 2020)

Licence, T., 'A New Source for the Vita Ædwardi Regis' in *Journal of Medieval Latin*, No.29 (2019) pp.1–19

Lot, F., ed. *Chronique de l'abbaye de Saint Riquier* (Paris; Picard, 1894)

Lowther, A. W. G., 'The Saxon Cemetery at Guildown, Guildford', in *Surrey Archaeological Collections, Vol. 39, pp. 1–50 (1931) and Vol.41, pp. 119–22* (1933)

Loyn, H. R., and A. L. Brown, eds., *The Governance of England. Vol 1: The Governance of Anglo-Saxon England, 500 – 1087*, repr. (London: Arnold, 1991)

Margary, I., *Roman roads in Britain*, 3rd edn (London; John Baker, 1973)

Marren, P., *Battles of the Dark Ages: British Battlefields AD 410 to 1065* (Barnsley: Pen & Sword Military, 2009)

Marsden, J., *Harald Hardrada: The Warriors Way* (Stroud: Sutton Publishing, 2007)

Marwood, G. W., *The Story of the Holy Trinity Church* (Chichester; Selsey Press, 1995)

Mason, E., *The House of Godwine: The History of a Dynasty* (Hambledon & London: Cambridge University Press, 2004)

Maund, K. L., 'The Welsh Alliances of Earl Ælfgar and his family in the mid-eleventh-century', in *Anglo-Norman Studies XI: Proceedings of the Battle Conference 1988* (Woodbridge, Boydell Press, 1989) pp.181–90

McKitterick, R., and T. Reuter, *The New Cambridge Medieval History: Volume 3, C.900–c.1024* (Cambridge University Press, 1995)

McLynn, F., *1066: The Year of the Three Battles* (London, BCA, 1999)

Missuno, M. B., 'Contact and Continuity: England and the Scandinavian Elites in the Early Middle Ages', in *Nordic Elites in Transformation c.1050–1250, vol II*, eds. K. Esmark, L. Hermanson & H. J. Orning (New York; Routledge, 2020)

Morillo, S., ed, *The Battle of Hastings: Sources and Interpretations* (Woodbridge: Boydell Press, 1996)

Morris, M., *The Norman Conquest* (London: Windmill, 2013)

Mortimer, R., ed, *Edward the Confessor: The Man and the Legend* (Woodbridge: Boydell Press, 2009)

Nelson, J. L., 'Early Medieval rites of Queen-making and the shaping of early medieval Queenship', in *Queens and Queenship in Medieval Europe*, ed A. J. Duggan (Woodbridge; Boydell, 1997) pp.301–15

Nelson, J. L., 'Rulers and Government', in *The New Cambridge Medieval History: Volume 3, C.900–c.1024*, ed. by Rosamund McKitterick and Timothy Reuter (Cambridge; New York: Cambridge University Press, 1999), pp. 95–129

Neveux, F., *A Brief History of the Normans: The Conquests that changed the face of Europe*, with trans by H. Curtis (London: Constable & Robinson, 2006)

Nicolle, D., *Medieval Warfare Source Book: Warfare in western Christendom* (London: Brockhampton Press, 1999)

O'Brien, H., *Queen Emma and the Vikings: The Woman Who Shaped the Events of 1066* (London, Bloomsbury Publishing, 2006)

Oman, C., *A History of the Art of War in the Middle Ages*, 2nd edn. (London, Methuen, 1924)

Oram, R., *David I: The King who made Scotland* (Stroud; Tempus, 2004)

Owen-Crocker, G. R., *King Harold II and the Bayeux Tapestry* (Woodbridge: Boydell Press, 2005)

'Oxford Dictionary of National Biography', <http://www.oxforddnb.com> [accessed 19 March 2019 to 12 April 2020]

Palle, L., *A History of the Kingdom of Denmark*, with trans by D. Hohnen (Copenhagen; Høst, 1960)

'Pastscape', <https://www.pastscape.org.uk/> [accessed 19 May 2019 to 16 January 2020]

Patourel, J. le., *The Norman Empire* (Oxford: Clarendon Press. 1976)

Patterson, B. R., *Harold and William: The Battle for England 1064–1066* (Stroud: Tempus, 2004)

Pearson, A., *The Roman Shore Forts: Coastal Defences of Southern Britain* (Stroud; History Press, 2002)

Pollock, J., *Harold Rex: Is King Harold buried in Bosham Church* (Bosham; Penny Publications, 4th ed 1996 suppl. 2002)

Poyntz-Wright, P., *Hastings* (Gloucester: Windrush Press, 1996)

'Prosopography of Anglo-Saxon England: Database Home' <http://www.pase.ac.uk/> [accessed 26 March 2019 to 10 April 2020]

Raper, W. A., 'On the silver pennies of Edward the Confessor found at Sedlescombe', in *Sussex Archaeological Collections, Vol.33* (1883)

Raraty, D. G. J., 'Earl Godwine of Wessex: The Origins of his Power and his Political Loyalties', *History*, 74, 1989, pp.3–19

Redgate, A. E., *Religion, Politics and Society in Britain 800–1066*, (London; New York: Routledge, Taylor & Francis, 2014)

Rex, P., *Edward the Confessor: King of England* (Stroud: Amberley, 2013)

Rex, P., *King and Saint: The Life of Edward the Confessor* (Stroud: History Press, 2008)

Rex, P., *1066: A new history of the Norman Conquest* (Stroud: Amberley, 2009)

Rex, P., *The Last English King: The Life of Harold II* (Stroud: History Press, 2008)

Roach, L., *Æthelred the Unready* (New Haven; London: Yale University Press, 2017)

Rodwell, W., 'New glimpses of Edward the Confessor's Abbey at Westminster', in *Edward the Confessor: The Man and the Legend*, ed. R. Mortimer (Woodbridge: Boydell Press, 2009) pp.151–67

Ronay, G., *The Lost King of England: The Eastern European adventures of Edward the Exile* (Woodbridge: Boydell Press, 1989)

Rumble, A.R., ed, *The Reign of Cnut: King of England, Denmark and Norway* (London: Leicester University Press, 1994)

Sawyer, P. H., *Anglo-Saxon Charters: An Annotated List and Bibliography*, 8 (London: Offices of the Royal Historical. Society, 1968)

Sawyer, P. H., *Kings and Vikings: Scandinavia and Europe AD700–1100* (London; Routledge, 1996)

Sawyer, P. H., ed. *The Charters of Burton Abbey* (New York: Oxford; Oxford University Press, 1979)

Stafford, P., ed. *A Companion to the Early Middle Ages: Britain and Ireland C.500–1100*, Blackwell Companions to British History (Chichester, U.K. ; Malden, MA: Wiley-Blackwell, 2009)

Stafford, P., 'Edith, Edward's Wife and Queen', in *Edward the Confessor: The Man and the Legend*, ed. by R. Mortimer (Woodbridge: Boydell Press, 2009) pp.119–38

Stafford, P., *Queen Emma and Queen Edith: Queenship and Women's Power in Eleventh-Century England* (Oxford: Blackwell Publishers, 2001)

Stafford, P., 'The King's Wife in Wessex 800–1066', *Past & Present* (1981) pp.3–27

Stafford, P., 'The Laws of Cnut and the history of Anglo-Saxon royal promises', in *Anglo-Saxon England, Vol. 10*, (1981) pp. 173–90

Stafford, P., *Unification and Conquest: A Political and Social History of England in the Tenth and Eleventh Centuries* (London: Edward Arnold, 1989)

Starkey, J, and M. Starkey., *The Battle of Hastings at Sedlescombe* (Sussex: Momentous Britain, 2018)

Stenton, F. M., *Anglo-Saxon England*, 3rd edn (Oxford: Clarendon Press, 1971)

Stevenson, J., ed. 'The History of Ingulf', in *Church Historians of England, Vol ii* (London, 1854)

Stevenson, W. H., 'An alleged son of King Harold Harefoot', in *English Historical Review, No.109* (1913) pp.112–17

'Steyning Museum' <http://www.steyningmuseum.org.uk/fecamp> [accessed 5 July 2019]

Strachan, I., *Emma: The Twice-Crowned Queen* (London.; Chester Springs, PA: Peter Owen, 2004)

Strickland, M., ed, *Anglo-Norman Warfare: Studies in late Anglo-Saxon and Anglo-Norman Military Organization and Warfare* (Woodbridge: Boydell Press, 1992)

H. Summerson, 'Tudor Antiquaries and the *Vita Edwardi*', in Anglo Saxon England, no.38, (2009) pp.157–84

Talvio, T., 'The design of Edward the Confessor's coins', in *Studies in Late Anglo-Saxon Coinage in memory of Bror Emil Hildebrand*, ed K. Jonsson (Stockholm; Numismatika' 1990) pp.487–99

Tanner, H. J., *Family, Friends and Allies: Boulogne and Politics in Northern France and England c.879–1160* (Brill, 2004)

Thacker, A. T., 'The Cult of King Harold at Chester', in The Middle Ages in the North-West, eds. T. Scott and P. Starkey (Oxford, 1995) pp.155–76

'Topographic-Map',<https://en-gb.topographic-map.com/maps/du6e/East-Sussex/> [accessed 11 October 2019 to 7 March 2020]

Trigg, J., *Battle Story: Hastings 1066* (Stroud: History Press, 2012)

Tyson, K., trans & transcript. *Carmen Widonis: The First History of the Norman Conquest* (Granularity, 2018)

Venning, T., *An Alternative History of Britain: The Anglo-Saxon Age* (Barnsley: Pen & Sword Military, 2013)

Walker, I. W., *Harold: The Last Anglo-Saxon King* (Stroud: History Press, repr. 2010)

Wareham, A., 'Transformation of Kinship and the Family in late Anglo-Saxon England', in *Early Medieval Europe, Vol 10*, (2001), pp. 375–99

Warren, P., *Battleground Britain: 1066 The Battles of York, Stamford Bridge and Hastings* (Barnsley, Pen and Sword Books, 2004)

Watkiss, L, and M. Chibnall, ed and trans, *The Waltham Chronicle: An account of the discovery of Our Holy Cross at Montacute and its conveyance to Waltham* (Oxford; Oxford University Press, 1994)

'Westminster Abbey', <http://www.westminster-abbey.org/abbey-commemorations> [accessed 28 August 2019]

Whitelock, D., ed and trans. *Anglo-Saxon Wills* (Cambridge; 1930)

Whittock, M., and H. Whittock, *The Viking Blitzkrieg 789–1098 AD.* (New York: The History Press, 2013)

Williams, A., *Æthelred the Unready: The Ill-Counselled King* (London: Hambleton, 2003)

Williams, A., *Kingship and Government in Pre-Conquest England, C.500–1066*, British History in Perspective (New York: St. Martin's Press; Macmillan, 1999)

Williams, A., 'Land and Power in the Eleventh Century: The Estates of Harold Godwineson', in *Anglo-Norman Studies III: Proceedings of the Battle Conference 1980*, (Woodbridge: Boydell Press, 1081), pp. 171–87

Williams, A., 'Some Notes and Considerations on Problems Connected with the English Royal Succession, 860–1066', in *Procedures of the Battle Conference on Anglo-Norman Studies, Vol. I* (Boydell Press, 1978), pp. 144–67

Williams, A., *The English and the Norman Conquest* (Woodbridge: Boydell Press, 2nd edn. 1997)

Williams, A., *The World before Domesday: The English Aristocracy 900–1066* (London: Continuum, 2008)

Williams, A., 'Thegnly piety and ecclesiastical patronage in the late old English kingdom', in *Anglo-Norman Studies XXIV: Proceedings of the Battle Conference 2001* (Woodbridge, Boydell Press, 2002) pp.1–24

Williams, A., A. P. Smyth, and D. P. Kirby, *A Biographical Dictionary of Dark Age Britain: England, Scotland, and Wales, C. 500–c. 1050* (Psychology Press, 1991)

Wilson, D. M., *The Bayeux Tapestry* (London: Thames & Hudson, 2nd edn. 2004)

Zaluckyj, S., *Mercia: The Anglo-Saxon Kingdom of Central England*, repr. (Little Logaston: Logaston Press, 2011)

Wolfram, H., *Conrad II, 990–1039: Emperor of Three Kingdoms*, with trans by D. A. Kaiser (Pennsylvania; Pennsylvania State University Press, 2006)

Wright, T., ed. *The Anglo-Norman Satirical Poets and Epigrammatists of the Twelfth Century, vol II* (London, Rolls Series, 1872)

Index

Fulford, Battle of, 218,
221–3, 225, 227, 230,
273, 295
Fulk of Mantes, son of
Godgifu, 268
Gainsborough, 30
Galmanho, York, 151
Gamal, thegn, 187–8, 192,
294
Gamelbearn, thegn, 192
Geffrei Gaimar, writer, 19,
36, 44, 59, 74, 93, 158,
213, 216, 248, 277
Geldesdon Hill, *see*
Guildown
Geoffrey Martel, count of
Anjou, 105, 128
Gerald of Wales, writer,
175
Germany Beck, *see*
Fulford, Battle of
Germany, 58, 67, 98, 118,
158–9, 198, 232, 261,
293
Gesta Danorum, text, 20,
92, 271, 276
Gesta Guillelmi, text, 17,
19, 178, 180, 234, 242,
282
*Gesta Hammaburgensis
Ecclesiae Pontificum,*
text, 20, 69
*Gesta Normannorum
Ducum,* text, 19, 178,
248
*Gesta Pontificum
Anglorum,* text, 19, 115,
124, 172
Gesta Regum Anglorum,
text, 18, 92–3, 99, 120,
146, 152, 240
Ghent, 37, 41
Gilfard, *see* Walter Giffard
Gillingham, 75
Giso, bishop of Wells, 172,
206
Glasbury-on-Wye, battle
at, 156
Glastonbury, 36, 48, 63,
81, 144, 206
Glonieorn, thegn, 192

Gloucester, 95, 101,
120–3, 126, 137, 146,
155, 174, 186, 191, 197,
292, 294
Gloucestershire, 36, 40,
94, 107, 109, 113, 122,
126–7, 143–4, 149,
164–5, 167, 219, 291
Glywysing, Welsh kingdom
of, 107
God Begot Manor,
Winchester, 95–6, 132–3
Godgifu, daughter of
Æthelred II and Emma,
38, 41, 71, 98, 112,
118–9, 157, 182, 268
Godgifu, wife of earl
Leofric, 163
Godiva, *see* Godgifu, wife
of earl Leofric
Godric, thegn, 171
Godstone, 262
Godwin Wulfnothson,
earl of Wessex, 9–13,
16, 26–31, 33, 45–7,
49–56, 58, 61, 64, 66–8,
72–3, 75–6, 79–81, 83,
85–6, 88, 91–2, 94–103,
106–7, 109, 111–2,
114–7, 120, 123–4, 126,
128–41, 145, 150–1,
154, 158, 163, 166, 168,
176, 189–90, 198, 201–
3, 219, 233, 236, 243,
265–6, 272, 275, 277–
87, 289–92, 294, 296–7;
ancestry of 23–6, 34,
40, 43–4, 57, 287; birth
of, 23, 25–6, 287; birth
of children, 53–5, 63,
287–90; in charters, 51,
57, 62, 64–5, 81, 87, 95,
130, 144; death of, 26,
146–9, 293; earldom
of, 46–9, 109, 127, 143,
148–9, 287; and Cnut,
40, 43–6, 48, 50–1,
59–60, and Edward (the
Confessor), 89, 92–4,
103–5, 110, 113, 115,
120–2, 125, 139–40;
and Harefoot, 70, 72–5,

78, 82; and Harthacnut,
68, 83–7; marriage of,
45, 49–53, 287
Godwin, abbot of
Winchcombe, 144
Godwin, son of Harold
Godwinson, 38
Gospatric, earl of
Northumbria, 188, 192
Gospatric, thegn, 154, 173,
188, 294
Granta, River, 35
Great North Road, 224,
240
Great Sanders Ridge, 254
Greenwich, 30, 57, 68
Gregorian Calendar, 13,
231
Gruffydd ap Llywelyn,
king of Powys and
Gwynedd, 156, 174–6
Gruffydd ap Rhydderch,
king of Deheubarth, 145
Guestling, estate, 239
Guildford, 73–6, 79, 85,
95, 119, 262, 290
Guildown, 74
Gunhild Godwinsdottir,
38, 53–5, 63–4, 101,
126, 149, 167, 262,
270–2, 280, 283, 289,
292, 297; birth of,
53–5, 63, 289; death of,
271, 280–1, 297; after
Hastings, 262, 270–1,
297
Gunhild, daughter of
Harold Godwinson, 38,
101, 276–7, 279, 281,
292, 297
Gunhild, sister of Cnut,
96, 104
Gunhilda, daughter of
Cnut and Emma, 64, 67,
82, 96, 159, 268
Guy of Amiens, bishop
and writer, 19, 235, 242,
246, 248, 250, 261, 263
Guy, count of Ponthieu,
178
Gwent, Welsh kingdom of,
107, 191

William II 'Rufus', king of England, 259, 264, 268, 274, 276–8, 297

William Malet, minister, 152, 206, 260

William of Jumièges, monk & chronicler, 19, 69, 72, 80, 178, 203–4, 211, 232, 237, 248, 274

William of Malmesbury, monk & chronicler, 18–9, 27, 40–2, 49, 59–61, 75, 80–1, 84, 92–5, 99, 115, 119–22, 124, 133, 139, 141, 144–5, 147, 151, 158, 160, 168, 173, 177–9, 192–4, 198, 201–3, 207, 209, 213, 226, 229, 239–41, 246–8, 250–1, 270, 275–8, 282, 285

William of Newburgh, writer, 20

William of Poitiers, writer, 17, 19, 72–3, 80, 89, 127–8, 177–9, 181–3, 200, 203, 217, 231, 234, 237, 242, 247–9, 251, 258, 265, 282

William, bishop of London, 116, 126, 140

William, I, king of England, the Conqueror, duke of Normandy, 9, 11–12, 16, 19–21, 71, 80, 87, 89, 96, 105, 108, 117–21, 127–31, 141, 147, 162, 177–83, 196, 200, 202–3, 206–7, 211–4, 216, 218, 230–51, 253, 255–6, 259–60, 262–6,

268, 270–2, 274–5, 277, 282, 292, 294–7

Willingdon, estate, 66, 148

Wilton Abbey, 55, 124–6, 132, 136, 143, 275–7, 292, 294, 297

Wiltshire, 26, 31, 33–4, 148–9, 164, 191–2, 207, 219, 263, 267

Wincanton, 33

Winchcombe Abbey, 144, 172

Winchelsea, 233, 238, 246

Winchester, 17, 26, 39, 46, 56–7, 64, 68–70, 72–3, 77–9, 82, 87–8, 91, 95–7, 101, 112, 132–3, 137, 139, 144, 146, 148, 162, 169–70, 172, 261–3, 274–7, 279, 289–93, 296–7

Winchester Annals, 146

Windsor, 146, 190

Wissant, 72, 75, 119

Witan (Council), 78, 83, 89, 92, 104, 117, 121, 133, 139, 152–3, 158, 183, 194

Witley, 66

Worcester, 17, 57, 84, 86, 97, 106, 108, 144, 153, 163, 170, 172–3, 290–1

Worcestershire, 40, 86, 101, 108, 113, 127, 143, 149, 219

Wulfhild, daughter of Æthelred II, 268

Wulfnoth Cild, ealdorman & father of Godwin, 9, 11, 23–5, 27–9, 34, 38, 45, 55, 66–7, 199; in

charters, 25; kinship of, 24–6, 40, 43; birth of, 25, 287; death of, 28, 287; outlawed, 28

Wulfnoth Godwinson, son of Godwin, 38, 108, 129, 140, 177, 182, 189, 271, 280, 284; in *Bayeux Tapestry*, 177, 182; birth of, 53–5, 290; death of, 278, 280, 297; given as hostage, 123, 126, 139; hostage in Normandy, 178, 182, 274, 277, 293–4, 297

Wulfsige, bishop of Lichfield, 144

Wulfstan, bishop of Worcester, 173, 202, 204, 209, 264, 276

Wulfstan, Lupus, archbishop of York, 45–6, 57

Wulfwig, bishop of Dorchester-on-Thames, 174

Wye, River, 155–6

Yaroslav I, the great, king of Russia, 42, 158, 160

York, 29, 32, 57, 67, 69, 80, 84, 91, 115, 144, 149, 151–3, 169, 172, 187, 192–3, 204–5, 213, 215, 217, 220–1, 223–6, 229, 240, 271, 280, 294–6

Yorkshire, 154, 164, 167, 207, 219, 224, 281

Yric of Hlathir, *see* Eric Hákonarson

Yrling, viking jarl, 103

Yser, River, 133